Eco-communities

An ebook edition of this book is available open access on bloomsburycollections.com. Open access was funded by the Bloomsbury Open Collections Library Collective.

Bloomsbury Open Collections is a collective-action approach to funding open access books that allows select authors to publish their books open access at no cost to them. Through this model, we make open access publication available to a wider range of authors by spreading the cost across multiple organisations, while providing additional benefits to participating libraries. The aim is to engage a more diverse set of authors and bring their work to a wider global audience.

More details, including how to participate and a list of contributing libraries, are available from bloomsbury.com/bloomsbury-open-collections.

BLOOMSBURY ACADEMIC
Bloomsbury Publishing Plc, 50 Bedford Square, London, WC1B 3DP, UK
Bloomsbury Publishing Inc, 1385 Broadway, New York, NY 10018, USA
Bloomsbury Publishing Ireland, 29 Earlsfort Terrace, Dublin 2, D02 AY28, Ireland

BLOOMSBURY, BLOOMSBURY ACADEMIC and the Diana logo
are trademarks of Bloomsbury Publishing Plc

First published in Great Britain 2025

Copyright © Jenny Pickerill, 2025

Jenny Pickerill has asserted her right under the Copyright,
Designs and Patents Act, 1988, to be identified as Editor of this work.

For legal purposes the Acknowledgements on pp. xxi–xxii constitute
an extension of this copyright page.

Cover design by Adriana Brioso
Cover image: Christie Walk, Adelaide, Australia, courtesy of Jenny Pickerill

This work is published open access subject to a Creative Commons Attribution-NonCommercial-NoDerivatives 4.0 International licence (CC BY-NC-ND 4.0, https://creativecommons.org/licenses/by-nc-nd/4.0/). You may re-use, distribute, and reproduce this work in any medium for non-commercial purposes, provided you give attribution to the copyright holder and the publisher and provide a link to the Creative Commons licence.

Bloomsbury Publishing Plc does not have any control over, or responsibility for,
any third-party websites referred to or in this book. All internet addresses given in this book
were correct at the time of going to press. The author and publisher regret any inconvenience
caused if addresses have changed or sites have ceased to exist, but can accept
no responsibility for any such changes.

A catalogue record for this book is available from the British Library.

Library of Congress Cataloging-in-Publication Data
Names: Pickerill, Jenny editor
Title: Eco-communities : surviving well together / edited by Jenny Pickerill.
Description: London ; New York : Bloomsbury Academic, 2025. |
Includes bibliographical references and index. | Summary: "This book critically explores the aims and practices of eco-communities worldwide. The book examines eco-communities through the lens of key three challenges: how eco-communities practice living together in non-conventional ways; how eco-communities challenge conventions, particularly mainstream approaches to time, economics, race, justice, democracy and aesthetics; and the challenge of replication and propagation"– Provided by publisher.
Identifiers: LCCN 2024057436 (print) | LCCN 2024057437 (ebook) |
ISBN 9781350528154 hardback | ISBN 9781350528192 paperback |
ISBN 9781350528161 epub | ISBN 9781350528178 pdf
Subjects: LCSH: Communal living | Sustainable living | Alternative lifestyles–Environmental aspects | Communities–Environmental aspects
Classification: LCC HQ970 .E36 2025 (print) | LCC HQ970 (ebook) |
DDC 307.77/4–dc23/eng/20250408
LC record available at https://lccn.loc.gov/2024057436
LC ebook record available at https://lccn.loc.gov/2024057437

ISBN:	HB:	978-1-3505-2815-4
	ePDF:	978-1-3505-2817-8
	eBook:	978-1-3505-2816-1

Typeset by Integra Software Services Pvt. Ltd.

For product safety related questions contact productsafety@bloomsbury.com.

To find out more about our authors and books visit www.bloomsbury.com
and sign up for our newsletters.

Eco-communities

Surviving Well Together

Edited by

Jenny Pickerill

BLOOMSBURY ACADEMIC
LONDON • NEW YORK • OXFORD • NEW DELHI • SYDNEY

To Tim and Toffee for bringing the fun to daily life.

Contents

List of Figures	xi
List of Tables	xiii
List of Contributors	xv
Acknowledgements	xxi
World Map of Eco-communities	xxiii

1 Collective dynamic socio-ecological experiments *Jenny Pickerill*   1

Part One Living ecologically: Generating socio-ecological transformations *Jenny Pickerill*   31

2 Does living sustainably suck? Reduced consumption and quality of life at Dancing Rabbit Ecovillage during the Anthropocene *Joshua Lockyer and Brooke Jones*   33

3 Understanding consumption reduction through the social practices of an Australian eco-community *Matthew Daly*   47

4 Reconfiguring more-than-human relations in eco-communities: Skillsets, empowerment and discomfort *Elisa Schramm*   67

5 Peopled environments: Eco-communities and their reconfigurations of nature *Jenny Pickerill*   83

6 Eco-communities and outsiders: Opportunities and obstacles to transforming the world *Jon Anderson*   99

Part Two Negotiating questions of inclusion *Jenny Pickerill*   113

7 Towards inclusive eco-communities: Socially and environmentally just sustainable futures *Tendai Chitewere*   115

8 Settling in colonial ways? Eco-communities' uncomfortable settler colonial practices *Adam Barker and Jenny Pickerill*   129

9 Eco-communities and feminism(s): Who cares? An ethnographic study of social practices in three French eco-communities *Nadine Gerner*   143

10	Uneven equity and sustainability in intentional communities in the United States: A national-level exploratory analysis *Christina Lopez and Russell Weaver*	157
11	Confronting racial privilege: Questioning whiteness in eco-communities *Jenny Pickerill*	173
12	In defence of eco-collaborative housing communities: Porous boundaries and scaling out *Anitra Nelson*	187

Part Three Doing it together: Collective governance *Jenny Pickerill*		201
13	Contingent, contested, political: Learning from processes of environmental governance in the Global South to understand eco-communities *Natasha Cornea*	203
14	Organizing together: Coexisting, time economies, money and scale in Barcelona eco-communities *Marc Gavaldà and Claudio Cattaneo*	215
15	How eco-communities grow through social learning, social permaculture and group transformation *Helen Jarvis*	227
16	Prompting spiritually prefigurative political practice: Collective decision-making in Auroville, India *Suryamayi Aswini Clarence-Smith*	241

Part Four Building diverse economies *Jenny Pickerill*		255
17	Escaping capitalism? Time, quality of life and hybrid economies *Kirsten Stevens-Wood*	257
18	Workshops and liberation in Freetown Christiania: Tensions in a post-growth community economy *Thomas S. J. Smith and Nadia Johanisova*	271
19	Community economies in eco-communities: Spaces of collaboration, opportunities and dilemmas *Jan Malý Blažek*	285
20	Being collectively transformational? *Jenny Pickerill*	299

Index	312

Figures

World map of eco-communities. (Source: Jenny Pickerill.)   xxiii

Chapter 2

1	Dancing Rabbit Ecovillage location map. (Source: Zach Rubin, PhD.)	36
2	Common house and main road at Dancing Rabbit Ecovillage. (Source: Joshua Lockyer.)	36

Chapter 3

1	Plan view of the ground floor of Murundaka. (Source: Matthew Daly.)	51
2	View of Murundaka from the back corner of garden. (Source: Matthew Daly.)	52
3	Outdoor common space. (Source: Matthew Daly.)	52

Chapter 4

1	Map of the three sites. (Source: Elisa Schramm.)	71
2	Uneven repair in Can Masdeu. (Source: Elisa Schramm.)	73
3	Inside one of Can Masdeu's compost toilets. (Source: Elisa Schramm.)	77

Chapter 5

1	Eco-communities in Britain. (Source: Jenny Pickerill.)	88
2	Tao and Hoppi's plot, Tir y Gafel, 2006. (Source: Jenny Pickerill.)	90
3	Tao and Hoppi's plot, Tir y Gafel, 2016. (Source: Jenny Pickerill.)	91
4	LILAC. (Source: Jenny Pickerill.)	93

Chapter 8

1	Carving into a house door at The Lama Foundation, New Mexico, USA. (Source: Jenny Pickerill.)	136

Chapter 10

1	Distribution of intentional communities in the contiguous United States. (Source: Christina Lopez and Russell Weaver.)	162
2	Heat map of intentional communities in the conterminous United States relative to selected natural and cultural features of potential interest for future research. (Source: Christina Lopez and Russell Weaver.)	165

Chapter 16

1	Awareness through the Body session, Auroville. (Source: Awareness through the Body, 2012.)	247

Chapter 18

1	Outline of the Freetown's location in central Copenhagen. (Source: Thomas S. J. Smith.)	272
2	The entrance to Christiania Bikes/Smedien. (Source: Thomas S. J. Smith.)	276
3	The Green Hall. (Source: Thomas S. J. Smith.)	278
4	Optimisten's main workshop space. (Source: Thomas S. J. Smith.)	279

Tables

Chapter 1

1 Different forms of eco-communities (Bang 2005; Dawson 2006; Fairlie 1996; Litfin 2014; Miller 2019; Pepper 1991)   8

Chapter 3

1 Murundaka vision statement (Murundaka Cohousing 2016)   51
2 Domains and sustainability practices at Murundaka   54
3 Key practices and elements in the creation and ongoing governance of Murundaka Cohousing Community   57
4 Key practices and elements in the provision of food in Murundaka Cohousing Community   61

Chapter 5

1 Examples of livelihoods engaged in by eco-community residents in Britain   87

Chapter 10

1 Overlap between selected planning concepts and ICs using real-world examples   160
2 IC and related concepts of communal/social arrangements, with relevant indicators   161
3 Indicators and data sources   163
4 Sustainability indicators in IC tracts and neighbouring tracts   166

Chapter 14

1 Example of negative Euros: Anti-monetary benefits and costs   221

Chapter 15

1 Australian Intentional Communities (IC) selected to represent eco-community activity in the Northern Rivers Region of New South Wales, listed to indicate discrete waves of development   231

Chapter 19

1 The diverse economy   287
2 Diverse economies in eco-communities   288

Contributors

Jon Anderson holds a Chair in Human Geography at the School of Geography and Planning, Cardiff University, UK. His research interests focus on the relations between culture, place and identity, particularly the geographies, politics and practices that emerge from these. His key publications include: *Understanding Cultural Geography: Places and Traces* (2010, 2015, 2022), *Surfing Spaces* (2023) and *Water Worlds* (with Kimberley Peters, 2014). Jon has a monograph on Literary Geographies coming out in 2025.

Adam J. Barker is a settler Canadian originally from the overlapping territories of the Haudenosaunee and Anishinaabe, near Hamilton, Ontario. His work focuses on the production of settler colonial space and identity, processes of social change and contemporary decolonization activism. Adam holds a PhD in Human Geography from the University of Leicester and an MA in Indigenous Governance from the University of Victoria (Canada). He is the author of *Making and Breaking Settler Space* (UBC Press, 2021) and co-author with Emma Battell Lowman of the book, *Settler: Identity and Colonialism, 2nd edition* (Fernwood Press, 2025).

Claudio Cattaneo has been a member of the Can Masdeu, a squatted eco-community and social centre in Barcelona since 2003 and, being a member of Research and Degrowth, is also a degrowth proponent. He holds a PhD from ICTA-UAB in ecological economics. He works as a researcher for Masaryk University, as a precarious professor in ecological economics for Universitat Autonoma where he directs the master in Political Ecology Degrowth and Environmental Justice and the online master on Degrowth, Ecology, Economics, Policy. His research interests span alternative and grassroots alternatives to the analysis of social metabolism of agrarian activity, to mobility and degrowth.

Tendai Chitewere is Professor in the School of the Environment and Director of the Center for Science and Mathematics Education at San Francisco State University. Her research critically examines the relationship between environmentalism, sustainable communities and capitalism, specifically as it intersects with racism, social injustice and persistent inequality. By defining the environment broadly, Dr Chitewere explores the deep tensions that challenge our abilities to address systemic social and environmental degradation. She holds a PhD in Anthropology as well as degrees in agriculture engineering and water resources.

Suryamayi Clarence-Smith is an activist-academic based in Auroville (India), the largest intentional community in the world. Her autoethnographic research on utopian and prefigurative practice in this community has been widely published: in the Alternatives to Capitalism in the 21st century series (Bristol University Press), where she published her monograph *Prefiguring Utopia: The Auroville Experiment*, the Ralahine Utopian Studies series (Peter Lang), *Sustainability Science* and *New Political Science,* amongst others. She is a faculty member of the California Institute of Integral Studies, and manages the Auroville Research Platform, an organization that facilitates research on Auroville. She holds a PhD in International Development from the University of Sussex, and a BA in Interdisciplinary Studies from the University of California, Berkeley.

Natasha Cornea is Associate Professor in Human Geography at the University of Birmingham. Her research explores everyday governance practices and the politics of urban environments, primarily in South Asia. Her governance research primarily examines the roles and influence of non-elite, non-state actors. She is also interested in how the environment, both as a socio-material system and an idea, becomes enrolled in the complex politics of urban life.

Matt Daly is Research Fellow with the Sustainable Buildings Research Centre, University of Wollongong (UOW). He holds a B.Eng (Environmental) (Hons I) from UOW and a PhD in Sustainable Futures from the University of Technology Sydney. Matt focuses on interdisciplinary and transdisciplinary research tackling complex and systemic problems in the housing and sustainable built environment space. He is passionate about exploring the worlds of those leading the way with sustainable houses and communities, and is also working to improve the basic standard of residential and commercial buildings. To this end, his research has explored both bottom-up niche innovations (e.g. community-led housing groups) and government-led policy responses, applying theories of social change, applied systems thinking, sustainability transitions and social practices. Matt has a long-standing interest understanding grassroots-led sustainability actions (such as the environmental impact of ecovillages and cohousing communities, and his PhD on sustainable practices). He's been a board member of Cohousing Australia since 2018, and convenes the Cohousing Australia Researcher Network. He's always interested in hearing from potential collaborators.

Marc Gavalda is Associate Professor in the Department of Economics and Economic History at the Universitat Autònoma de Barcelona. He is a researcher in environmental conflicts associated with Energy, Territory and Indigenous Peoples in the Amazon, and author of books such as 'La Recolonización' (2003), 'Viaje a Repsolandia' (2006) 'Patagonia Petrolera' (2008) and 'Gas Amazónico' (2013). He is the founder of the audiovisual collective Alerta Amazónica, and director of Punta de lanza (2020), Lágrimas de aceite (2017), Asfaltar Bolivia (2015), Alerta Amazonica (2013), Los Nahua 20 años después (2012), Patagonia petrolera (2008), Tentayapi, el pueblo intacto (2005) and Vivir sobre el Pozo (2002). He also directs television programmes on Barcelona's community television Lamosca.tv. He is an active member of the Okupat Kan Pasqual Social Center.

Nadine Gerner (MA) holds a double degree from the University of Münster, Sciences Po Lille and Toulouse. Throughout her Social Sciences course she specialized in sustainable development and gender studies, which led to her interest in degrowth and ecofeminism. Her quest for practices of degrowth brought her to study eco-communities in France through an ecofeminist lens. Nadine is a lecturer at various German universities where she teaches ecofeminism, care, social reproduction and degrowth. She is currently completing a PhD in the field ecofeminist activism. She is the author of German introductory book on ecofeminisms *Ökofeminismus: Zwischen Theorie und Praxis (2024)*. She also organizes transdisciplinary and activist conferences on expropriation and socialization for a democratic economy. Nadine likes to give workshops on ecofeminism and considers herself as a scholar activist. Therefore, she is organized in the climate justice movement, takes part in feminist campaigns, lives in a houseproject in Berlin and works in a feminist bar collective.

Helen Jarvis is Professor Emerita, Social Geography Engagement, Newcastle University: she gained her PhD from the London School of Economics in 1997. She has long been drawn to new forms of communalism around collaborative housing and resilient eco-communities in both her university research and teaching. She has gained practical insights of collective decision-making and group-work from periods of 'research in residence' with iconic intentional communities, including Christiania, Denmark, and Findhorn, Scotland, and comparative eco-community studies conducted in Britain, Australia and the United States. Helen is deeply committed to engaging community stakeholders in collaborative research and providing students with community-engaged learning. She is regularly invited to speak publicly about alternative housing and sustainable de-growth by grassroots community groups as well as academic institutions overseas. She has published three books on Cities, Gender, Work/Life Balance and Social Reproduction. She has a monograph on communities organizing for social and environmental justice coming out in 2026.

Nadia Johanisova (PhD) is Associate Professor at the Faculty of Social Studies at the Masaryk University, Brno, Czech Republic. She has a degree in biology from the Charles University in Prague and a PhD in environmental humanities from the Masaryk University. She has taught and written about critical economics, degrowth and 'different economies', variously designated as community economies, eco-social enterprises and social solidarity economies, and has researched such projects in the Czech Republic and in the UK, with particular emphasis on their environmental and degrowth dimensions. She is the author and co-author of books, book chapters and papers in English, Czech and Spanish.

K. Brooke Jones received an MA in Applied Anthropology from the University of North Texas, focusing on the relationship between humans and the environment. During graduate school she worked with the Maya Research Program conducting ethnographic research under the direction of Dr Grace Lloyd Bascopé. Her thesis, *Toward Sustainability: Assessing Progress at Dancing Rabbit Ecovillage*, was based on over two years of ethnographic research at Dancing Rabbit Ecovillage in Missouri, USA, in collaboration with Joshua Lockyer and under the direction of Dr James R. Veteto. Brooke currently serves as the Grants Development Officer for First Nations Development Institute; a national Native nonprofit working to uplift and sustain the lifeways and economies of Native communities throughout the United States.

Joshua Lockyer is Professor of Anthropology at Arkansas Tech University. He is the author of *Seeing Like a Commons: Eighty Years of Intentional Community Building and Commons Stewardship in Celo, North Carolina* which received the 2021 Timothy Miller Outstanding Book Award from the Communal Studies Association. He is also co-editor, with James R. Veteto, of the volume *Environmental Anthropology Engaging Ecotopia: Bioregionalism, Permaculture, & Ecovillages* along with numerous other articles and book chapters. He has been conducting engaged and activist scholarship with intentional communities, including Celo Community, Dancing Rabbit Ecovillage and Earthaven Ecovillage, for over twenty years.

Christina Lopez is an environmental geographer and earned her MS and PhD in geography at Texas State University in San Marcos, Texas, USA. Her research focuses on ecological intentional communities, environmental volunteerism and environmental values. She has held positions at several environmental organizations, such as the Plum Creek Watershed Partnership, Colorado River Alliance and the National Wildlife Federation. Christina also teaches environmental geography at Texas State University and currently works on the Clean Coast Texas project at the Meadows Center for Water and the Environment.

Jan Malý Blažek is an economist and social geographer with a PhD in environmental studies and an assistant professor at the Faculty of Architecture, Brno University of Technology, Czech Republic. Jan was the principal investigator of the interdisciplinary research project that explored the potential and barriers of introducing participatory housing in the Czech Republic through action research with city officials and residents. He also works in the interdisciplinary studio/collective MEZE on municipal strategic planning on climate change and housing, and is co-author of the comic book *How to Design a City for Life* (Prague: Heinrich Böll Stiftung, 2021). The chapter is an original result of his dissertation thesis on the economy of European eco-communities. It was intended to be published first in this book, but due to the delay in its publication, it was included in the dissertation thesis defended in 2024 as 'forthcoming chapter'. It was written as part of the Masaryk University's special research support for student projects, MUNI/A/1460/2021, 'Challenges of sustainable society through the lenses of humanities and social sciences'.

Anitra Nelson is an activist-scholar, Honorary Principal Fellow at the Informal Urbanism Research Hub in the Melbourne School of Design at the University of Melbourne (Australia). She lived in eco-communities in Australia for a decade and has stayed in intentional communities in the United States and Europe. She has an associated research interest in nonmonetary ('real value') economies. Works include

Small Is Necessary: Shared Living on a Shared Planet (2018, Pluto Press), on eco-collaborative living for sustainability, and *Housing for Degrowth: Principles, Models, Challenges and Opportunities* (co-editor, 2018, Routledge) including analyses of collaborative living. Her book *Beyond Money: A Postcapitalist Strategy* (2022, Pluto Press) draws selectively on such experiences and knowledge. She is an active member of the International Network of Urban Research and Action, on the editorial board of *Human Geography* and is a series editor for both the Palgrave Macmillan (Springer) Alternatives and Futures: Cultures, Practices, Activism and Utopias series and the Pluto Press Fireworks series. See more at https://anitranelson.info/

Jenny Pickerill is Professor of Environmental Geography at the University of Sheffield, England. Her work explores alternatives to capitalism that generate environmental and social justice. This has included working with environmentalists, experimental eco-communities, anarchist projects, social justice campaigns, self-build eco-housing and activists moving towards anti-colonialism. Her published books include *Eco-homes: People, Place and Politics* (2016), *Anti-War Activism: New Media and Protest in the Information Age* (2008, with Gillan and Webster) and *Cyberprotest: Environmental Activism Online* (2003), and co-edited several collections including *Occupy! A Global Movement* (2015), *Research Ethics and Social Movements: Scholarship, Activism & Knowledge Production* (2015) and *Low Impact Development* (2009). She has published over fifty articles and book chapters on eco-housing, eco-communities, social justice and environmentalism.

Elisa Schramm is a postdoctoral researcher in human geography at the University of Amsterdam. She holds a PhD from the University of Oxford in geography and the environment and her interests lie in understanding processes of transformation towards post-growth and post-capitalism, focused in particular on questions of dwelling (eco-communities and housing cooperatives) and mobilities (transport cooperatives). Her previous work has built on more-than-human geographies, STS and non-representational theories as well as economic geography and sociology.

Thomas S.J. Smith is a researcher, writer and editor based in northern Spain. He received his PhD in geography and sustainable development from the University of St Andrews, and has since held numerous roles including postdoctoral researcher in environmental studies at Masaryk University, Brno, and Marie Skłodowska-Curie postdoctoral fellow in geography at Ludwig Maximilian University (LMU), Munich. He is a member of the Community Economies Institute (CEI) and on the board of the Sustainable Consumption Research and Action Initiative (SCORAI). His research interests relate to social ecological transformations, economic localization and post-growth economics.

Kirsten Stevens-Wood is Senior Lecturer at Cardiff Metropolitan University based in the School of Education and Social Policy. Kirsten has been researching Intentional Communities since 2014 and is the lead for the Intentional Communities Research group, an international interdisciplinary group of academics and researchers. Her research encompasses diverse forms of collective and communal living from ecovillages to communes and protest communities. She is principally an ethnographic researcher and has completed a PhD exploring Creativity and experimentality in intentional communities. She is a qualified community development worker and an editor for the Diggers and Dreamers collective.

Russell Weaver, PhD, is a human geographer and Director of Research at the Cornell University School of Industrial and Labor Relations Buffalo Co-Lab. He was previously an Associate Professor at the Texas State University Department of Geography, where he taught courses in community geography, community development, urban planning, geographic thought and quantitative data analysis. His research programmes are aimed at understanding and contributing to pathways for context-sensitive, sustainable and equitable community change. Weaver is the lead author of the book *Shrinking Cities: Understanding Urban Decline in the United States*. Find him on Twitter @RustBeltGeo.

Acknowledgements

This book has been a highly collective effort over many years. What started as a loose idea emerging from a research project on affordable eco-homes (funded by the Churchill Trust, 2010) was extended through my fieldwork with British and Australian eco-communities in 2016. The project coalesced through a residential workshop on 'Eco-communities: Inclusive, creative and self-provisioning approaches' in Berlin in 2019 (funded by the Independent Social Research Foundation) and a seminar series on 'Eco-communities in an urban future' (funded by the Urban Studies Foundation, 2019–20). The majority of authors shared an early version of their chapters at these events, while some joined later as I discovered their research.

Thanks are due especially to the numerous and worldwide eco-community residents who have spent time, shared reflections and welcomed us to work with them over many years. I am also indebted to the patience of the twenty-one authors who stuck with me through numerous delays while I tried to balance being the Head of the Department of Geography at the University of Sheffield during multiple Covid lockdowns and still see this book through to completion. I am also privileged to work in such a fantastic academic department with inspiring colleagues who have put up with me talking about eco-communities for years.

I have had the good fortune of benefiting from two key international networks and associated conferences that share my fascination with eco-communities. The Intentional Communities annual conferences, run by Kirsten Stevens-Wood from Cardiff Metropolitan University, have been a vital source of connections, feedback and joy. The International Communal Societies Association (ICSA) conferences (particularly at Findhorn, Scotland in 2013 and in Denmark, 2022) have deeply informed my understandings of eco-communities, their possibilities and challenges. I am honoured to now be a board member of ICSA and look forward to co-organizing future events. This book, and particularly my chapters in it, has been significantly improved through feedback from numerous iterations of talks I have given at York, Glasgow, Newcastle, Edinburgh, Manchester and Sussex universities in the UK; Macquarie and Wollongong universities in Australia; University College Cork Ireland; and the University of Amsterdam, Netherlands.

Finally, there are always those crucial people who support any author during their writing. My partner Tim and Toffee our Labrador have patiently waited for me numerous times while I promised I would 'definitely finish work soon'. Naomi Hart, a lifelong friend and fabulous artist who shares my passion for all things ecological. Jessica Dubow, a colleague, friend and fellow troublemaker, has spurred me on in completing this book, even when I thought I really couldn't write any more. My wonderful colleague Matt Watson greatly improved my chapters with his excellent constructive insights, and numerous conversations with Jenny Atchinson about peopled landscapes pushed my thinking forward. Last, but definitely not least, thanks to Adam Barker, an amazing co-author who I have had the great fortune to work with for many years, and who also provided editorial assistance for this book.

I hope that you find the eco-communities explored in this book as fascinating and inspiring as I do.

World Map of Eco-communities

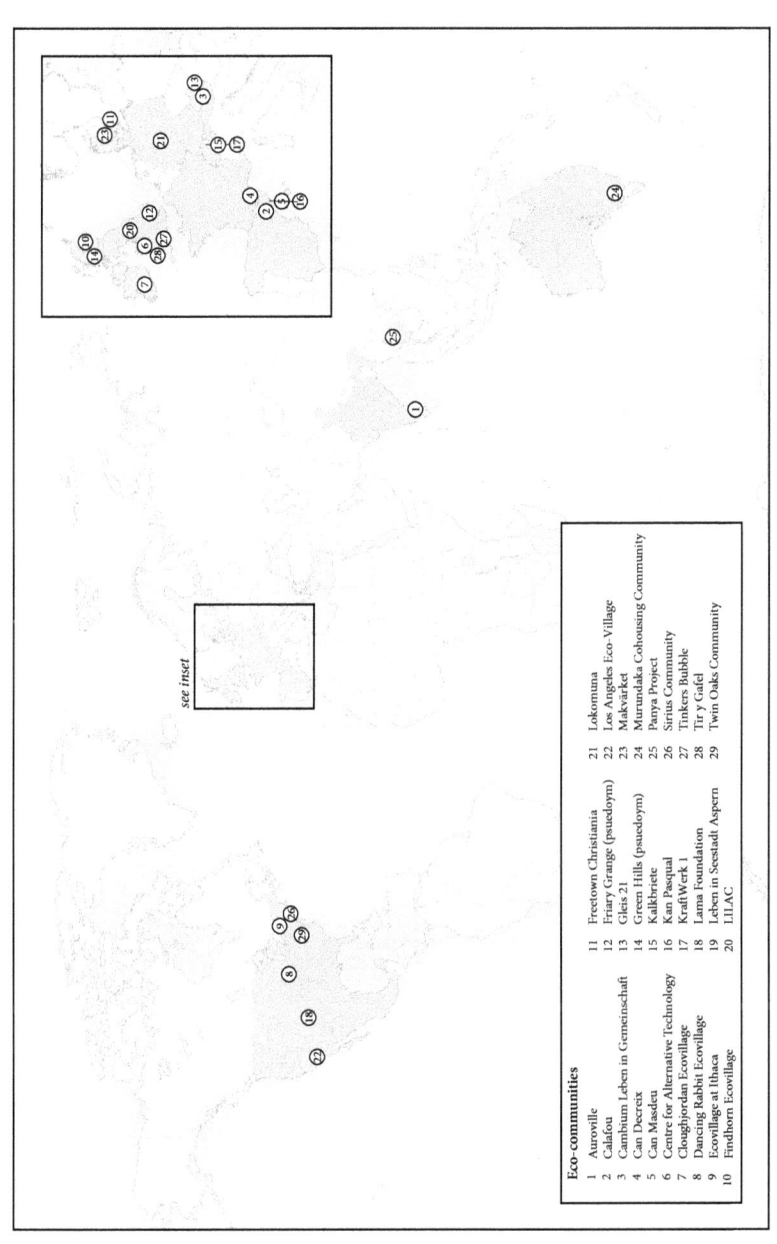

1

Collective dynamic socio-ecological experiments

Jenny Pickerill

Introduction

Eco-communities can inspire, provoke and challenge us to live more environmentally harmonious and collective lives. They are practical, ongoing experimentations on how we might survive well together – humans and all living beings on this planet (Gibson-Graham et al., 2016). Eco-communities answer the call to find 'new ways to live with the earth, to rework ourselves and our high energy, high consumption, and hyper-instrumental societies adaptively' (Plumwood 2007, 1).

Using an image of Findhorn eco-village (Scotland) IPPC Working Group III report (2022) advocated for innovative ecologically focused experimental systems-orientated approaches educating and demonstrating positive examples of change. Eco-communities are a vital example of this whole systems-oriented approach. They experiment in building new material infrastructures (houses, energy generation, food production, water and sewage systems) and social infrastructures (collective decision-making structures, systems of sharing, ways of being in common).

Eco-communities are examples of grassroot efforts at socio-ecological transformation – self-organized practices, infrastructures and spaces that seek to transform ways of being, living and working (Chatterton and Pusey 2020; Renau 2018). They are part of broader social movements and activist initiatives that seek to build post-capitalist alternatives, which are a 'reflective recalibration of economic, political and social institutions to support a temporally and spatially equitable, sustainable and dignified survival of the human and of non-human species' (Schmid 2019, 1).

While many eco-communities – certainly those explored in this book – attempt to transform all elements of their daily lives (a holistic and interconnected reworking of how we dwell, eat, work, educate, reproduce, age, etc.), these processes are always incomplete, in-the-making, unfinished and messy (Schelly et al., 2024). In part this is because humans are dynamic, non-rational and contradictory beings, but also because the creation of alternatives always struggle in tension with, against and beyond capitalism and the associated structures colonialism, the state, patriarchy, racism and heteronormativity.

A central question running through all the chapters in this book is the challenge of community living, particularly how gender and race can remain intractable points of difference and exclusion. The ways eco-communities confront these questions, or rather where fault lines of communal life hinder the tackling of knotty problems, are as interesting as their apparent successes. Indeed, what even constitutes success in eco-communities is rarely defined and even less often evaluated.

This struggle with the moments of incompleteness and the demands of living in community is what makes working with eco-communities so fascinating (Shannon et al., 2021). This book is not about whether or not eco-communities have achieved an end goal of a utopian collective ecological life; rather, it explores the ongoing processes of navigating tensions and contradictions that nonetheless create hope that we might be able to live otherwise and to be involved in world-making projects (Tsing 2015). Indeed, because eco-communities are experimental and ongoing, there can be unexpected consequences, or surprising outcomes (Hong and Vicdan 2016; Schelly et al., 2024).

This book, then, is about the 'now'. It exposes what is possible in these moments of polycrises – the climate emergency, inequity and the resulting poverty, the rise of fascism, and refugee abandonment – what hope is there, and what do eco-communities' practical and social experimentations teach us, *and* reveal, about how we live?

Eco-communities regularly challenge convention, particularly approaches to time, economics, justice, democracy and cultural norms. Eco-community residents are more than aware of the difficulties they face (there are numerous highly reflexive pieces written by residents such as Blue 2024; Kinkade 1994; Lanphear 2014; Walker 2005; Würfel 2012), and authors in this book work *with* participants in exploring these tensions. There are elements of eco-communities which have already received significant attention, including motivating values (Kirby 2003), interpersonal relations and communications (Christian 2003), novel decision-making structures (Rau and Koch-Gonzalez 2018), stages of formation (Bang 2007; Christian 2003), practices of sharing and commons (Jarvis 2019), layout and design (Chatterton 2015; McCamant and Durrett 1988), how to build eco-homes (Pickerill 2016), reducing reliance on fossil fuels (Copeland et al., 2023), permaculture (Birnbaum and Fox 2014; Pickerill 2013; Veteto and Lockyer 2008) and food self-sufficiency (Brombin 2015; Sanford 2014; Ulug et al., 2021). We know, therefore, that collective living can be a cost-effective way of life (Chatterton 2013), reduce feelings of loneliness (Glass 2020), increase quality of life (Puplampu et al., 2020), and can create meaningful relationships (Kunze 2020; Wechuli 2017).

There has been less attention paid to the tensions, negotiations and compromises inherent to socio-ecological transformations (explored here in the section 'Living Ecologically'). The questions of who lives in them (section 'Negotiating questions of inclusion'), how collective governance practices are framed and managed (section 'Doing It Together'), the financial necessity of meeting basic costs and building livelihoods are often continuous and acute (section 'Building diverse economies'). Running through all these section are interrogations of whether, and in what ways and in what ways, eco-communicates adequately reflect on questions of class, race and ethnicity, economics, age, spirituality, gender, disability, relationships to the state, non-humans, legality and replicability. While some of these questions are finally beginning to receive the attention they deserve (such as Ergas' [2021] exploration of gender inequality in eco-communities), there is much work still to be done.

The majority of chapters in this book explore everyday dynamics that reveal how socio-ecological change is manifest, and the complex processes of experimenting, learning, failing and abandoning new approaches. There remains a partiality to eco-community research, including in this book, not just because the definitional boundaries are fuzzy, but also due to a predominance of work from the Global North, and a tendency for academics to work with established large-scale eco-communities. The work shared here is all grounded in actually existing real-world empirical examples. It takes a pragmatic approach because while utopian imaginations can be inspiring there is a vital necessity to ground, detail and demonstrate what is possible in the contemporary moment. Here, the necessity of hope or the envisioning of a better future lives alongside the proximate and contingent day-to-day. This book takes an interdisciplinary, but social science-focused, approach to examining eco-communities, and shares an emphasis on using qualitative, ethnographic and participatory methodologies.

Post-capitalist possibilities

This book is part of what Erik Olin Wright (2010) calls a radical epistemology and an emancipatory social science that purposefully diagnoses and challenges, designs and then shares alternatives. As evidenced by the diverse disciplinary homes of the authors in this book (Geography, Sociology, Anthropology, Political Science, Architecture and Design) eco-communities are researched (empirically and conceptually) through multivarious interdisciplinary perspectives. This includes chapters focusing on social practice theories, environmental governance processes, measures of consumption, social learning and settler colonialism.

Despite this diversity, the analytical framework that shapes this book and its arguments is rooted in a broad post-capitalist ethics. Post-capitalism is the active search for, and experimental prefiguration of, liberatory worldmaking that challenges the domination of capitalism and its associated interlocking forms of oppression such as colonialism, patriarchy, racism and heteronormativity. A post-capitalist ethics particularly builds on anarchist and feminist (and to a lesser extent post-structural Marxist) interventions which question existing societal norms and structures. An examination of the *potential* of alternatives to capitalism is emerging as a nascent theory of social change, a (albeit partial and fragmented) conceptualization of utopian intent and a grounded-theory of how to generate the necessary socio-ecological transformations to realize this potential (Feola et al., 2021).

Far from a unified theory, the post-capitalism which shapes analysis in this book is inspired by three contentions. First, that anarchist articulations of anti-state, anti-capitalist, non-violent change with its emphasis on mutual aid, free association, co-operation and solidarity practices enable grassroots collective action (Smessaert and Feola 2023). Anarchist emphasis on collectivity, reciprocity, communal ownership (anti-private property) and the rejection of systems of hierarchical rule fuel many social movements (Springer 2012). The anarchist concept of integrality (Bookchin 1990; Reclus 1884), akin to acknowledging the interdependence of all living things and a holism in how we need to understand the world, is already a central tenet in social science research, especially geography (Smessaert and Feola 2024). The anarchist focus on building new relations (with each other, more-than-humans, and environments) provides a multi-scale spatiality for everyday radical transformative change (Newman 2010). Anarchism offers two further concepts that are central to post-capitalism: prefiguration and interstituality. As Monticelli (2024) aptly explores, prefiguration is the enaction in the present of how we would like the future to be. It is a focus on the *here* and *now*. Interstituality is the recognition that social change often takes place in the 'cracks' of seemingly hegemonic systems and rarely from large-scale revolution or overthrow of the state (Holloway 2010; Monticelli 2018).

Second, that feminists argue we should pay attention to how power is often gendered in society *and* how processes of social reproduction (i.e. all activities which support the reproduction of labour, including childbearing and care work) are rarely recognized or valued in capitalist economies (Di Chiro 2019; Harcourt 2019). By challenging the division between public and private spaces (such as the home), highlighting inequalities and inequities, and detailing the differentiated everyday experiences of women, people of colour, LGBTQ+ and other marginalized or minoritized peoples, feminism complicates and extends post-capitalist imaginaries.

Third, in anarchism and feminism there is an explicit recognition of diversity – of place, people, values and beliefs, systems of organization, daily life and experiences (especially of capitalism). Post-capitalism is inspired by this attention to diverse ways of being in the world that challenges any universalist impulse (Schmid and Smith 2021). There is a political emphasis on diverse ontologies and diverse economies. Recognition of the pluriversality of ontologies (ways of defining what exists) enables both a celebration of a world of multitudes (Escobar 2020; Pickerill 2024) and the possibility of an 'onto-shift' (Bollier and Helfrich 2019) where there is a change in how we understand and organize the world. Rather than seek to build a one-size-fits-all alternative, the need for differentiated and diverse experiments (in this case eco-communities) is advocated, where there are places of interconnection between them and also spaces of disjuncture. Similarly, the diverse economies approach expands what is considered to constitute 'the economy' by identifying the diverse economic forms that create, restrict, support, avoid, co-exist and challenge capitalist practices (Gibson-Graham 2006). This requires a 'reading for difference' of the 'capitalist' landscape and a rethinking of political agency (Margarida Fernandes Esteves et al., 2023). This approach calls for 'appreciating the heterogeneity of perspectives and methods that flourish' (Gibson 2014, 286) in the quest for worldmaking *otherwise*.

This post-capitalist ethics shapes the questions we ask and what are looking for in eco-communities. That is a quest to make visible and resist power dynamics, absences and inequalities in eco-communities *alongside* recognizing acts that creatively generate new relations that enable innovative ways of being, living, working and surviving. The tension, then, that persists throughout this book, is a deliberate recognition that socio-ecological transformation is imperfect, always-in-the-making and messy. Thus, alongside the call to critically examine what eco-communities achieve, we need to interrogate where they fail: not as a way to dismiss them as inadequate change makers, but to creatively *work with* them in their already-existing attempts to move forward and build alternative worlds. Indeed, eco-communities can reveal spaces of potential intervention in capitalism, even if they are (not yet) able to fully mobilize in such spaces of opportunity.

This approach is underpinned by three political impulses. First, a conscious choice of *which* eco-communities are engaged with in this book. We are purposefully working with those who express post-capitalist ethics (even if just implicitly), are aware of their challenges and contradictions, and want to (in the main) become more inclusive, collective, ecological, financially autonomous and participatory (Lallement 2024). These eco-communities demonstrate a desire for broader-scale change, beyond being privileged 'lifeboats' solely for their residents. This choice deliberately excludes those eco-communities with explicit eco-fascist, far-right, white supremacist or capitalist intentions. Although as we explore, we actively critique some eco-communities that exhibit some of these worrying political tendencies in order to question whether this is intentional (and thus problematic) or unconscious slippage (which can be made visible and rectified). Likewise, as eco-communities remain prone to capitalist co-optation, we seek to constructively identify where a post-capitalist ethics is being eroded, weakened or undermined, in order to encourage rectification or at least recognition of the direction of travel for the community (Hollender 2016).

Second, we deliberately focus on eco-communities which seek to change *all* their relations. That is those who acknowledge the interdependencies and integrality of changing how humans operate in the world require new relationalities with each other, more-than-humans, places, environments and ontologies. In turn, generating and sustaining new relations will look and feel different across places and peoples. This recognizes that eco-communities need to prioritize differently given their diverse contexts; be that national politics, legal structures, societal norms or experiences of oppression. Such an approach not only values the (geographical) diversity integral to a post-capitalist ethics; it also (see Chapter 5) engages those contexts in which a community's appreciation of the longer – and often hidden – histories of place is limited. All of this complicates attempts at comparative analysis. The aim is not to directly compare and contrast eco-communities with each other, but rather to identify commonalities and trends to answer broader questions about whether and how eco-communities contribute to socio-ecological transformations.

Third, in the quest to interrogate the why, how, what and implications of eco-communities, we retain a hopeful ethics in celebrating what is achieved as much as identifying limitations or failures. This positivity is a political choice in an era of polycrisis and a stance against the at-times overly pessimistic doom-laden criticality of academia. Here there is a political impulse to seek, identify and share what we (collectively) *can* do to survive well together; what options are being experimented with in spite of their apparent limitations. This is a political choice to identify hope as much as hopelessness, to read the world for possibilities as much as pitfalls. We retain a critical analysis in this evaluation of what kinds of alternatives are being shaped by eco-communities. Indeed the anarchist and feminist perspectives employed here demand critical reflections on such imaginaries. But crucially, that some eco-communities might struggle in their navigation of, for example, class inclusivity is identified as a point of learning, not a reason to discard eco-communities wholesale as a failed political project.

The constituency of many eco-communities as ostensibly middle class (as defined by education, profession, wealth and values) has long been acknowledged (Pickerill 2016). What is interesting is less the identification of the absence of class diversity and more how it is being tackled (Bell 2020). Taking a hopeful, future-orientated stance requires working on navigating tensions, not just naming them. There are calls to recognize the heterogeneity and contradictions behind class categories, and for residents to use their class privilege and wealth, to wield their power for liberation for all. Simultaneously, Cardwell (2024) ran a fascinating and thought-provoking participatory workshop with British eco-community members which revealed how value differences between social classes result in contrasting approaches to authority, governance and conflict. She demonstrated how class identities can shape our implicit values, which coalesce into collective assumptions of appropriate behaviour. By identifying some of these assumptions she revealed how and why working-class values, practices and activities are too often deemed ill-fitting with established eco-community social infrastructures, resulting in either working-class people feeling out of place and not belonging, or in their active exclusion for 'inappropriate' behaviour. This slow hard process of working carefully in participatory and embodied ways with eco-communities to become self-aware of class bias and difference is vital, to be celebrated, and achieved far more than a harsh academic critique which fails to suggest any pathways forward.

A post-capitalist ethics, then, creates space for nuance, messiness, recognition of absences and work-yet-to-be-done, but maintains a future-orientated momentum that asserts a need to always continue in seeking more just equitable and ecological worlds.

Experimental eco-communities

The concept of community can be understood as a 'mode of relating' (Calhoun 1998, 391). It can be experienced as a sense of belonging, a form of identity, a place of sharing or as a mode of interdependency. Community-based politics can be divisive, and communities are understood here as 'sites of contestation, difference, tension, and distinction' (Taylor Aiken et al., 2017, 463). There are an infinite number of forms of community – of place, of interest, of choice, of practice, etc. If communities share a deliberate geographical proximity, an intertwining and overlapping of daily lives, and shared purpose, some experience this as insular 'stifling, oppressive, dogmatic, fixed' (Swyngedouw, quoted in Nelson, Chapter 12). This understanding of community is of closed, reactionary and politically regressive spaces.

Community initiatives have been criticized for being post-political for their focus on symptoms rather than structural causes (Taylor Aiken 2017). For example, community projects which focus on litter-picking rather than waste reduction. Indeed, there has been a tendency for the notion of community to be mobilized as a way to relocalize environmental governance. This enables active participation at a 'meso' scale, generates activities and activism, but simultaneously risks delimiting the scale at which politics is concerned (such was the criticism of the Transition Towns movement, Taylor Aiken 2019).

Community governance, or governance via communities, holds inherent risks of exclusion, of homogeneity and of unequal power relations (Kumar and Taylor Aiken 2021). For example, Morrow and Martin (2019), in researching urban food harvesting, confirmed white people had privileged access to space while Black people suffered policing and surveillance. As Hubbard (2024) argues 'some communities are more able to enact alternatives than others'. This inequity in power relations can be as a power-over other communities, but also often acts as unequal power dynamics *within* communities (Pickerill 2021). Community, then, is not a normative ideal. Yet, 'community' retains its potential for enabling a certain form of organizational power, of forging connections between people, and creating a powerful 'geo-political architecture' (Wills 2012, 114). As Kumar and Taylor Aiken (2021) argue community is most powerful when understood and practised as 'fluid bonds of solidarity'.

The challenge then is how eco-communities, which tend to be geographically proximate with shared values, can avoid being closed entities wielding unequal power. As Miller (2019) argues, community need not be essentialist, but rather can be a powerful political project of togetherness. Community 'calls us to continually ask and struggle over questions of *who* to care for and *how*' (Miller 2019a, 118). Community can be a shared condition of being-in-common that remains open to how commonality is defined and experienced (Kunze 2020). As Nelson (Chapter 12) argues, there is a need to focus on and examine 'best practice' eco-communities if we are to find those most likely to generate the progressive, inclusive, plural and open approaches to world-making otherwise that we are seeking. Throughout this book eco-communities that fall short of this potential are analysed not because they have failed, but in recognition of messy empirical worlds, and to support and identify how they can continue to be improved, always acknowledging that being-in-common is a dynamic ongoing process.

Eco-communities, then, are forms of community that share an explicit intention to reduce their environmental impact while meeting human needs. They are sites of collaboration and collective housing and living that develop experimental approaches to ecology, economy, community and consciousness (Kunze 2012; Litfin 2014). Eco-communities,

> are those that strive to be self-sufficient, environmentally sustainable, and generally have a low impact on the Earth. Communities are generally designed (physically and socially) to be environmentally responsible. The participants often choose to work on the land or limit other economic activities … These communities strive to produce their own food and energy, usually through alternative means and renewable energies: solar, wind, and water.
>
> (Lopez and Weaver 2019, 200)

Key aspirations of an eco-community include (but are not always present): a culture of self-provision and self-reliance; minimal environmental impact and minimal resource use; low-cost affordable approaches; extended relations of mutual care for others;

progressive values (e.g. towards gender equality); and an emphasis on collectivist and communal sharing.

Eco-communities of various forms have existed for decades (Kanter 1972; McCammant and Durret 1988; Miller 2019b; Pepper 1991). Yet despite many challenges and a high rate of failure, there are now an increasing number of eco-communities worldwide (Magnusson 2018). Eco-communities are deliberately defined here as a broad concept that encompasses eco-villages (Bang 2005), intentional communities (Meijering et al., 2007), co-housing (Bunker et al., 2011; LaFond and Tsvetkova 2017; McCammant and Durret 1988) and low impact developments (Fairlie 1996), among others (Crabtree-Hayes 2023) (Table 1). As this diversity suggests, eco-communities are best understood as a worldwide network (Bang 2007; LeVasseur 2013). There are a variety of global organizations that seek to support, represent and advocate for this network including the Global Ecovillage Network, the Foundation for Intentional Community, Diggers and Dreamers, Europtopia, CoHousing Research Network and the International Communal Studies Association.

Table 1 Different forms of eco-communities (Bang 2005; Dawson 2006; Fairlie 1996; Litfin 2014; Miller 2019; Pepper 1991)

Type of eco-community	Brief description
Commune	Co-operative living without any private homes, all spaces are shared.
Eco-village	A community with shared values around environmental issues as a core focus. Interested in establishing long-term basic services such as housing, food provision, livelihoods, education, etc.
Ecological intentional community/ intentional eco-community/ Sustainability-orientated intentional communities	Diversity in aims but often include becoming more socially, economically and ecologically sustainable. Structured around particular core goals and shared values and intentions. Reducing environmental damage is a core goal.
Eco-collaborative housing communities	Self-governing, resident-designed multiple-household communities sharing certain spaces and facilities.
Ecologically sustainable communities	Reducing environmental impact is a core goal, but there might not necessarily be articulated shared values and intentions beyond the ecological.
Eco-housing project	Multiple housing project focused on high-quality environmental design and building.
Co-housing	Co-operative living where people have private homes but share facilities (e.g. energy/ heat production, waste management, laundry, gardens, meeting rooms, childcare, communal kitchen).
Low-impact development	Low visual impact by blending with surroundings, built from local, recycled or natural materials, small-scale and environmentally efficient. Autonomous in the sense that they generate their own energy (through wind, solar or water power) and deal with their waste (through recycling and composting). Tends to be rural, off-grid with a large emphasis on agricultural work.

There are relatively few large (over 400 people) eco-communities. Notable examples include Findhorn, Scotland (Meltzer 2015); Ecovillage at Ithaca, USA (Chitewere 2017); Damanhur, Italy (Fois 2019); Zurich housing co-operatives, Switzerland; Christiania, Denmark (Jarvis 2013); and Auroville, India (Devon 2019). Most are smaller with between 30 and 100 inhabitants. For example, Sieben Linden, Germany, has 150 participants (Andreas and Wagner 2012); Twin Oaks, USA, has 100 residents (Kuhlmann 2000); LILAC, England has 50 members (Chatterton 2015); and Dancing Rabbit, USA, has 30 people on site (Lockyer 2017).

While these eco-communities are mostly situated in Europe: Germany, Switzerland, Czech Republic, England, Wales, Scotland, Ireland, Denmark and France, the book includes examples from the United States, Thailand, India and Australia. This book deliberately includes a wide range of well-known, established eco-communities such as Findhorn (Jarvis, Chapter 15), Auroville (Clarence-Smith, Chapter 16), Dancing Rabbit, USA (Locyker and Jones, Chapter 2), Lama Foundation, USA (Barker and Pickerill, Chapter 8), Christiania (Smith and Johanisova, Chapter 18), and Centre for Alternative Technology, Wales (Anderson, Chapter 6). But it also explores smaller or emerging examples including Tir y Gafel, Wales (Pickerill, Chapter 5), Murundaka Cohousing Community, Australia (Daly, Chapter 3), Panya Project, Thailand (Barker and Pickerill, Chapter 8), Tinkers Bubble, England (Maly Blažek, Chapter 19), Cloughjordan Ecovillage, Ireland (Nelson, Chapter 12), and Can Decreix, France (Schramm, Chapter 4).

Despite the breadth of the definition and examples, there are six shared characteristics of eco-communities: collectivity and collaboration, being experimental, being dynamic and ongoing, centring an environmental praxis, being anti-capitalist and a future-oriented approach.

Collectivity and collaboration

Eco-communities are about building and living overlapping lives, finding ways to exist together and mutually support each other (Meltzer 2005). There is an ethos of do-it-together, a sociality which facilitates mutual support and extended relations of care (Bang 2005). Eco-communities have strong relational cultures of interdependence and collectivist values (Arrigoitia and West 2021; Van Schyndel Kasper 2008). These are practised and reinforced by developing 'interpersonal competences' (Schwab and Roysen 2022) and participatory democracy (Sullivan 2016). There is an emphasis on equity in participation; collective decision-making approaches which seek to resist hierarchies such as sociocracy (Rau and Koch-Gonzalez 2018). This intense collaboration is often reliant upon, but also Co-constitutes the development of a collective identity (Ergas 2010). Central to this collaboration is a quest to share – resources, materials, spaces, skills and care obligations (Jarvis 2013). Eco-community living, then, is shaped by numerous reciprocal actions (Meltzer 2005) and increases members' wellbeing (Grinde 2018).

Experimental

Eco-communities are also experimental spaces of invention and innovation (Clarence-Smith 2023; Fois 2019; Stevens-Wood 2020). They 'understand themselves as experimental responses to the violence of environmental and social crises and as demonstration sites and models for broader social change' (Sanford 2017, 8). For example, many experiment in non-market (non-monetary) activities to create new forms of economic sustainability (Blažek 2016). Being experimental requires diverse skills, engaging with risk and ongoing processes of learning. As a result, residents tend to avoid skills specialization, develop broad expertise, and learn through doing. As Lennon and Berg (2022) reflect in their analysis of how eco-communities in Norway are perceived externally, this emphasis on being experimental tends to create a sense of distinction from conventional society (an 'othering') and residents are considered either entrepreneurial or idealistic by wider society.

Dynamic and ongoing

Given this experimental approach it is not surprising that eco-communities are also dynamic, in constant flux, messy spaces of doing, making and creating. Hence there are many unknowns as eco-communities experiment which create tensions and contradictions, but as Sekulova et al. (2017) argue there is also a richness and diversity of texture and possibilities. They are unfinished materially, socially and economically. Eco-communities evolve through different phases, such as pioneering, maturity and stability and old age, but are never static (Bang 2007).

Environmental praxis

Eco-communities actively reduce their environmental impact in novel ways through an ecosophical approach that seeks ecological harmony (Anderson 2017). They practise low-impact lifestyles by sharing common infrastructures, resources and in urban areas dense housing arrangements. Their emphasis on self-sufficiency seeks to meet many of their needs onsite (such as food, livelihoods, childcare) which further reduces environmental impact from goods distribution, commuting and packaging (Sanford 2017). Many rural eco-communities are deliberately land-based with self-sufficient agriculture and permaculture practices (Stevens-Wood 2020). Material infrastructures (such as novel eco-home designs: Walker 2005) are used to reinforce changes to social practices to encourage environmentally sustainable praxis (Roysen and Mertens 2019). This way, novel ecosystems of practices are coalesced which 'foster "social learning" by providing environments where people can engage in, learn, and reproduce new practices and skills' (Temesgen 2020, 4).

Eco-communities have been highly successful in dramatically reducing environmental impacts and CO_2 emissions (Copeland et al., 2023; Daly 2017). Radical reductions in environmental impacts were recorded in Sirius Community, Earthaven and Ecovillage at Ithaca (all in the United States) (Sherry 2019), and 'per capita resource consumption for inhabitants of Dancing Rabbit Ecovillage is less than ten percent of the average American in most major categories' (Boyer 2016, 47). Similar radical reductions have been calculated at The Self-Sustaining Village (Denmark) – with a carbon footprint that is 60% below national average (Gausset and Jensen 2024) and Sieben Lindens ecological footprint is less than a third of the German average (Würfel 2012).

Anti-capitalist and diverse livelihoods

While many eco-communities might not articulate themselves as explicitly anti-capitalist, the majority start from a quest to remove themselves from capitalist extractive systems *and* create alternative beyond capitalist relations through diverse livelihoods and non-monetary systems (Baker 2013). Eco-communities often encourage home- or land-based livelihoods, minimize economic needs, and some share income. This is differently articulated as voluntary simplicity (Sanford 2017; Vannini and Taggart 2013) or moving towards post-capitalism (Chatterton and Pusey 2020). These approaches share a quest to disrupt and dismantle existing capitalist systems, but these attempts will likely always be partial, incomplete and fragmented. As Winters (2016) explores in how Christiania residents opposed a new cycle path through the community, this can result in seemingly surprising contradictions, but is actually a resistance to neoliberal approaches to environmental governance and a reassertion of autonomous, grassroots and anti-capitalist ethics. At the same time, also in Denmark, there is a mainstreaming of eco-communities via top-down municipal support and professional community builders (Nielsen-Englyst and Guasset 2024).

Future-oriented

The final shared characteristic of eco-communities is in being future-oriented (Würfel 2012). Eco-communities are engaged in both prefigurative actions and building towards more environmentally and socially just futures (Litfin 2014). Eco-communities are invested in processes of social change and transformation (Meltzer 2005). They seek to enact collective change with the potential to demonstrate, influence and inspire others beyond the boundaries of their community site. This is evidenced in Dancing Rabbit, USA, who emphasize 'sharing their experiences and lessons with broader publics through media, research, and educational programs' (Lockyer 2017, 519). It is also illustrated in the variety of eco-community locations. Most established and large eco-communities are located in rural areas because of the space, privacy, freedom and lower land costs available (e.g. Findhorn, Scotland). But in addition to some long-running urban sites (e.g. Christiania in Copenhagen was formed in 1971, and UfaFabrik in Berlin in 1979), there has been a purposeful increase in urban experiments. These include LILAC, England (Chatterton 2015), Kailash Eco-village and Los Angeles Eco-Village, USA, and Cascade CoHousing and Christie Walk, Australia (Cooper and Baer 2019). This emphasis on urban sites recognizes the necessity to shape sustainable urbanism, but also that urban eco-communities can attract greater political attention through proximity.

Critically questioning eco-communities

While these six shared characteristics of eco-communities suggest a progressive, inclusive and successful approach to socio-ecological transformations, empirical research reveals multiple challenges and limits to eco-community living. As Blue (2024) attests, eco-communities struggle with homogeneity, internal crisis, lack of succession planning, unresolved conflict and burnout. The premise of this book is to interrogate the why, how, what and implications of eco-communities. This interrogation, however, is undertaken with care; working with eco-community residents and their own critical self-awareness, with a generosity in reading for hopeful possibilities of agency, as much as for systemic failings and struggle, and as future-orientated. That is, critically questioning eco-communities *in order to* seek world-making otherwise as an assertively political endeavour.

Building on what is already researched and known about eco-communities (briefly summarized above), this book asks four critical questions: (1) Can eco-communities generate socio-ecological transformations, and if so how and in what form?; (2) Who lives in eco-communities and what are the implications of this demographic composition?; (3) What does it entail to organize via collective governance practices?; and (4) How do eco-communities operate financially and generate money and livelihoods?

There is an overarching concern here with what kinds of alternative worlds are being made and shaped by eco-communities, and therefore what the broader implications are of some of the messiness, partiality and exclusions of eco-communities. To put it simply, if eco-communities are incomplete utopian experiments in what ways are they useful as aspirational 'models', tools or learning spaces of surviving well together?

Transformative potential

In examining the generation of socio-ecological transformations, Lopez and Weaver (Chapter 10) conducted a quantitative analysis of eco-communities in the contiguous United States. They develop proxy indicators to measure the success of eco-communities against the environmental and social goals that most aspire to in their values and mission statements. Their findings suggest that intentional communities 'have fewer negative environmental impacts relative to their conventional neighbouring communities', but are less inclusive, affordable and diverse.

Anderson (Chapter 6), therefore, asks whether eco-communities 'change the world' or 'simply the world of their participants'? Anderson categorizes into three groups those who engage in or encounter eco-communities: insiders (key committed participants), thresholders (share values, but less involved) and outsiders (observers or temporary visitors). He focuses on outsiders and how transformative their encounters with eco-communities are for them.

Researching with the Centre for Alternative Technology (CAT) in Wales – an established and long-running residential and environmental education centre – over seven years, Anderson has previously demonstrated how insiders and thresholders experienced the eco-community as deeply transformative in changing daily practices, adoption of eco-technologies and benefitting from the collectivity of community. However, while outsiders were initially excited, hopeful and inspired by the variety of green infrastructures, technologies and innovations offered at CAT they were ultimately disappointed by the possibilities presented. Outsiders, already interested in socio-ecological transformations enough to visit, yearned for more radical up-to-date innovations and were dismayed by the familiarity of some of the technologies (wind power, recycling systems, etc) and the contradictions of the epistemic and physical distance between a remote rural eco-community and their everyday lives as outsiders.

Perhaps most revealing was that outsiders were either already familiar with, or unconvinced by, the technological innovations being displayed and understood these technologies as being inadequate and *not* the most transformative element of eco-communities. They realized not just that socio-ecological transformations could not be led or solely about technological innovation, but that what made CAT interesting were the practices of residents – the collectivity, sharing of skills and responsibilities, engagements with nature etc – that were less visible to visitors. It was the transformative potential of 'community' that the outsiders were inspired by, but which at CAT they only caught tantalizing glimpses. This distinction is crucial to understand not just for education endeavours, but in acknowledging what is most valuable in what eco-communities offer.

Lockyer and Jones (Chapter 2) work with members of Dancing Rabbit Ecovillage, Missouri, USA, to explore how they have been particularly successful in reducing consumption and the impacts on how members felt and experienced quality of life. The authors identify aspects of eco-community living that enhanced quality of life – togetherness, sociality, mutual support, care and concern (beyond the heteronormative notion of family) and closeness to nature. Yet unsurprisingly there was a shared struggle with the unfinished, still-in-progress experimental elements of material life where the incompleteness of structures led to inconvenience, dirt and battles with pests (sparrows, rats and mice). Some members also bemoaned the lack of privacy, autonomy and racial diversity. Ultimately the trade-off at Dancing Rabbit is accepting fewer material infrastructures, convenience and things, in exchange for the benefits of togetherness and collectivity.

There is also an important focus on mental health and an acknowledgement of the need to shift expectations about how happiness is achieved. As Lockyer and Jones argue, while life in an eco-community 'does not suck', it might do for those less willing to sacrifice any elements of comfort or convenience for their values. Therefore, the possibilities offered by Dancing Rabbit for radically reducing consumption might not be translatable to conventional society.

Sticking with the focus on consumption, Matthew Daly (Chapter 3) works with a purpose-built suburban co-housing eco-community in Melbourne, Australia, to demonstrate the potential to change everyday social practices of consumption. Residents did directly change their food provisioning through communal gardening, prioritizing localization of supply and an increase in the consumption of organic goods. Most residents credited the act of living together in an eco-community as enabling these new and changed practices.

Yet the impact on consumption practices was only indirect. Residents were actively involved in the formation and design stages of the community, particularly its material infrastructures. Yet this does not directly result in more sustainable consumption. It shifts the priorities of the community in creating infrastructures of opportunity (like the large garden, rain water tanks or photovoltaic energy generation). Daly argues that these institutional governance and new systems' approaches to sustainability are just as vital as the direct material changes evidenced by food provisioning practices. It is in this mix of replacing, or substituting, less sustainable practices, alongside developing new practices, that eco-communities demonstrate the possibilities and hopefulness of socio-ecological transformation.

These chapters suggest that eco-communities enable transformation within their borders, but struggle to shape broader-scale change. By design, eco-communities operate at a community scale (also called human scale) and therefore it is 'common to dismiss these initiatives for being too marginal and for failing to attend to deeper structural problems' (Schwab and Roysen 2022, 2). It is assumed by critics that transformations can only occur if initiatives are 'scaled-up' and amplified. Two assumptions are made here: first, that eco-communities only benefit residents, and second that scales of transformation and structures of human agency are effective only to the level of the local, rather than influence the global as well (Schmid 2019).

The validity of the first assumption very much depends on the specific eco-community. As Kehl and Then (2013) found, in their analysis of German cohousing, there are examples where the borders of eco-communities are tightly closed, and where a lack of social integration with neighbours led to the benefits of eco-community practices being confined to residents. Yet there are more examples that demonstrate how eco-communities deliberately seek to share their spatial, ecological, social and economic benefits through porous borders, and act as activist-hubs for numerous political campaigns. Perhaps unsurprisingly, those eco-communities with predominantly private ownership of property are least likely to share their benefits, while those with mixed and all-tenant tenures facilitate greater beyond-border sharing (Thörn et al., 2020). As eco-communities benefit internally from economies of scale, there is an even greater benefit when they reach out to share these facilities and activities beyond their borders.

The second assumption, however, is more complicated. Here, a belief in a vertical hierarchical ordering of scale presupposes that eco-communities' efforts at 'growing, spreading, replicating' (Schmid and Taylor Aiken 2023, 6) through horizontality will be deficient, because it cannot tackle the embedded vertical power relations of existing capitalist structures of scale. Those who argue that hopeful sites of possibility can generate broader transformations 'remind [us] that although hierarchies are socially produced, a transformation beyond growth and accumulation inevitably originates from within given socio-spatial relations and is thus conditioned by present institutional orders' (Schmid 2019, 8). In simpler terms, we cannot simply ignore the way capitalist structures constrain efforts at post-capitalist transformation.

Nelson (Chapter 12) argues for a new unit of analysis through which to understand the beyond-border impact of these eco-communities. She uses best practice examples in Ireland, Switzerland and Germany to demonstrate the centrality of tenure to inclusivity, porous boundaries to participation, and articulates 'scaling-out' rather than 'up' as a post-capitalist act. Nelson also examines the centrality of working *with* the state (be that municipal government, planners, housing professionals and financers). Her chapter seeks to remind us that these communities have to operate within, alongside and beyond ongoing capitalist processes of housing, inequality, marginalization, poverty, racism and that consequently eco-communities alone are unlikely to be able to erase or move beyond these existing structural tensions in society.

As Schmid and Taylor Aiken (2023) caution, we need a 'literacy of scaling' that critically reflects on what practices should be scaled, and with what transformations they promote. There is a risk within the call for amplifying and 'scaling-up' all hopeful practices, that the necessary bonds of solidarity, empathy and trust get ignored or are lost; indeed, the emphasis on scaling-up often sacrifices the very prefigurative approaches on which eco-communities depend. This not only obstructs any meaningful transformation but also simultaneously devalues 'the already existing forms of care, solidarity and survival that are not made prominent or foregrounded, and yet these hidden histories and practices of sustainability are often highly resourceful and proven to function as a reservoir of living well together' (2023, 6). Schmid and Taylor Aiken (2023) call instead for a 'tactical scaling' mindful of what might be achieved but also lost through such processes.

Yet as Jonas (2006) argues, geographers have created a false site-versus-scale dualism. This not only simplifies the debate about amplification, reducing it to a question of whether a singular 'site' (such as an eco-community) can ever harness enough influence to challenge embedded power structures, it also assumes scalar hierarchies to be fixed and vertical. Instead, Schmid (2019) suggests that understanding scale as a 'site ontology' (a singular site but with known relations beyond its borders) acknowledges that the question need not be about the possibility of 'scaling-up' (vertically to the 'global'), but rather 'scaling-out' through these relations, as 'sites themselves are expressions of powerful socio-spatial relations' (Schmid, 2019, 8). Eco-communities do not exist outside of these relations to others nor are they (as outlined below in discussions of homogeneity) devoid of power in these relations. Therefore, the possibility of eco-communities contributing to socio-ecological transformations beyond their borders is reliant on how they employ these relations to navigate the challenges to the changes they advocate (Nicolosi and Feola 2016). This more nuanced approach to scale shapes the discussion of what eco-communities can offer in this book, with socio-ecological transformations understood through a multitude of different relational possibilities.

Extending this rationale, in Chapter 5, I explore how eco-communities reconfigure society-environment relations. Creating new ways to overcome a perceived separation between people and the environment, eco-communities develop non-dualistic ontologies (ways of defining what exists). In other words, what living in-relation-to, interrelated and interdependent with all beings means in practice. This chapter starts from a recognition that socio-ecological relations are dynamic, multiple and hybrid, and constituted through mutual interdependencies. It details how three British eco-communities are developing the concept of peopled landscapes that demonstrate how they are living in mutual interdependence with 'the environment'. Focusing on extended relations rather than scale enables analysis of how eco-communities might transform places (within and beyond their borders). But even here there are curious limits. While new relationalities are developed and 'scaled-out' eco-communities have tended to build these by ignoring social relations with those already in place.

The social specifics of place are erased and remade anew by eco-communities, with existing place-based knowledges subordinated while simultaneously privileging environmental relations. This creates a disconnect between a place and an eco-community: 'advocates of sustainable living generally tend of value connection to place. Yet usually, the process of founding an intentional community, especially a rural one, involves plans to relocate' (Freifelder 2022, 12). This is especially problematic given the colonial implications of settling on Indigenous land (explored further in Barker and Pickerill, Chapter 8; see also Jazeel 2023, for discussion of the neo-coloniality of Auroville).

Places, particularly eco-communities, should be created which benefit all, not just a few, especially as eco-communities are always remaking places to which others already relate (Sack 2001). For Larsen and Johnson (2012), a progressive place is open, and encourages sharing, compassion, tolerance and an acknowledgement of interdependence with others. As is detailed in this book, eco-communities do not always adequately understand place, its existing relationalities or the political need to retain an openness. Assessing the transformative potential of eco-communities requires also, therefore, thinking critically about what is erased or lost in these processes.

Homogeneity

A significant critique of eco-communities is their apparent homogeneity. Eco-communities tend to represent a narrow demographic of the population – often highly educated, white, able-bodied and with a greater proportion of women (Chitewere 2017). There are also expectations that residents need to be physically fit and emotionally resilient (Laughton 2008). This homogeneity prevents those who do not see themselves represented in such communities from joining, excluding them from the potential benefits of eco-community living. A lack of diversity also limits the likely applicability of any innovations for broader populations.

That many eco-communities are internally demographically and ethnically similar is often a purposeful choice. Residents construct collective identities built around shared values (often egalitarianism and environmentalism), and as Rubin (2021) outlines at Dancing Rabbit, USA, erect barriers to deliberately exclude newcomers who might disrupt this identity and undermine collective intentions. Bresson and Labit (2020) in their analysis of French collaborative housing note 'a rather robust socio-cultural homogeneity, which probably strengthens the social cohesion' (128) and Tummers and MacGregor (2019, 13) agree that 'most co-housing projects have a homogeneous population; there is an (unintentional) lack of socio-cultural and economic diversity'.

Even where a demographic cohort might numerically dominate, such as the prevalence of women, gendered assumptions from conventional society tend to be retained and difficult to challenge. Gerner (Chapter 9) critically examines how gender and patriarchy are understood and challenged in eco-communities. She argues that gender and associated questions about care work and social reproduction have largely been ignored. Using ethnographic qualitative research with three French eco-communities, Gerner demonstrates a gap between discourse and action. The eco-communities centred on the importance of caring relationships, including self-care, and care that extends to non-humans and for a valuing of a variety of care work. Yet through a focus on unpaid care work – cleaning, health choices, child-raising and food sourcing and production, Gerner narrates a persuasive neoliberal individualism which negates the possibility of radically renegotiating gender.

Despite developing infrastructures which supported care through practices of sharing that enabled individuals to do less, stubborn assumptions remain about binaries of differences between gendered bodies and competencies, and almost a complete absence of consideration of queer or non-heterosexual configurations. More worrying is how rarely materials or practices were altered in order to enable or support gender-neutral implications. This common approach to gender in eco-communities was considered 'natural', ignoring social, power and privilege as structures and left for the individual to challenge. Gerner, then, articulates the significant work to be done in eco-communities to challenge both the thinking and the practices bound up in the concept of gender. Where numbers are very few, such as disabled residents, there is often a complete lack of accommodation for their needs in material or social infrastructures (Bhakta and Pickerill 2016).

There is also a particular and noticeable absence of engagement in eco-communities with questions of race. As Bledsoe et al. (2022) make clear if racialization underpins capitalism (most succinctly expressed as racial capitalism – that capitalism is explicitly built and reliant upon extracting labour and resources from the most marginalized in society, predominantly Black people), then 'establishing non-capitalist economies entails attending explicitly to the question of race' (281), and to ignore questions of racial difference in the generation of socio-ecological transformations risks inadequately understanding the processes at play.

Chitewere (Chapter 7) uses her extended ethnographic work in the Ecovillage at Ithaca, EVA, as an experience from which to call for eco-communities to attend to systemic and structural inequalities, racism and injustices that contribute to social and environmental degradation. She argues that the lack of racial and ethnic diversity in many eco-communities prevents them from being the powerful exemplars of sustainable transformation to which many aspire. Eco-communities are trapped by historic and ongoing infrastructures of white supremacy and segregation that they, albeit sometimes inadvertently, can perpetuate and sustain. Chitewere argues eco-communities remain inwardly focused at the cost of participating in social movements for environmental justice. Distinguishing between de jure (legally recognized practices) and de facto (practices not recognized legally, but which occur regardless), she argues that some eco-communities engage in de facto segregation – subtle practices that exclude people of colour from the ecological concerns that affect their communities.

To develop inclusive eco-communities Chitewere offers the mnemonic device AIM HIGHER: Active alliances and listening; Inward avoidance; Make the political personal; Hire broadly; Investigate and integrate; Greater circle of social relationships; Helping to heal, Environment broadly defined and Racism matters. Only by purposefully and actively engaging with social justice movements can inclusive models of surviving well together be built.

As I (Chapter 11) go on to examine, many eco-communities that do acknowledge a lack of racial diversity rely on the provision of more affordable housing as their 'solution', failing to understand the broader tensions of sense of belonging and social justice needs. Examining the overlaps between white environmentalisms and racial exclusions in eco communities I detail the consequences of a subordination of social justice in residents' practices. Being radically anti-racist, challenging neo-liberal and colonial frameworks, and working with Black, Indigenous and other People of Colour environmental projects is identified as crucial to ensuring eco-communities reach their potential of generating socio-ecological transformations.

In Chapter 8, Barker and I also use the framework of settler colonialism to ask critical questions about eco-communities' entanglements with colonialism, dispossession of Indigenous lands, and white supremacy. We identify several problematic practices including the private purchase and occupation of unceeded Indigenous lands, cultural appropriation of Indigenous knowledge and culture, co-option of relationships with 'nature', and racism. While seemingly often unintentional we call for greater self-reflection on the ways eco-communities can reinforce processes of settler colonial dispossession and suggest different place-relationship possibilities.

Organizing collectively

Eco-community living is slow and hard work, but tends to get romanticized as a simple life. As discussed in this book, residents struggle with the collectivity and the work, and practices are adjusted, abandoned or people leave. Many eco-communities rely on volunteers to do the necessary manual labour, which also raises questions about long-term feasibility (Laughton 2008). In many eco-communities there are elements of self-denial – a foregoing of some comforts, materials, mobilities – which require voluntarily giving up what might be perceived as important components of quality of life (Pickerill 2015).

Kallis et al. (2012) argue eco-communities are inadequate in tackling our current crises for two reasons 'one of false extrapolation and one of political naiveté' (174). The first is that voluntary simplicity fails to take account of the extent to which eco-community living, 'relies on the surplus – and the products and infrastructures – provided by the rest of the industrial economy' (174), and secondly that scaling up to the societal level would require significant hardship for residents (because it would by design disrupt the industrial economy), hardships that non-dedicated people are unlikely to accept. Indeed, there is likely to be a large gulf between those who choose to make radical changes in their everyday by living in eco-communities and the challenge of convincing those less interested to adopt new practices.

Schramm (Chapter 4) explores how such a 'sustainable' equitable life is materialized in eco-communities. She argues that much analysis of eco-communities focuses on inter-human relations (such as decision-making processes) and ignores the agency of non-humans and the centrality of how eco-communities function. Using ethnographic research with Can Decreix (France), Can Masdeu and Calafou (both near Barcelona, Catalonia), Schramm conceptualizes material practices as 'more-than-human-compositions' where humans and non-humans interact and come together to produce 'outcomes' that shape the eco-community, such as compost toilets, methods of building and other material infrastructures.

In exploring how skillsets are learnt and shared, Schramm demonstrates how non-human elements limit, surprise and shape outcomes – such as even plastering – and that humans learn to accept that lack of control they have and enjoy the freedom and errors that result. These different engagements with non-human materialities were also evident in how some eco-community members experienced bodily discomfort in, for example, reliance on collective compost toilets. This discomfort, especially in the long term, led some residents to reconfigure the novel infrastructural materialities (by building private dry toilets) to seek greater comfort – challenging the acceptability of innovative practices. Ultimately, therefore, Schramm provides the much-needed detail on *how* innovative material practices evolve while also raising crucial questions about the durability of some practices.

Jarvis (Chapter 15) examines how eco-communities sustain as collective entities through deep social learning. Social learning is the non-linear process of learning from, and with others, through observation and replication. Focusing on lived experiences in six Australian eco-communities and the Findhorn Foundation (Scotland), she asks how living and working in a group creating 'community glue' can become transformational. This social learning requires a shift from individuality to acknowledging the systems of interdependence and commitment 'to intentions consciously negotiated in ethical discernment with others'. Through a series of vignettes, Jarvis produces examples of this group-work which shifts between shallow but necessary outreach activities to attract new members and develop their inter-personal competence, to deep sustained engagement that requires time and space to manifest sometimes unexpected transformations. Despite these processes of social learning, as eco-communities become more popular their radical intent can diminish, to the extent that they begin to adopt neoliberal principles of home ownership, work and individualization (Sargisson 2012). Some have adopted these approaches to financially survive – using the income generated to attend to maintenance issues, others in attempts to attract new residents who are less willing to sacrifice private financial capital. Other eco-communities are struggling with an ageing residential cohort and a reliance on manual labour to provide their livelihood. Only relatively recently has the model of senior co-housing been adopted in the UK, for example, with the first example being New Ground, in London (Chaudhuri 2023). These questions of resilience and ability to be self-sustaining over extended periods require innovative inclusive ownership models and open discussion about ageing.

In governing collectively, Cornea (Chapter 13) draws on India to open up three complementary lines of analysis of eco-communities; how they govern, their relationships to the state, and possibilities and limitations of seeking to replicate practices, infrastructures and/or technologies from eco-communities into other places. First, Cornea's articulation of the complexity of how environmental governance works – as a messy everyday practice of compromise, negotiation and disorder – aptly describes governance in eco-communities. As Cornea notes, 'governance as practiced will always vary from governance as prescribed'. She calls for a careful analysis of how uneven power relations and processes of control shape the practical norms, rules and regulations, which unfortunately can work against the communities' quest for equitable environmentally sustainable ways of living. In other words, we must interrogate governance in eco-communities through their everyday practices, the implementation and also ask how community members become (or not) governable.

Second, eco-communities often have difficult relationships with the state. Yet as Cornea notes, residents will act strategically in relation to the state when needed, 'whilst serving as alternatives to the state at other points'. How eco-communities engage in the state influences many aspects of their continuation, such as planning approval, accessing welfare, health and educational systems, pensions, energy, water and sewerage infrastructure, as well as those who have benefitted from government grants (LILAC, Lammas). Yet there has been relatively little academic analysis of these engagements with the state. Finally, Cornea's nuanced conceptualization of governance complicates the simple advocation of replicating practices, infrastructures or technologies which have been proved to work in eco-communities in other places. Cornea acknowledges the social and material histories of particular places and how environmental governance emerges through complex socio-technical configurations which are dynamic, heteregeneous, lived, fluid, and spatially and temporally variable. This complicates and should inform the likely (im)possibilities of scaling up/out, or replicating seemingly successful elements of eco-communities.

Gavaldá and Cattaneo (Chapter 14) examine and reflect on how Can Masdeu and Kan Pasqual (Barcelona) self-organize and govern internally in four broad aspects of everyday life: co-existence and collectivity; developing time economies; monetary flows and anti-monetary benefits; and the importance of scale. Gavaldá and Cattaneo argue that despite adopting consensus approaches, decision-making remains problematic because of uneven manifestations of power and the ongoing tensions between individual and community needs. A balance has also yet to be achieved between political activity planning and attending to the emotional needs and dynamics of the group. A successful organizational change has been in shifting economic practices to be time-based rather than profit-driven to balance community contributions with externally paid employment, to value anti-monetary benefits and celebrate diverse economies.

Clarence-Smith (Chapter 16) uses an autoethnography of Auroville, India, to examine the role of spirituality in governance, specifically in participatory decision-making. Spiritually informed practices of collective silence, and using spiritual prompts in a variety of exercises were intended to shape and aid working group consensus decision-making. Although not all participants wanted to engage in the process, many felt that it was necessary to focus on the spiritual in order to create the space and potentially to radically transform what strategic action was taken. As Clarence-Smith demonstrates, while the outcomes of this balance between spiritual ideals and practical material governance can appear loose and not immediately attributable to spirituality, the very attempt to develop spiritually informed political praxis is an important process if communities are ultimately to develop radically different ways of collectively being and doing.

Building economies

This final section explores how eco-communities reconfigure their engagement with the capitalist economy, work and labour. Stevens-Wood (Chapter 17) examines the attempts of an eco-community to develop post-capitalist economic relations which reframe how time, work and quality of life are understood and valued. At Friary Grange (a pseudonym) 'work' includes the fifteen hours a week each member is meant to commit to the functioning of the community (meal preparation, admin, animal care, food production, maintenance, etc.), external paid employment (to cover additional food costs, materials, bills, etc.) and the less visible work of child or elder care.

Stevens-Wood works through three consequences of this approach to work and the economy. First, she explores how 'not all time is equal' in how the inequalities of capitalist society are perpetuated by the need for members to continue paid external employment, and the tension this creates in the demands to also fulfil community work obligations. Unlike the examples Gavaldá and Cattaneo (Chapter 14) discuss, at Friary Grange it is not possible to 'buy out' a member's contribution to community work.

Second, most members have made a deliberate trade-off – reducing their income in exchange for a higher quality of life. Like Lockyer and Jones's (Chapter 2) exploration of Dancing Rabbit Ecovillage, Friary Grange residents experienced an improved quality of life from reduced income and consumption despite having to make-do-and-mend, and the physical labour of maintaining an old building and 70 acres of land. Finally, this approach to work enabled members to challenge the dominant socio-economic system and its requirement to work-to-live, even if they were only able to do so partially. This hybrid approach with its messy compromises is a pragmatic reality for many eco-communities seeking a sustainable life and self-sufficiency, and despite its tensions is a hopeful example of the complexity of building diverse economies.

Thomas Smith and Nadia Johanisova (Chapter 18) use seven vignettes of different forms of economic practices in Freetown Christiania (Denmark) to demonstrate the wide diversity of economic activity from commercial (and now international) initiatives, workers' cooperatives, social enterprises, self-employment and informal collectives. As Smith and Johanisova demonstrate, many have complex overlaps with state institutions, banks, funders and conventional legal structures. While many residents have sought to reconfigure what 'work' is, few generate much surplus and even fewer financial plans for later life. Broader financial sustainability remains unclear.

Finally, Jan Malý Blažek (Chapter 19) argues that eco-communities have lots of great radical ideas, but they are not implemented to the best extent of their possibilities. Blazek draws on over forty eco-community examples across six European countries to critically examine economic experimentation, what he calls economic playgrounds. Eco-communities are spaces of dilemma and compromise, and the extent of economic novelty (economic playground experimentations) is largely determined by their initial driver – be that housing provision, ecological protection or political imperative.

Conclusions

In a sharp open letter to the intentional communities movement in North America, Blue (2024), an experienced eco-community resident, argued that eco-communities do not adequately deliver on their promise of socio-ecological transformation. Blue blamed their homogeneity, isolation, insularity, micro-scale, individualist ownership structures and ineffective governance. Eco-communities had become about making and maintaining nice places to live – 'little islands in a rising sea, scattered and struggling' – with a lack of theory for how eco-communities will change the world. Blue called for new strategies that could generate collective capacity for movement building (particularly towards social justice goals), national resource sharing and solidarities, and a clearer sense of purpose.

It is timely, then, for this book to examine what socio-ecological transformations eco-communities offer. Yet, eco-communities do not lack theories of change. In fact the Global Ecovillage Network has carefully developed a theory of regeneration and Whole System Design which explicitly details how eco-communities transform ecological, cultural, economic and social practices to regenerate the world (GEN 2024). Other scholars have employed socio-technical transitions theory to detail how eco-communities (among other grassroots change makers) change social relations through processes of knowing, doing, framing and organizing (Pel et al., 2020).

Using a post-capitalist ethics eludes generating a neatly coherent or cohesive theory of transformation, and is deliberately cognizant of the partiality and nascent characteristics of eco-communities' politics and properties of transformation. Instead, this book dwells on the contradictions, cracks, messiness and unfinished nature of eco-communities. It recognizes eco-communities as making important interventions in worldmaking otherwise, but also the ever-present risk of distasteful elements – eco-fascism, white supremacy – gaining discursive and practical footholds. While hopeful and future-orientated, we intend this book to contribute constructively and with care, *with* residents, to critically reflect on all that eco-communities offer, and in what can be understood about the possibilities of building a socially just and ecologically regenerative world.

References

Anderson, J. (2017) 'Retreat or re-connect: How effective can ecosophical communities be in transforming the mainstream?', *Geografiska Annaler: Series B, Human Geography* 99(2), pp. 192–206.

Andreas, M. and Wagner, F. (2012) '"For whom? For the future!" Ecovillage Sieben Linden as a model and research project', *RCC Perspectives* (8), pp. 135–48.

Arrigoitia, M.F. and West, K. (2021) 'Interdependence, commitment, learning and love: The case of the United Kingdom's first older women's co-housing community', *Ageing & Society* 41(7), pp. 1673–96.

Baker, T. (2013) 'Ecovillages and capitalism. Creating sustainable communities within an unsustainable context', in Lockyer, J. and Veteto, J.R. (eds.) *Environmental Anthropology Engaging Ecotopia: Bioregionalism, Permaculture and Ecovillages*. Oxford: Berghan Books, pp. 285–300.

Bang, J.M. (2005) *Ecovillages: A Practical Guide to Sustainable Communities*. Gabriola Island: New Society Publishers.

Bang, J.M. (2007) *Growing Eco-Communities: Practical Ways to Create Sustainability*. Edinburgh: Floris Books.

Bell, K. (2020) *Working-Class Environmentalism*. New York: Springer.

Bhakta, A. and Pickerill, J. (2016) 'Making space for disability in eco-homes and eco-communities', *The Geographical Journal* 182(4), pp. 406–17.

Birnbaum, J. and Fox, L. (2014) *Sustainable Revolution: Permaculture in ecovillages, urban farms and communities worldwide.* Berkley, CA: North Atlantic Books.

Blažek, J. (2016) 'Economic micro-systems? Non-market and not-only-for-profit economic activities in eco-communities', *Human Affairs* 26(4), pp. 377–89.

Bledsoe, A., McCreary, T. and Wright, W. (2022) 'Theorizing diverse economies in the context of racial capitalism', *Geoforum* 132, pp. 281–90.

Blue, S. (2024) *Where Do We Go from Here: Open Letter to the Intentional Communities Movement.* https://www.ic.org/sky-blue-where-do-we-go-from-here. Accessed 1 November 2024.

Bollier, D., (2019) *Free, Fair, and Alive: The Insurgent Power of the Commons.* Gabriola Island: New Society Publishers.

Bookchin, M. (1990) *The Philosophy of Social Ecology: Essays of Dialectical Naturalism Black Rose.* Montreal: Black Rose.

Boyer, R.H.W. (2016) 'Achieving one-planet living through transitions in social practice: A case study of Dancing Rabbit Ecovillage', *Sustainability: Science, Practice and Policy* 12(1), pp. 47–59.

Bresson, S. and Labit, A. (2020) 'How does collaborative housing address the issue of social inclusion? A French perspective', *Housing, Theory and Society* 37(1), pp. 118–38.

Brombin, A. (2015) 'Faces of sustainability in Italian ecovillages: Food as "contact zone"', *International Journal of Consumer Studies*, 39(5), pp. 468–77.

Bunker, S., Coates, C., Field, M. and How, J. (2011) *Cohousing in Britain: A Diggers & Dreamers Review.* London: Diggers and Dreamers Publications.

Calhoun, C. (1998) 'Community without propinquity revisited: Communications technology and the transformation of the urban public sphere', *Sociological Inquiry* 68(3), pp. 373–97.

Cameron, J. and Gibson-Graham, J.K. (2022). 'The diverse economies approach', in Stilwell, F., Primrose, D. and Thornton, T. B. (eds.) *Handbook of Alternative Theories of Political Economy.* Cheltenham: Edward Elgar Publishing, pp. 329–42.

Cardwell, E. (2024) Class and Community workshop, at UK Intentional Communities Conference, Braziers Park, Oxfordshire, 20 July.

Chatterton, P. (2013) 'Towards an agenda for post-carbon cities: Lessons from Lilac, the UK's first ecological affordable cohousing community', *International Journal of Urban and Regional Research*, 37(5), pp. 1654–74.

Chatterton, P. (2015) *Low Impact Living: A Field Guide to Ecological, Affordable Community Building.* London: Routledge.

Chatterton, P. and Pusey, A. (2020) 'Beyond capitalist enclosure, commodification and alienation: Postcapitalist praxis as commons, social production and useful doing', *Progress in Human Geography* 44(1), pp. 27–48.

Chaudhuri, A. (2023) 'We have brothers, sons, lovers – but they cant' live here!' The happy home shared by 26 women, *The Guardian*, 24 August. https://www.theguardian.com/lifeandstyle/2023/aug/24/we-have-brothers-sons-lovers-but-they-cant-live-here-the-happy-home-shared-by-26-women.

Chitewere, T. (2010) Equity in sustainable communities: Exploring tools for environmental justice and political ecology. *National Resources Journal* 50(2), p. 315.

Chitewere, T. (2017) *Sustainable Communities and Green Lifestyles: Consumption and Environmentalism.* London: Routledge.

Christian, D.L. (2003) *Creating a Life Together: Practical Tools to Grow Ecovillages and Intentional Communities*. Gabriola: New Society Publishers.

Clarence-Smith, S.A. (2023) *Prefiguring Utopia: The Auroville Experiment*. Bristol: Bristol University Press.

Cooper, L. and Baer, H.A. (2019) *Urban Eco-Communities in Australia: Real Utopian Responses to the Ecological Crisis or Niche Markets?* New York: Springer.

Copeland, C., MacKerron, G. and Foxon, T.J. (2023) 'Futures for Findhorn: Exploring challenges for achieving net zero in an ecological intentional community', *Futures* 149, 103155, pp. 1–18.

Crabtree-Hayes, L. (2024) 'Establishing a glossary of community-led housing', *International Journal of Housing Policy* 24(1), pp. 157–84.

Daly, M. (2017) 'Quantifying the environmental impact of ecovillages and co-housing communities: A systematic literature review', *Local Environment* 22(11), pp. 1358–77.

Dawson, J. (2006) *Ecovillages: New Frontiers for Sustainability*, Schumacher Briefing No. 12. Vermont, VT: Chelsea Green Publishing.

Devon, C. (2019) *Auroville or the Quest for a Better World: Past, Present, Future*. New York: Discovery Publisher.

Di Chiro, G. (2019) 'Care not growth: Imagining a subsistence economy for all', *The British Journal of Politics and International Relations* 21(2), pp. 303–11.

Ergas, C. (2010) 'A model of sustainable living: Collective identity in an urban ecovillage', *Organization & Environment* 23(1), pp. 32–54.

Ergas, C. (2021) *Surviving Collapse: Building Community toward Radical Sustainability*. Oxford: Oxford University Press.

Escobar, A. (2001) 'Culture sits in places: Reflections on globalism and subaltern strategies of localization', *Political Geography* 20(2), pp. 139–74.

Escobar, A. (2020) *Pluriversal Politics: The Real and the Possible*. Durham, NC: Duke University Press.

Fairlie, S. (1996) *Low Impact Development: Planning and People in a Sustainable Countryside*. Oxford: Jon Carpenter.

Feola, G., Vincent, O., and Moore, D. (2021). (Un)Making in sustainability transformation beyond capitalism. *Global Environmental Change* 69, 102290, pp. 1–12.

Fois, F. (2019) 'Enacting experimental alternative spaces', *Antipode* 51(1), pp. 107–28.

Freifelder, R. (2022) 'Sense of place and land back in a transient culture', *Communities Magazine* 195 (Summer), pp. 12–17.

Gausset, Q. and Jensen, P.D. (2024) 'Living sustainably in a Danish eco-community: How social and physical infrastructures affect carbon footprints', *npj Climate Action* 3(1), p. 33.

GEN (2024) 'Concepts: Regeneration', https://ecovillage.org/about/about-gen/concepts/. Accessed 1 November 2024.

Gibson-Graham, J.K. (2006) *Postcapitalist Politics*. Minneapolis, MN: University of Minnesota Press.

Gibson-Graham, J.K., Cameron, J. and Healy, S. (2016) 'Pursuing happiness: The politics of surviving well together', in Pike, D., Nelson, C. and Ledvinka, G. (eds.) *Essays on Happiness*. Perth: University of Western Australia Press, pp. 116–31.

Gibson, K. (2014) 'Thinking around what a radical geography "must be"', *Dialogues in Human Geography* 4(3), pp. 283–7.

Glass, A.P. (2020) 'Sense of community, loneliness, and satisfaction in five elder cohousing neighborhoods', *Journal of Women & Aging* 32(1), pp. 3–27.

Grinde, B., Nes, R. B., MacDonald, I. F. and Wilson, D. S. (2018) 'Quality of life in intentional communities', *Social Indicators Research* 137(2), pp. 625–40.

Harcourt, W. (2019) 'Feminist political ecology practices of worlding', *International Journal of the Commons* 13(1), pp. 153–74.

Hollender, R. (2016). 'A politics of the commons or commoning the political? Distinct possibilities for post-capitalist transformation', *Spectra* 5(1), https://vtechworks.lib.vt.edu/items/9600ff59-2386-46a8-b7fc-e68627890db7.

Holloway, J. (2010) *Crack Capitalism*. London: Pluto Press.

Hong, S. and Vicdan, H. (2016) 'Re-imaging the utopian: Transformation of a sustainable lifestyle in ecovillages', *Journal of Business Research* 69(1), pp. 120–36.

Hubbard, E. (2024) Bioregioning: Building more just and sustainable livelihoods? PhD thesis, University of Sheffield.

IPCC (2022) *Climate Change 2022: Mitigation of Climate Change. Contribution of Working Group III to the Sixth Assessment Report of the Intergovernmental Panel on Climate Change*. Shukla, P.R., Skea, J., Slade, R., Al Khourdajie, A., van Diemen, R., McCollum, D., Pathak, M., Some, S., Vyas, P., Fradera, R., Belkacemi, M., Hasija, A., Lisboa, G., Luz, S., Malley, J., (eds.) Cambridge and New York: Cambridge University Press.

Jarvis, H. (2013) 'Against the "tyranny" of single-family dwelling: Insights from Christiania at 40', *Gender, Place & Culture* 20(8), pp. 939–59.

Jarvis, H. (2019) 'Sharing, togetherness and intentional degrowth', *Progress in Human Geography* 43(2), pp. 256–75.

Jazeel, T. (2023) 'IN THE SHADOW OF "THE CITY" YET TO COME: Auroville, Developmentalism and the Social Effects of Cityness', *International Journal of Urban and Regional Research* 47(2), pp. 258–78.

Jonas, A.E. (2006) 'Pro scale: Further reflections on the'scale debate'in human geography', *Transactions of the Institute of British Geographers* 31(3), pp. 399–406.

Kallis, G., Kerschner, C. and Martinez-Alier, J. (2012) 'The economics of degrowth', *Ecological Economics* 84, pp. 172–80.

Kanter, R.M. (1972) *Commitment and Community: Communes and Utopias in Sociological Perspective* (Vol. 36). Cambridge, MA: Harvard University Press.

Kehl, K. and Then, V. (2013) 'Community and civil society returns of multi-generation cohousing in Germany', *Journal of Civil Society* 9(1), pp. 41–57.

Kinkade, K. (1994) *Is It Utopia Yet? An Insider's View of Twin Oaks Community in Its 26th Year*. Twin Oaks, VA: Twin Oaks Publishing.

Kirby, A. (2003) 'Redefining social and environmental relations at the ecovillage at Ithaca: A case study', *Journal of Environmental Psychology* 23(3), pp. 323–32.

Kuhlmann, H. (2000) 'The illusion of permanence: Work motivation and membership turnover at twin oaks community', *Critical Review of International Social and Political Philosophy* 3(2–3), pp. 157–71.

Kumar, A. and Taylor Aiken, G. (2021) 'A postcolonial critique of community energy: Searching for community as solidarity in India and Scotland', *Antipode* 53(1), pp. 200–21.

Kunze, I. (2012) 'Social innovations for communal and ecological living: Lessons from sustainability research and observations in intentional communities', *Communal Societies* 32(1), 50–67.

Kunze, I. (2020) '"A new we": Post-individualistic community-based initiatives as social innovations? Empirical observations in intentional communities', in Jansen, B. (ed.) *Rethinking Community through Transdisciplinary Research*. London: Palgrave Macmillan, pp. 285–305.

LaFond, M. and Tsvetkova, L. (2017) *Co-Housing Inclusive: Self-Organised, Community-Led Housing for All*. Berlin: ID22: Institute for Creative Sustainability.

Lallement, M. (2024) *A Desire for Equality: Living and Working in Concrete Utopian Communities*. Bristol: Bristol University Press.

Lanphear, F. (2014) *Songaia: An Unfolding Dream*. Bothell, WA: Songaia Press.
Larsen, S.C. and Johnson, J.T. (2012) 'Toward an open sense of place: Phenomenology, affinity, and the question of being', *Annals of the Association of American Geographers* 102(3), pp. 632–46.
Laughton, R. (2008) *Surviving and Thriving on the Land: How to Use Your Time and Energy to Run a Successful Smallholding*. Totnes, Devon: Green Books.
Leafe Christian, D. (2003) *Creating a Life Together: Practical Tools to Grow Ecovillages and Intentional Communities*. Gabriola Island: New Society Publishers.
Lennon, A. and Berg, N.G. (2022) 'Alternative places for alternative people? A changing ecovillage discourse from Othered lifestyle to another rurality', *Journal of Rural Studies* 95, pp. 302–15.
LeVasseur, T. (2013) 'Globalizing the ecovillage ideal: Networks of empowerment, seeds of hope', in Lockyer, J. and Veteto, J.R. (eds.) *Environmental Anthropology Engaging Ecotopia: Bioregionalism, Permaculture, and Ecovillages*. New York: Berghan Books, pp. 251–68.
Litfin, K.T. (2014) *Eco-Villages: Lessons for Sustainable Community*. Cambridge: Polity Press.
Lockyer, J. (2017) 'Community, commons, and degrowth at Dancing Rabbit Ecovillage', *Journal of Political Ecology* 24(1), pp. 519–42.
Lopez, C. and Weaver, R. (2019) 'Placing intentional communities in geography', *Journal of Geography* 118(5), pp. 197–209.
Mafle Ferreira Duarte, L.G., Sahakian, M. and Ferreira Neto, J.L. (2021) 'Empowerment in an ecovillage: Unveiling the role of power relations in social practices', *Community Development* 52(5), pp. 592–606.
Magnusson, D. (2018) 'Going back to the roots: The fourth generation of Swedish eco-villages', *Scottish Geographical Journal* 134(3–4), pp. 122–40.
Malpas, J. (2014) *Thinking Topographically: Place, Space and Geography*. Downloaded from http://jeffmalpas.com/downloadable-essays.
Margarida Fernandes Esteves, A., Henfrey, T., Lucas Dos Santos, L., Leal, L. (Eds.) (2023) *Solidarity Economy: Alternative Spaces, Power and Politics*. Milton Park: Routledge.
McCammant, K. and Durret, C. (1988) *Cohousing: A Contemporary Approach to Housing Ourselves*. Berkeley, CA: Ten Speed Press.
Meijering, L., Huigen, P. and Van Hoven, B. (2007) 'Intentional communities in rural spaces', *Tijdschrift Voor Economische en Sociale Geografie* 98(1), pp. 42–52.
Meltzer, G. (2005) *Sustainable Community: Learning from the Cohousing Model*. Crewe, Cheshire: Trafford Publishing.
Meltzer, G. (2015) *Findhorn Reflections: A Very Personal Take on Life inside the Famous Spiritual Community and Ecovillage*. Graham Meltzer (self-published). CreateSpace Independent Publishing Platform.
Miller, E. (2019) *Reimagining Livelihoods: Life beyond Economy, Society, and Environment*. Minneapolis: University of Minnesota Press.
Miller, T. (2019) *Communes in America, 1975–2000*. Syracuse: Syracuse University Press.
Monticelli, L. (2018) 'Embodying alternatives to capitalism in the 21st century. *TripleC: Communication, Capitalism & Critique*', *Open Access Journal for a Global Sustainable Information Society* 16(2), pp. 501–17.
Monticelli, L. (2024) 'Prefigurative politics within, despite and beyond contemporary capitalism', in Monticelli, L. (ed.) *The Future Is Now: An Introduction to Prefigurative Politics*. Bristol: Bristol University Press.
Morrow, O. and Martin, D.G. (2019) 'Unbundling property in Boston's urban food commons', *Urban Geography* 40(10), pp. 1485–505.

Mychajluk, L. (2017) 'Learning to live and work together in an ecovillage community of practice', *European Journal for Research on the Education and Learning of Adults* 8(2), pp. 179–94.

Newman, S. (2010) *The Politics of Postanarchism*. Edinburgh: Edinburgh University Press.

Nicolosi, E. and Feola, G. (2016) 'Transition in place: Dynamics, possibilities, and constraints', *Geoforum* 76, pp. 153–63.

Nielsen-Englyst, C. and Gausset, Q. (2024) 'From countercultural ecovillages to mainstream green neighbourhoods—a view on current trends in Denmark', *Npj Climate Action* 3(1), p. 60.

Pel, B., Haxeltine, A., Avelino, F., Dumitru, A., Kemp, R., Bauler, T., Kunze, I., Dorland, J., Wittmayer, J. and Jørgensen, M.S. (2020) 'Towards a theory of transformative social innovation: A relational framework and 12 propositions', *Research Policy* 49(8), 104080, pp. 1–13.

Pepper, D. (1991) *Communes and the Green Vision: Counterculture, Lifestyle and the New Age*. London: Merlin Press.

Pickerill, J. (2013) 'Permaculture in practice', in Lockyer, J. and Veteto, J.R. (eds.) *Environmental Anthropology Engaging Ecotopia: Bioregionalism, permaculture, and ecovillages*. New York: Berghan Books, pp. 180–94.

Pickerill, J. (2015) 'Cold comfort? Reconceiving the practices of bathing in British self-build eco-homes', *Annals of the Association of American Geographers* 105(5), pp. 1061–77.

Pickerill, J., (2016) *Eco-Homes: People, Place and Politics*. London: Bloomsbury Publishing.

Pickerill, J. (2021) 'Hopefulness for transformative grassroots change', *Environmental Policy and Governance* 31(3), pp. 249–51.

Pickerill, J. (2024) 'Unsettling geography: Enacting the politics of Indigenous ontologies', *Agoriad: A Journal of Spatial Theory* 1(1), pp. 1–19.

Pickerill, J., Chitewere, T., Cornea, N., Lockyer, J., Macrorie, R., Malý Blažek, J., and Nelson, A. (2024) 'Urban ecological futures: Five eco-community strategies for more sustainable and equitable cities', *International Journal for Urban and Regional Research* 48(1), pp. 161–76.

Pisters, S.R., Vihinen, H. and Figueiredo, E. (2020) 'Inner change and sustainability initiatives: Explore the narratives from eco-villages through a place-based transformative learning approach', *Sustainability Science* 5(2), pp. 395–409.

Pitzer, D.E., Janzen, D.E., Lewis, D. and Wright-Summerton, R. (2014) 'Communes and intentional communities', in Parker, M., Cheney, G., Fournier, V. and Land, C. (eds.) *The Routledge Companion to Alternative Organization*. London: Routledge, pp. 89–104.

Plumwood, V. (2007) 'A review of Deborah Bird Rose's reports from a wild country: Ethics of decolonisation', *Australian Humanities Review* 42(August), pp. 1–4.

Puplampu, V., Matthews, E., Puplampu, G., Gross, M., Pathak, S. and Peters, S. (2020) 'The impact of cohousing on older adults' quality of life', *Canadian Journal on Aging/La Revue canadienne du vieillissement* 39(3), pp. 406–20.

Rau, T.J. and Koch-Gonzalez, J. (2018) *Many Voices One Song: Shared Power with Sociocracy*. Amherst, MA: Sociocracy for All.

Reclus, E. (1884) 'Anarchy: By an anarchist', *Contemporary Review* 45, pp. 627–41.

Renau, L.D.R. (2018) 'Ecovillages in Spain: Searching an emancipatory social transformation?', *Cogent Social Sciences* 4(1), 1468200, pp. 1–12.

Rice, J., Long, J., and Levenda, A. (2022) 'Against climate apartheid: Confronting the persistent legacies of expendability for climate justice', *Environment and Planning E: Nature and Space* 5(2), pp. 625–45.

Rose, D. (2004) *Report from a Wild Country: Ethics for Decolonisation*. Sydney: University of New South Wales Press.

Roysen, R. and Mertens, F. (2019) 'New normalities in grassroots innovations: The reconfiguration and normalization of social practices in an ecovillage', *Journal of Cleaner Production* 236, 117647, pp. 1–8.

Rubin, Z. (2021) '"We do this at Dancing Rabbit": Recruitment and collective identity processes in the ecovillage', *Journal of Contemporary Ethnography* 50(4), pp. 443–65.

Sack, R.D. (2001) 'The geographic problematic: empirical issues.' *Norsk Geografisk Tidsskrift-Norwegian Journal of Geography* 55(3), pp. 107–16.

Sanford, A.W. (2014) 'Being the change: Food, nonviolence, and self-sufficiency in contemporary intentional communities', *Communal Societies* 34(1), pp. 28–53.

Sanford, A.W. (2017) *Living Sustainably: What Intentional Communities Can Teach Us about Democracy, Simplicity, and Nonviolence*. Lexington, KY: University Press of Kentucky.

Sanford, A.W. (2019) *Living Sustainably: What Intentional Communities Can Teach Us About Democracy, Simplicity, and Nonviolence*. Lexington, KY: University Press of Kentucky.

Sargisson, L. (2012) 'Second-wave cohousing: A modern utopia?', *Utopian Studies* 23(1), pp. 28–56.

Schelly, C., Rubin, Z. and Lockyer, J. (2024) 'The paradox of collective climate action in rural US ecovillages: Ethnographic reflections and perspectives', *npj Climate Action* 3(1), p. 17.

Schmid, B. (2019) 'Degrowth and postcapitalism: Transformative geographies beyond accumulation and growth', *Geography Compass* 13(11), e12470, pp. 1–15.

Schmid, B. and Smith, T.S. (2021) 'Social transformation and postcapitalist possibility: Emerging dialogues between practice theory and diverse economies', *Progress in Human Geography* 45(2), pp. 253–75.

Schmid, B. and Taylor Aiken, G. (2023) 'A critical view on the role of scale and instrumental imaginaries within community sustainability transitions research', *Area*, 55(4), pp. 506–13.

Schramm, E. (2021) The space-time of post-capitalist transformation: More-than-human affects in French and Catalan eco-communities. PhD thesis, Oxford University.

Schwab, A.K. and Roysen, R. (2022) 'Ecovillages and other community-led initiatives as experiences of climate action', *Climate Action* 1(1), pp. 1–4.

Sekulova, F., Anguelovski, I., Argüelles, L. and Conill, J. (2017) 'A "fertile soil" for sustainability-related community initiatives: A new analytical framework', *Environment and Planning A* 49(10), pp. 2362–82.

Shannon, J., Hankins, K.B., Shelton, T., Bosse, A.J., Scott, D., Block, D., Fischer, H., Eaves, L.E., Jung, J.K., Robinson, J. and Solís, P. (2021) 'Community geography: Toward a disciplinary framework', *Progress in Human Geography* 45(5), pp. 1147–68.

Sherry, J. (2019) 'The impact of community sustainability: A life cycle assessment of three ecovillages', *Journal of Cleaner Production* 237(10), 117830, pp. 1–13.

Smessaert, J. and Feola, G. (2023) 'Beyond statism and deliberation: questioning ecological democracy through eco-anarchism and cosmopolitics. *Environmental Values* 32(6), pp. 765–93.

Smessaert, J. and Feola, G. (2024) 'Becoming-interdependent: Democratic Praxis in-against-and-beyond capitalism in agrifood collectives', *Antipode*.

Springer, S. (2012). 'Anarchism! What geography still ought to be', *Antipode* 44(5), pp. 1605–24.

Stevens-Wood, K. (2020) 'These communities are experimenting with greener and fairer ways of living', *The Conversation,* 10 July. Available at: https://theconversation.com/these-communities-are-experimenting-with-greener-and-fairer-ways-of-living-129374.
Sullivan, E. (2016) '(Un)Intentional community: Power and expert knowledge in a sustainable lifestyle community', *Sociological Inquiry* 86(4), pp. 540–62.
Taylor Aiken, G. (2017) 'The politics of community: Togetherness, transition and post-politics', *Environment and planning A* 49(10), pp. 2383–401.
Taylor Aiken, G. (2019) 'Community as tool for low carbon transitions: Involvement and containment, policy and action', *Environment and Planning C: Politics and Space* 37(4), pp. 732–49.
Taylor Aiken, G., Middlemiss, L., Sallu, S. and Hauxwell-Baldwin, R. (2017) 'Researching climate change and community in neoliberal contexts: An emerging critical approach. *Wiley Interdisciplinary Reviews: Climate Change* 8(4), p. e463.
Temesgen, A.K. (2020) 'Building an island of sustainability in a sea of unsustainability? A study of two ecovillages', *Sustainability* 12(24), pp. 10585.
Thörn, H., Larsen, H.G., Hagbert, P. and Wasshede, C. (2020) 'Co-housing, sustainable urban development and governance: An introduction', in Hagbert, P., Larsen, H.G., Thörn, H. and Wasshede, C. (eds.) *Contemporary Co-Housing in Europe: Towards Sustainable Cities?* Milton Park/New York: Routledge, pp. 1–19.
Tsing, A.L., (2015) *The Mushroom at the End of the World: On the Possibility of Life in Capitalist Ruins.* New Jersey, NJ: Princeton University Press.
Tummers, L. and MacGregor, S. (2019) 'Sustainable beyond wishful thinking: A FPE perspective on commoning, care, and the promise of co-housing', *International Journal of the Commons* 13(1), pp. 1–22.
Ulug, C., Trell, E.M. and Horlings, L. (2021) 'Ecovillage foodscapes: Zooming in and out of sustainable food practices', *Agriculture and Human Values* 38(4), pp. 1041–59.
Van Schyndel Kasper, D. (2008) 'Redefining community in the ecovillage', *Human Ecology Review* 15(1), pp. 12–24.
Vannini, P. and Taggart, J. (2013) 'Voluntary simplicity, involuntary complexities, and the pull of remove: The radical ruralities of off-grid lifestyles', *Environment and Planning A* 45(2), pp. 295–311.
Veteto, J.R. and Lockyer, J. (2008) 'Environmental anthropology engaging permaculture: Moving theory and practice toward sustainability', *Culture & Agriculture* 30(1–2), pp. 47–58.
Walker, L. (2005) *Ecovillage at Ithaca: Pioneering a sustainable culture.* New Society Publishers.
Wechuli, Y. (2017) 'Neighborly assistance: High expectations of multi-generation cohousing projects', *Working with Older People* 21(3), pp. 133–9.
Wills, J. (2012) 'The geography of community and political organisation in London today', *Political Geography* 31(2), pp. 114–26.
Wimbush, T.P. (2021) *The Lammas Ecovillage: Deep Roots and Stormy Skies.* England: FeedARead Publishing.
Winter, A. (2016) '"Environmental sustainability? We don't have that here": Freetown Christiania as an unintentional eco-village', *ACME: An International Journal for Critical Geographies* 15(1), pp. 129–49.
Wright, E.O. (2010) *Envisioning Real Utopias.* London: Verso.
Würfel, M. (2012) 'The ecovillage: A model for a more sustainable, future-oriented lifestyle?', *RCC Perspectives* 8, pp. 11–17.

Part One

Living ecologically: Generating socio-ecological transformations

Jenny Pickerill

A defining rationale of eco-communities is that they generate socio-ecological transformations which reduce their environmental impact, and many have achieved significant savings in CO_2 emissions. This has been achieved through radical changes in what environmental resources are required and needed (through a reduction in the use of energy-intensive technologies, consumption and travel), and in switching the types of resources used (away from fossil fuel energies towards renewable sources, collecting rainwater, etc). These are combined through the building of off-grid material infrastructures (such as micro-renewable energy generation), sharing common infrastructures (e.g. sharing laundry facilities) and social infrastructures (such as childcare) which result in radically reducing the use of fossil fuel energies and in reduced overall resource use, even when these changes are achieved indirectly (as Daly, Chapter 3, explores).

These successes, however, belie a complexity which is explored in this section. There are numerous tensions and compromises which have to be navigated to achieve a more ecological way of life, and these changes are often hard to develop, learn, practise and sustain. If residents struggle with these processes and practices, then the likelihood of them being more broadly adopted and facilitating socio-ecological transformations beyond eco-communities diminishes. Some of these difficulties are because of the dynamic ongoing experimental nature of eco-communities means that infrastructures are unfinished, incomplete and partial, but even when completed several require daily manual labour. As Kallis et al. (2012) have argued those not committed to an ecological life are unlikely to voluntarily accept hardships, discomfort or sacrifice to achieve it. A key concern for the contributors in this section is the practical obstacles that participants encounter generating more ecological lives, and what is required to navigate them.

The challenge in living ecologically, however, is more than one of practical or infrastructural changes; it is also about how everyday life is experienced, enjoyed, felt and understood. There are those who happily seek a voluntary simplicity that might result in some physical hardships – such as having to manually collect wood for heating and cooking, or limited availability of lighting in evenings. However, residents tend to seek an enhancement in other aspects of life to compensate such as an improved social quality of life in terms of enjoyment, happiness, togetherness and more-than-human relations.

These social elements are more nebulous, subjective, less visible, intangible and much harder to quantify. But they are the very reason residents can endure these radical changes to their daily lives and many credit the collectivity, mutual support and solidarity they offer as crucial to facilitating more ecological lives. For the eco-communities examined in this section living ecologically often requires compromises and navigating challenges encountered in generating a multitude of material and social changes. Residents make trade-offs between their intent and practical limitations of personal discomfort or more-than-human surprises, navigating what gives them joy, emotionally sustains them, and what they can physically endure. As these chapters demonstrate, living ecologically is as much about changes in social relations and what constitutes a community, than it is about material innovations.

2

Does living sustainably suck? Reduced consumption and quality of life at Dancing Rabbit Ecovillage during the Anthropocene

Joshua Lockyer and Brooke Jones

Introduction

Humans in the most affluent societies are out of balance with the planet and, in the process of creating that imbalance, we are eroding both our own quality of life and the conditions that made our affluence possible. Based on changes in atmospheric chemistry and the declining diversity of terrestrial and marine life on the planet – changes that are largely due to increased human consumption of natural resources – geologists are currently debating whether the present time should be designated a new geologic epoch. The Anthropocene is a designation indicating that human actions have become the dominant force on the planet, a force strong enough to destabilize the conditions under which all civilizations have arisen (Crutzen 2006; Kress and Stine 2017; Lewis and Maslin 2015). At the same time, a growing body of research has demonstrated that people in industrialized societies have not increased in happiness despite their levels of material consumption increasing (Jackson 2009; Kasser 2002). Something is out of balance here; we consume in pursuit of happiness and we are consuming ourselves out of a livable planet without much to show for it in terms of enhanced quality of life. Who is doing the challenging work of trailblazing pathways that will enable us to transition out of this mess?

This chapter is based on research we conducted at Dancing Rabbit Ecovillage, an intentional eco-community located in Missouri, USA, between 2010 and 2019. Our research included a two-year period during which one of us (Jones) lived and conducted intensive ethnographic data collection in the community while the other (Lockyer) visited frequently, assisted with research, and brought groups of students to experience the ecovillage and help with data collection. The basic question we seek to address here, phrased colloquially, is: 'does living intentionally and more sustainably suck?' Our analysis suggests that the quality of life experienced at Dancing Rabbit, while multidimensional and far from straightforward, is still relatively high despite significant reductions in resource consumption achieved by community members.

Eco-communities

Beginning in the 1990s, a growing number of intentional communities, many of them referring to themselves as ecovillages, began to adopt an explicit focus on providing contexts in which people might experiment with living in more ecologically sustainable and socially connected ways (Litfin 2014; Miller 2019; Sanford 2017). Driven by concerns about the environmental impact of high consumptive lifestyles and attendant social alienation and experienced declines in quality of life, ecovillages, cohousing communities, transition towns and other eco-communities provide a context in which people try out new lifestyles that are more sustainable and fulfilling. A quotation from the Global Ecovillage Network's website, illustrates these aspirational goals: '*Ecovillages are living laboratories* pioneering beautiful alternatives and innovative solutions. They are rural or urban settlements with vibrant social structures, vastly diverse, yet *united in their actions towards low-impact, high-quality lifestyles*' (Global Ecovillage Network 2018, emphasis by the authors).

Similar aspirational claims are made by the Cohousing Association of the United States and Transition US:

> *Cohousing communities are intentional, collaborative neighborhoods* created with a little ingenuity. They bring together the value of private homes with the benefits of more sustainable living. That means residents actively participate in the design and operation of their neighborhoods, and share common facilities and good connections with neighbors. All in all, *they stand as innovative and sustainable answers to today's environmental and social problems*
> (The Cohousing Association of the United States 2018, emphasis by the authors)

> *The Transition Movement is a vibrant, grassroots movement that seeks to build community resilience in the face of such challenges as peak oil, climate change and the economic crisis.* It represents one of the most promising ways of engaging people in strengthening their communities against the effects of these challenges, *resulting in a life that is more abundant, fulfilling, equitable and socially connected.*
> (Transition US 2018, emphasis by the authors)

Recent scholarship on contemporary eco-communities highlights the broad variety of experiments in more sustainable living that intentional communitarians are undertaking and makes the case that these communities are creating models for sustainability that are applicable far beyond the confines of intentional communities themselves. For example, Sanford concludes her book *Living Sustainably* by stating: 'Their experiments in nonviolence, interdependence, and voluntary simplicity, enacted in specific contexts and geographies, help us imagine new pathways of living and being together sustainably' (Sanford 2017; for similar claims, see also Boyer 2016; Daly 2017; Grinde, Nes, MacDonald, and Wilson 2017; Litfin 2014; Nelson 2018).

Literature produced by practitioners in these communities makes similar claims about reduced environmental footprints and the applicability of the experiments being undertaken to broader publics, suggesting that these communities offer desirable alternatives to mainstream lifestyles that can lead to broader socio-ecological transformations. Addressing her fellow communitarians in the afterword to her book *Together Resilient,* Ludwig writes,

> The vast majority of us are hard-working, deeply grounded, and incredibly caring people who have figured out some really important things about how to live, how to prosper on less, how to be more conscious and responsible humans. … You've taken seriously enough the economic and ecological challenges that are trashing the world that you've made your life into a vessel for real change.
>
> (Ludwig 2017)

However, very few of these accounts of contemporary eco-communities are supported by systematic data collection and analysis demonstrating that the models being created are sustainable *and* desirable. Our research, including this chapter combined with earlier publications (Jones 2014; Lockyer 2017, 2018), aims to make a modest contribution in this area through an in-depth study of Dancing Rabbit Ecovillage.

Dancing Rabbit Ecovillage

Dancing Rabbit Ecovillage is an intentional community of approximately fifty people[1] situated on a 280-acre land trust in rural northeast Missouri, USA (see Figure 1 and 2). Located on rolling prairies near the centre of North American continent, Dancing Rabbit is situated in a landscape transformed by over a century of industrial scale development (see Mutel 2008 for a history of the ecological destruction of prairie ecosystems). At a significant distance from any large population centres and the attendant suburban sprawl, the ecovillage is surrounded by a landscape dominated by large-scale farms mostly engaged in industrial monocrop agriculture. Accompanying this, the introduction of non-native species and the suppression of periodic fire that is a natural part of prairie ecosystems (along with the earlier removal of indigenous people and the destruction of the North American bison) generated a landscape devoid of much of its original biodiversity. This is the landscape that Dancing Rabbit's founders chose to inhabit when they started the community.

The community was founded in the mid-1990s by a small group of people who, while completing graduate school together in California, decided that they needed to move beyond protesting ecological destruction to start modelling a more sustainable, more fulfilling way of life. They chose rural Missouri for their experiment for a number of reasons. One was the local presence of other communal groups, including a 1960s commune called Sandhill Farm and a large number of Mennonite communities, from

---

[1] This figure is approximate and includes full members of the community who signed membership agreements following a period of trial membership as well as a number of long-term visitors who may be completing apprenticeships or trial memberships. The total population varies from season to season and year to year.

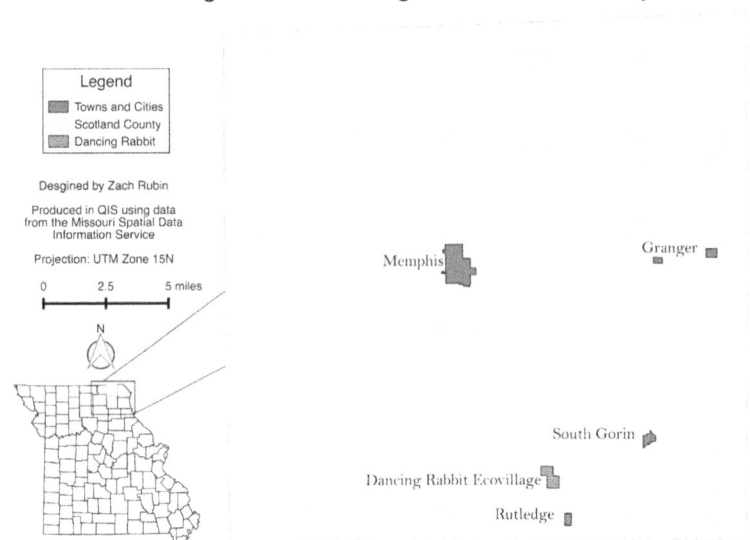

Figure 1 Dancing Rabbit Ecovillage location map. (Source: Zach Rubin, PhD.)

Figure 2 Common house and main road at Dancing Rabbit Ecovillage. (Source: Joshua Lockyer.)

whose accumulated wisdom about communal living they might learn. Another reason for choosing this location was the relative dearth of zoning and building codes which often present obstacles to experiments in sustainable living. A third reason was the opportunity to take advantage of the federal government's Conservation Reserve Program which would provide funding to enable the community to commence the process of rehabilitating the over-exploited industrial farmland they purchased (Lockyer 2018).

The founders of Dancing Rabbit articulated their mission statement and sets of 'ecological covenants' and 'sustainability guidelines' to embody their aspirations and goals. Dancing Rabbit states that their mission is 'To create a society, the size of a small town or village, made up of individuals and communities of various sizes and social structures, which allows and encourages its members to live sustainably. To encourage this sustainable society to grow to have the size and recognition necessary to have an influence on the global community by example, education, and research' (Dancing Rabbit Ecovillage 2020a). The community's approach to fulfilling this mission is, in turn, guided by more specific sets of rules and principles.

The community's 'ecological covenants' provide binding rules that community members are expected to abide by when they are accepted into membership in the community. Their ecological covenants include commitments to:

- Not keep or use a personal vehicle on site; instead, members use a small number of cooperatively owned vehicles
- Not use fossil fuels for heating and cooling buildings, providing refrigeration, or heating water; in the absence of sound alternatives, some fossil fuel use is allowed for cooking
- Engage in only organic gardening and agricultural production
- Use only renewable resources for electricity production[2]
- Use only local/reclaimed/certified sustainable timber for building construction
- Reclaim organic and recyclable wastes; this includes human waste which the community composts (paraphrased from Dancing Rabbit Ecovillage 2020b).

Dancing Rabbit's 'sustainability guidelines', also subscribed to by new community members, provide general guidance for organizing life's activities in the ecovillage within a more global context. They include agreements to:

- Look holistically at issues of sustainability to create a sustainable culture that takes into account all impacts of its actions
- Rely only upon renewable resources and use them at a rate less than their replacement
- Understand and minimize negative impacts on global ecological systems

---

[2] This covenant was modified fifteen years after the community was founded when they decided to connect to the grid for more regular access to electricity. This decision was made with the caveat that they send twice as much renewably generated electricity into the grid as they take from it, a goal that the community has achieved only irregularly.

- Preserve and rebuild healthy ecosystems and have a positive impact on biodiversity
- Create closed resource loops where byproducts are reintegrated as useful resources, thus minimizing waste products
- Avoid exploiting people and other cultures
- Achieve negative population growth from reproduction (paraphrased from Dancing Rabbit Ecovillage 2020c).

These covenants and guidelines set the stage not only for individual household design and consumptive activities but also for group endeavours at Dancing Rabbit such as building a collective, renewable energy micro-grid in the community and restoring their common land through reforestation and other land use management practices (see Lockyer 2018).

Increased Ecological Sustainability at Dancing Rabbit

Part of our research programme at Dancing Rabbit aimed to help them assess their progress towards some of their goals of living in a more ecologically sustainable manner. To this end, we collected data on the average per capita resource consumption of Dancing Rabbit Ecovillage members and compared the numbers from our data collection with per capita averages for the United States. Summarizing the results of this part of our research (Jones 2014; Lockyer 2017), including data on travel, fossil fuel and electricity usage, water consumption, vehicle ownership and solid waste production, the members of Dancing Rabbit Ecovillage consume approximately 10 per cent of the resources of the average North American in multiple key areas.

However, it became clear that if Dancing Rabbit was to have an influence on the world as suggested in their mission statement, if they wanted to be a model for broader socio-ecological transformations, we would also need to analyse how the members of Dancing Rabbit *felt* about and *experienced* living a lifestyle characterized by such low rates of consumption. Dancing Rabbit could not be a model for other people or other communities if members were miserable living a low consumption lifestyle. In other words, we would need to determine not only if the members of the ecovillage were living in more ecologically sustainable ways but if they were able to also maintain a relatively high quality of life.

Quality of life at Dancing Rabbit

Our analysis of experienced quality of life at Dancing Rabbit Ecovillage is based on twenty-two in-depth ethnographic interviews with members of the community, representing approximately two-thirds of the total full members of the community that were present at the time of the research. Our interviews included two quantitative questions that asked people to rank their quality of life in the ecovillage on a set scale, as well as twelve open-ended questions focused on people's lived experience in the ecovillage. In designing our questions, we drew upon on a citizen science study of Seattle, USA, that sought to develop data and strategies for assessing and increasing the city's ecological sustainability and livability (Sustainable Seattle 2004). Seattle is widely known as an environmentally conscious city and the aims of Sustainable Seattle's study paralleled our research on Dancing Rabbit (albeit in a larger context) and offered methodology and indicators that were easily replicable.

Our first quantitative question – 'Do you think Dancing Rabbit is a good place to live?' – asked respondents to rank their life in the community on a five-tiered scale. Possible answers included: not at all, somewhat, neutral, good and extremely good. Eighty-eight per cent of our respondents ranked Dancing Rabbit as either 'good' or 'extremely good' and no one gave it a ranking below neutral. This is very similar to the rankings given by respondents to the Sustainable Seattle survey where 91 per cent of respondents indicated that Seattle was a 'good' or 'extremely good' place to live.

Our second quantitative question – 'How happy are you with life at Dancing Rabbit right now?' – asked respondents to rank their happiness with life in the community on a 10-point scale, going from 1 being least happy to 10 being most happy. The average respondent ranking on this scale was 7.3 with only two respondents giving rankings of 5 or under. We do not have comparative data for this question, but we do intend to return to the community and ask both of our quantitative questions after a ten-year time period to gain a more longitudinal perspective on these topics.

While our quantitative data paint a relatively straightforward, largely positive picture of experienced quality of life at Dancing Rabbit, the results of our open-ended, qualitative questions add depth and nuance to this picture. Our qualitative analysis reveals that experienced quality of life is multi-dimensional and far from straightforward.

Every person we interviewed mentioned things about living at Dancing Rabbit that enhanced their quality of life and things that detracted from their quality of life. People most often identified things in the collective social realm that enhanced their quality of life in the ecovillage. For example, one respondent stated, 'I really, really like living with like-minded people. I like the social aspect and I like supporting each other in what we want to do in the world .... I am very satisfied with the sense of support and continuity of connection I feel in community.' Similarly, another respondent said, 'We're doing important work, and there's a deep satisfaction that I take in what we're doing ... It's this really important sustainability project and that makes a really big difference for me.' For both of these respondents, it is clear that being part of the group social endeavur that is the ecovillage enhances their experienced quality of life.

If our respondents had a strong tendency to appreciate the togetherness aspect of ecovillage life as a positive contribution to their quality of life, they also tended to identify challenges in the material, physical realm as things that detract from their experienced quality of life. One of our interviewees stated:

> Some things are kind of hard about living here. It's dirty, there are ticks, there are chiggers,[3] and like flies in the poopers, you've gotta go get sawdust sometimes when all you want to do is go to the bathroom, there's just a level of inconvenience here that unless there's a really strong values alignment I don't think people would be happy living here.

Another one of our respondents indicated a similar experience. 'I think living in a partially done house has been hard. And my quality of life will go up by a notch once the house is really done.' For the participants in our research, it is the unfinished, still-in-process, experimental components of material life in the ecovillage that are challenging. Many community members spend years building their own homes, leaving themselves more exposed to the elements than was the case before they moved to Dancing Rabbit. Furthermore, their agreement to forgo certain conveniences that are common in life outside the ecovillage – flush toilets for example – leads to frustration that can detract from quality of life. However, it is clear that ecovillage members are willing to trade some challenges and frustrations for a chance to live with like-minded people in a collective pursuit of a life that more closely conforms to their values.

Our analysis also identified that something one person experienced as enhancing quality of life in the ecovillage was sometimes the same thing that detracted from quality of life for another person. For example, one respondent reflected the above-identified positive valuation of social aspects of life in the ecovillage. 'I also feel that my social time coincides with my work and so I'm out in the garden working and yet I'm with my friends. I'm doing my childcare and I find that incredibly fulfilling. And … my jobs very much overlap with my social life. And I absolutely love that, I thrive on it.' However, another respondent indicated that the intensity of social interactions was especially challenging for her.

> For an introvert it can be really difficult to have lots of people in and out and, in my situation where I am eating now at the common house, that can be difficult for me socially to have a lot of interactions and then when I actually want to be social … then I don't have energy for it so that can be a challenge.

Elsewhere in the interview, this latter respondent placed a positive value on the collective, social aspects of life in the ecovillage, but it is clear that for her as a self-identified introvert, the intensity of social interactions could reach a threshold beyond which she experienced their impact as negative.

This last point leads us to another unmistakable finding from our analysis of our qualitative interviews: the same thing could both enhance and detract from experienced quality of life for the same individual. We illustrate this finding with three examples, each containing quotations from the same interview with one community member. The first example involves a respondent identifying social aspects of ecovillage life as simultaneously fulfilling and challenging.

---

[3] Chiggers are tiny organisms often found on tall grasses and weeds such as those on the Missouri prairies. They mature to become mites whose bites cause unbearable itching and large red bumps.

It's also full of unexpected delight, people really appreciate little things and they tell you so, again it's that there's a connection, people can tell if I look miserable walking down the street, people evince concern. That doesn't happen anywhere else. So, there's a level of care and support that's deeper than family … It just comes back to the depth of connection that is incredibly fulfilling.

Later in the interview, the same individual states:

I miss the ability to do what I want when I want to …. There is an ease that comes from not needing to care about what the neighbors might think or how what you do will impact somebody, you can just do what you want to do…. I miss being able to just have like a box within which I can just do whatever I want.

Another respondent emphasized the double-edged-sword nature of collective ecovillage life, this time in light of what it is like to raise a child in the community. On one hand, the social support and connections are positive: 'So … connections for my family, like so much support for everyone in my family. There's men's group, and [my daughter]'s connections with both other kids and adults, is super important to me.' On the other hand, this respondent found that the community around him was not as diverse as it might otherwise be outside of an ecovillage context and he experienced this as a negative:

Definitely racial and cultural and ethnic diversity are missing. That is, and has always been disappointing to me and my disappointment kind of grows around that. Largely because raising a child here, I just feel like I want her to experience the fullness of life and if you're around a bunch of white people it's not very full.

Other researchers have commented critically on the relative lack of attention to equity and diversity in intentional communities and the ways in which this can prevent them from becoming the broadly attractive alternatives they may wish to be (Chitewere 2010; Tummers and MacGregor 2019). We know from our research that this is something that is acknowledged by and of concern to many intentional community members and it is clearly a challenge that needs to be more fully addressed.

A third and final example focuses on the physical, material realm mentioned above. In this participant's experience, being close to nature is both inspiring and incredibly challenging. 'Oh, when the cool wind blows on a hot day …. I think that living within the limits of nature really enhances my quality of life because I feel more in tune with my true nature. [When] I am not living outside of nature and not fighting nature, [life] feels more complete.' Yet, while this person might find himself living in tune with nature when a cooling breeze blows, it is not an all-encompassing nature that provides comfort as is apparent from the next quote from the same interview. 'The sparrows, we call them flying rats, they are a pest along with the actual rats and mice.' Again, for those who are building their own homes, and who may find themselves more exposed to the elements than they did in their life prior to joining the community, this aspect of ecovillage life can be especially challenging.

Another one of our findings is that the participants in our research have chosen to make trade-offs. The ecovillagers in our study are willing to sacrifice some degree of quality of life in one area in order to do something meaningful according to their values:

> The one thing that … I've been thinking on a lot lately is like it's a trade-off, you know, like if you think you need air conditioning, you know, your carbon footprint is gonna go up or if you think you need to eat meat more often, same thing. So it's a balancing act for everyone and … so like I said it's a balancing act and I think that comes down to every aspect of sustainability. You gotta balance your quality of life with like your guilt or your conscience or something.

For the ecovillagers at Dancing Rabbit, making a sacrifice in one area – in living with fewer physical comforts than they were previously used to, or living a more socially intensive life than they may be comfortable with – is seen as a necessary price to pay for doing what they see as the ethically appropriate course of action of deliberately attempting to live in a more ecologically sensitive manner.

One final theme is that many respondents identified their internal state of mind as posing the greatest challenges to and opportunities for enhanced quality of life at Dancing Rabbit. For these people, the ability to experience high quality of life is located as much in their psyche as it is within the larger ecovillage milieu around them.

> There are definitely things [about Dancing Rabbit] that I could say I would really like to have them change but I can just as easily imagine that to achieve my optimal level of happiness is more about my own inner work. My own ability to be compassionate. My own ability to be appreciative for the things that I have. I mean I have it really good compared to the vast majority of humans throughout human history so, if the little 1% of things could get better I don't know that that matters nearly as much.

> My level of happiness is mostly me defining what I need to be happy. Yeah, so if I let myself start thinking in a negative way or start redefining preferences as needs then I can make myself unhappy; in fact, I am good at doing that. I think we are culturally prepped to do that to ourselves, the culture sort of does it. If I am careful with that then nothing prevents me from being happy here, you know.

These two final quotations from our interviews raise the important point that an essential part of achieving a more ecologically sustainable and personal fulfilling lifestyle, especially for the more affluent people in the more affluent societies, will be adjusting expectations and cultural mindsets. This is especially true relative to an understanding of what might constitute one's fair share of resources in a globally interconnected world as well as beliefs about what one truly needs to be happy.

Fewer material things and a happier life?

It is useful to put our analysis of experienced quality of life at Dancing Rabbit Ecovillage in a comparative context. Two recent studies attempted to analyse quality of life in contemporary intentional communities. Both of these studies were based on surveys distributed to intentional community members by researchers working at a distance and provide an informative comparative context for our more in-depth, ethnographic research.

First, Grinde et al. (2017) surveyed more than 900 members of intentional communities around the world, finding that intentional community members experienced high 'meaning in life' and high 'satisfaction with life' relative to other demographic groups that were asked the same set of questions in other studies. They also found that intentional community members overwhelmingly reported that their life had improved since they joined an intentional community. They concluded that 'sustainability, in the form of a communal lifestyle of low ecological footprint, may be promoted without forfeiting wellbeing' (Grinde et al., 2017, 625). Our research clearly supports this conclusion and adds qualitative depth to it. People at Dancing Rabbit live communally and have a decreased environmental impact compared to the average North American and they have a relatively high quality of life, however complex and multidimensional their experience of it may be.

Second, Mulder et al. (2006) sent a set of survey questions to people who live in intentional communities and people who live in 'unintentional' communities and compared the answers of the two sets of people. One conclusion that these authors reached is that 'ICs [intentional communities] have a better balance between built, human, social, and natural capital than unintentional communities and ... this results in higher QofL [quality of life]' (Mulder et al., 2006, 13). Our analysis does not clearly support this conclusion. It is clear that the built environment, or at least the perpetually incomplete nature of it, is consistently challenging for many members of Dancing Rabbit. While the ecovillagers in our study clearly valued having access to the natural world, they sometimes got too much of it due in part to the incomplete, experimental nature of their built environment. The lack of congruence of our findings with Mulder et al. may be in part a result of divergent nature of Dancing Rabbit compared with the intentional communities those authors surveyed. It is clear that Dancing Rabbit is a younger intentional community with less completed infrastructure and a more radical commitment to experimental building than the communities they focused on.

The results of our analysis are in closer alignment with Mulder et al.'s second conclusion that in intentional communities, 'social capital is substituted for built capital, thereby reducing the level of material throughput' (Mulder et al., 2006, 13). The participants in our research often expressed that being in community with others offset many detrimental effects associated with less access to infrastructure and other material things. For the members of Dancing Rabbit, the fact that they were intimately joined with others in full-time pursuit of a less consumptive lifestyle made any decreased access to material amenities more bearable and meaningful. However, such lack of access was challenging and was often seen as a necessary, if not entirely desirable, trade-off.

Conclusions

If we return to the question from the start of this chapter – does living sustainably suck? – the answer is not entirely straightforward. The participants in our research repeatedly expressed frustration and challenges directly associated with trying to construct a life in an ecovillage. At times, these challenges and frustrations became quite salient even to the point of leading them to wonder if the trade-offs they chose were appropriate. However, on the balance, our participants indicated that their choices went further to enhancing their quality of life than to detracting from it, especially in terms of allowing them to live a life aligned with their values. The answers to our quantitative questions support the qualitative interpretation that, in the final analysis, living more sustainably mostly does not suck.

However, our analysis does leave some questions unanswered. For example, is improved quality of life in intentional communities translatable beyond the immediate context or does it only work for those who already see living more sustainably as a path to improved happiness by aligning their lives more closely with their values? There are many who would find that life at Dancing Rabbit, with its attendant rules, guidelines and reduced access to material amenities and consumption, contributed to a significant decrease in quality of life. Our results might also be different if we were able to expand our sample to include all members of the ecovillage as well as people who resigned from community membership. A few community members chose not to participate in our interviews; were they disgruntled with life in the ecovillage but still supportive enough of the overall mission that they chose not to participate because they didn't want their views to detract from an otherwise positive image? Were we to interview people who left community, what would they say? Did they leave at least in part because their quality of life had sunk to levels where the trade-offs were no longer worth it?

Equally, our research presents a relatively small snapshot of time of the community. Some of the people we interviewed alluded to a 'honeymoon' period that they experienced during the time immediately preceding and immediately following their acceptance into the community. We did not ask people directly about how their experienced quality of life changed over time. If we did ask such a question, would we find a significant drop off in experienced quality of life after joining the community? We would also like to note that, since the time of our research, the community has been challenged by at least two significant events, one internal in source and one external, that may significantly affect experienced quality of life there. One of these challenges involved significant criminal charges against a long-term community member and we are aware that a degree of social conflict arose in the community in the aftermath of these charges. The other event is the ongoing challenges surrounding the Covid-19 pandemic. This has been especially challenging for Dancing Rabbit because so much of their life is focused on close social interaction among members. It has also been challenging because such a significant part of the community's income and mission focuses on putting on programmes for non-community members who wish to come to the village to learn from Dancing Rabbit's example or to explore the possibility of joining the community. There is no doubt that were we to replicate our data collection in the community in the present, our results would be at least somewhat different.

In the end, we feel that our general conclusion that living more sustainably mostly does not suck for the members of Dancing Rabbit Ecovillage suggests that the community can contribute to broader socio-ecological transformation. There is almost certainly a large chunk of the population in affluent societies who would be willing to make the trade-off of living a less consumptive lifestyle in order to address their real environmental concerns. That their trade-off does not necessarily need to include a great reduction in quality of life can be inspiring. Indeed, the high number of participants in Dancing Rabbit's visitor programmes indicates that there are many people out there seeking just such inspiration so that they may, if not join an ecovillage, contribute to positive socio-ecological transformations in their own way and in their own communities.

References

Boyer, R.H.W. (2016) 'Achieving one-planet living through transitions in social practice: A case study of Dancing Rabbit Ecovillage', *Sustainability: Science, Practice, and Policy* 12(1), pp. 47–59.

Chitewere, T. (2010) 'Equity in sustainable communities: Exploring tools from environmental justice and political ecology', *Natural Resources* 50(2), pp. 315–39.

The Cohousing Association of the United States (2018) Available at: https://www.cohousing.org/. Accessed 4 October 2018.

Crutzen, P.J. (2006) 'The "Anthropocene"', in Ehlers, E. and Krafft, T. (eds.) *Earth System Science in the Anthropocene*. Berlin: Springer, pp. 13–18.

Daly, M. (2017) 'Quantifying the environmental impact of ecovillages and co-housing communities: A systematic literature review', *Local Environment* 22(11), pp. 1358–77.

Dancing Rabbit Ecovillage (2020a) *Dancing Rabbit Mission Statement*. Available at: https://www.dancingrabbit.org/about-dancing-rabbit-ecovillage/vision/mission-statement/. Accessed 14 July 2020.

Dancing Rabbit Ecovillage (2020b) *Ecological Covenants*. Available at: https://www.dancingrabbit.org/about-dancing-rabbit-ecovillage/vision/ecological-covenants/. Accessed 14 July 2020.

Dancing Rabbit Ecovillage (2020c) *Sustainability Guidelines*. Available at: https://www.dancingrabbit.org/about-dancing-rabbit-ecovillage/vision/sustainability-guidelines/. Accessed 14 July 2020.

Global Ecovillage Network (2018) *What Is an Ecovillage?* Available at: https://ecovillage.org/global-ecovillage-network/about-gen/. Accessed 18 September 2018.

Grinde, B., Ban Nes, R., MacDonald, I. and Wilson, D. (2017) 'Quality of life in intentional communities', *Social Indicators Research* 137(2), pp. 625–40.

Jackson, T. (2009) *Prosperity without Growth: Economics for a Finite Planet*. London: earthscan.

Jones, K.B. (2014) *Toward Sustainable Community: Assessing Progress at Dancing Rabbit Ecovillage*. Master's thesis. University of North Texas.

Kasser, T. (2002) *The High Price of Materialism*. Cambridge, MA: The MIT Press.

Kress, W., Stine, J. and Stine, J.K. (Eds.) (2017) *Living in the Anthropocene: Earth in the Age of Humans*. Washington, DC: Smithsonian Books.

Lewis, S.L. and Maslin, M. (2015) 'Defining the Anthropocene', *Nature* 519(7542), pp. 171–80.

Litfin, K.T. (2014) *Ecovillages: Lessons for Sustainable Community*. Malden, MA: Polity Press.

Lockyer, J. (2017) 'Community, commons, and degrowth at Dancing Rabbit Ecovillage', *Journal of Political Ecology* 24(1), pp. 425–66.

Lockyer, J. (2018) 'Community, commons, and ecological restoration at Dancing Rabbit Ecovillage', *Rootstalk: A Prairie Journal of Culture, Science, and the Arts* 5(1), pp. 41–52. Available at: https://rootstalk.grinnell.edu/past-issues/volume-v-issue-1/community-commons-ecological-restoration/.

Ludwig, M. (2017) *Together Resilient: Building Community in the Age of Climate Disruption*. Rutledge, MO: Fellowship for Intentional Community.

Miller, T. (2019) *Communes in America, 1975–2000*. Syracuse: Syracuse University Press.

Mulder, K., Costanza, R. and Erickson, J. (2006) 'The contribution of built, human, social and natural capital to quality of life in intentional and unintentional communities', *Ecological Economics* 59(1), pp. 13–23.

Mutel, C. (2008) *The Emerald Horizon: The History of Nature in Iowa*. Iowa City, IA: University of Iowa Press.

Nelson, A. (2018) *Small Is Necessary: Shared Living on a Shared Planet*. London: Pluto Press.

Sanford, W. (2017) *Living Sustainably: What Intentional Communities Can Teach Us about Democracy, Simplicity, and Nonviolence*. Lexington, KY: The University of Kentucky Press.

Sustainable Seattle (2004) *Sustainable Seattle, 1998: Indicators of Sustainable Community. A Status Report on Long-Term Cultural, Economic, and Environmental Health for Seattle/King County*. Available at: http://www.sustainableseattle.org/component/content/article/44-regional-indicators/123-1998report. Accessed 1 April 2013.

Transition US (2018) *About Us: Bringing a New World to Life*. Available at: http://www.transitionus.org/about-us. Accessed on 18 September 2018.

Tummers, L. and MacGregor, S. (2019) 'Beyond wishful thinking: A FPE perspective on commoning, care, and the promise of co-housing', *International Journal of the Commons* 13(1), pp. 62–83.

3

Understanding consumption reduction through the social practices of an Australian eco-community

Matthew Daly

Introduction

There has never been a more pressing time to re-imagine how we live with, and on, the Earth. In less than a century, the relationship between humankind and the natural world has undergone the most rapid transformation in human history (Steffen et al., 2004). From an environmental perspective, the effects have been devastating. Humanity has exceeded seven of eight global-scale safe and just Earth system boundaries (Rockström et al., 2023), and has a global consumption footprint which exceeds the earth's biocapacity for regeneration by 75 per cent, meaning we would need the equivalent 1.75 Earths to sustain current lifestyles (WWF 2022). The environmental impacts of consumption are felt on a global scale, yet the ultimate drivers of a large proportion of consumption are local, and ultimately occurring at the household level. Research estimates that roughly 65 per cent of global greenhouse gas (GHG) emissions, and between 50 per cent and 80 per cent of total land, water and material use, stem from household consumption (Ivanova et al., 2016). The indirect emissions associated with carbon embedded in goods and services are estimated to account for between 70 per cent and 80 per cent of household GHG emissions (Capstick et al., 2014).

The consumption of goods and services is a daily activity, carried out in order to satisfy needs and wants in a manner that is generally perceived to maintain or improve quality of life. The interplay between the personal, the social, the systemic and the related environmental and ecological impacts is complex. The impacts of household consumption are highly variable globally, and within individual societies, due to different lifestyles and consumption patterns across households (WWF 2022). This opens up the possibility of achieving significant change in these patterns, with rapid reductions in environmental impacts (Newton 2011). This idea, that residents of eco-communities can change their household practices to minimize their environmental impact, is the focus of this chapter, and is one of the core drivers for the socio-ecological transformations that many eco-communities are striving towards.

Existing consumption patterns are shaped and guided by existing structures and socio-technical systems in which they are embedded. Changing these systems to address the environmental challenges will require a reconfiguration of existing patterns of consumption, involving major innovations within, and changes to, the socio-technical systems that structure society (Geels et al., 2015). While this is a difficult task, the local and everyday nature of consumption implies that changes in consumption patterns do not necessarily need to stem from global or national initiatives. Shifting the consumption embedded in existing domains of everyday practice and routine, such as mobility, food and energy use and provision, can have a significant environmental impact (Tukker et al., 2010), and these are aspects of lifestyle which individuals or households can often significantly influence (Hertwich and Peters 2009).

It can be problematic to shift the burden of responsibility for reducing emissions to the individual or community. Unfortunately, the responses of governments and corporations to date have been inadequate, leading to a flourishing of individual and grassroots initiatives to reduce the environmental impacts of consumption (Penha-lopes and Henfrey 2019). Fortunately, there is evidence to suggest that in many cases there can be multiple benefits – a double dividend – from pursuing more sustainable household practices (Grinde et al., 2017; Jackson 2005), which suggests that some level of individual action need not be viewed only as burdensome on the individual or household.

Within this context, eco-communities represent real-world examples of people intentionally enacting such changes in their own households and communities, seeking alternatives to the existing consumption practices of the household. Evidence suggests eco-community residents are able to significantly reduce their ecological footprints, with a systematic review finding that communities had on average halved their ecological footprints (Daly 2017). Approaches communities have taken to do this include: adopting more sustainable technologies, reducing individual house sizes through the efficiency of shared space, encouraging pro-environmental practices amongst residents, greater sharing of goods and resources, and encouraging post-modern worldviews and post-materialist values that reduce consumption needs by prioritizing wellbeing rather than material goods and possessions (Daly 2018; Grinde et al., 2017; Meltzer and Metcalf 2005; Sherry and Ormsby 2016). Importantly, this can happen while also bringing wellbeing and social benefits to the community members (Grinde et al., 2017).

This chapter takes a distinct approach to understanding sustainability in eco-communities, drawing on social practice theories to explore consumption in terms of the routine, repeated practices (Shove, Pantzar and Watson 2012) that are enacted in the daily lives of community residents. First, the concept of social practices and approaches to intervention are introduced before consumption reduction in the eco-community of Murundaka Cohousing Community is explored.

Sustainable practice interventions

Scholars of socio-ecological transitions have argued for attention to be given to both transformations in socio-technical systems, and the practices of daily life (Geels et al.,

2015). Within this space, social practice theory (SPT) is an approach to understanding everyday sustainability that places practices, their elements and how they change, as the focus of analysis of everyday life. Individuals are decentred, becoming instead 'carriers or hosts of practices' (Shove et al., 2012, 7). In doing so, the focus shifts to the understood ways of 'doing' everyday social practices, and the inconspicuous consumption linked to these practices, rather than the behaviours and decision-making of individuals, or the material infrastructures and social norms that shape actions (Shove et al., 2012; Spurling et al., 2013).

Social practices are understood as a combination of interconnected elements, typically: materials, meanings and competencies (Shove et al., 2012). A practice can be described both as a practice-as-entity which represents a certain pattern of elements generally recognizable as constituting a practice, and also as a practice-as-performance; the dynamic combining of those elements in the actual 'doing' of the practice (Schatzki 1996). Consumption can then be understood as a moment in the performance of a practice (Spurling et al., 2013).

Consider showering as an example (Shove and Walker 2010). Whenever someone has a shower, they combine the materials (water, electricity/gas for hot water, soap, a dedicated shower space), meanings (cleanliness, freshness, relaxation) and competencies (how to use soap and wash oneself, how to make oneself presentable for the day ahead) that make up the practice of showering. The practice-entity of showering can be described as above; however, it is only through enacting this practice – as a performance, that the links between the elements of showering are reinforced or changed, and also that the hot water and soap are consumed. This provides a better reflection of how people typically understand daily life, as they generally think about heating their house, rather than consuming gas or electricity, for example. For this reason, Spurling et al. (2013) argue that social practices, and in particular the practice-as-entity which is the socially embedded underpinning of behaviour, are a better target for interventions to improve sustainability.

Changes to any element of practice can change – slightly or significantly – the way that practice is performed, and hence the impact of that practice. Practices are almost always interlinked, or 'bundled' to varying degrees with other practices in wider systems of practice, through co-location or sharing of elements (Shove, Pantzar and Watson 2012). Therefore, changes in one element, or practice, can have a wider rippling effect.

The strong emphasis practice theory places on the social context to help explain action gives it a natural affinity for the study of community-based initiatives, and how practices change within them (Middlemiss 2011). Eco-communities present themselves as excellent cases for research taking an SPT approach to understanding sustainable consumption. They are conscious attempts by members to adopt a mode of sustainable living as an alternative to the mainstream (Metcalf 2004). This is a deliberate attempt by the community to intervene in social practices. Research focusing on intentional communities is growing, though still limited (e.g. Pickerill 2015; Roysen and Mertens 2019).

Exploring how eco-community members adopt alternative modes of sustainable living places a focus on how these communities 'intervene' in daily practices.

Interventions in practice have been characterized as occurring via three different mechanisms (Spurling et al., 2013):

- recrafting – changing the elements that make up a practice,
- substituting – discouraging unsustainable practices in favour or existing or new alternative practices,
- changing the interlocking – changing the bundling of practices to change the demand for the practice itself.

These three mechanisms are all explored in the case study discussed in this chapter, to better understand how interventions in practice can encourage more sustainable household consumption. Within this research, sustainable consumption is understood through the evaluation frameworks of:

- new economics (Seyfang 2009) – key indicators being localization, reducing ecological footprints, community-building, collective action, and building new infrastructure of provision, and
- lowering carbon footprints for consumers (Schanes, Giljum and Hertwich 2016) through categories of direct reduction, indirect reduction, direct improvement and indirect improvement.

These two frameworks were used in this research to analyse the potential impacts of the sustainability practices discussed by community members.

Murundaka Cohousing Community

Murundaka is an urban cohousing project that has explicitly attempted to create a community that allows its members to live in a more sustainable manner. Their community vision has eight points, and specifically includes living sustainably (Murundaka Cohousing 2016). The full vision is shown in Table 1.
Murundaka was established in 2011 as an all-rental housing cooperative. All residents are members of Earth Common Equity Rental Cooperative (Earth Co-op), a housing co-operative that first formed in 1986, although most residents joined around the time when Murundaka was developed. Earth Co-op is one of more than a hundred Victorian housing cooperatives that operate under the Common Equity Housing (CEHL) programme. Murundaka consists of twenty households and approximately thirty-five to forty community members.

Murundaka is located in the middle-ring suburbs of Melbourne, 16 km from the city centre. It is located on a street that feels typically suburban Australian, with two-lanes, wide grassed verges and footpaths on either side, mostly single-storey detached red-brick houses with large front yards and some townhouse developments. More detail on the history of the community can be found in the thesis by Daly (2018) and the Murundaka website.[1] For further scholarship on the Melbourne region and eco-community type projects, see Palmer (2020).

The community design was based on cohousing principles (McCamant and Durrett 2011), and has a large, centrally located common house with two apartment wings (containing eighteen apartments in total) clustered around the communal building (see Figure 1). A shared parking lot adjoins the street on the south-west corner of the block and the shared backyard is situated on the north-east corner. A gate connects the backyard to an adjacent public park. Figures 2 and 3 show a number of images of

Table 1 Murundaka vision statement (Murundaka Cohousing 2016)

Our Vision

- We are a cooperative community, relating to each other with respect, compassion and support.
- We acknowledge the traditional owners on whose land we are living and working, and pay our respects to their Elders past and present.
- We live sustainably: Conscious of ourselves, our local community, the world and our legacy for the future through our individual and collective actions.
- We live with integrity: Balancing rights and responsibilities and behaving with authenticity.
- We are self-reflective and outward-looking: Curious, courageous, collaborative, valuing the cohesion of the group and the wisdom of all.
- We are part of our broader communities: Learning from and engaging in dialogue and action.
- We have fun: Encouraging trust and harmony through play, spontaneity and creativity.
- The statements represent our vision of what we want to be together and who we are already. We'll aim high and forgive each other when we fall short.

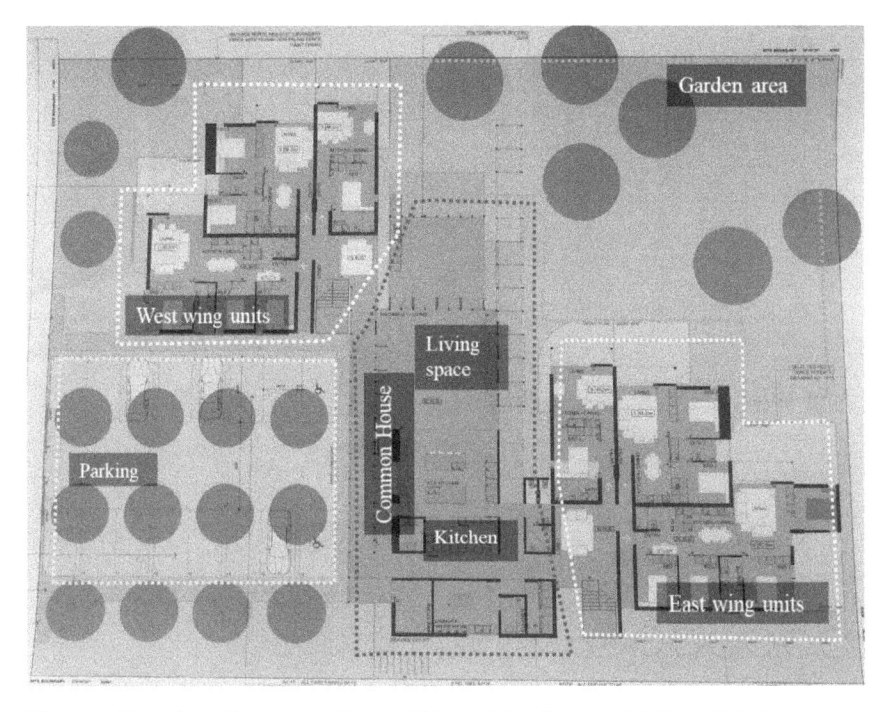

Figure 1 Plan view of the ground floor of Murundaka. (Source: Matthew Daly.)

Figure 2 View of Murundaka from the back corner of garden. (Source: Matthew Daly.)

Figure 3 Outdoor common space. (Source: Matthew Daly.)

the community buildings and space. At the time of research, the surrounding area was slowly undergoing a change in character, as free-standing homes on large lots of land were being replaced by denser rows of townhouses. However, the tall and bulky street frontage of the Murundaka buildings was a bold contrast to the predominant form and character of its neighbourhood, at least initially.

Research approach

To understand sustainable practice at Murundaka, the author conducted interviews with community members (nine individual, one group interview), housing and urban development professionals with involvement with Murundaka (six interviews), documentary analysis, and participant observation during two separate stays on the community totalling seven nights.

All gathered data were thematically analysed and grouped into different 'sustainability practices' within a number of practice domains. For each practice, key elements were identified as important to the sustainability of that practice, or key to differentiating that practice entity from more mainstream arrangements. While this analysis is grounded in the participants' understanding of both their everyday actions as eco-community members and how this compares to 'mainstream' practices, it is important to have a reference point for what is a 'mainstream' practice. In this case, work by Waitt et al. (2012) on sustainable household capability provided a useful Australian reference point. The analysis is arranged into 'sustainable practice tables' for each domain (Tables 3 and 4 below). The tables show the key elements for each practice, along with describing the type of intervention in practice, and the sustainability impact.

Practising sustainability in an eco-community

The Murundaka community had diverse views on what living sustainably meant to their own lives, and how this part of the community vision, and living at Murundaka, impacted their personal everyday practices. Through discussions with residents about living sustainably, many practices across multiple consumption domains emerged (Table 2).

These practices provide insight into the everyday household consumption practices that can evolve and stabilize (at least provisionally) within a niche environment that allows experimentation with new forms of sustainable lifestyles. Those practices in bold in Table 2 emerged as being distinct and particularly significant; a valuable insight when considering sustainability practices that may be encouraged on a wider scale. Typically, their significance was either because of their direct impact on the reduction of the community's environmental footprint, or indirectly because of their role in enabling the community to govern practice within it. Although indirect, these practices supported sustainable living by circulating 'sustainable elements' or influencing the overall practice system within the community. The sections below will focus on creating home and community, and food provisioning. Both of these

Table 2 Domains and sustainability practices at Murundaka

Domains	Murundaka Practices
Creating home/community	Creating a cohousing community
	Materializing a cohousing community
	Community formation (joining and leaving)
Governing home/community	Community Decision-Making
	Visioning & Reflection
	Mindful communication
Dwelling the house	Energy provisioning
	Provisioning the home (acquiring)
	Clothes swapping
	Disposing of waste
	Heating and cooling the home
Food	Growing food
	Shopping for food
	Dining
Transportation/Moving Around	Car Sharing
	Bike Riding

are linked to consumption, and the community members saw them as contributing to their sustainable living practices.

Creating home and community

The story of the formation of Murundaka, as is often the case with intentional communities, is long. Earth Co-op, from which it eventually grew, was one of many housing cooperatives formed in the Australian state of Victoria in the late 1980s; however, it had an environmental consciousness which set it apart from many of its contemporaries. Two early members of Earth Co-op would later become founding members of Murundaka. They had experienced life in intentional communities in other parts of Australia, but didn't think Melbourne would be receptive to an inner-city intentional community in the 1980s. By 2005, Earth Co-op had come under the umbrella of CEHL. Coop members were also founding members of the Sustainable Living Foundation (SLF), which amongst its many activities had a green building group which had been exploring the concept of cohousing. A 'set of ingredients' began to emerge once two neighbouring properties to an Earth Co-op house became available for purchase, and serious discussions began convincing CEHL to pursue a cohousing development.

The coming together of multiple meanings was key to the cohousing formation. Many of the Murundaka core group shared the vision of creating a social and cultural alternative to that which exists in mainstream society. In particular, the role of housing in perpetuating a structure which wasn't addressing key social and environmental issues:

> [W]e all take for granted the way we have been brought up and corralled, and manipulated and sold and marketed and campaigned, and just structured into the intentional way we live in suburbia. It's someone else's intentions but it doesn't often address deep needs, and it doesn't address sustainability needs.
> (Founding member)

Creating an intentional community was seen as a means of addressing environmental ('the climate emergency') and social issues ('a whole range of other social problems'). In particular, cohousing was seen as a form of intentional community that could present a mainstream solution to these issues, accessible to a wide array of people. These meanings were reflected early (interim) core values of sustainability, inclusiveness and social justice (including equity and access). The community was established as an all-rental cooperative, proactively structuring accessibility for households with low incomes, or lacking in financial wealth into the community model. Other aspects of social inclusion and equity, such as gender and race, weren't a focus during discussions on environmental and consumption practices.

These meanings, crucial during the conceptualizing and forming stages, took more specific form during the design and construction. They reflected an underlying desire of many members to challenge the existing speculative, individualized housing development paradigm, and adopt cohousing design principles (McCamant and Durrett 2011). The site layout was designed to encourage 'accidental' social interaction, residents traded private space to create more communal spaces, and ecologically sustainable design principles guided the design.

Along with shared meanings, the founders could also draw on a bedrock of key competencies (or skills) necessary to make the project happen. Founding members had first-hand experience living within intentional communities of Northern NSW, along with knowledge gained from a cohousing study tour of the United States. The development was designed by external architects engaged by CEHL; however, the forming members were knowledgeable enough to shape the design to (largely) reflect their vision of incorporating cohousing design principles such as integration of private and communal spaces. Crucially, the networks formed through activities, such as the SLF green building group, gave access to other people with specific skills (e.g. legal, planning and financial) that were needed to drive or influence the formation process.

The material reality of the land and eventual built form were also crucial elements in the eventual creation of Murundaka. Inner-city suburban land was crucial for the cohousing vision, but was more expensive and came with added planning restrictions and complications. The particular land helped to crystallize the vision of the founding members, linked to Earth Co-op and CEHL, and shaped the future of the community as a rental cooperative.

---

[1] https://www.murundakacohousing.org.au/about

Similarly, the construction of the buildings of the community allowed the concept of the cohousing community to become reality. The physical buildings allowed residents to start cohabitating, turning the concept of cohousing living into the reality of sharing communal spaces and negotiating the day-to-day realities of co-located living. The shared communal space was vital in the creation of a community from the people who, when first moving in, were to some extent just people living close together in a new development:

> So it's the community ... It does become the glue, definitely. And just the physical availability of space makes things happen. It's quite amazing. It's a catalyst.
> (Giselle, 6 years)

Table 3 summarizes the practices discussed in this section and highlights the key elements that were crucial in the way the practice was performed at Murundaka, or most significant in the way that practice differed from more mainstream forms of the practice. The table also comments on the type of intervention occurring within the practice, and the sustainable consumption significance of that practice.

The practices discussed show Murundaka members in the process of creating what Kunze (2012) described as a living laboratory of communal and ecological living. They are also perhaps the clearest examples of the community members intervening with the aim of improving the sustainability of their lifestyles. These community creation practices are not necessarily directly linked with greater sustainable consumption. Rather they are distinctive, non-mainstream practices unusual because of who the carriers and practitioners are – the future community members. In many ways this is also a historical practice, as once the community moved in, many of these elements became less relevant. Governance and ongoing maintenance of the community become the priority. However, the process of creation was so influential in both the physical and social fabric of the community, that it was an underlying presence in almost all aspects of daily practice.

In the case of Murundaka, the practice of intentional, or deliberate, creation of a community development or multi-unit complex is uncommon in mainstream Australian society. This practice can firstly be understood as changing the way certain practices are sequenced, by bringing the future resident into the formation and design stages of a new multi-unit development. It also represents a shifting of who performs this bundle of practices, from housing developers building for an individualized market to the group of individuals who would be living in the community. This resulted in an eco-community design that would not otherwise have been provided by the housing market, specifically addressing the needs of that community. Secondly, the prioritization of specific values (meanings) in the design – generous communal spaces, and a design that encourages social interaction – recrafted individual elements of the design practice resulting in smaller private dwellings, and generous shared spaces (material). This materialization of the community structures would go on to impact both the ways that community members would interact in those spaces, and the ways that energy was consumed throughout the community.

Table 3 Key practices and elements in the creation and ongoing governance of Murundaka Cohousing Community

Practices	Domain : Creating home and community			
	Elements			
	Materials	Competencies	Meanings	Type of intervention into 'mainstream' practice	Sustainability impact of practice

Creating an intentional community (Murundaka)	• Land of appropriate size and location – inner-city
	• Geographical location
	• Shared communal space in home design
		• Skills to turn ideas into visions and plans
		• Experience in communal living
		• Understanding of cohousing (Study tours and resources)
		• Group organization, and working collaboratively
		• Ability to connect and network with people
		• with legal, planning and financial skills
		• Experience working in housing cooperative
			• Shared Meaning
			• Creating a social and cultural alternative to mainstream society
			• Community as a means of addressing environmental and social issues
			• A mainstream solution to social sustainability
			• Core values of:
			  • sustainability
			  • inclusiveness
			  • social justice (including equity and access
				• Changing the sequencing in the process of community and home creation (changing how practices interlock) by having future residents involved during the formations stages	• Providing an alternative system for the provision of housing
					• Community building by developing social network around developing the community/housing
					• Collective action – strong sense of acting collectively – enabling collaboration to make effective decision about thing that effect their lives and engage with local government and local policy

Domain: Creating home and community

Practices	Elements			Type of intervention into 'mainstream' practice	Sustainability impact of practice
	Materials	Competencies	Meanings		
Materializing a cohousing community	• Sufficient and appropriate land • A mix of private space in homes for increased common space (give up the 'stuff room') • Specific style layout • Money (government contribution, housing cooperative) • Located in inner-city – Close to 'everything' • Location makes use of wider 'communal spaces' – parks etc.	• Organizational structure of community • Cohousing design principles • Social contact design principles • Know how shared by completed cohousing communities • Participatory design	• Design to encourage social interaction • Downsizing of private space to maximize communal space • Ecologically sustainable design principles • Challenge the existing housing development paradigm	• Recrafting by introducing new elements material, meaning and competencies into the design of community housing	• Community building through creating inclusive and cohesive spaces for the members • Indirect reduction – Changes in the behaviour of using space - sharing space makes more efficient use of space, e.g. reducing wasted heating and cooling energy

The sustainability impact of this practice is linked to the way the priorities driving the development are changed when the proponents become the future residents. As the construction of a housing development creates infrastructures that are material elements constituent in many practices, and particularly durable ones, there is a large potential to influence the sustainability of many practices in this way. A well-designed, and smaller, private dwelling requires less energy to heat and cool to comfortable temperatures. The provision of spacious and secure bike parking makes cycling an easier, and less resource intensive, transport option. These are just some examples of how the built form of the community can influence household consumption over the life of the building.

Food provisioning practices

The second domain considered here is that of food provisioning, which can be directly linked to significant environmental impact. As a consumption category, food is a priority action area that accounts for 16 per cent of Australian per capita GHG emissions (Hertwich and Peters 2009; Tukker et al., 2010).

Two of the Murundaka Sustainability Goals[2] directly addressed the food provisioning practices within the community. These were:

- To develop and keep our gardens and open spaces for recreation and food production
- To be mindful of sourcing of food and other goods locally and to utilize cooperative purchasing

The influence of these goals could be seen in the material availability of space available for food production, as well as representing a codification of certain meanings as important in the sourcing of food. Many residents of Murundaka considered food provisioning practices as important for living a sustainable lifestyle.

Most residents discussed gardening as an important practice for personal sustainability. A communal vegetable garden and chicken coop took up a large proportion of the backyard area (see Figure 3). One of the community's initial ambitions was to produce 10 per cent of their food on-site. Many residents talked of using the garden to supplement parts of their meals, and mostly for common meals, though they didn't think they were reaching the 10 per cent target. There were a number of residents who were 'really passionate about growing [their] own food' (resident member), with different meanings contributing to this passion.

> I'm really passionate about the composting system and getting that really happening well and giving the earth more ... just making it really fertile ....
> (resident member)

---

[2] Sustainability goals separate from the community vision were displayed on large posters in the Common House.

Some were concerned by food security and increasing self sufficiency, while others focused on personal responsibility for their food supply chain, or a desire for locally grown, organic food.

> I found that things happen naturally just by being around people, it wasn't someone preaching to me that I should live my life a certain way, just by being around people, it all became organic … and now Greg and I are prioritising eating organic over eating cheaply which we used to always just prioritise eating cheaply.
>
> (resident member)

These meanings led to a consideration of the material elements involved in the gardening practices. The consolidated sharing of space by the community allowed food to be grown on a larger scale. A large area in the communal backyard was dedicated to gardening, with vegetable plots, compost bins, a chicken run and six rainwater tanks. Residents discussed how much they appreciated the large garden space, compared with previous experience in smaller share-house gardens, or even growing plants in pots. The community was able to share tools and resources used for gardening. It also had the labour of a large group of willing gardeners, with the garden group having between five and ten members. The garden group met roughly monthly for 'working bees'.[3] Having others to share the work was empowering, enabling different types of practice:

> Anyway so here, you know, we can share the work. And things that I cannot do on my own I can do.
>
> (resident member)

Two residents had experience and training in permaculture principles, and had had taken a leading role with food growing practices at Murundaka. The gardening experience of other residents varied, some had been growing their own small gardens for a long time, whilst some just enjoyed gardening and were happy to contribute labour and learn from others. Competence and know-how were unequally spread throughout the community. Yet by gardening communally everyone was able to benefit from a garden that used permaculture knowledge. Murundaka land was also used to host a large variety of workshops. The workshops, as well as the monthly gardening group working bees, provided opportunities for hands-on participation and learning-by-doing, and was an important mechanism for the spread of know-how within the community.

Table 4 summarizes the practices and elements, including the type of innovation or intervention occurring within the practice, and the sustainability significance of that practice.

Food provisioning practices, particularly growing their own food, were passionately discussed by many Murundaka residents. In terms of impacts on sustainability, this is

---

[3] Voluntary time performing manual tasks in the garden.

Table 4 Key practices and elements in the provision of food in Murundaka Cohousing Community

Practices	Domain: food provisioning				
	Elements			Type of intervention into 'mainstream' practice	Sustainability impact of practice
	Materials	competencies	Meanings		
Growing food	• Large communal backyard dedicated to garden • Shared gardening equipment & tools • Pool of willing labour • Plentiful compost • Rainwater tanks	• Permaculture, gardening and composting knowledge • Cooking for seasonal vegetables • Preserving of excess food	• Self-sufficiency and personal responsibility (grow own food) • Local, organic food is desirable	• Recrafting of elements of growing food to increase the scale. • Substitution of growing own food instead of buying food from existing networks	• Building new infrastructures of provision – through alternative food supply chains • Localization – increasing self-reliance, reducing supply chain length • Reducing ecological footprint of consumption • Indirect reduction – growing your own food – Home-grown produce reduce transportation requirements (both distribution and personal shopping) • Direct improvement – more efficiently produced food – Organic agriculture delivers benefits, e.g. reduces non-renewable energy use by lowering agrochemical need

the introduction of a new means of provisioning, and a localization of the supply chain for food needs. This can have both direct sustainability improvements, mainly through organic production, and lead to indirect reductions in transport requirements. As an intervention in practice, growing food directly competes with food shopping for the 'role' of providing the food for household meals. Food grown in the garden has a negligible transport footprint, and when grown organically is likely to represent a more environmentally beneficial form of production. The food production at Murundaka represented an intervention by the community to substitute growing food rather than buying it. There were also examples of recrafting existing practices, particularly through shifting meanings – a community goal was set to achieve 10 per cent of food consumption from the garden – and sharing competencies related to food production.

Conclusion

The introduction to this book described eco-communities as an example of a whole systems-oriented approach to sustainability. This is reflected in the potential breadth of impact across different aspects of daily life and consumption domains (as illustrated in Table 2). This chapter conceives of eco-communities as an intervention in multiple interlinked systems of consumption practice. Community residents seek to change and govern these practices in order to to live more sustainably. It emphasized that the community took intentional actions to shape these practices, while at the same time being the people enacting these practices on a daily basis. In this way, the community members are in a somewhat unusual position of being both practitioners and policymakers of their everyday life.

In food provisioning, the community established a vision (meaning), but also the mechanisms – such as working bees – to help the community members work towards the vision. Becoming more self-sufficient in food production can have a direct impact on reducing community member's ecological footprints. However, to a large extent the community practices related to creating community were not directly related to reductions in ecological footprint; they do not directly improve any of the priority areas for sustainable consumption action (Tukker et al., 2010). SPT research in the context of sustainable consumption has tended to emphasize the link to material resources (Røpke 2009). Yet, it was clear that the practices that are not commonly performed by mainstream communities of this scale – positioning the community members as active participants in the development, advocating for their values in the design process, along with community governance practices – are critical in enabling the community to realize their sustainability visions. Food production on-site would have been more limited without the large, consolidated and shared garden space, and the process of creating the community-embedded food sustainability within the community visions. The community creation practices enabled and supported sustainable elements being integrated into the practice ecosystems of Murundaka.

This is an important consideration, as sustainability advocates have tended to focus on directly reducing environmental impacts (Capstick et al., 2014). Yet indirect impacts can be crucial. Capstick et al. (2014) conceptualized the type of radical change required to move towards sustainability as both 'radical environmental impacts' and 'radical institutional impacts'. The role that supporting and enabling practices play in the eco-communities specifically supports the arguments of Seyfang (2009); that community-building, collective action and directing attention towards providing new systems of provision are all crucial parts of ecological citizenship for sustainable consumption.

The answer to the question – how do the residents of eco-communities establish daily practices that differ from mainstream communities (in a sustainable way)? – is deceptively simple. To say that they differ because they directly intervened to make them different may seem disingenuous; however, this ignores the difficulty of changing everyday practices in a lasting manner.

Some of the interventions involved replacing – to a certain extent – less sustainable practices with more sustainable ones. This can be seen in the case of increasing the quantity of local food production. Along with this, the community introduced novel practices into existing processes around creating home and community, which enabled a different approach to housing to be taken. This can be seen as giving community members a role as being not only practitioners of their everyday lives, but 'policymakers' as well. The creation of the eco-community, as well as the ongoing governance, provides a process for the community to intervene in the institutions and infrastructures that support certain (often unsustainable) arrangements of practice. It is not only what eco-communities are doing, but the way they are doing it, that helps in chasing their sustainability visions.

References

Capstick, S., Lorenzoni, I., Corner, A. and Whitmarsh, L. (2014) 'Prospects for radical emissions reduction through behavior and lifestyle change', *Carbon Management* 5(4), pp. 429–45.
Daly, M. (2017) 'Quantifying the environmental impact of ecovillages and cohousing communities: A systematic literature review', *Local Environment: The International Journal of Justice and Sustainability* 22(11), pp. 1358–77.
Daly, M. (2018) 'The most powerful form of activism is just the way you live': Grassroots intentional communities and the sustainability of everyday practice. PhD Dissertation. University of Technology Sydney. Available at: https://opus.lib.uts.edu.au/bitstream/10453/127745/7/02whole.pdf.
Geels, F.W., McMeekin, A., Mylan, J. and Southerton, D. (2015) 'A critical appraisal of Sustainable Consumption and Production research: The reformist, revolutionary and reconfiguration positions', *Global Environmental Change* 34(September), pp. 1–12.
Grinde, B., Nes, R.B., MacDonald, I.F. and Wilson, D.S. (2017) 'Quality of life in intentional communities', *Social Indicators Research* 137(2), pp. 625–40.
Hertwich, E. G. and Peters, G. P. (2009) 'Carbon footprint of nations: A global, trade-linked analysis', *Environmental Science & Technology* 43(16), pp. 6414–20.
Ivanova, D. et al. (2016) 'Environmental impact assessment of household consumption', *Journal of Industrial Ecology* 20(3), pp. 526–536.
Jackson, T. (2005) 'Live better by consuming less? Is there a "double dividend" in sustainable consumption?', *Journal of Industrial Ecology* 9(1), pp. 19–36.

Kunze, I. (2012) 'Social innovations for communal and ecological living: Lessons from sustainability research and observations in intentional communities', *Communal Societies: Journal of the Communal Studies Association* 32(1), pp. 50–67.

McCamant, K. and Durrett, C. (2011) *Creating Cohousing: Building Sustainable Communities*. Gabriola Island: New Society Publishers.

Meltzer, G. (2005) *Sustainable Community: Learning from the Cohousing Model*. Trafford Publishing.

Metcalf, B. (2004) *The Findhorn Book of Community Living*. Findhorn: Findhorn Press.

Middlemiss, L. (2011) 'The power of community: How community-based organizations stimulate sustainable lifestyles among participants', *Society & Natural Resources* 24(11), pp. 1157–73.

Murundaka Cohousing (2016) *Murundaka Cohousing Community*. Available at: https://www.murundakacohousing.org.au/. Accessed 23 February 2018.

Newton, P. (2011) 'Consumption and environmental sustainability', in Newton, P. (ed.) *Urban Consumption*. Collingwood: CSIRO Publishing, pp. 1–25.

Palmer, J.S. (2020) 'Realising collective self-organised housing: A network agency perspective', *Urban Policy and Research*. Abingdon-on-Thames: Routledge 38(2), pp. 101–17.

Penha-lopes, G.P. and Henfrey, T. (2019) *Reshaping the Future: How Local Communities Are Catalysing Social, Economic and Ecological Transformation in Europe*. Brussels: ECOLISE.

Pickerill, J. (2015) 'Cold comfort? Reconceiving the practices of bathing in British self-build eco-homes', *Annals of the Association of American Geographers* 105(5), pp. 1061–77.

Rockström, J., Gupta, J., Qin, D., Lade, Steven J., Abrams, Jesse F., Andersen, Lauren S., Armstrong McKay, David I., Bai, X., Bala, G., Bunn, Stuart E., Ciobanu, D., DeClerck, F., Ebi, K., Gifford, L., Gordon, C., Hasan, S., Kanie, N., Lenton, Timothy M., Loriani, S., Liverman, Diana M., Mohamed, A., Nakicenovic, N., Obura, D., Ospina, D., Prodani, K., Rammelt, C., Sakschewski, B., Scholtens, J., Stewart-Koster, B., Tharammal, T., van Vuure, D., Verburg, Peter H., Winkelmann, R., Zimm, C., Bennett, Elena M., Bringezu, S., Broadgate, W., Green, Pamela, A., Huang, L., Jacobson, L., Ndehedehe, C., Pedde, S., Rocha, J., Scheffer, M., Schulte-Uebbing, L., de Vries, W., Xiao, C., Xu, C., Xu, X., Zafra-Calvo, N. and Zhang, X. (2023) 'Safe and just Earth system boundaries', *Nature* 619(April), pp. 102–11.

Roysen, R. and Mertens, F. (2019) 'New normalities in grassroots innovations: The reconfiguration and normalization of social practices in an ecovillage', *Journal of Cleaner Production* 236, p. 117647.

Røpke, I. (2009) 'Theories of practice – New inspiration for ecological economic studies on consumption', *Ecological Economics*. Elsevier B.V. 68(10), pp. 2490–7.

Schanes, K., Giljum, S. and Hertwich, E.G. (2016) 'Low carbon lifestyles: A framework to structure consumption strategies and options to reduce carbon footprints', *Journal of Cleaner Production* 139(December), pp. 1033–43.

Schatzki, T. (1996) *Social Practices: A Wittgensteinian Approach to Human Activity and the Social*. Cambridge: Cambridge University Press.

Seyfang, G. (2009) *The New Economics of Sustainable Consumption*. Basingstoke: Palgrave Macmillan (Energy, Climate and the Environment Series).

Sherry, J. and Ormsby, A. (2016) 'Sustainability in practice: A comparative case study analysis of the ecoVillage at Ithaca, Earthaven, and Sirius', *Communal Societies: Journal of the Communal Studies Association* 36(2), pp. 125–51.

Shove, E. and Walker, G. (2010) 'Governing transitions in the sustainability of everyday life', *Research Policy* 39(4), pp. 471–6.

Shove, E., Pantzar, M. and Watson, M. (2012) *The Dynamics of Social Practice: Everyday Life and How It Changes*. Online. London: SAGE Publications.
Spurling, N., McMeekin, A., Shove, E., Southerton, D. and Welch, D. (2013) *Interventions in Practice: Re-Framing Policy Approaches to Consumer Behaviour*. Manchester: University of Manchester, Sustainable Practices Research Group.
Steffen, W., Steffen, W., Sanderson, A., Tyson, P., Jäger, J., Matson, P., Moore, B., Oldfield, F., Richardson, K., Schellnhuber, H. John, Turner, B. L. and Wasson, Robert J. (2004) *Executive Summary: Global Change and the Earth System – A Planet under Pressure*. Stockholm: International Geosphere-Biosphere Programme.
Tukker, A., Tukker, A., Cohen, Maurie J., Klaus, H. and Mont, O. (2010) 'The Impacts of household consumption and options for change', *Journal of Industrial Ecology* 14(1), pp. 13–30.
Waitt, G., Caputi, P., Gibson, C., Farbotko, C., Head, L., Gill, N. and Stanes, E. (2012) 'Sustainable household capability: Which households are doing the work of environmental sustainability?', *Australian Geographer* 43(1), pp. 51–74.
WWF (2022) *Living Planet Report 2022 – Building a Nature- Positive Society, Wwf*. R.E. Almond et al. (eds.) Gland, Switzerland: WWF. Available at: www.livingplanetindex.org.

4

Reconfiguring more-than-human relations in eco-communities: Skillsets, empowerment and discomfort

Elisa Schramm

Introduction

Eco-communities have long been known for shifting everyday practices towards more sustainable and communal alternatives. In so doing, they have significantly reduced environmental impacts, while also showing much creativity and innovation around the ways in which they engage with technologies, objects, plants and animals in everyday life. Eco-community residents have for instance experimented with permaculture, repair practices and the construction of their own infrastructures. They have also produced their own goods using 'locally available, low-cost materials and basic skills' (Bobulescu and Fritscheova 2021, 2), such as with 'bioconstruction', pedalling washing machines and solar ovens.

Yet, despite the centrality of such material practices to eco-community life, they have received little attention in the literature (excepting: Pickerill 2015a, 2015b; Vannini and Taggart 2015), particularly compared to 'social' practices pertaining to the organization of communal life. In this chapter, I want to emphasize the importance of attending to material practices in eco-communities and show how eco-community life is lived differently as compared to the 'mainstream', thanks to, in large part, altered everyday material practices.

I do so in the context of a wide body of literature that has problematized the relative neglect of 'non-humans' and the pervasive ontological dichotomizations between nature-society and technology-society in the social sciences (Haraway 2008; Latour 1993; Whatmore 2006), including more-than-human approaches to geography (see Greenhough 2014).[1] This body of work has instead sought to show the ways in which

---

[1] For Greenhough (2014, 5) more-than-human approaches to geography are characterized by five key elements: '(i) an interest in unpacking assemblages of bodies, knowledges, and properties; (ii) a non-anthropocentric perspective on whom (or what) should matter politically; (iii) a recognition of non-human agency; (iv) a conviction that space and time should be defined relationally [...]; a recognition of humans' limited capacities to represent the world coupled with an imperative to hone new sensitivities, skills and affectual capacities'.

non-humans are unpredictable, lively and highly relevant for politics, life and the study of social phenomena (Marres 2012, 4). Importantly, agency is understood here less as any non-human's inherent ability to act but is rather situated in the contingent coming together of various, heterogeneous co-actors, including non-humans (e.g. plants, animals, tools, technologies), shaping a particular outcome such as a material practice. The liveliness and unpredictable confluence of such heterogeneous forces, including the human, that constitute climate change, and the coronavirus pandemic are cases in point, but so are weeds, decaying walls and malfunctioning compost toilets. As Timothy Morton (2012, 164) so evocatively puts it, these examples demonstrate that 'humans are not running the show' and neither do they (completely) in eco-communities. But what such an appraisal of non-humans means has rarely been examined in the context of eco-communities, starting with the relative scarcity of work focusing on material practices.

Following on from this, I argue that examining more-than-human relations in material practices taking place in eco-communities is a fruitful line of inquiry, that gives much insight into how sustainable, equitable life is *materialized* in eco-communities and the difficulties that might emerge in doing so. Studying more-than-human relations in eco-communities is also important because of how they have been reconfigured compared to Western society at large. Eco-communities have *qualitatively* changed their way of relating to objects and technologies, especially when considering the high-tech fixes within capitalism that mainly seek to replace current technologies with putatively more sustainable ones, arguably leading to a 'change of no change' (Marres 2012). Put differently, eco-communities challenge the assumption that technological shortcuts such as electric cars will enable ecological modes of living. *What, then, does studying 'more-than-human relations' in material practices teach us about eco-community life? How exactly are more-than-human relations in eco-communities reconfigured vis-à-vis a capitalist mainstream?*

After going into further depth with the theoretical background and the chosen field sites, I answer these questions by showing three ways in which more-than-human relations in material practices are key to understanding dynamics in eco-communities. First, I focus on skills and the process of 'enskilment' as a ubiquitous way of attuning oneself to non-humans on-site, focusing on infrastructural repair. Second and continuing with this example, I show how unequal power relations between residents emerged directly out of differential capacities to attune oneself to non-humans. Finally, I consider issues of discomforts and foreground in this context the human body in relation to non-humans and argue that discomforts play an important role in shaping the particularities and community dynamics of different eco-communities. Overall then, I demonstrate the ways in which socio-ecological transformations involve different, and more attentive ways of engaging with various everyday technologies, objects, plants and animals. I conclude by highlighting some of the generative questions raised by a more-than-human perspective on eco-communities.

Theoretical background

Much of the literature on eco-communities has not yet taken into consideration what it might mean to examine eco-communities beyond the classical ontological separations of nature/society/technology that are typical of Western modernist thought. As Bruno Latour (1993) has argued, nature/society and technology/society are not separate 'domains of reality'; rather, their dichotomizations are best understood as historically contingent phenomena. In other words, the fact that Western modes of thinking 'split' nature and/or technology as separate from society is not 'reality' per se, but rather the result of Western history and culture. In this sense, it is extremely common to cast non-humans as passive, predictable and irrelevant to politics (Marres 2012), an immutable 'ground' to human action (Tsing 2015, 21). Humans are, in this understanding, foregrounded over many other active world-making projects (Tsing 2015, 21), such as those of other animals and plants, with whom we share this planet and who create their own 'worlds' for their own survival and flourishing, e.g. beavers building dams.

Importantly, this problematic relationship with non-humans – as predictable and unlively resources – is arguably at the heart of the climate and ecological crisis, with fossil-fuelled capitalism as its key feature (Head and Gibson 2012, 699). Thus, if capitalist modes of living have been characterized by a conceptual and practical deadening of non-humans, what other relationships with non-humans are possible, and what kind of relationships with non-humans have eco-communards built up? How can a more ecological way of living acknowledge and work with existing more-than-human interdependencies? Considering the myriad of unusual everyday practices, eco-communities appear a fertile ground for generating knowledge about different ways of relating to non-humans in everyday life.

Even though it has been frequently highlighted that eco-communards have found ways to 'harmlessly integrate' their activities 'into the natural world' (Gilman and Gilman 1991, 10), there has been relatively little effort to concretize what this means in *everyday practice* (exceptions are Pickerill [2015a, 2015b] and Vannini and Taggart [2014]). There has also been attention to the reduced environmental and carbon footprint of eco-communities (e.g. Lockyer 2017), but relatively little insight into the nitty-gritty details of how this was achieved. Conversely, an emerging body of literature in eco-communities has examined 'inter-human' practices, such as how skills for participatory decision-making processes were acquired (e.g. Ulug, Trell and Horlings 2021). In some accounts, material skills have been mentioned but not elaborated on, including composting, bioconstruction, and using dry toilets and solar panels (see Roysen and Martens 2019). Brombin (2019) has taken a first step in this direction by examining transformed relations with 'natural' entities, such as water and plants, but a further examination of the role of various technologies and objects is equally important.

How then to conceptualize material practices in eco-communities, under consideration of more-than-human liveliness? With Latour (2010), I propose conceptualizing practices as more-than-human *compositions*, drawing attention to the active re-configurative efforts that characterize many practices in eco-communities; that is, everyday practices are continuously altered and adapted so as to enable a more sustainable way of living. This conceptualization significantly departs from approaches which consider a different relationship to 'nature' in abstracted terms by focusing on *everyday* entanglements. Furthermore, rather than simply determining which non-humans 'are' sustainable (e.g. chestnut shampoo or organic food), based on the assumption that every non-human has fixed attributes, focusing on the *composition* of particular practices helps draw attention towards more-than-human relations in the eco-communities' particular contexts (e.g. it depends *how* the shampoo is used, or vegetables are grown). This also allows us to ask if practices are 'well or badly composed' (Latour 2010, 474), including how humans experience them.

In such compositions, human intentions still play a role, but, as Jensen and Morita (2015) suggest, it is valuable to consider the 'incessant interplay between *(intended) design* inscriptions and the varied, unpredictable, and often overlooked responses of other actors, especially a motley crew of non-humans'. Put differently, various non-humans may as much 'object' to human plans (Bingham 1996) as facilitate them to varying extents.

Field sites

I base this chapter on ethnographic fieldwork conducted in three field sites in South-West France and Catalonia during 2018 and 2019. These included the degrowth house Can Decreix in Cerbère, France, the anarchist 'rurban' squat Can Masdeu on the outskirts of Barcelona and the post-capitalist eco-industrial colony Calafou near Vallbona d'Anoia, some 60 km west of Barcelona (see Figure 1). All three arguably belong to the lively alternative 'scene' of the wider Barcelona area's community initiatives (Sekulova et al., 2017), to which Sekulova et al. (2017, 2362) also count Can Decreix, with its strong ties to Catalonia – indeed its name means 'house of degrowth' in Catalan. The wider Barcelona area has also been home to decades-long squatting cycles (Debelle et al., 2018), to much housing (Larsen 2019) and anti-austerity activism (Díaz-Parra and Mena 2015) and a strong non- and post-capitalist economy (Balaguer Rasillo 2021; Conill et al., 2012). Thus, while eco-communities are unique in their dedication to comprehensive ecological living, they fit into a wider tapestry of alternative community initiatives in the wider Barcelona area.

Still, residents in all sites were overall privileged in familiar ways, with most being white, middle-class and European, highly educated, often with master's degrees and PhDs. Furthermore, most seemed unencumbered by health and mobility issues. Importantly also, at least two-thirds of residents in Calafou and Can Masdeu were men, which may be related to gendered dynamics of care and responsibilities and a masculinist appeal to a putatively harsh lifestyle in eco-communities.

All sites engaged in a wide array of rather unusual material practices, including the use of compost toilets and wood stoves, on-site beer or wine production, extensive repair and maintenance work and bioconstruction, gardening, agroecology and self-made irrigation systems, washing dishes with buckets and communal showers. Can Decreix experimented most with unorthodox innovations such as solar ovens, ash soap, composting, wild plants and shampoo alternatives (see Schramm 2023). Meanwhile, Calafou had repurposed its vast industrial space (28,000 m^2), formerly a textile factory, to build a wood workshop, an electronics workshop, a brewery and other spaces to experiment with free computer software, growing mushrooms, making soap and cutting glass and ceramics.

In this context, I conducted participant observation, giving priority to attuning myself to non-humans while learning new (manual) skills (Greenhough 2014,

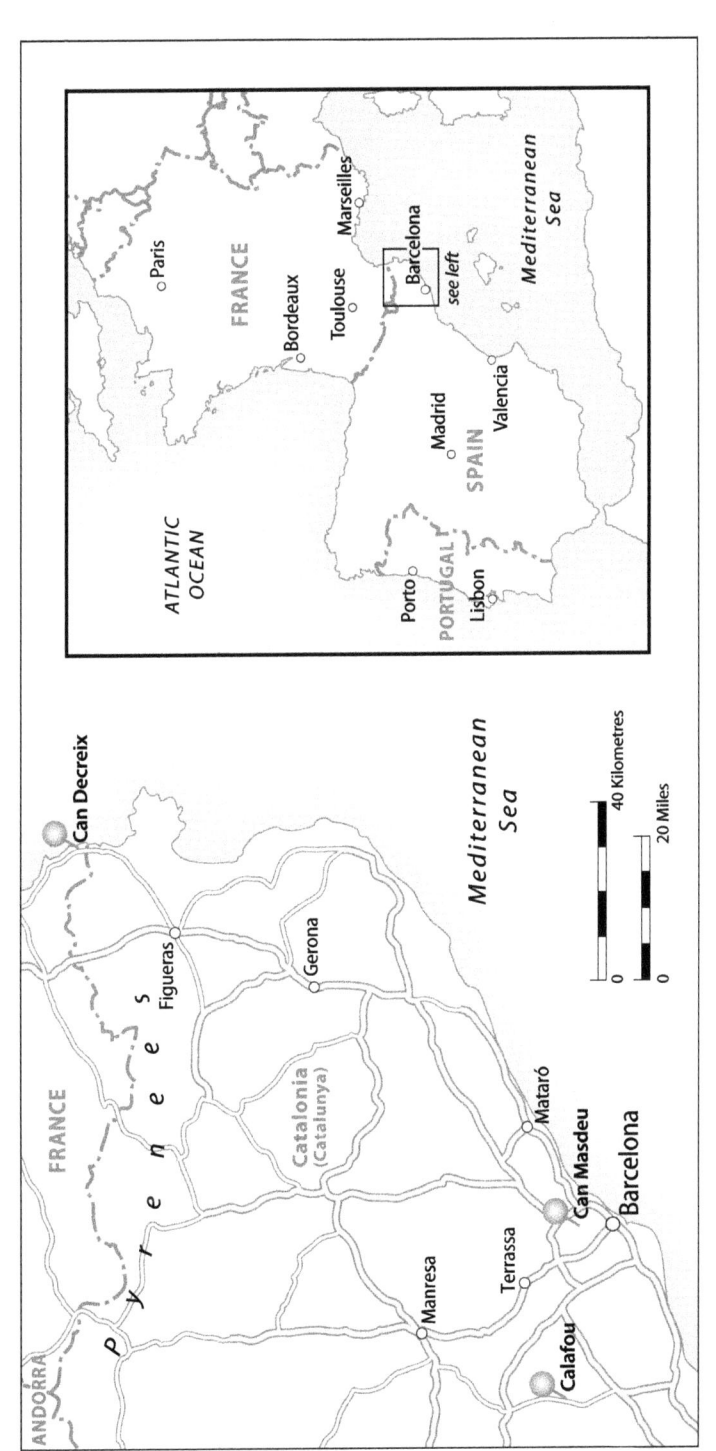

Figure 1 Map of the three sites. (Source: Elisa Schramm.)

115). I also conducted eighty-four interviews with sixty-one long-term inhabitants and volunteers, focusing on material practices and everyday habits that residents and visitors were engaged in. I inquired about their practical know-how and enjoyment of and difficulties with practices. I also asked participants to bring a photo or video of a non-human (Rose 2016, 315–6), to centre non-humans more strongly and help elicit 'everyday, taken-for-granted things' in participants' lives.

In the following, I demonstrate three ways in which considering practices as more-than-human compositions yields interesting insights into eco-community living, focusing on skills and 'enskilment', power relations and inequalities, and discomforts.

Skills and 'enskilment'

The process of 'skilling' was key in the three sites and functioned through a process of attuning to, and responding to non-humans' affordances and resistances in practice. Crucially, through skilling themselves eco-community residents and visitors helped reconfigure everyday more-than-human relations in *qualitatively* different ways, facilitating ways of 'composing' that were distinct from the capitalist mainstream. I argue that residents thanks to skilled practice actively materialized eco-community life *in practice*, with repair and rehabilitation practices being perhaps the most obvious example, enabling the sites' very inhabitation.

Indeed, in the eco-communities visited, skilled (material) practices were ubiquitous and wide-ranging (see previous section). These activities took up significant though varying amounts of time, much more for instance than assemblies and consensus decision-making processes. Visitors and volunteers were directly bound up in such practices. Introducing them to the sites was therefore largely an introduction to particular *skillsets*, often with more experienced community residents guiding novices (Ingold 2000).

This introduction to skillsets can be understood as 'enskilment', that can be understood as the 'evolving and functionally adaptable fit that emerges between an organism and the constraints of his/her environment as they progressively attune to' the latter (Ingold 2000 in Woods et al., 2021, 2). This understanding stands in contradistinction to approaches which emphasize an individual acquiring mental rules, divorced from context. Enskilment therefore implied gaining an embodied understanding of the affordances and recalcitrances of non-humans in practice (Krzywoszynska 2017), as I learnt while I was taking part in bio-construction practices.[2] With rather awkward gestures, I applied bio-paste mass to walls, fitting stones and paste into holes into walls, using a 'mosaic' technique. I therefore let myself be schooled by non-human collaborators, attuning myself to bio-paste and walls: '*I am never quite sure how much mass exactly to put on, but over time, I start to get a bit of a*

---

[2] 'Bio-construction' practices usually consist of mixing sand, water and clay and sometimes straw, lime and stones, to avoid using cement. This technique was used to repair walls, pavements and staircases.

feel for it, hitting the paste hard against the wall. Still, I feel like my paste looks not quite as good as those of others' (Field Notes 25/10/2018, see Figure 2). Furthermore, the '*paste fell to the ground*' frequently, contravening my design intentions. Such instances of non-human recalcitrance occurred very frequently, producing unexpected fumes while brewing beer, spillages in precariously built pipelines and languishing vegetables, demonstrating how crucial non-human 'collaboration' is to enabling alternative practices on-site.

While I found such non-human resistances rather embarrassing, for more advanced learners, enskillment often entailed a more positive assessment of 'failure', which in turn seemed to improve some volunteers' ability to relate to materials. Pauline, a volunteer in Can Decreix, explained that she did not '*enjoy doing things if I have to do it [sic] in a very specific way [...] because then, I'm nervous about that it's not gonna be right, instead of like, [...] it's ok that it's not perfect, then you're gonna enjoy the process*'. She had therefore gained a greater sense of enjoyment from non-human surprises and considered errors 'vital to the process of making, rather than obstacles to be overcome' (Carr and Gibson 2016, 303). This also encouraged her 'creative autonomy', including relishing the 'imperfections' (Edensor 2020, 270) of her work.

Figure 2 Uneven repair in Can Masdeu. (Source: Elisa Schramm.)

Importantly, accepting flaws meant a relation in which non-humans were controlled *less*. Rather than 'trying to efficiently orchestrate categories of material culture' (Hitchings 2012, 378), to the slightly more initiated, attunement implied that materials 'were allowed to persuade people into a more enjoyable experience of non-human agencies'. Infrastructural repair therefore consisted of a *co-composition* of humans and non-humans, rather than a design imposition from the former onto the latter. Such insights are particularly important in the context of attitudes to the environment within the capitalist mainstream that are characterized by attempts at high level of control over non-humans and little space for close more-than-human attunements during production and consumption practices.

This qualitatively different relationship to non-humans was very apparent to visiting craftspeople: Axel, a Scandinavian restoration carpenter visiting Can Masdeu, seemed used to repair work as the domain of specialized workers such as himself, efficiently and flawlessly working with virgin materials. He experimented with building a brick porch (not his area of expertise), which, he argued, left him with '*a big freedom, because then I can do – less good work [...] Here I got the chance [...]to just try it out. And if it goes wrong, then I re-do it.*' This professed sense of freedom stood contrasted with his regular work, where both getting paid and him being '*too proud*' would stand in the way of the generative possibilities of failure. The freedom to experiment with materials with comparatively limited skillsets, and an affirmation of DIY/DIW ('Do-it with', Vannini and Taggart 2015, 123) culture was therefore often a joyful experience, creating novel more-than-human relations, in an attempt to live more sustainably whilst escaping capitalist markets.

In summary, projects of alterity such as eco-communities depend on an attunement to non-humans in skilled practice, to materialize a different way of living. The examples in this section may seem minute, small-scale or even in the final instant down to human design rather than non-human recalcitrance. Still, if non-humans refuse to comply with human design intentions, as they frequently did, then these alternative infrastructures would simply not come to be, at least not in their particularities. This also implies that to transform our lifestyles to be truly ecological, it is necessary to think both which materials are sustainable and which practices with the latter are appropriate – which implies getting used to imperfections, failure and the joy of trying anew.

Power relations and inequalities

More than uncontentious reconfigurations, material practices and the skill levels required to perform them created their own politics, particularly in terms of power dynamics and in-group tensions. Non-humans and unequal abilities of attunement through enskilment were therefore not external to political processes, conflicts or decision-making processes on-site, but co-constituted them directly.

These dynamics arguably emerged from the sense of empowerment that some professed through their attunement to more-than-human collaborators: David in Calafou highlighted a sense of independence after improving his infrastructural repair skills. He noticed that his attitude had changed from asking others for help towards:

D: 'you inform yourself, starting with Youtube [...] And now more than knowing how to do things, it was, like, I already saw myself being able to do a thing, you know?

E: Before knowing how to do it?

D: [...] Before knowing how to do it. My predisposition was very different [...] when you are insecure about doing something, you are going more slowly. [...] when you grab the power, [...] you can get [still] things wrong [...] but the attitude behind it is very different, no?'

Becoming part of new collaborations with materials was thus perceived as an enhanced 'power of acting'. David moved from requiring 'guided attention' to a greater facility for 'wayfinding', an 'actively self-regulating individual who relies on perception, cognitions, emotions and actions, finding their way through the task'(Woods et al., 2021, 5).

This sense of empowerment is, however, perhaps best understood in ambivalent terms, with power and by extension empowerment both a 'productive force that produces the power to act' and 'power over' (Nightingale 2019, 18) other humans, who did not necessarily share this sense of empowerment, nor the same levels of capability, dexterity and experience around infrastructural repair. These differential levels of empowerment therefore led to at times conflictual interhuman dynamics: inequalities in people's ability to attune themselves to non-humans had often created tensions. Fernando in Calafou pointed out that those *'who did not have these capacities need much more time, it takes much more out of them, and in some way, this has created differences, between us, and has created a lot of conflict'*. This meant that everyday life, but especially the rehabilitation of flats, which usually preceded a permanent residence in Calafou, implied differing levels of effort for residents. Fernando had for instance helped two new arrivals build their chimney, noting that another resident had commented that *'you put the chimney up in two days, others need a month'*.

Furthermore, whilst Can Masdeu residents usually rotated yearly between different commissions, Enzo's expertise in infrastructural repair was valued to the point of him becoming a permanent member of the infrastructural commission. In this capacity, he ended up initiating and contributing disproportionately to various infrastructural projects on-site, including a small brewery, his own one-bedroom cottage and a ramp for disabled access to the site. Skill as the (empowering) capacity to participate in the world's unfolding (Krzywoszynska 2017, 128) was thus not equally distributed amongst the community and instead led to a specialization of tasks, along with informal hierarchies (Pusey 2010, 187). This also implies significant differences between residents in their ability to shape infrastructural features of the site.

While the infrastructural projects above may seem rather innocuous, differences in the ability to attune oneself coalesced around and arguably cemented familiar inequalities, including gender inequalities. Many of the more skilled members were men, which at least in Can Decreix had led to the construction of a particularly exclusionary infrastructure, namely a pee toilet that could only be used standing up (see also Pickerill 2015a). This, unsurprisingly, proved difficult for most women to use. Only when a greater number of female volunteers arrived in Can Decreix, was the design made more inclusive.

Finally, these differences in empowerment/attunement also emerged as a source of tension during consensus decision-making processes, whereby a democratic decision is reached by reaching a consensus within the group: Fernando explained that '*maybe if I have an opinion about rehabilitation or about a structure, [...], one listens more to a person that more or less understands than to another [less experienced person], no? But also, it's also understanding that not everybody knows the same things.*' As such, 'wayfinders' like Fernando found themselves uniquely positioned to shape democratic processes, yielding power as experts in basic democratic decision-making processes. This appears to reproduce dynamics in contemporary representative democracies (Lane et al., 2011; Wynne 1992). What is at stake, then, is the role of expertise in consensus decision-making practices, an issue that has to my knowledge not been studied in the context of eco-communities. It is a particularly important issues given how empowerment/attunement to non-humans often seemed to reproduce existing inequalities. Examining attunement to non-humans on-site is therefore a promising way of elucidating interpersonal relationships within eco-communities. Such a perspective adds to literatures that have examined internal conflicts, without reference to what these conflicts were about (e.g. Cunningham and Wearing 2013; Magnusson 2018). It also underscores that the transformative processes towards more socio-ecological modes of living may be easier for some to participate in than for others.

Discomforts

Finally, specific more-than-human relations may also be experienced as undesirable, uncomfortable or inconvenient. I understand discomfort here as a more-than-human relation between 'a body and its proximate environment', rather than a determined feature of a particular object (Bissell 2008, 1703). Discomforts thus constitute another important way that non-humans come to matter to eco-community life, actively shaping the radical potential of such sites (see Schramm 2024). While an evolution in the sense of comfort of eco-community residents has been highlighted (Pickerill 2015b; Vannini and Taggart 2016), I wish to emphasize that this varied significantly between residents and evolved over time. Furthermore, the collective management of varying and evolving levels of discomfort was also a source of tension and conflict. I will illustrate these points using the example of the compost toilet.

In all three eco-communities, compost toilets, dry toilets or outdoor urinals (Figure 3) were commonplace, with no flush toilets in use. Its most common form consisted of an outdoors compost toilet, situated in a small structure, where sawdust, twigs or another carbon source were added to excrements or urine, landing in big underground containers. This mixture would slowly turn to compost, with the containers emptied every half year to two years.

In this context, visitors in Can Decreix often admitted feeling uncomfortable around compost toilets, with many mentioning feeling uneasy about '*rats*' (Axel), '*spiders*' (Antonio), a '*wobbly*' toilet seat (Patricia), or about opening '*the lid and there's this immediate warmth coming up*' (Gabriella). Others highlighted a lack of privacy, apprehension while on one's period and other hygiene concerns. As Peter, a volunteer,

Figure 3 Inside one of Can Masdeu's compost toilets. (Source: Elisa Schramm.)

pointed out, such *'resistances and hurdles'* occurred even with a *'small group of highly motivated'*, implying that even strong values around environmental living were insufficient to overcome such sensations of discomfort, at least not initially.

Discomfort was not, however, a universally shared experience, with some coming to view compost toilets as a common-sense solution to *'avoid having to shit into drinking water'* (Enzo). But these varied responses give an indication of how some more delicate more-than-human relations may shape the extent of eco-communities' reconfiguration vis-à-vis mainstream modes of living. They foreground more strongly the (human) body, eliciting responses to specific more-than-human configurations, in ways only partially connected to 'will' and 'intention'.

With longer-term residents, another issue emerged, namely that compost toilets were located quite far from the main buildings, necessitating a relatively far walk, especially in Calafou. Calafou resident Ana Maria, who had previously lived in a squat in Barcelona with a toilet in the middle of the main room, only protected by a curtain, now found herself craving *'a shower in the house. [...] I want good heating and I want a sewer [...] I am beginning not to want to spend my entire day making an effort for my basic necessities.'* Ana Maria's example highlights how discomfort evolves over time, with David Bissell (2008, 1703), emphasizing that the more-than-human relation between body and environment is an 'embodied contingency', requiring frequent adjustments, as both bodies and their environments change.

Ana Maria's candour seemed relatively unusual, with some hinting at other residents' discomforts, rather than admitting to it themselves. More often, inconvenience and discomforts were apparent in evolving toilet practices, with residents adapting the technology itself to *their* needs (in contradistinction to visitors' attempts to attune their bodies to unfamiliar objects). In its simplest form, Can Masdeu resident Pablo emptied '*a bottle with pee in the outdoor sink behind the compost toilet*' (Field Notes 29/10/2018) one morning, in an apparently routine gesture. In Calafou, residents increasingly built make-shift dry toilets in their own flats, demonstrating how comfort was actively produced through adjustments. This, however, also led to a significant individualization and duplication of key infrastructures, which some viewed rather critically.

There were even discussions to reintroduce '*water treatment plants*' for flush toilets in Calafou, an idea that Ralph, a new arrival, firmly opposed. Similarly, Enzo in Can Masdeu darkly imagined that others '*probably want to flush it, they probably want to put bleach down there*' in their quest of '*moving towards normality*', illustrating the contentiousness different experiences of discomfort caused. More than simply a matter of people not believing anymore in particular values,[3] this example shows that *eco-community* living requires frequent collective renegotiations over which particular more-than-human compositions should be adjusted, removed or added over time, to enable comfort.

These collective negotiations (and sometimes their absence) are key to eco-community life in practice. While such tendencies may seem like an inevitable return towards a more 'normal' life, they were in fact highly contested, conflictual and often non-linear. Overall, an emphasis on the body-environment relationship draws attention to the specificities of alternative living in eco-communities. Here, the non-humans render these spaces more or less radical and/or sustainable, with every 'alternative' practice constituting to some degree of compromise between values and ideals.

Conclusion

In this chapter, I argued for a greater consideration of more-than-human relations in everyday material practices as a counterpoint to nature-society and society-technology dichotomizations that characterize much of the eco-communities literature. I sought to demonstrate this by sketching out three ways in which more-than-human relations come to matter in eco-community life and politics, with implications for how socio-ecological transformations are practised in everyday life. I furthermore contend that such a lens raises generative questions, deepening our understanding of eco-communities, though the specificity of the Catalan/French context and the relative privilege of residents potentially limit their wider applicability.

First, I focused on processes of 'enskilment', that are ubiquitous and central to the functioning and particularities of eco-communities. Enskilment is an apprenticeship in the affordances and recalcitrances of non-humans, with which practices were co-composed in everyday life. It is also a fraught, unpredictable process, that has

---

[3] Though especially in Can Masdeu, different degrees of commitment to values around sustainable, communitarian living were obvious.

often been taken for granted. Skilled labour was furthermore the basis that enabled residents to reconfigure the material fabric of eco-community sites vis-à-vis a capitalist mainstream, evading capitalist markets as they built their own 'stuff', relying on used materials and embracing flaws in design. In so doing, residents also built up more-than-human relations that were more cognizant of interdependencies, less wasteful and more appreciative of non-humans' liveliness. This demonstrates that socio-ecological transformations may require more attentiveness, curiosity and patience with materials in everyday life.

Second, I showed that unequal abilities in attuning oneself to non-humans during enskilment led to interhuman tensions and conflict. Rather than being outside of politics, non-humans *were* the stuff of politics, particularly with regards to power politics, and in-group inequalities. More concretely, some residents' greater ability to attune themselves to non-humans, led to an enhanced ability to shape one's physical surroundings as well as of consensus decision-making processes, which sometimes created tension and conflict. These inequalities in empowerment occurred frequently along familiar contours of inequalities, most notably gender, with problematic consequences for collective governance and wider transformative processes. This raises questions such as: How might eco-community residents successfully address such inequalities in attunement/empowerment? What levels of specialization or diversification of skills work best in eco-communities? How to best approach expertise in consensus decision-making processes?

Third, I focused on discomfort as another way of how non-humans come to matter to eco-communities' life and politics. Discomforts as the dynamic relation between bodies and their proximate environment were experienced differently by different bodies, evolving over time and sometimes leading to the adoption of new technologies. Again, these differences led to tensions, conflicts and resentment between residents and contributed to processes of (contested) deradicalization, an important element to consider in wider socio-ecological transformations. Focusing on the body-environment relationship also raises other as-of-yet unexamined lines of inquiry in the context of eco-communities: What happens to bodies in eco-communities with age, illness, disability, pregnancy and with children? What to do with bodies worn out, when through years of repetition, a practice becomes unbearable? How is it possible to potentially recover more energy and joy in those practices?

In summary, focusing on more-than-human relations revealed the extent to which the particular features of the sites and their radicality vis-à-vis the mainstream are the result of complex negotiations between residents with differential abilities and desires to relate to non-humans in everyday practice. An attention to more-than-human relations in everyday practices can therefore help elucidate conflict, tension and breakdown in eco-communities.

References

Balaguer Rasillo, X. (2021). 'Alternative economies, digital innovation and commoning in grassroots organisations: Analysing degrowth currencies in the Spanish region of Catalonia', *Environmental Policy and Governance* 31(3), pp. 175–85.

Bingham, N. (1996) 'Object-ions: From technological determinism towards geographies of relations', *Environment and Planning D: Society and Space* 14(6), pp. 635–57.
Bissell, D. (2008) 'Comfortable bodies: Sedentary affects', *Environment and Planning A* 40(7), pp. 1697–712.
Bobulescu, R. and Fritscheova, A. (2021) 'Convivial innovation in sustainable communities: Four cases in France', *Ecological Economics* 181(C)(November 2020), p. 106932.
Brombin, A. (2019) 'The ecovillage movement: New ways to experience nature', *Environmental Values* 28(2), pp. 191–210.
Carr, C. and Gibson, C. (2016) 'Geographies of making: Rethinking materials and skills for volatile futures', *Progress in Human Geography* 40(3), pp. 297–315.
Conill, J., Cárdenas, A., Castells, M., Hlebik, S. and Servon, L. (2012) *Otra vida es posible. Prácticas económicas alternativas durante la crisis*. Barcelona: Editorial UOC.
Cunningham, P.A. and Wearing, S. (2013) 'The politics of consensus: An exploration of the Cloughjordan ecovillage, Ireland', *Cosmopolitan Civil Societies: An Interdisciplinary Journal* 5(2), 1–28.
Debelle, G., Cattaneo, C., Gonzalex Garcia, R., Barranco, O. and Llobet Ribas, M. (2018) 'Squatting cycles in Barcelona: Identities, repression and the controversy of institutionalisation', in Martínez-López, M.A. (ed.) *The Urban Politics of Squatters' Movements*. New York: Palgrave Macmillan, pp. 51–73.
Díaz-Parra, I., and Mena, J.C. (2015). 'Squatting, the 15-M movement, and struggles for housing in the context of the Spanish social crisis', *Human Geography* 8(1), pp. 40–53.
Edensor, T. (2020) *Stone: Stories of Urban Materiality*. Singapore: Palgrave Macmillan.
Gilman, D. and Gilman, R. (1991) *Eco-Villages and Sustainable Communities*. Langlay, WA: The Context Institute.
Greenhough, B. (2014) 'More-than-human geographies', in Lee, R. et al. (eds.) *The SAGE Handbook of Human Geography*. Los Angeles, London, New Delhi, Singapore, Washington, DC: Sage, pp. 94–120.
Haraway, D. (2008) *When Species Meet, Environmental Philosophy*. Minneapolis, MN, and London: University of Minnesota Press.
Head, L. and Gibson, C. (2012) 'Becoming differently modern: Geographic contributions to a generative climate politics', *Progress in Human Geography* 36(6), pp. 699–714.
Hitchings, R. (2012) 'People can talk about their practices', *Area* 44(1), pp. 61–7.
Ingold, T. (2000) *The Perception of the Environment: Essays on Livelihood, Dwelling and Skill*. London and New York: Taylor & Francis.
Jensen, C.B. and Morita, A. (2015) 'Infrastructures as ontological experiments', *Engaging Science, Technology, and Society* 1, pp. 81–7.
Krzywoszynska, A. (2017) 'Empowerment as skill: The role of affect in building new subjectivities', in Bastian, M. et al. (eds.) *Participatory Research in More-than-human worlds*. London and New York: Routledge, pp. 127–41.
Lane, S.N., Odoni, N., Landström, C., Whatmore, S.J., Ward, N. and Bradley, S. (2011) 'Doing flood risk science differently: An experiment in radical scientific method', *Transactions of the Institute of British Geographers* 36(1), pp. 15–36.
Larsen, H.G. (2019) 'Barcelona: Housing crisis and urban activism', in *Contemporary Co-Housing in Europe*. Abingdon-on-Thames: Routledge, pp. 74–94.
Latour, B. (1993) *We Have Never Been Modern*. Cambridge, MA: Harvard University Press.
Latour, B. (2010) 'An attempt at writing a compositionist manifesto', *New Literary History* 41, pp. 471–90.
Lockyer, J. (2017) 'Community, commons, and degrowth at Dancing Rabbit Ecovillage', *Journal of Political Ecology* 24(1), pp. 519–42.

Magnusson, D. (2018) 'Going back to the roots: The fourth generation of Swedish eco-villages', *Scottish Geographical Journal* 134(3-4), 122–40.

Marres, N. (2012) *Material Participation: Technology, the Environment and Everyday Publics*. London and New York: Palgrave Macmillan.

Morton, T. (2012) *Hyperobjects: Philosophy and Ecology after the End of the World*. Minneapolis, MN: University of Minnesota Press.

Nightingale, A.J. (2019) 'Commoning for inclusion? Commons, exclusion, property and socio-natural becomings', *International Journal of the Commons* 13(1), p. 16.

Paton, D. (2013) 'The quarry as sculpture: The place of making', *Environment and Planning A* 45(5), pp. 1070–86.

Pickerill, J. (2015a) 'Bodies, building and bricks: Women architects and builders in eight eco-communities in Argentina, Britain, Spain, Thailand and USA', *Gender, Place and Culture* 22(7), pp. 901–19.

Pickerill, J. (2015b) 'Cold comfort? Reconceiving the practices of bathing in British self-build eco-homes', *Annals of the Association of American Geographers* 105(5), pp. 1061–77.

Pusey, A. (2010) 'Social centres and new cooperativism of the common', *Affinities: A Journal of Radical Theory, Culture, and Action* 4(1), pp. 1–24.

Rose, G. (2016) *Visual Methodologies: An Introduction to Researching with Visual Materials*. 4th edn. Los Angeles, London, New Delhi, Singapore, Washington, DC: Sage.

Roysen, R. and Mertens, F. (2019) 'New normalities in grassroots innovations: The reconfiguration and normalization of social practices in an ecovillage', *Journal of Cleaner Production* 236(November), 117647, pp. 1–8.

Schramm, E. (2023) 'Examining the role of minor experiments in French and Catalan eco-communities: Between critique and post-capitalist world-building', *Journal of Political Ecology* 30(1), p. 559.

Schramm, E. (2024) 'The comfortable endurance of sustainable practices: Values, affect and community dynamics in Catalan eco-communities', *Cultural Geographies*, 14744740241269155, pp. 1–19.

Sekulova, F., Anguelovski, I., Argüelles, L. and Conill, J. (2017) 'A "fertile soil" for sustainability-related community initiatives: A new analytical framework', *Environment and Planning A* 49(10), pp. 2362–82.

Tsing, A.L. (2015) *The Mushroom at the End of the World: On the possibility of life in capitalism ruins*. Princeton, NJ, and Oxford: Princeton University Press.

Ulug, C., Trell, E.M. and Horlings, L. (2021) 'Ecovillage foodscapes: Zooming in and out of sustainable food practices', *Agriculture and Human Values* 38(4), pp. 1041–59.

Vannini, P., and Taggart, J. (2014) 'Do-it-yourself or do-it-with? The regenerative life skills of off-grid home builders', *Cultural Geographies* 21(2), 267–85.

Vannini, P. and Taggart, J. (2015) *Off the Grid: Re-Assembling Domestic Life*. New York and London: Routledge.

Vannini, P. and Taggart, J. (2016) 'Onerous consumption: The alternative hedonism of off-grid domestic water use', *Journal of Consumer Culture* 16(1), pp. 80–100.

Whatmore, S. (2006) 'Materialist returns: Practising cultural geography in and for a more-than-human world', *Cultural Geographies* 13(4), pp. 600–9.

Woods, C. T., Rudd, J., Gray, R. and Davids, K. (2021) 'Enskilment: An ecological-anthropological worldview of skill, learning and education in sport', *Sports Medicine – Open* 7(1), p. 33.

Wynne, B. (1992) 'Uncertainty and environmental learning: Reconceiving science and policy in the preventive paradigm', *Global Environmental Change* 2(2), pp. 111–27.

5

Peopled environments: Eco-communities and their reconfigurations of nature

Jenny Pickerill

Introduction

Standing in a barn on a Welsh farm in Pembrokeshire I felt increasingly uncomfortable. I was facilitating the local consultation of a new eco-community being built next to Glandwr village. We had invited local residents to a presentation and Q&A about the project. Things were not going well. A woman from the audience was screaming at me that I was going to ruin her life. Turning the farm near her house into an eco-community would, in her mind, bring unwanted outsiders, dogs, cars and noise to the village. After the consultation I received letters from locals arguing I was destroying Welsh rural life and its traditions. Locals seemed most upset by the potential change to their landscape view. They objected to the idea that homes would be visible from the other side of the valley and that the sheep farm would be no more.

This story is my recollection of a moment in the early years of Tir y Gafel, now an established eco-community in west Wales. While the environmentalists argued they were saving a degraded farm and building climate change-resilient homes and livelihoods, locals were appalled at the very idea of such change. For local residents, some planners and politicians, the proposal for a new eco-community was a worrying disruption of their village and existing landscape.

I want to use such an example as way to understand how the notion of the 'environment' itself is disrupted and reconfigured by eco-communities. Part of the local resistance to Tir y Gafel was a belief that people should not live and build in greenfield rural areas, except in ways that fit existing visions and uses of a landscape, in this case sheep farming. At the same time, those advocating for Tir y Gafel eco-community were deliberately seeking to repopulate the landscape and create a diverse peopled environment. They were re-envisioning both what the environment looks like and people's relations to it; the possibilities of creating a place of co-existence and co-habitation between humans and non-humans through social models of radical sustainability (Ergas 2021). This disruption of the fallacy of a society-environment dualism and the creation of new society-environmental relations and diverse ecologies is in keeping with many academics' calls for a more social, constructivist and nuanced understanding of how humans relate to the environment; 'we need to rebuild a place for people in the conservation landscape' (Adams 2006, 160). However, as Jørgensen (2017) demonstrates, changes to existing landscapes even when known to be ecologically positive can meet resistance if they clash with what existing residents perceive to be 'natural'.

Eco-communities, as a form of environmentalism, offer an opportunity to explore what relating differently to the environment might entail and its consequences (Kirby 2003; Sanford 2017). It is important to understand what these different relations might practically entail, and what resistance and conflict they might generate (Wright 2010). These processes of transformation also lead to questions of inclusion, of who gets to participate and co-exist in these peopled environments (Ergas 2021; Gibson-Graham and Miller 2015; Pooley 2021).

Dualisms and diverse ontologies

Eco-communities' reconfiguration of the environment can be understood as a critique of the notion of a society-environment dualism, a perceived separation between people and the environment. Despite academic recognition that the environment is produced, rather than a given, through human and non-human relations (Soper 1999) and there is no such thing as an external, abstract, untouched 'nature' as discrete from humans (Lorimer 2015), this dualism remains hegemonic because of its economic and political power, as it makes it easier to exploit the environment as a 'resource' (Harvey 2005). This dualism is therefore maintained by hegemonic capitalism and its political supporters as a way to further commodify nature.

Historically some environmentalists have sought to protect places and ecosystems they have defined as 'pristine', 'wilderness' and 'untouched' (Castree's 'first nature' [2013]) by territorializing them and seeking to exclude human activities – an ecocentric perspective that argues that nature has an intrinsic value which must be protected from human use. But there is increasing recognition that such an approach rests on misunderstandings of what 'the environment' is.

Diverse ecological ontologies (ways of defining what exists) require us to develop ways of living in mutual interdependence with all (multi)species acknowledging the agency of more-than-human beings, and start from the premise that the society-environment relationship is mutually constitutive (Rzedzian 2019). Geographers have worked through post-structuralism to develop more-than-human geographies that examine a variety of relational interconnections between humans, animals and all life including plants (see for example: Whatmore 2017). Escobar (2020), in his development of a pluriverse politics ('a world where many worlds fit'), identifies multiple emerging alternatives, including elements of eco-communities and the Right of Nature movements (where nature becomes a rights-bearing entity), as challenging the modernist politics of ontological dualism by drawing on radical relationality where 'all entities that make up the world are so deeply interrelated that they have no intrinsic separate existence by themselves' (p.xiii).

Gibson-Graham and Miller (2015) suggest that to create this 'thoroughly ecological community of life' (p.7) requires making the 'complexities of our interdependencies' (p.8) visible. The environment has endured a process of 'discursive enclosure' (p.8) from social relations. This has reduced non-humans to an objective ontological category of which their primary use is as extractive resources. As part of this 'all more-than-human life was relegated to the domain of passive objects' (p.9) and humans privileged as singular, distinctive and self-contained beings. Instead, we need to acknowledge, 'see, think and feel' (p.9) the diverse ecological ontologies and multispecies interdependences that humans have with all other more-than-human life, abandoning any society-environment dualism.

There are examples where diverse ecological ontologies have been made explicit, in permaculture, biomimicry and the Right to Nature movements. Eco-communities are another example of how the theoretical challenge of how we live as a multispecies community can be put into practice. What living in-relation-to, interrelated and interdependent with all beings (being-in-common) means in practice. This challenges humans to reconceive our perceived separateness from the environments on which our lives depend, and provokes questions of agency: of who gets to participate in these new society-environment reconfigurations.

As Garforth (2018) argues, the debate is not what is or is not 'the environment' or 'nature', but about how to create 'space to acknowledge multiplicity, complexity, hybridity ... [which] open up to more demanding and rigorous questions about how we might live better with all the beings that matter' (p.152).

Peopled environments

One way that diverse ecological ontologies are being practised is through peopled environments – where the role that people have in generating our existing environments (such as farming landscapes) is assertively acknowledged *and* the centrality of humans to creating, managing and supporting a flourishing of biodiversity is understood and valued (Atchison et al., 2024; Hunter 1995). Of course, biodiversity has flourished without humans for most of its existence and most likely will after we have gone, but in the anthropocene human activity *is* central to its recovery because nowhere is free from human influence.

The concept of peopled environments builds on the nascent and emerging use of the term 'peopled landscapes' (Selman 2008; Ward 1999). 'Peopled landscapes' has been primarily used as a way to acknowledge Indigenous occupation and therefore the shaping of pre-colonial places (Haberle and David 2012; Hallam 2002), or self-built unofficial housing that has informally shaped many landscapes (Hardy and Ward 1984). But for many interested in environmentalism 'people' tend to still be constructed as an external threat from which we must protect, for example, forests (Nagendra et al., 2013).

Underpinning the advocation of a peopled environment are three assertions: acknowledging the ways environments have already been shaped by humans (and vice versa), the belief that humans are necessary, indeed crucial to processes of actively recreating abundant biodiversity and ecological survival in this anthropocene era; and that it is politically dangerous to remove people from the environment because such processes of exclusion are too often racially weaponized.

First, in Britain and elsewhere, there is plenty of evidence illustrating how current landscapes have legacies of past clearances, agricultures, industrial interventions, dams, pollution and more. There is a tension between accepting that much of our environment has been ecologically destroyed and acknowledging the cultural history, layers of interwoven characteristics of years of human endeavour, that have shaped the landscape as it now appears. Indeed, removing humans from the environment 'goes against the grain of a progressively holistic approach to landscape as a synthesis of culture and nature' (Procter 2014, 77). A focus on non-peopled environments also risks misdirecting attention to environments 'elsewhere', as Jørgensen (2015) argues, 'the idea of the wild without people leads us to undervalue the wild where people are' (487).

Second, eco-community advocates have long argued for a repopulating of rural spaces – for a peopled landscape where humans can be self-sustaining but do so only by creating abundant biodiversity (Fairlie 1996; Ward 1999). Eco-communities are interested in a broad variety of environments and places to be (re)peopled – rural, degraded, urban, brownfield sites – which starts from conceptualizing 'the environment' and its value as being all around us at all times. Finally, it is not realistically possible to seek to remove people from the environment without risking evoking dangerous eco-fascist and anti-population growth approaches, which tend to target economically or racially marginalized people (Moore and Roberts 2022).

Therefore, the concept of peopled environment signifies a political and practical imperative to develop forms of co-existence and practices of being-in-common with all living things. It recognizes that environments are dynamic, always emerging and evolving. This approach recognizes humans in the broader political project of environmentalism for practical and ethical reasons, and in so doing positions humans as having a crucial complex role which cannot be reduced to a singular notion of conceiving humans as innately or irrevocably environmentally 'damaging'. Taking seriously the inseparability of people from the environment *per se* requires new experiments in creating lived-in peopled environments. Of course, any discussion of (re)peopling environments raises questions about who gets to determine what is environmentally progressive and what risks such approaches might generate. The risks of resource extraction, capitalist accumulation and ecologically damaging practices are precisely the practices that eco-communities are working against, but other risks remain in the implementation of this approach, to which we will return below.

Eco-communities as experimental spaces

Eco-communities are part of a broader milieu of alternative spaces (such as squats, protest camps, etc.) where non-conventional practices and experimentations emerge (Escobar 2020). Eco-communities have often deliberately built non-conventional infrastructures, different values and competencies, and generate new routines and habits. This chapter examines the ways in which eco-communities are demonstrating what some of the diverse ecological ontologies of mutual interdependence look like, and working through the tensions involved.

This chapter draws upon empirical qualitative ethnographic research (interviews, participant observation and photography) conducted with twelve eco-communities in Britain: Beach Hill Community, Brithdr Mawr, Findhorn Eco-Village, Fireside Co-operative, Green Hills (pseudonym), Hockerton Housing Project, Tir y Gafel, Lancaster Co-housing, Landmatters, LILAC, Springhill Cohousing, Steward Woodland Community, The Yard, Threshold Centre, Tinkers Bubble and Trelay (Figure 1).

These eco-communities are building, making and enacting new socio-materialities. Their practices can be categorized into five main activities, which is the self-provision of: homes, livelihoods, infrastructures, production and education. What is notable about all of these practices of provision is that the key requirements for daily life are self-organized, generated collectively and all concentrated in one place. It is this locally bounded concentration which is a key defining feature of how eco-communities work (Litfin 2014).

For homes this involves self-building a broad variety of forms of shelter, from temporary canvas benders to highly technological eco-houses. For livelihoods, eco-community residents often traverse between engagement in capitalist and community economy practices (explored further in Chapters 17, 18 and 19). As Table 1 illustrates residents tend to concentrate on creating site-based livelihoods (such as producing food for sale), or in using skills they have developed within the eco-community to generate a livelihood, but some are engaged in employment that is off-site. The difficulty of making a living from the land means that over time residents tend to drift away from land-based activities to diverse forms of income generation.

For infrastructures most eco-communities have had to build their own energy, water, waste, sewerage and transport systems. Those that are off-grid have obviously had to do more including building compost toilets, using spring water and installing renewable energy systems. But even those with access to grid-infrastructures have sought to build different infrastructures – such as Lancaster Co-housing having very limited car parking, but a large bike shed and encouraging residents to cycle to town rather than drive. In self-provisioning production, many eco-communities intend to be as self-sufficient as possible, producing their own fruit, vegetables, eggs

Table 1 Examples of livelihoods engaged in by eco-community residents in Britain

Site-based livelihoods	Site-skills livelihoods	Off-site livelihoods
Basket weaving	Permaculture teaching	Shop work
Farm produce sales + box schemes	Planning consultancy	Academia
Educational tours	Spiritual healing	Medical professional
Holiday accommodation	Construction teaching	
	Carpentry	

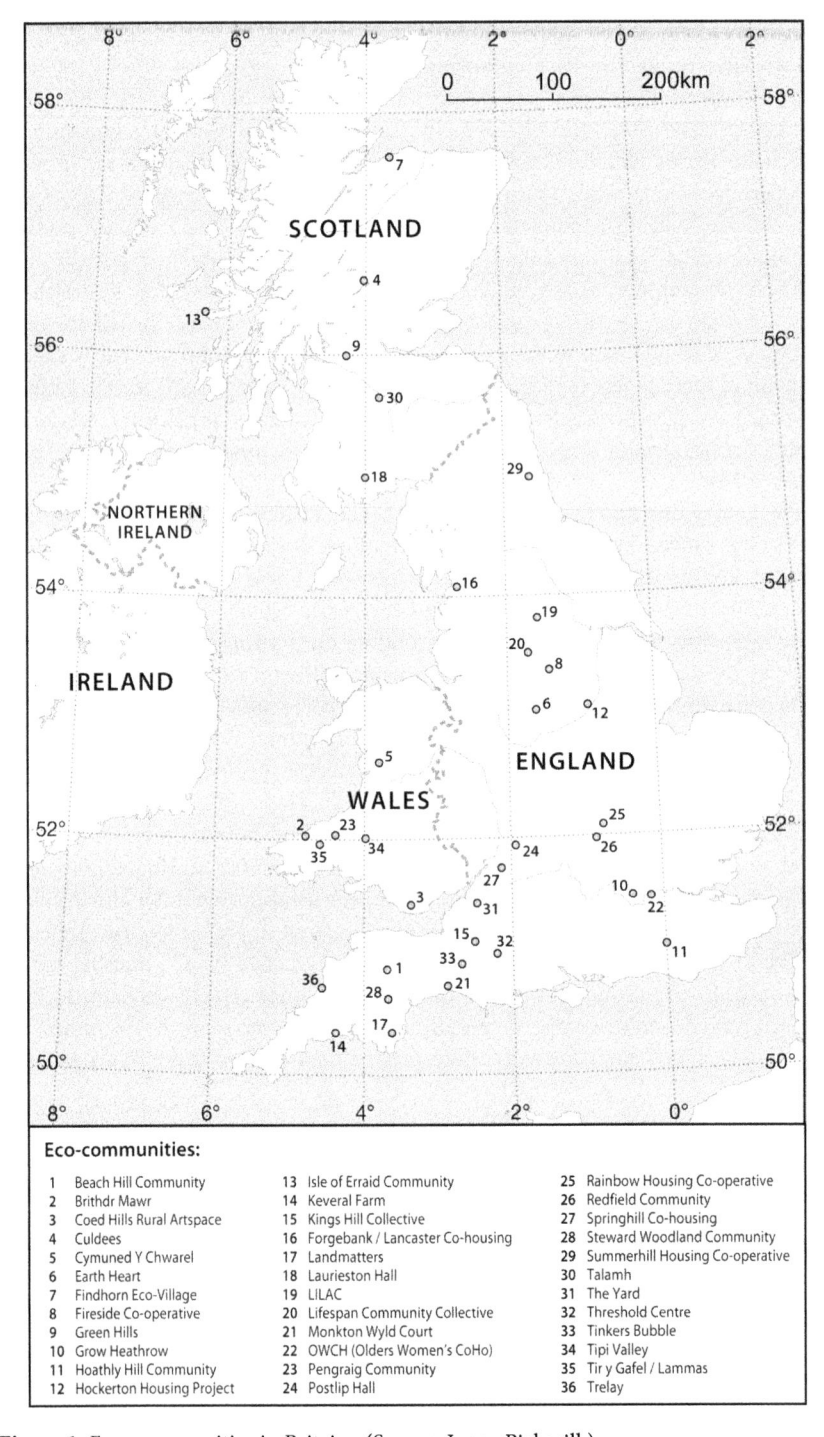

Figure 1 Eco-communities in Britain. (Source: Jenny Pickerill.)

Eco-communities:

1. Beach Hill Community
2. Brithdr Mawr
3. Coed Hills Rural Artspace
4. Culdees
5. Cymuned Y Chwarel
6. Earth Heart
7. Findhorn Eco-Village
8. Fireside Co-operative
9. Green Hills
10. Grow Heathrow
11. Hoathly Hill Community
12. Hockerton Housing Project
13. Isle of Erraid Community
14. Keveral Farm
15. Kings Hill Collective
16. Forgebank / Lancaster Co-housing
17. Landmatters
18. Laurieston Hall
19. LILAC
20. Lifespan Community Collective
21. Monkton Wyld Court
22. OWCH (Olders Women's CoHo)
23. Pengraig Community
24. Postlip Hall
25. Rainbow Housing Co-operative
26. Redfield Community
27. Springhill Co-housing
28. Steward Woodland Community
29. Summerhill Housing Co-operative
30. Talamh
31. The Yard
32. Threshold Centre
33. Tinkers Bubble
34. Tipi Valley
35. Tir y Gafel / Lammas
36. Trelay

and meat. Needs for purchasing goods off-site are deliberately limited either by this self-production or by self-limiting consumption. Finally, for education, there are numerous examples of eco-community residents developing home-schooling or choosing non-conventional schools for their children (Kraftl 2013). Many eco-communities also operate as sites of education for visitors, running tours, workshops and research.

Lived-in landscapes

While it is useful to detail how eco-communities operate through varied practices of self-provisioning, it is necessary to examine whether these practices fundamentally shift how people relate to the environment and to each other; whether these practices produce new society-environment relations, and reconfigure existing social relations. Crucial to such an analysis is an understanding of who is involved in these new relations. Using three examples of practices of self-provisioning, it is possible to identify how relations have been reconfigured. All three eco-communities briefly discussed here produce lived-in peopled environments, disrupting conventional understandings of what nature, environment, landscapes and farmland could and should be. These examples also illustrate how eco-communities are attempting to attend to issues of affordability, but have been less successful at taking disabled or ageing bodies into account (see Bhakta and Pickerill 2016; Laughton 2008).

Producing food at Tir y Gafel

Tir y Gafel, established in 2009, is an eco-community of nine smallholdings of households living off-grid in Pembrokeshire, West Wales. Just as Anderson (Chapter 6) explores, there is a particular geographical context to eco-communities in rural West Wales. The founders of Tir y Gafel were English and despite having lived in Wales for several years did not initially speak Welsh. Their choice to locate in a nation without reference to its distinctive Welsh culture, which has long been threatened by English migration, caused much of the initial resistance they encountered. The linguistic, cultural and political questions of what it means to be Welsh, especially only a decade after the creation of the National Assembly for Wales (established 1999), were largely ignored by the eco-community (Chetty 2022). Indeed, Tir y Gafel sought to establish itself without reference to questions of Welsh devolution, the fight to maintain the Welsh language, or how the Welsh identity has often been bound up in the rural identity of sheep farming (Welstead 2021). In this Tir y Gafel mirrors many other eco-communities' colonial practices (explored further by Barker and Pickerill, Chapter 8), especially in the cultural context and how and why certain Welsh landscapes are protected so fiercely against seemingly progressive environmental projects (Mason and Milbourne 2014).

Tir y Gafel has been disrupting these conventional understandings of productivist and extractivist farming, moving towards intensive multi-crop production and regenerative agriculture. They have diversified the landscape from a sheep farm to one populated with willow, fruit trees, vegetable patches, cows, geese, chickens and sheep (Figures 2 and 3) and are trying to create 'a food and fuel rich landscape' (Dale and Dale 2015, 38). Permaculture is used as a design principle and a practice, evidenced in how everything has multiple uses (a pond will collect rainwater and hold fish), there are closed loops of resource use (no waste), and wild areas are as important as production areas. For residents it is this enlivening of biodiversity which is,

> the most important thing about this place is the increasing abundance of nature ... I'm always amazed by the different insects, the different birds, the little critters that I see ... I'm just loving seeing that from the degraded landscape into one that's becoming really abundant ... just multitudes of life as it's recovering.
> (Hoppi, Tir y Gafel, interview)

This is not just an ecological restoration project, or a small holding, it is driven by a desire to enable people to live off the land, deliberately populate rural spaces, and regenerate degraded environments (Wimbush 2012, 2021). It is about creating an active, lived-in landscape, where humans coexist with nature. Projects like Tir y Gafel are also driven by a quest to open the countryside to as many people as possible. Rural sites outside of permitted development zones are significantly cheaper and, once purchased, the model of One Planet Development (the Welsh planning regulations that formalized a particular version of Low Impact Development into a set of planning criteria) requires

Figure 2 Tao and Hoppi's plot, Tir y Gafel, 2006. (Source: Jenny Pickerill.)

Figure 3 Tao and Hoppi's plot, Tir y Gafel, 2016. (Source: Jenny Pickerill.)

livelihood generation to be on-site (Thorpe 2014). By self-producing for most of their needs, little money is needed to purchase additional goods. The premise is that projects like Tir y Gafel are affordable to establish and to sustain (Shirani 2020).

Of course, Tir y Gafel is not without its problems. Like most eco-communities it is always in process and experimental. Managing land using permacultural organic approaches and manual labour is unsurprisingly hard work. It is this need for solid graft, day in day out, and the pressures of complying with One Planet Development planning regulations that has encouraged a tendency to individualize labour. Social organization for the project was unplanned and the resulting conflict around communal decisions has caused residents to retreat to their plots to focus on their own practices of provisioning. The focus on society-environment relations was reinforced by the short timeframe (five years) in which residents had to meet the One Planet Development criteria, or risk losing their planning permission. These criteria were environmental rather than social. Tir y Gafel had also been designed as separate plots, rather than sharing land in common, and without prior agreement about how decisions would be made communally. Together these factors resulted in changes to environmental relations but limited the possibilities of social collectivity and collaboration. New society-environmental relations have been built, but in the case of Tir y Gafel there is little evidence of new social relations. Or rather they have disrupted conventional ways of relating to the environment, but maintained individualized ways of interacting with each other.

Building infrastructures at Green Hills

Green Hills is an eco-community that is entirely off-grid. Its location is deliberately vague as it has been built without planning permission. However, in a similar vein as Tir y Gafel, its founders migrated to the area and connections to the cultural histories of the place have been built over time as they settled there, rather than shaping its original intent or design. In other words, initially there was a disconnect between the specific cultural history of the place and the newly emerging eco-community.

Will and May (founders and residents) rely on a wind turbine and solar panels for electricity, and bottled gas and a wood stove for heating water and cooking. Rainwater is pumped into their house, but spring drinking water has to be collected from a well tap down the hill. They have gradually built the infrastructure themselves, over years:

> Every now and again we have one of those little landmark moments like 'oh that tap's suddenly been put in' or 'that pipe has been put in'. So getting the water from A to B is suddenly a lot easier. I think about when we were first here and water had to be brought in from offsite, because there's no mains water here and, now we've got a well with a pump that takes the water to inside to a sink in Matt and Jo's house and to a tap outside the front of our house. It's only a matter of time before I put a pump on our house that'll bring that water inside our house as well.
>
> (Will, Green Hills, interview)

They do not have a bathroom, but do have a compost toilet and separate urinal spots in the woods. The infrastructure that Will and May have self-built forces them into certain environmentally sustainable practices. It is hard, for example, to waste quality drinking water because while rainwater is available for cooking and sinks, drinking water has to be manually collected and there is no toilet to flush it down. In other words, it is easier to be ecological than not. Likewise, because they have uneven electricity supply, especially in winter, there are limits to what can be powered. Will and May have restricted the number of phone chargers so that mobile phones deliberately have to be rotated to be charged. This sometimes causes tensions in the family, especially between the teenage children, but it also enforces the necessity of limits.

While these limits are hard to transgress they do have unintended implications. Domestic tasks take longer because of a lack of convenient infrastructures and these limits mean that the family do not have a fridge because there is not enough electricity to power it. The lack of a fridge means they have to go to the shop more often, normally by car, to buy perishable goods. Another family on-site built a more sophisticated house, with spring water piped into the kitchen sink, and more space and facilities. When May was asked what she would like she responded 'a fridge, a washing machine, a bathroom' (May, Green Hills, interview). In time the demands and expectations are likely to ratchet up rather than stay stable.

At Green Hills society-environment relations were reconfigured but with a focus on changing resource flows rather than biodiversity and therefore demonstrates a different shift in relations. In terms of social relations, Green Hills' income was shared, all tasks were intended to be distributed equally (including childcare and cooking), and decisions were made collectively using consensus.

Constructing homes at LILAC

LILAC is a twenty-household co-housing eco-community in West Leeds built in 2013. Unlike Tir y Gafel and Green Hills, a co-founder of LILAC was born locally and the eco-community invested many years in collaboratively co-designing an approach to fit with, and reflect, its specific urban location (Chatterton 2014). It is a good example through which to explore how new social relations of sharing, through home design, enable a reduction of environmental impact (Chatterton 2013). LILAC is a dense urban development and therefore not surprisingly homes have been designed to share common energy infrastructure (mains connection and photovoltaic panels) and a SUDS waste water management system. But residents also share gardens, bike sheds, laundry, car park, a common house and spare bedrooms located in some blocks' hallways (Figure 4). The sharing of a laundry (and a contract preventing residents having their own washing machines), common house and the shared four guest rooms have enabled the individual houses to be smaller. The structural design of the site and homes reduces the overall environmental impact.

This design, however, also influenced other daily practices of households. For example, residents share what jobs they would like help with, or to ask to borrow a piece of equipment using a *WhatsApp* group. Alan describes how daily tasks get shared:

> There's a lot of efficiency of co-housing, of sharing errands. Frequently people say oh I'm just nipping to the supermarket, does anybody want anything? There's a lot of efficiencies of time use and so energy as well. And with that, with informal and formal child care as well, and then also sharing of tools and resources, of bikes and tents and many things. So that makes life easier and can have a better standard

Figure 4 LILAC. (Source: Jenny Pickerill.)

of living really with better stuff, because we share them and have a bit more time – which I hadn't appreciated how extensive that would be before we moved in.

(Alan, LILAC, interview)

There are weekly communal meals and residents also share each other's houses when guests visit:

> One of the things that we didn't even talk about and didn't anticipate was how much, when we're away, we'd lend each other our houses or flats for when people come and visit.
>
> (Alan, LILAC, interview)

In order to maintain these shared spaces, there are team task work groups. Resident contributions to this communal work are uneven and those who work full-time off-site claim they do not have time. As Fran says, 'it's possible that we made a mistake from the beginning. Perhaps only people who work part time or less can be part of it' (interview). While LILAC has actively sought to create new social relations, which have implications for society-environment relations, there are residents who have struggled with this new sociality and sharing. Fran, a co-founder, decided that she could no longer cope with sharing:

> I love the flat, I love parts of LILAC, but some of the behaviour of people drives me bonkers. One of them that comes to mind is soap in the soap dispenser in the washing machine. How most people would put it in carefully into the correct bit, people here throw it in, because it's all over the floor, it's in the wrong things … and it will just sit there and it'll go in mine as well as theirs … Sometimes I think just get over it, it's just a bit of soap, and other times I want to throw it at somebody.
>
> (Fran, LILAC, interview)

The ethics of sharing at LILAC extends beyond the design of the homes themselves to include the way in which the project was funded to be affordable. LILAC uses a solidaristic funding model (a Mutual Home Ownership Model) where the wealthier residents subsidize those less well off. All residents pay 35 per cent of their annual income to live at LILAC and therefore the overall costs are shared unevenly between the community. This was because, as Alan put it, 'none of us wanted to live with just rich people' (Alan, interview). LILAC has, therefore, structured new society-environment relations through its careful building designs, which reduced resource use and enabled sharing and informal and spontaneous collectivity. Despite this careful design, however, tensions still emerged which tested the effectiveness of reconfiguration – with one resident ultimately moving out to live alone.

Conclusions

Despite Gibson-Graham and Millers' (2015) call to develop diverse ontologies that make visible and support the mutual interdependencies of human and more-than-human life, there remains a risk that peopled environments centre humans and that this approach maybe too anthropocentric, undermining the agency of more-than-humans. While residents at Green Hills learnt to be affected by the environmental limits of uneven energy supplies (while also craving more sophisticated infrastructures), there were also limits to their recognition of multispecies interdependence. Animals were, in the main, used as a productivist resource at Tir y Gafel and Green Hills with little evidence of new ethical engagements with more-than-human beings.

Questions also remain about who is able to participate in these experimental eco-communities. Residents at Tir y Gafel and Green Hills are reliant on high levels of physical and mental health (Laughton 2008; Leafe Christian 2003) which prioritize the able-bodied (Bhakta and Pickerill 2016). Financially, affordability was tackled at LILAC but unfortunately the model is so complicated that it has not been replicated by other eco-communities.

In addition to these risks about multispecies interdependence and participation, there is a broader question about the effectiveness of these reconfigured relations in shifting understandings beyond the eco-communities themselves, and in how sustainable they are over time for residents. There remain two key pressures on these new relations: a difficulty sustaining them over time against a drift towards individualization, greater comfort and activities off-site, and an ongoing challenge to engage non-residents in these new ways of relating.

Rural eco-communities, such as Tir y Gafel, encountered stronger resistance from local communities to their new radical relationalities, but also had greater autonomy in designing and developing new modes of living and in how they self-provisioned and built new socio-materialities. The resistance Tir y Gafel encountered illustrates how embedded perceptions of a society-environment dualism are, and how challenges to this can trigger conflict. What is at stake cannot simply be resolved by demonstrating and enacting diverse ecological ontologies or advocating for peopled environments.

Urban eco-communities, like LILAC, which made the most of a dense plot and the sharing and sociality it enabled, encountered less local resistance but had to contend with residents spending more time off-site and therefore had to navigate tensions about commitment to communal activities and projects. For all examples here, approaches evolved over time, with some pressure at Green Hills to adopt less radical physically easier practices and a creeping individualization at Tir y Gafel. Eco-communities are challenging fundamental assumptions of conventional society and established ways of being, so it is unsurprising that the broader impact will be slow and limited.

While the examples from eco-communities shared here offer hope for new society-environment relations, they also demonstrate that any attempt to create these modes of co-existence and make visible our mutual interdependencies is a political act, unfinished, ongoing, slow and always vulnerable to tensions and contradictions. Most effort, especially in LILAC and Green Hills, has been put into reconfiguring human-to-human relations in ways that reduce environmental exploitations. Less attention has been paid to engaging in and making visible non-human agencies.

These examples have demonstrated that humans are more than an interventional and destructive presence in the environment, but rather an intrinsic and co-constitutive part of it, and that this presence is a political relation. The eco-communities' experimentation in forging new society-environment and social relations is always a matter of tension and inconsistency. Indeed, being otherwise does not itself resolve conflict or settle contradictions, but is a vital step in realizing these relations differently. While these eco-communities offer hope, we need further examples of what coexistence might involve and require in practice, and for these to be critically and empirically explored so that we can better envision the potential of creating an 'ecological community of life' (Gibson-Graham and Miller 2015).

References

Adams, W. (2006) *Future Nature: A Vision for Conservation*. London: Earthscan.

Atchison, J., Arnold, C., Gibbs, L., Gill, N., Hubbard, E., Lorimer, J., Pickerill, J. and Watson, M. (2024) 'Peopled landscapes? Questions of coexistence and future sustainabilities in invasive plant management and rewilding', *People and Nature* 6(2), pp. 458–73.

Bhakta, A. and Pickerill, J. (2016) 'Making space for disability in eco-homes and eco-communities', *The Geographical Journal* 182(4), pp. 406–17.

Castree, N. (2013) *Making Sense of Nature*. London: Routledge.

Chatterton, P. (2013) 'Towards an agenda for post-carbon cities: Lessons from LILAC, the UK's first ecological, affordable, cohousing community', *International Journal for Urban and Regional Research* 37(5), pp. 1654–1674.

Chatterton, P. (2014). *Low Impact Living: A Field Guide to Ecological, Affordable Community Building*. Milton Park: Routledge.

Chetty, D. (Ed.) (2022) *Welsh (plural): Essays on the Future of Wales*. London: Repeater Books.

Dale, J. and Dale, S. (2015) *Wild by Design*. Booklet.

Ergas, C. (2010) 'A model of sustainable living: Collective identity in an urban ecovillage', *Organization and Environment* 23(1), pp. 32–54.

Ergas, C. (2021) *Surviving Collapse: Building Community toward Radical Sustainability*. Oxford: Oxford University Press.

Escobar, A. (2020) *Pluriversal Politics: The Real and the Possible*. Durham, NC: Duke University Press.

Fairlie, S. (1996) *Low Impact Development: Planning and People in a Sustainable Countryside*. Oxford: Jon Carpenter.

Garforth, L. (2018) *Green Utopias: Environmental Hope before and after Nature*. New York: John Wiley & Sons.

Gibson-Graham, J.K. and Miller, E. (2015) 'Economy as ecological livelihood', in Gibson, K., Bird Rose, D. and Fincher, R. (eds.) *Manifesto for Living in the Anthropocene*. Brooklyn, New York: Punctum books, pp. 7–16.

Haberle, S.G. and David, B. (2012) *Peopled Landscapes: Archaeological and Biogeographic Approaches to Landscapes*. Canberra: ANU Press.

Hallam, S.J. (2002) 'Peopled landscapes in southwestern Australia in the early 1800s: aboriginal burning off in the light of Western Australian historical documents', *Early Days: Journal of the Royal Western Australian Historical Society* 12(2), p. 177.

Hardy, D. and Ward, C. (1984) *Arcadia for All: The Legacy of the Makeshift Landscape*. Cambridge: Mansell.

Harvey, D. (2005) *Spaces of Neoliberalization: Towards a Theory of Uneven Geographical Development* (Vol. 8). Stuttgart: Franz Steiner Verlag.
Hunter, J. (1995) *On the Other Side of Sorrow: Nature and People in the Scottish Highlands.* Edinburgh: Birlinn.
Jørgensen, D. (2015) 'Rethinking rewilding', *Geoforum* 65(October), pp. 482–8.
Jørgensen, D. (2017) 'Competing ideas of "natural" in a dam removal controversy', *Water Alternatives* 10(3), pp. 840–52.
Kirby, A. (2003) 'Redefining social and environmental relations at the ecovillage at Ithaca: A case study', *Journal of Environmental Psychology* 23(3), pp. 323–32.
Kraftl, P. (2013) *Geographies of Alternative Education: Diverse Learning Spaces for Children and Young People.* Bristol: Policy Press.
Laughton, R. (2008) *Surviving and Thriving on the Land: How to Use Your Time and Energy to Run a Successful Smallholding.* Totnes: Green Books.
Leafe Christian, D. (2003) *Creating a Life Together: Practical Tools to Grow Ecovillages and Intentional Communities.* Gabriola Island: New Society Publishers.
Litfin, K.T. (2014) *Eco-Villages: Lessons for Sustainable Community.* Cambridge: Polity Press.
Lorimer, J. (2015) *Wildlife in the Anthropocene: Conservation after Nature.* Minneapolis, MN: University of Minnesota Press.
Mason, K. and Milbourne, P. (2014) 'Constructing a "landscape justice" for windfarm development: The case of Nant Y Moch, Wales', *Geoforum* 53(May), pp. 104–15.
Moore, S. and Roberts, A. (2022) *The Rise of Ecofascism: Climate Change and the Far Right.* New York: John Wiley & Sons.
Nagendra, H., Mondal, P., Adhikari, S. and Southworth, J. (2013) 'Peopled parks: Forest change in India's protected landscapes', in Brondízio, E. and Moran, E. (eds.) *Human-Environment Interactions.* Dordrecht: Springer, pp. 113–39.
Pooley, S. (2021) 'Coexistence for whom?', *Frontiers in Conservation Science* 2, 726991, pp. 1–7.
Procter, E. (2014) 'Rewilding: An alternative view', *Landscapes* 15(1), pp. 77–81.
Rzedzian, S.H. (2019) Promoting and defending the rights of nature in ecuador: Divergent environmentalisms and counter-hegemonies. PhD thesis, University of Newcastle.
Sanford, A.W. (2017) *Living Sustainably: What Intentional Communities Can Teach Us about Democracy, Simplicity, and Nonviolence.* Lexington, KY: University Press of Kentucky.
Selman, P. (2008) 'What do we mean by sustainable landscape?', *Sustainability: Science, Practice, & Policy* 4(2), pp. 23–8.
Shirani, F., Groves, C., Henwood, K., Pidgeon, N. and Roberts, E. (2020) 'What counts as success? Wider implications of achieving planning permission in a low-impact ecovillage', *Environmental Values* 29(3), pp. 339–59.
Soper, K. (1999) 'The politics of nature: Reflections on hedonism, progress and ecology', *Capitalism Nature Socialism* 10(2), pp. 42–70.
Thorpe, D. (2014) *The 'One Planet' Life: A Blueprint for Low Impact Development.* London: Routledge.
Ward, C. (1999) 'A peopled landscape', in Worpole, K. (ed.) *Richer Futures: Fashioning a New Politics.* London: Routledge, pp. 84–98.
Welstead, W. (2021) '"Green desert" or "living landscape": Sheep and people in the Welsh uplands', in *Writing on Sheep.* Manchester: Manchester University Press, pp. 96–103.

Whatmore, S. (2017) 'Hybrid geographies: Rethinking the "human" in human geography', in Anderson, K. and Braun, B. (eds.) *Environment: Critical Essays in Human Geography*. London: Routledge, pp. 411–28.
Wimbush, P. (2012) *The Birth of an Ecovillage: Adventures in an Alternative World*. England: FeedARead Publishing.
Wimbush, T.P. (2021) *The Lammas Ecovillage: Deep Roots and Stormy Skies*. England: FeedARead Publishing.
Wright, E.O. (2010) *Envisioning Real Utopias*. London: Verso.

6

Eco-communities and outsiders: Opportunities and obstacles to transforming the world

Jon Anderson

Introduction

Eco-communities that function as both residential and environmental education centres are crucial in empowering socio-ecological transformation (see Ibsen 2013; Xue 2014). As such these centres can be understood as socio-spatial practices that seek to not only resist the industrialization of people and the planet, but also offer functioning, ecological, alternatives. However, like many political acts, eco-centres face tensions at the heart of their transformative project: do they operate to 'change the world' or simply the world of their participants? This question raises the important issue of the function of political chapter examines these questions in relation to one specific eco-community that functions as both a residential and environmental education centre: The Centre for Alternative Technology (CAT), Machynlleth, UK. Established in the 1970s by Gerard Morgan-Grenville (see CAT 2015a), CAT describes itself as the 'major centre for environmental inspiration' in Britain (CAT 2015b, no page). Today CAT functions as an education and residential community, with over 100 employees and volunteers. The Centre experiments with a range of alternative technologies, including photovoltaics, solar thermal, biomass, combined heat and power, air source heat pumps, reed bed systems, and wind turbines (CAT 2015a, no page). The Welsh Institute for Sustainable Education is part of the Centre, which supplements existing experimentation with postgraduate and practical courses (e.g. in installing photovoltaic technologies), whilst also functioning as a conference and wedding venue (see CAT 2015a; CAT 2015c). The site is open to the public and houses a well-established on-site community for up to 16 residents (CAT 2015d, no page).

This chapter argues that eco-centres like CAT are examples of spatial practice. Spatial practices are acts that take and make locations, socially ordering and geographically bordering sites in line with specific ideologies and cultural preferences (Anderson 2021). In this way, spatial practices are fundamental to any form of protest, as it is in space that political power is made manifest (Thrift 2000), and it is inevitably *with* space that any act fuelled by a 'desire to transgress the current state' of affairs must engage (Jordan 2002, 12). In social movements (see della Porta and Diani 2006; Ruggerio and Montagna 2008), perceived threats to and injustices within the contemporary system can mobilize individuals to engage in actions which seek to change the cultural geographies of a location, re(b)ordering them in line with alternative aims and objectives. These spatial practices therefore seek to literally change the world. The success of these practices can be understood in terms of two interconnected criteria. Firstly, they can be understood in terms of their duration. In line with the terms used by Hakim Bey with reference to 'autonomous zones' (2003, 2007), these socio-spatial practices can be temporary or permanent in nature. 'Temporary' autonomous zones are socio-spatial practices that intentionally, or due to intervention from the state, tend towards the 'creation of momentary, self-governing spaces' (Armitage 1999, 117). Examples may include the lifetime of a protest, sit-in, or action camp (see Anderson 2004; Halvorsen 2015). As Bey acknowledges, such spatial practices can occur as one-off events, or more 'periodically', perhaps being annual protests (such as May Day or anti-G8 protests) or regular 'flash' protests by (semi)-organized cells or groups (Bey 2003). However, it is also possible for socio-spatial practices that seek to transgress the current system to be more durable in nature. As Bey states, 'not all ... autonomous zones are "temporary". Some are (at least by intention) more-or-less "permanent"' (Hermetic Library 1993, no page).

Allied, and perhaps broadly aligned, to these temporal criteria are constituencies attracted to these socio-spatial practices. Employing the categories first developed by May and Nugent (1982; but also developed by scholars including: Grant 2002; Maloney et al., 1994), this chapter identifies that a second key criteria for understanding socio-spatial practices are the constituencies to which they are aligned and subsequently generate: namely, insiders, thresholders, and outsiders. Insiders are those individuals who are deeply committed and converted to a cause, and participate in a campaign, movement, or specific 'autonomous zone' for a lengthy period. Insiders are privy to the logics and strategies associated with decision-making, and form part of the 'inner circle' of the group in some or all of its operations. Thresholders are those who share the general values of the spatial practice but are not always involved in the action. This constituency balances irregular involvement within the action with competing obligations of job, family, or other interests that may run counter to the values and objectives of the transgressive practice. Thresholders are thus in a liminal position in relation to alternative and mainstream society, they are betwixt and between positions, enjoying and enduring a foot in both camps. Outsiders refer to those individuals who may be (un)sympathetic observers, temporary participants, or visitors to these transgressive practices. Outsiders are unlikely to be aware of more 'backstage' aspects of decision-making or more intimate social dimensions of activities, but nevertheless consume the public face of the practice and can be converted or alienated to the cause through this engagement.

Identifying both the duration and constituency of these spatial actions, and how they interweave in practice, will help determine their significance in changing the world. From these criteria we can ask, for example, whether socio-ecological utopia exist to the change the world of outsiders, thresholders, or insiders? We can consider how temporary actions evolve into more durable, permanent spatial practices, and which constituency is most attracted to the cause. The chapter will demonstrate how, while outsiders were initially excited, hopeful and inspired by the variety of green innovations offered at CAT, they were also dismayed by the familiarity of some of the technologies on show. The chapter will go on to outline how, for this group, what made CAT interesting were the practices of residents – the conviviality and skill-sharing that were, unfortunately, less visible to outsiders. The chapter concludes by suggesting that when the transformative potential of eco-communities are considered it is important to reflect on all aspects of 'community' practice involved in these actions, rather than reducing alternatives to the narrow implementation of technology in the conventional sense.

Researching CAT as a permanent autonomous zone

The Centre for Alternative Technology was set up in 1973 and has been in sustained operation since that time. CAT can be understood as a socio-spatial practice with an established degree of durability and, in line with Bey's broad vocabulary, a 'permanent autonomous zone'. CAT is located in a disused slate mine in the Dyfi Valley, mid Wales, and the choice of this specific somewhere to ground this ecotopia was not random. Aligning with Meijering et al.'s broad argument that, 'eco-villages … withdraw from mainstream urban society, challenging norms of urban life … and creat[ing] their own places in rural areas' (2007, 43), CAT colonized what the early founders considered to be a figurative and material 'crack' in contemporary society in which to realize a socio-spatial critique of modern industrialization and militarization (Bey 2003). Indeed, for any outsider, the location of the Centre for Alternative Technology could indeed be seen to be relatively remote. CAT is located approximately twenty miles north from the University town of Aberystwyth (Aberystwyth has a permanent population of just over 10,000 people (City Population 2023a), with over 8000 further residents studying temporarily at the University (Prifysgol University Aberystwyth 2023)). Aberystwyth is the largest settlement within ninety minutes travel time of CAT (the predominant mode of travel in the area would be by road, with only one key rail line connecting the town to the midlands of England, over 100 miles away). The nearest settlement to CAT is Machynlleth, approximately three miles away in distance, and only accessible by road. Machynlleth itself is a market town of approximately 2000 inhabitants (City Population 2023b); its small population is constituted predominantly by English-speaking urban residents, and Welsh-speaking farmers who work its hinterland (see Davies 2010). Today, Machynlleth functions as part of a wider tourist trail which caters to UK and international visitors, and is dominated by Eryri National Park (Snowdonia) to the North and the coastal villages of Cardigan Bay. In the context of the 1970s, the founders of CAT considered the abandoned slate mine in the Dyfi Valley north of Machynlleth as an ideal space of escape from the mainstream; to use Bey's terms, it was a site beyond the gaze of the State's 'mapmakers' (2003, 101), a fold in the map so peripheral and, 'so vacant, that whole groups [could] move into [it] and settle down' (Bey quoted in Hermetic Library 1993, no page). Indeed, in both a cultural and a spatial sense, the location remains distant and different from contemporary, industrial urbanism; as one city-based visitor noted in a contemporary focus group, 'I knew it was rural, but nothing can prepare you for the remoteness of its location' (Anonymized focus group response, for details see below).

With respect to intentional communities in general, such distance and difference from the mainstream – what Sargisson terms 'estrangement' – secure the opportunity to not only generate a new group identity for those establishing the community, but also a vital criticality of the spaces left behind; in short, it promotes 'fresh perception of the limits of the possible' (Sargisson 2007, 393). In line with Bey's notion of the permanent autonomous zone, the Centre's permanence in this distanced and differentiated location 'serve[s] a vital function' for many groups with different degrees of affiliation to socio-ecological transformation (Bey quoted in Hermetic Library 1993, no page). CAT functions as a 'homeplace' for 'insiders' who live and work there (see Anderson 2007), a 'meetingplace' for thresholders – or in Bey's words the 'wide circle of friends and allies who may not actually live full-time on the "farm" or in the "village" but are nevertheless committed to their goals, at least in principle' (Hermetic Library 1993, no page). CAT also functions for 'outsiders' from mainstream society. Visitors can enter CAT with day passes; engage with the exhibits, technologies, and information in the Centre; as well as use the café, shop and public event facilities. These outsiders may be looking for validation of their nascent ecological interest, advice on particular technological problems they are facing, or simply visiting CAT as part of the tourist trail of Ceredigion, mid Wales.

In order to gain critical insight into the long-term transformative potential of this socio-ecological utopia, this chapter draws on extensive research at the Centre. First, three months of participant observation was undertaken within CAT's resident community and work organization, with the author undertaking thirty in-depth interviews with a range of volunteers, employees and long-term residents of the Centre (these interviews were split 50% identifying as male and 50% female, and all were white in their ethnicity). During this period of participant observation, interviews were also undertaken with regular visitors and CAT members attending their annual conference (n=12, with a ratio of 60:40 female: male, and 100 per cent white). Day trips to the Centre were also held with postgraduate students over seven academic years (2009–15 inclusive), totalling 150 students in all (overall, 50 per cent of these students identified as male, and 50 per cent female; 40 per cent were white British, and 60 per cent non-White, non-British). Focus groups were held with students following each visit, and participants were invited to write reflexive journals of their experiences (see Anderson 2012b). These methods combined to generate a wide variety of experiences of the Centre, from participants who were later categorized into 'insider', 'thresholder' and 'outsider' constituencies. In general, insider participants dominated the resident community and work organization interviews; thresholders were mainly positioned by their status as regular visitors to the Centre and CAT conference attendees; whilst outsiders tended to be positioned as 'normal' students enrolled in postgraduate study.[1] As outlined, this chapter draws particularly on the

---

[1] These students were registered on a taught 'sustainability' degree, twenty-five were regular visitors to CAT (and categorized as thresholders), and the remainder categorized as outsiders. All students agreed to allow their thoughts to be included in published study, co-creating the terms of anonymity and identification that have been implemented in this paper.

outsider group in an attempt to understand the relative success (or otherwise) of this attempt at socio-ecological transformation with respect to the perceptions and prejudices of this constituency.

Curating alternative technologies?

For those who live, work and regularly visit CAT it is possible to experiment with the 'alternative technologies' being explored on-site. In this sense, technology, from the Greek *techne* (i.e. art, skill, or craft) and *logos* (i.e. the way of representing or naming the accomplishments gained), can be understood as the products and practices (techne) as well as the subsequent narratives (logos) used by CAT to (b)order the world to alternative ends. As introduced elsewhere (Anderson 2007, 2012a), CAT has created a range of green architectures (following Horton 2003) which facilitate ecological living – the Centre has developed a community of like-minded people who are supportive in practical, psychological and emotional terms when trying to live differently in the world. For this constituency, the socio-ecological utopia promised by this permanent spatial practice is substantially realized. For insiders and thresholders, therefore, CAT has changed their world; as the following student thresholders articulate:

> The place has inspired me since my first visit in March 2008 for my first course, and every time I go there I discover something new and interesting.
> (Anonymized focus group respondent [FG])

> For me CAT radiates waves of hope for better lifestyles and occupies a special place in my life. I feel a prosperous atmosphere there, very inspiring indeed. Something related with its practice makes me sense a different atmosphere there.
> (Anonymized field diary entry [FD])

CAT's realization of ecotopian objectives in practice offers a compelling escape for insider and thresholder constituencies. Its difference and distance from the industrial urban mainstream enable and infuse a general sense of back-to-the-land arcadia for those directly involved in its alternative spaces. Beyond these groups, outsiders have the potential to be converted to CAT's convivial community (and thus evolve from being outsiders-to-thresholders and -insiders through their visits). However, to what extent does the estrangement that is so vital to the Centre's establishment help outsiders in this potential conversion? When anticipating their visit, the outsiders in this study had positive expectations about the Centre: the promise of ecotopia existing in the hills of mid-Wales was a tantalising one.

> CAT's website clams that they, '*offer solutions to some of the most serious challenges facing our planet and the human race, such as climate change, pollution and the waste of precious resources*' I was really looking forward to seeing how CAT would demonstrate [at the macro-scale] that it was possible to provide enough [green]

energy to supply the needs of a small neighbourhood and eventually a country, and [at the micro-scale] how grey-water installation systems could channel my old bath water to the toilet and garden.

(FD)

I understood that the staff at The Centre for Alternate Technology were investigating alternative technologies to finding practical solutions to the problems of the 21st century and preserve the planet for future generations. The underlying factors causing global warming, ozone depletion, deforestation, and peak oil crisis could be tackled if CAT had found ways to expand the use of renewable energy systems. So when I was given the opportunity to visit CAT with my classmates, I gladly took it.

(FD)

The promise of a portal into an alternative paradigm of living was therefore appealing to these outsiders. CAT's own marketing, allied to an awareness of the need for sustainable alternatives, created a sense of hope among these visitors that real answers to society's problems could be found at the Centre. This hope was maintained upon arrival; CAT's location in the remote rural lent an air of difference and opportunity to those arriving from the city:

I found it really idyllic. ... the birds were just there, the woodland meant you did kind of feel like you were in this little heaven; really rustic and just out in the middle of nowhere ... it felt serene and just really cut off from everything.

(FG)

I was impressed by the low visual impact created by the Centre, especially given its elevated position. While the funicular railway station was visible from the road, most of the other buildings are further back into the disused quarry site and shielded by the vegetation. ... In particular I liked their use of turfed roofs, ... it reminded me that these 'alternative' techniques are relatively popular in regions such as Scandinavia, and are now increasingly mainstream in the UK – from the get-go it inspired me to 'turf' the roof of my garage to improve the appearance of my garden and hopefully increase biodiversity.

(FD)

These outsiders' initial impression of the CAT site reinforced its distance and difference from the industrial urban spaces with which they were more familiar. However, this 'estrangement' – the remoteness of CAT's chosen location and the low impact 'footprint' of its buildings – did not alienate or isolate these visitors; rather, it complemented their expectations that have been cultivated by CAT's marketing image. It suggested that real solutions may be possible in this alternatively imagined world; as one responded stated, 'you arrive on site and think: "this is sustainability!"' (FG). Following a short introduction to the history of the site from an insider employee, outsiders were free to tour the public areas where a range of ecological techniques (from recycling to alternative energy systems) were displayed; in these areas, as one respondent explains:

> You can just turn around and there will be some sort of a sustainable system in practice. There was a line of recycling bins as well as sustainable use of flushing system in the toilet. It just makes you think 'why didn't I think of that?'.
>
> (FD)

> I found these displays the most interesting, I enjoyed discovering how things work and I liked seeing something interesting happen, much like a youngster watching an experiment in a science lesson!.
>
> (FG)

At first sight, many outsiders in this study appreciated the tactile, clear demonstrations of sustainable practice on display; however, on closer inspection some also felt that the technologies on view were not as innovative or alternative as they anticipated. Despite acknowledging their own better-than-average understanding of environmental issues, respondents nevertheless felt that the technologies on display were not as advanced or cutting-edge as the website marketing had led them to believe, as the following respondents articulate:

> The most interesting displays were the hands-on exhibits but they were more suitable to children. I enjoyed the principles they presented, yet they taught me little in respect to knowledge I already had.
>
> (FD)

> The public displays were clearly aimed at a much younger audience.
>
> (FG)

Not only did respondents feel that the displays may have been pitched at a school-age constituency, they also commented that the technologies showcased had not kept up with the pace of change and technological advancement they were familiar with in their own lives:

> What was disappointing was the lack of alternative advice available – there was nothing new being said. It was the standard advice on switching lights off, turning taps off while brushing teeth, composting food waste etc.
>
> (FD)

> On the whole I thought the presentation of displays were quite out-of-date, the displays seen to be something that I would of looked at when I went to school and with the recent development of technology such as the progressions of mobile phones and wireless technology, none of these technological advances seem to have impacted or influenced the Centre.
>
> (FD)

> CAT was built in the 70s and the displays and information being presented was out-of-date for the 21st century lifestyles we all live in. ... All the ideas had good intentions when they were first conceived but these had not been developed and moved forward into the technological generation.
>
> (FD)

Thus, as they toured the site, these outsiders underwent a change in identification. Their initial connection with 'alternative' technologies such as the low-impact constructions they encountered upon arrival they assumed would be 'built' upon with more innovative techniques and solutions on-site. However, in practice the technologies they witnessed were felt to be already mainstream, or even outmoded, as one respondent stated: 'I found it hard to be inspired by ... out of date technology' (FD). Through the absence of any narrative that aligned these products and practices with a specific educational purpose or age-group constituency, distance and difference had been created between insiders and outsiders, where connection had been possible. CAT had somehow failed to capitalize on the opportunity to inspire these respondents on what it means to be green, and as such, an estrangement had been generated that compounded rather than challenged these individuals' identity as outsiders.

These respondents also began to contemplate what message CAT's location sent in terms of contemporary sustainability, mobility and modern travel. As one individual stated: 'It invites me to question whether travelling for 6 hours was worth the amount of carbon emissions to visit a centre that was out-of-date and irrelevant to today's lifestyle' (FG). Individuals also reflected on whether it may be possible to realize a green life in practice ('although well-meaning in its aim of spreading the message about sustainable living, CAT appears to be presenting the idea that leading a sustainable life means *having* to live up a hill in a rural part of the country' (FD, emphasis in original)). To paraphrase Sargisson (2007, 393), difference and distance can often promote critique, and the estrangement these outsiders felt in relation to CAT's ability to convincingly curate an 'alternative' technology message prompted them to question the Centre's version of a green life. Some indeed interpreted CAT's vision as solely an escape for the few, rather than a solution for the many:

> Whilst it appeared that they were purveying a message that sustainable measures should be universally implemented, they ensured segregation from society through locating deep in the Welsh hillside. ... this segregation is a form of 'green elitism' giving the impression that to be truly green you must live outside of society.
>
> (FD)

> I left feeling that the only way I can be green is to have more financial independence and stability ... I will have to get a very well-paid job and be rich!.
>
> (FD)

These outsiders' estrangement from the public displays led them to regard the (backstage) architectures that provide the mainstay for CAT's insider and thresholder groups as a bolthole for a minority, rather than a template for a collectivised majority;

indeed one concluded that they could only mimic such solutions through working in the mainstream, then retreating from it. These critiques fuelled estrangement from the cultural and physical (b)orders of the site, fostering isolation from it rather than close identification with it, as the following respondents put it:

> The physical space that CAT inhabited and the displays they showcased contributed to the epistemic distance which I felt. The physical location of the centre – even down to the point that it was situated atop a large hill added to the epistemic distance; for me it was somehow separate from my everyday reality.
>
> (FD)

> I was a little disappointed that the experience is so different to the images presented. It felt to me like stepping backwards in time, not forwards
>
> (FD)

> I returned home … harbouring the burden that such places as CAT might see their own defeat due to their isolation.
>
> (FD)

Thus although estrangement may be 'fundamental to utopianism' (Suvin 1973) from an insider or thresholder perspective, when seeking to engage outsiders such difference and distance are a constant threat. Although at times estrangement can induce hope and expectation in outsiders due precisely to its difference from the mainstream, connections need to be nurtured and maintained if these opportunities are not to mutate into significant obstacles. Without the curation of a convincing message that resonated with the public image of the site, CAT failed to capitalize on its opportunity, and caused these outsiders to critique their (b)orders. Building bridges between insider and outsider groups in the context of eco-communities is thus fraught with fragility, or to use Sargisson's words, 'estranged relationships are complex and difficult' (2007, 393). Yet, although the outsider community at large may be heterogeneous and complex, it is not always, as Sargisson puts it, 'strange and unknown' (2007, 393). In the final section of this chapter, I draw on knowledge offered by the particular outsider group accessed by this project to 'contemplate' ways in which it may be possible to counter their estrangement and re-instil identification with sustainable living.

Reaching the outsider: Connecting through communities

As we have seen, the outsider group accessed in this study felt little affinity with the products and practices on public display at CAT, a feeling that developed into a lack of connection with the Centre as a whole. As demonstrated elsewhere (Anderson 2012a, 2017), this lack of identification is in sharp contrast with the strong affinity developed by insiders and thresholder constituencies. The outsiders in this study were keenly aware that they were missing something that these other constituencies had access to:

I find it difficult to imagine [CAT] as an eco-community ... I mean there are real people living on-site but it was so difficult for us to see any of that experience. ... I can't help but feel we missed the most important part.

(FG)

It would have actually been really useful to have more time to spend talking to [insiders and thresholders] about the way they live and interact as a community and their way of life.

(FG)

These comments suggest that although the products on display at CAT may not have been compelling, the collective, day-to-day practices undertaken by those on-site may have been. The problem remained that these everyday practices were often backstage; they were literally and materially 'outside' the normal public spaces of the site. As such, only glimpses of these practices were possible for these outsiders. As the following respondents articulate:

What I found more interesting and vibrant was the means by which the people on site were living, in close community and in harmony with the land and each other.

(FD)

I came away feeling very positive, not so much about the energy efficiency or the education resources, but more so about the community spirit and networks. Whilst walking around I could sometimes see people doing little tasks or jobs as part of maintaining the grounds such as carving into a large rock, felling some trees, working together in the restaurant, moving waste around the site or cultivating the allotment. I guess this was kind of like a 'real life in action' exhibition without those mannikins behind a glass screen you get at most museums. I found this fascinating and truly appealing.

(FD)

These people [you could see] were learning from the land and learning off each other, they were working together with possibly no prior knowledge of the task in hand but nonetheless they were learning from that experience and in the process were supplying themselves with much needed resources. They all looked happy and content to be doing what they were doing, nothing seemed like a chore. This community spirit ... in itself is 'sustainable development'.

(FD)

They may have succeeded in developing a resource-efficient way of dwelling, but more importantly they have been able to establish a community spirit based on the values of sustainability. It is this community spirit which I admire.

(FD)

Regardless of the physical and cultural estrangement of CAT, what these respondents identified with was the possibility of alternative practices that defined the people and place of the site as a community. When these 'green architectures' were glimpsed, it was as if these respondents' outsider position (regardless of whether this was an identity they had chosen or been relegated to by Centre itself) was transgressed. Seeing a range of 'old technologies' being put to work, albeit (re-)contextualized in an unfamiliar environment, re-connected these individuals to the promise and reality of green living.

Although these glimpses of the insider life were appreciated, it was acknowledged that it may be difficult and unappealing for those on-site to continually 'display' themselves to visiting publics, in the stead of existing interactive installations. It was, however, suggested that the potentially revolutionary 'reality' of life on-site could be 'televized' in other ways:

> So many of the displays in isolation don't show that much, but maybe if they showed a video of them living, 'a week in the life' video maybe, so you can say 'right, see how we do things? This is how these technologies fit into our lives', that could give a sense of it.
>
> (FG)

> If they want to make it really interesting, they should try to integrate how the community and the practices come together and show it in an holistic way, that would have a bigger impact.
>
> (FD)

It is notable that these outsiders' implicit allusion to 'reality TV', and the associated norms of mainstream twenty-first-century life, is considered to offer a potential means through which to generate connection with and combat estrangement from this eco-community. In looking to what is familiar to the outsider, and trying to find commonalities between this and insider life, means that difference and distance can be harnessed to motivate social and ecological transformation, rather than hinder it.

> I think the importance of the community is underestimated in the aim for sustainable development. I believe CAT does have some value in the shaping of sustainable development as it can demonstrate that shared objectives between the individuals of a community result in effective strategies and initiatives …. It is therefore a pity that the people of CAT seem to conceal this community spirit from visitors, as this is where the real value of the centre lies.
>
> (FD)

Conclusion

Eco-communities that function as both residential and environmental education centres can be vital in showcasing and progressing socio-ecological transformation. Sites such as CAT therefore function for multiple constituencies; whilst the residential aspect of their operation functions primarily for insider groups and on occasion thresholder constituencies, the education aspect is oriented predominantly towards outsider groups. In this way, the education function of the centre secures financial resilience for the residential community, creating the possibility that the site is not temporary in nature, but becomes a permanent autonomous zone. The education aspect of the development also offers the potential to recruit outsiders by offering alternative practices, products and narratives which can inspire and mobilize individuals onto a trajectory of green living. However, as we have seen in this chapter, this opportunity to recruit and inspire is often a temporary and fragile one; in the absence of compelling technologies which can connect with the contexts of outsiders' lives, these individuals' hearts and minds may be lost, and their financial contributions too.

However, as we have seen in this chapter, the day-to-day lives of eco-communities can themselves be compelling to outsider constituencies. Although often different and distant from the mainstream, their attempts to foster interdependence between people and place is the vital 'technology' – i.e. task *and* narrative – which can successfully convince others that this is 'how the[ir] world ought to be (too)' (Chatterton 2016, 403). Eco-communities thus offer an alternative to relegating outsiders to spectators of displays or consumers in on-site cafes and shops, and thus reducing them into 'the status quo of intense individualism, corrosive consumerism and financial austerity' (Chatterton 2016, 404). Through sharing their practice and actively considering how their experiences could inspire outsiders to refashion technologies for their own circumstances, eco-communities are positioned with a real opportunity, and indeed responsibility, to progress socio-ecological transformation by 'infiltrating, countering and corroding the dominant regime as they connect' outsiders into a different future (Chatterton 2016, 411; see also Scott-Cato and Hillier 2011).

References

Anderson, J. (2004) 'Spatial politics in practice: The style and substance of environmental direct action', *Antipode* 36(1), pp. 106–25.

Anderson, J. (2007) 'Elusive escapes: Everyday life and ecotopias', *Ecopolitics Online* 1(1), pp. 64–82.

Anderson, J. (2010) 'From "zombies" to "coyotes": Environmentalism where we are', *Environmental Politics* 19(6), pp. 973–92.

Anderson, J. (2012a) 'Managing trade-offs in "Ecotopia": Becoming green at the "centre for alternative technology"', *Transactions of the Institute of British Geographers* 37(2), pp. 212–25.

Anderson, J. (2012b) 'Reflective journals as a tool for auto-ethnographic learning: A case study of student experiences with individualised sustainability', *Journal of Geography in Higher Education* 36(4), pp. 613–23.

Anderson, J. (2017) 'Retreat or re-connect: How effective can ecosophical communities be in transforming the mainstream?', *Geografiska Annaler: Series B, Human Geography* 99(2), pp. 192–206.

Anderson, J. (2021) *Understanding Cultural Geography: Places & Traces*. London: Routledge.

Armitage, J. (1999) 'Ontological anarchy, the temporary autonomous zone, and the politics of cyberculture: A critique of Hakim Bey', *Angelaki: Journal of the Theoretical Humanities* 4(2), pp. 115–28.

Bey, H. (2003) *T.A.Z. The Temporary Autonomous Zone, Ontological Anarchy, Poetic Terrorism*. New York: Autonomedia.

Bey, H. (2007) *The Periodic Autonomous Zone*. Available at: http://www.hermetic.com/bey/periodic.html. Accessed June 2007.
Centre for Alternative Technology (1995) *Crazy Idealists? The CAT Story*. Machnylleth: Centre for Alternative Technology.
Centre for Alternative Technology (2007) *What Do We Do?* Available at: http://www.cat.org.uk/information/aboutcatx.tmpl?init=1. Accessed July 2007.
Centre for Alternative Technology (2015a) *What We Do*. Available at: https://content.cat.org.uk/index.php/about-cat-what-do-we-do. Accessed March 2015.
Centre for Alternative Technology (2015b) *How CAT Started*. Available at: https://content.cat.org.uk/index.php/how-cat-started. Accessed March 2015.
Centre for Alternative Technology (2015c) *CAT Venue Hire*. Available at: http://venuehire.cat.org.uk/. Accessed March 2015.
Centre for Alternative Technology (2015d) *CAT Site Community*. Available at: https://content.cat.org.uk/index.php/site-community. Accessed March 2015.
City Population (2023a) *Aberystwyth, Community in Wales*. Available at: https://www.citypopulation.de/en/uk/wales/admin/ceredigion/W04000359__aberystwyth/. Accessed June 2023.
City Population (2023b) *Machynlleth, Community in Wales*. Available at: https://www.citypopulation.de/en/uk/wales/admin/powys/W04000326__machynlleth/. Accessed June 2023.
Chatterton, P. (2016) 'Building transitions to post-capitalist urban commons', *Transactions of the Institute of British Geographers* 41(4), pp. 403–15.
Davies, E.H. (2010) *The Communities of Machynlleth: Parallel Lives?* Undergraduate Dissertation (unpublished): School of Geography and Planning, Cardiff University. Available from Author.
Della Porta, D. and Diani, M. (2006) *Social Movements: An Introduction*. Oxford: Blackwell.
Grant, W. (2002) *Pressure Groups and British Politics*. London: Macmillan.
Halvorsen, S. (2015) 'Encountering occupy London: Boundary making and the territoriality of urban activism', *Environment and Planning D: Society and Space* 33(2), pp. 314–30.
Hermetic Library (1993) *Permanent TAZs*. Available at: http://hermetic.com/bey/paz.html. Accessed March 2015.
Horton, D. (2003) 'Green distinctions: The performance of identity among environmental activists', in Szersynski, B., Heim, W. and Waterton, C. (eds.) *Nature Performed: Environment, Culture and Performance*. Oxford: Blackwell, pp. 63–77.
Ibsen, H. (2013) 'Walk the talk for sustainable everyday life: Experiences from eco-village living in Sweden', in Soderholm, P. (ed.) *Environmental Policy and Household Behaviour: Sustainability and Everyday Life*. London: Routledge, pp. 129–47.
Jordan, T. (2002) *Activism! Direct Action, Hacktivism and the Future of Society*. London: Reaktion Books.
Maloney, W., Jordan, G. and McLaughlin, A. (1994) 'Interest groups and public policy: The insider/outsider model revisited', *Journal of Public Policy* 14(1), pp. 17–38.
May, T. and Nugent, T. (1982) 'Insiders, outsiders and thresholders: Corporatism and pressure group strategies in Britain', *Political Studies Association Conference*, University of Kent, April 1982.
Meijering, L., Huigen, P. and Van Hoven, B. (2007) 'Intentional communities in rural spaces', *Tijdshrift voor Economische en Sociale Geographie* 98(1), pp. 42–52.
Pepper, D. (2005) 'Utopianism and Environmentalism', *Environmental Politics* 14(1), pp. 3–22.

Prifysgol Abcrystwyth University (2023) *Prifysgol Aberystwyth University homepage*. Available at: https://www.aber.ac.uk/en/. Accessed June 2023.

Ruggiero, V. and Montagna, N. (2008) *Social Movements: A Reader*. London: Routledge.

Sargisson, L. (2007) 'Strange places: Estrangement, utopianism, and intentional communities', *Utopian Studies* 18(3), pp. 393–424.

Scott-Cato, K. and Hillier, J. (2011) 'How could we study climate related social innovation? Applying Deleuzean philosophy to transition towns', *Environmental Politics* 19(6), pp. 869–87.

Suvin, D. (1973) 'Defining the literary genre of Utopia: Some historical semantics, some geneology, a proposal, and a plea', *Studies in the Literary Imagination* 6(2), pp. 121–45.

Thrift, N. (2000) 'Entanglements of power: Shadows', in Sharp, J., Routledge, P., Philo, C. and Paddison, R. (eds.) *Entanglements of Power: Geographies of Domination/Resistance*. London: Routledge, pp. 269–78.

Xue, J. (2014) 'Is eco-village/urban village the future of a degrowth society? An urban planner's perspective', *Ecological Economics* 105(C), pp. 130–8.

Part Two

Negotiating questions of inclusion

Jenny Pickerill

Eco-communities require changes in social relations as much as material innovations to reduce their environmental impact and to navigate and sustain the often-radical changes in daily practices to achieve this. Yet *who* constitutes the 'social' – as in the demographic characteristics of eco-community residents – and the implications of these demographics, have only been superficially examined. While many eco-communities assert (in their own literatures, and in interviews) the vitalness of enabling participation of all, in practice eco-communities enact many forms of exclusion. As Lopez and Weaver (Chapter 10) demonstrate, eco-communities are less inclusive, affordable and diverse than their conventional neighbours.

While rarely overt, these exclusions diminish the likelihood of large-scale socio-ecological transformations not just in limiting who participates, but in how such transformations are designed, what issues are prioritized, and what envisioned outcomes look like. If these sought-after transformations are designed by and for white, able-bodied, highly educated people, then they are less likely to be relevant to those who do not fit these categories. Furthermore, any 'outcomes' will likely enhance the lives of this already-privileged cohort and generate inequalities in society. As Rice et al. (2022) argue processes of climate apartheid – where certain places benefit from improved ecological housing, green transport options and climate change resilience infrastructures, while other places do not – benefit the already wealthy and privileged and further marginalization and injustice elsewhere. There is already evidence (documented by Chitewere, 2017) that eco-communities such as Ecovillage at Ithaca, USA, have led to forms of green gentrification.

A key stumbling block for eco-communities in negotiating questions of inclusion is in how processes of participation have been conceived and understood. There are three tendencies here which the contributors in this section explore. First, eco-communities tend to privilege the importance of shared (inward-looking) collective identity over tackling social justice concerns. Living ecologically requires shared intent and the collective navigation of hardships, which is easier to achieve if residents share values and beliefs. This means that often environmental concerns are prioritized, and there is a subordination of social or environmental justice. Second, there is often a failure to challenge embedded assumptions of gender, class and racial difference. For example, notions of care remain gendered (with women assumed to be most competent). There is little engagement with intersectionalities, or in challenging the structural and systemic processes of patriarchalism, neoliberalism, racism, white supremacy or settler colonialism. This means that power inequities are rarely made visible, acknowledged or not challenged systemically. Third, any acknowledgement of the systemic inequalities of society is identified only in so far as to defend eco-communities' lack of engagement with questions of inclusion. Here eco-communities' progress is positioned as hindered by these broader structures, and eco-communities *as* progressive for being slightly-better-than conventional society, rather than as able to, or intended to, be spaces and places of deep societal change.

These tendencies need to be challenged in order to facilitate more impactful, wide-reaching and effective socio-ecological transformations. Authors suggest a range of interventions, including active alliances, assertive anti-racism, naming whiteness and decolonialization.

7

Towards inclusive eco-communities: Socially and environmentally just sustainable futures

Tendai Chitewere

Introduction

If eco-communities intend to be models for a sustainable way to live, they must become proactively inclusive of racially and ethnically diverse peoples and the causes that affect their everyday lives. By so doing, they can more convincingly illustrate their effort to address the interconnectedness of social and environmental ecosystems.

This chapter stems from two years of ethnographic research in Ecovillage at Ithaca (EVI), located in Upstate New York, USA. EVI is situated on Cayuga Lake, one of five Finger lakes carved by glaciers, and flanked by beautiful waterfalls, meadows and brilliantly coloured autumn leaves. A common bumper sticker reads 'Ithaca is Gorges'. Two prestigious private campuses, Cornell University and Ithaca College, sit across the hill from EVI. Ithaca is often listed among the top liberal cities to live because of its carsharing programmes (Stasko et al., 2013), community focus (Frantz 2021) and experiments with alternative currency – Ithaca Hours (Grover 2006; Jacob et al., 2004). The founders of EVI chose to settle here precisely because of the liberal and environmentally friendly atmosphere (Chitewere 2017).

I use the term 'eco-communities' loosely to include projects that are intentionally created to be community or cooperative-minded and ecologically conscientious in their daily interactions. Generally, eco-communities recognize that our everyday life is interconnected with the well-being of other species and that decisions we make in one area of life – vegetarianism or carsharing – can have a positive impact on the environmental protection of the other. Environmental justice activist Dana Alston's (1991) urging that we consider the environment where we work, live and play, is reflected in the ethos that environmentalism needs to be practical, holistic and inclusive. Yet eco-communities remain deficient in the kind of participatory diversity that would manifest the broad impacts of eco-communities models as exemplars of sustainable living.

Eco-communities and multi-racial environmental justice movements pursue common goals. Both share the search for clean air and water, space to grow food, access to safe jobs, schools and communities, and the ability to live healthy productive lives.

Eco-communities and environmental justice activists together *could* make a powerful force for lasting structural change. In collaboration, these groups would not only carry significant political power addressing past environmental degradation, but model the kind of holistic social and ecological transformation needed to create a sustainable future.

The Foundation for Intentional Community (FIC), a central clearing house for intentional communities, acknowledges both their goals and shortcomings. It is important and fair that the statement (below) of good intentions that followed the George Floyd murder by police (Taylor 2020) not become another unimplemented pious statement of platitudes. The moment provides the impetus to discuss what went wrong and what we can do about it.

> Social justice is one of FIC's core values, yet, admittedly, we could have done more sooner and can do more now to help transform systems of oppression.
>
> We acknowledge that the majority of intentional communities in our network are predominately white, with significant cultural, financial and other barriers existing that make it difficult for people of color to start and/or join intentional communities. It is our responsibility to build a more aware and inclusive organization, as well as aid the communities in our network in addressing issues of racism and oppression.
>
> We recognize we have a long way to go in these endeavors. Unlearning and dismantling white supremacism and privilege is a continuous practice. We are committed to the long journey of creating a more just world for all.
>
> (FIC Staff and Board of Directors, 2020)

Indeed, there is much work to be done and we need everyone's help to heal and reimagine a social and environmentally sustainable society. Unfortunately, Black, Indigenous, People of Colour remain marginalized or invisible in some mainstream environmental efforts. Divisions that created the racially separate suffrage movement, environmental movement, climate change movement and eco-communities movement remain stubbornly segregated by race and ethnicity. This separation is reflected in a long history of formal (de jure) and informal (de facto) segregation patterns that replicate the racially stratified society we live in today. Segregation creates deep problems that do not simply end on their own, rather they become 'natural' and 'expected' so that we no longer recognize them (that's just the way it has always been). The hesitancy of eco-communities to embrace the experiences of Black and other people of colour has hurt both efforts, producing two parallel movements that at best duplicate energies, and at worse, benefit one at the cost of the other. These movements cannot succeed separately. Racial and economic injustice contributes significantly to social and environmental degradation and instability, consequently need to be understood and addressed.

The realization that anti-Blackness and systemic racism are a hindrance for a sustainable future makes it clear that if they are to contribute to the sustainable future, eco-communities need to proactively consider how their efforts may contribute to perpetuating white supremacy and segregation, and actively work to change this (Ross 2020). Given the commitment of eco-community participants to critically thinking about their everyday life: social structures of sharing, shared governance, etc., and the growing numbers of people who are looking to join or contribute to these projects, I believe eco-communities can rise to the challenge of contributing to social and ecological justice through becoming more inclusive.

Ecological intentional communities

Eco-communities are part of a long history of intentional alternatives to mainstream social, economic and environmental housing trends in the Global North. Responding to overwhelming social and ecological degradation, eco-communities have identified themselves as social experiments for what is possible. However, 'they remain incomplete, partial, and sometimes problematic' (Pickerill 2015, 32). Through their commitment to change, they identify challenges to overcome and the structural changes necessary to effect change. For example, well-intentioned efforts to model cooperative living, address environmental degradation, and be inclusive of Black, Indigenous People of Colour (BIPOC), were hampered by individual and societal forces that reinforce housing segregation even when the opposite was sought (Trounstine 2018). While some EVI residents wanted to live in a diverse community, they had ironically moved away from diverse communities in order to join EVI (Chitewere 2017). Critical examination of eco-communities might reveal ways to overcome the deep structural inequalities that prevent all people from experiencing a way of life that is sustainable. Change is needed not only on the individual and communal level, but on the city, state and federal levels of government. We cannot wait for eco-communities to get it right before scaling up – climate justice action is urgent.

It complicates their mission that eco-communities exist within a time and place that contain and use the infrastructure of white supremacy. Specifically, the history of colonialism, slavery, genocide and segregation is a significant part of the landscape of communities (Florida and Mellander 2015; Glotzer 2020; Paisley 2003; Samkange 1967). The present is intimately connected to the past and is visible in the ways our communities and environments have been shaped (Kovács, and Hegedűs 2014; Massey and Denton 1993; Rothstein 2017). Our everyday lives are mediated through a cultural lens that has built, supported and maintained white supremacy. This legacy is toxic to our collective effort to create a sustainable future, maintains collective social and ecological suffering, and requires hard work to end. The cost of white supremacy is not just the loss of valuable lives, environmental destruction and meaningful contributions, but inhibits our ability to solve our most pressing problems. Additionally, desires for social and environmental sustainability that includes clean air and water, healthy food and meaningful work are universal regardless of race or class. Racial and ethnic diversity provides rich knowledge, deep experience and creative ideas to solve these complex social and ecological problems.

If eco-communities argue that a different way to live is necessary, BIPOC have generations of experience that illustrates this very point. Racial discrimination, segregation and marginalization have relegated BIPOC to some of the most marginal and toxic environments around the world (Alexander 2010; Feagin 2013; Silver and Danielowski 2019; Taylor 2014) and that knowledge matters. For example, an environmental justice perspective on organic food consumption reminds us that farm worker health and wellbeing are equally important. Environmental justice broadens and deepens our ability to make authentic progress towards sustainability (Taylor 2000). Environmental justice activists and scholars have for decades engaged in public protests demanding the clean-up of hazardous waste in neighbourhoods and schools, improvements to health (Wilson et al., 2020), access to clean water (Campbell et al., 2016), an end to corporate pollution, access to green space and parks (Flores et al., 2018), equal opportunity in education, employment and housing, protections from gentrification in communities, and an appreciation for sustaining community (Agyeman and Evans 2004; Chitewere et al., 2017).

Eco-communities and environmental justice

As highlighted in several chapters in this volume, eco-communities have produced an important body of knowledge, such as the potential to challenge lifestyles in the Global North, modelling reduced energy consumption, increased value of sharing (Mychajluk 2017), local food production and consumption, and experimenting with innovative green building (Moos et al., 2006). By presenting these projects as models for sustainable living and examples of transformed social and ecological value, eco-communities are presented as ideal responses to: social and environmental degradation, a climate crisis that threatens to wreak havoc across the globe, and as important projects to help guide us to a better, sustainable way of life than we have now.

Lamentably, many findings have been uncritically positive, avoiding uncomfortable realities and missing an opportunity to problem solve (Andreas 2013; Chitewere 2017; Litfin 2014; Walker 2005). One explanation is that eco-communities are often considered separate from environmental justice efforts, or outside the scope of what is possible. For example, very little public discussion has considered that eco-communities are overwhelmingly white and upper middle class. During two years of living and studying EVI, residents often expressed genuine concern that they were unintentionally exclusionary but struggled to find a solution (Chitewere 2010). The *Communities Magazine* issue on *Class, Race, and Privilege* (2018) has been one of its most popular and is one of the few available for free. The need for more research that addresses critical questions around systemic racism, structural inequality and environmental injustice is urgent because understanding the problem allows us to get closer to a solution.

The intense energy needed for inward-facing practices of creating and maintaining a smaller version of the outside society means eco-communities remove themselves from the work of creating sustainability in a diverse and complex world. This presents a challenge for the movement because it is not possible to separate where and how we live from race and racism. Environmental justice activists and scholars have argued for decades that the two are not separate, and that in order to solve our ecological crisis, we need to confront the crisis of racism. By not engaging in dialogues about anti-Blackness, racism, inclusion, sustainability and justice, eco-communities miss the opportunity to understand and participate in conversations aimed at establishing lasting change. If eco-communities want to have an impact they must embrace social and ecological justice movements. This is not a new call. In the first article, in the first issue of *Communities Magazine* in 1972, Chris Elms warned of this dilemma.

> While the white stockbroker is too busy hustling his money to take time out to move against the war, the white communard is too busy working his garden. While gardening is certainly more laudible than money grubbing, what bugs me is the common element: both are white (and not lower class, either) and both are too busy with their own thing to come to the aid of less privileged non-whites (or poorer whites).
>
> (Elms 1972, 4)

Without inclusive engagement, eco-communities not only fail to meet their own internal goals of sustainable living, but also fail in their efforts to model how to live sustainably. Although scholars have attempted to point out the need for sustainable community efforts to be inclusive of social justice (Agyeman et al., 2016; Chitewere 2010), these efforts continue to be marginal to the mounting praise for eco-communities.

Scholars of colour have often been marginalized when they raise the concern of social and environmental injustice. The result has been the continuation of two parallel movements that are often segregated along racial lines – an environmental movement that is predominantly white and an environmental justice movement that is predominately BIPOC. Eco-communities have the opportunity to engage in deep, difficult conversation about what it means to create a sustainable way to live with a diverse population marginalized by white supremacy. Environmentalists of colour recognize that a commitment to the environment is not simply about solving problems in one's backyard. Without becoming inclusive, eco-communities risk repeating the mistakes of past segregation, consciously or unconsciously, creating a form of white flight – *green flight*. Or perhaps more importantly, focusing so much on their own community that environmentalism becomes *only in my backyard*, rather than contributing to building the kind of sustainable community we all seek.

Racism, housing, and sustaining segregated community

Twenty years ago, Massey and Denton noted:

> Most Americans vaguely realize that urban America is still a residentially segregated society, but few appreciate the depth of Black segregation or the degree to which it is maintained by ongoing institutional arrangements and contemporary individual actions.
>
> (Massey and Denton 2019, 1)

A brief history of housing in the United States highlights the need for eco-communities to pursue inclusive housing. The argument that eco-communities are meant to model a sustainable way to live, not address racial inequality is common. However, for BIPOC, housing and the environment are intricately linked to structural racism (Feagin 2013; Gregory 1999; Massey and Denton 1993). Given the long history of colonialism and slavery, it is an expression of white privilege to ignore this reality. It would also be a missed opportunity for eco-communities to contribute to solving important problems. In this section, I argue that structural racism manifests itself in formal and informal exclusionary housing practices (Ratcliffe 2002). The United States is not alone in the violent appropriation of Indigenous people's lands by white settlers or the enslavement of peoples of African descent, processes that produced disconnected families and communities, and environmental injustices (Osidipe 2011; Reeve and Robinson 2007). Any attempt to model a way to live sustainably in the future needs to acknowledge this past.

Feagin's (1999) works on systemic white racism argue that 'contemporary housing discrimination and residential segregation are the modern descendants of Monticello's Spartan slave quarters' perpetuating anti-Black racism and discrimination, that 'from the time of slavery, race came to be associated with place, and place came to signal race. This was true on plantations and in all cities and states, where there have always been places of racial inclusion and exclusion' (85). The practice is deeply engrained in our culture such that although surveys by the Pew Research Foundation found racially diverse communities are increasingly desirable (Taylor et al., 2008), we continue to see an increase in racial segregation across rural and small towns in the United States. An apartheid system began in the 1896 Supreme Court case of Plessy v. Ferguson. The Court ruled that the treatment of Plessy, a Black passenger who sat down in a 'whites only' section of a public train and was arrested, did not violate the 13th amendment to the US constitution that barred slavery, or the 14th Amendment granting equal protection to African Americans. The court argued the 14th Amendment was meant to provide *legal equality* but not *social equality*. This support for white supremacy invokes historic images of 'white only' drinking fountains, but continues today in more subtle forms of being excluded such as experiences of microaggressions, gaslighting or denied sense of belonging (Lewis et al., 2021; Orfield 2004).

The Supreme Court overturned Plessy v. Ferguson in the 1954 Brown v. The Board of Education decision, concluding that schools that separated whites from African Americans were inherently unequal. While the decision ended some forms of race-based discrimination in public education, and some amenities, housing continued exclusionary practices and high levels of racial segregation (Feagin 1999). Many of those practices have endured through urban renewal (Webster et al., 2002), or where Black parents are less likely to be told of gifted programmes for their child when considering schools with large white populations. Spatial segregation creates situations where whites have very little interaction with BIPOC; 'Since most Whites reside in highly segregated neighborhoods, their understanding of Americans of color and, thus, of critical racial issues is often severely limited' (Feagin 1999, 85). Without interactions with people of colour, 'most whites must rely heavily on the mass media to provide the main window through which they presume to see the Black world' (85). Specifically, Feagin argues that while Blacks experience interactions with whites through jobs, grocery stores and in education, whites have significantly less experience interacting with Blacks. This lack of experience and empathy makes it difficult to argue the case for inclusion because defensiveness and white fragility (DiAngelo 2018; Lodge

2016) override the reality that a large population is excluded from the conversation. Moreover, this pattern has been repeating itself for generations. The murder of Trayvon Martin, a young unarmed African American who was visiting his relatives in their gated community, illustrates that gated communities may not offer the same sense of security suggested by many of their proponents (Gooblar 2002).

In the Color of Law, Rothstein (2017) describes de facto (held by fact, but not a legal right) segregation as subtle and pervasive because it occupies the silent, but widely understood practice of exclusion. De facto segregation happens through unspoken cultural understandings and expectations such as white families living in separate communities or moving away from a neighbourhood when the Black population increases. Societal and individual practices maintain and normalize this segregation. Thus, the US Fair Housing Act (1968) did not suddenly reverse the desire for whites to live separately from people of colour. More subtle means had been quickly adopted after the Second World War and the 1954 Supreme Court decision. While de jure (held by a legal right) segregation was expressed in the form of Jim Crow and Sundown laws, de facto included white flight that pulled families, businesses, tax bases and investments out of the city and into suburbs leaving urban centres to deteriorate economically and later socially. These practices, often with government incentives, created urban ghettos that contained people who had limited resources to leave and even fewer ways to survive within them.

The rise of privately governed residential spaces became widespread in and outside of the United States (Blakely and Snyder 1997; Kovács and Hegedűs 2014; Webster et al., 2002) along with the debate on whether gated communities were exclusionary or positively contributed to creating a sense of community for those within them (Sakip et al., 2012). As people of colour moved into the suburbs, whites sought ways to further separate themselves. The privatization of public spaces is a central feature of these fortified enclaves (Caldeira 2000), but such spatial distinction is not limited to stone walls and iron gates. Promoted as green amenities in the city, privately owned publicly open spaces reinforce de facto segregation because these public urban parks are located in spaces that are white (Reeves et al., 2020; Schindler 2017). Therefore, while eco-communities are not engaged in de jure segregation, they are almost inevitably examples of de facto segregation. The design, structure and lack of diversity may communicate that people of colour do not belong. That the priorities of eco-communities are different from the social and environmental problems BIPOC face and are therefore outside of the white view is an example. De facto segregation suggests that when these grievances are raised they would be unfairly arbitrated. In Europe, the people who self-report experiences of housing discrimination rarely file complaints because they do not believe anything will be done, and instead fear retaliation (Silver and Danielowski 2019). European nations have only recently adopted a Racial Equity Directive to actively monitor and combat racial discrimination (Silver and Danielowski 2019). But one of the problems in Europe is the lack of evidence of racial or ethnic discrimination because of resistance to collecting racial data, leaving concerns of structural racism unexamined (Chopin et al., 2014).

Research is needed to provide a critical analysis of eco-communities. Such research could provide insight into how to become inclusive and have a greater impact. We know that environmental justice concerns are not different from the concerns of eco-communities (Chitewere and Taylor 2010). Critical research could shed light on the mechanisms that kept environmental justice at the margins of eco-communities. Such research offers an opportunity for eco-communities to join the robust environmental justice discussions on racial inclusion in sustaining all our future.

Towards inclusive eco-communities

Eco-community residents have, in spite of many oversights, created a unique opportunity to effect change, potentially on a large scale; and the road to an inclusive eco-community movement could be transforming. Through commitment and hard work, these communities could model a way of life that avoids and mitigates the mistakes of the past and present. Eco-communities are physically and socially constructed to do just this; it is this promise that first interested me (and the people I speak with in ecovillages) in studying ecovillages as solutions to structural social and environmental problems. From their origins, eco-communities boldly propose an alternative to the cultures and institutions that have contributed to social and ecological degradation. Countless studies illustrate that eco-communities are willing to call out ecological waste, sacrifice comfort for a sustainable future and take on uncomfortable challenges. While individual communities are engaged in decision-making at the neighbourhood level, local, national, and global levels, participants in eco-communities recognize that our ecosystems are interconnected and interdependent. What better place to start than the realization that our lives cannot be separated from the local and historical context that shaped them?

The following nine suggestions offer a starting place to **AIM HIGHER** by addressing structural inequality and system racism, and strive for inclusivity in eco-communities.

1. Active Alliances and Listening. Before eco-communities can teach and model sustainability, they can learn from others. The concerns of eco-communities are frequently the same as environmental justice activists. Since eco-communities have tended to emphasize or embrace separateness, a good place to start is to work to make active alliances with inclusive organizations. Solidarity and strength can be built through alignments with the work environmental justice organizations have been doing for a long time. Similarly, a lot can be learned by listening to people with different cultural experiences and scholars of colour. Reconsider how we define expertise, especially as it relates to housing, the community and the environment.

2. Inward Avoidance. Eco-communities must abjure the practice of focusing inward. As argued elsewhere, the work within eco-communities can be all-consuming, leaving participants with little energy to engage in struggles outside their neighbourhood. Eco-communities would benefit if they recognize themselves as inseparable from the ongoing struggles for social and ecological justice that confront structural and systemic inequality. Negotiating inclusion is to develop relationships with social and environmental justice groups within the larger society in order to build solidarity, broaden the understanding of the problems communities face, and participate in mutual causes while avoiding replicating efforts, or worse, competing against each other.

3. Make the Political Personal. Participate in the decision-making process in the larger society. Supporting elected officials and board members who represent the voices of those often ignored. Proactively advocate and support the inclusion of diverse participants in conversation and planning. Elect candidates who fight for social justice. As gentrification continues to displace people of colour and low-income households, work with these groups to support sustainable housing for everyone. De jure and de facto segregation has made it easy for eco-communities to create their own healthful spaces to live. This knowledge can be used to intentionally erode structures of segregation and build alliances with marginalized groups. Sometimes to take a step forward, a step back to reflect is useful.

4. Hire Broadly. Economic justice is equally needed for a sustainable future, and eco-communities can use their resources to support these efforts. Specifically, eco-communities should align themselves with the struggles for environmental justice that take a holistic approach to understanding the relationship between employment opportunities, living conditions and the environment. Act by including people of colour when hiring architects, planners, facilitators and lawyers. By working against pesticides, we protect farm workers who are often people of colour, from toxic pollution. We need to support existing groups and their causes, because their causes are our causes.

5. Investigate and Integrate. Eco-communities identify as experimental. Thus they would benefit from self-reflection, forthcoming about what works and what does not, and sharing how they adjust. Scholars could be helpful by providing critical feedback. Applications of scientific research could help ensure replicable models through documenting processes, testing hypotheses, collecting data, sharing findings and adjusting failures. For example, little is known about how long residents live in a community, why they leave, etc. Embrace of critique and meaningful debates can be tools for progress and evolution.

6. Greater Circle of Social Relationships. As articulated by the FIC, it is high time eco-communities 'help to transform systems of oppression'. A good place to start is where we live. We must strive for a lifestyle that embraces diversity at the individual and community levels. Expanding our circle of acquaintances will increase our empathy for the struggles of others. Friendships outside our familiar circles introduce us to different experiences and perspectives. Briggs (2007) shows interracial friendships act as bridges to increase access to information and reduce inequalities. Create community where you live. Karen Kerney's (1998) artwork on 'how to build community' is inspiring. Meet your neighbours and get to know the people in your community and advocate for social and ecological change.

7. Help to Heal. The world needs help to solve its most pressing problems, but we also need to help heal the pain of injustice. We all need to commit to pro-active inclusion, combatting anti-Blackness, becoming anti-racist and advocating for social justice if we care about a sustainable future. Incorporating reading groups, implicit bias training, etc. alongside consensus building will prepare all of us to understand how exclusion hurts our shared cause. Several scholars have written extensively on white privilege (Pulido 2017), not belonging (Ahmed 2012), castes (Wilkerson 2020) and structural racism (Feagin 2013), and de facto segregation (Rothstein 2017). A myriad of organizations, classes, businesses and individuals are working on racial, social and environmental justice. Let us argue for sustainable housing to be recognized as a basic human right, then act to make that a reality.

8. Environment Broadly Defined allows us to recognize the interconnectedness between the physical world around us and the social interactions that moderate that world. The ripples that eco-communities create sometimes bump against difficult realities. We are stronger when we collectively confront those challenges, whether they be critiques of green consumerism or fighting the closure of a local free clinic, with the aim of making life better for everyone.

9. **Racism Matters.** Recognize and respond to racism in our everyday life and in the institutions and structures that perpetuate it. The reality of our world is that historical injustices are carried forward and while we might not have had a direct hand in the origins of systemic racism, its persistence hurts us all. Models of sustainable ways to live benefit from acknowledging and in their own way, committing and contributing to ending racism.

Conclusion

Imagine the features we cherish about eco-communities expanded on a large scale so everyone, regardless of race or class, can live in a way that is good for the community and the environment. By focusing outward, on being members of the greater public, we can collectively strengthen the democratic systems already in place. By joining environmental justice struggles, we maximize the voices demanding change, reduce redundancies of time and energy, and build social cohesion. Winning the fights to stop pollution in environmental justice communities improves the quality of life for everyone. People who join eco-communities are not afraid to explore new challenges or invest their time to experimenting with creating change. Eco-community participants understand nonviolent communication, practise active listening and consensus building, and care about the future of the ecosystem, not just our place in it. Through critical research, listening and learning from people of colour, and engaging with social and environmental justice groups, eco-communities can make valuable contributions to modelling a way to live in an uncertain future.

References

Agyeman, J. and Evans, B. (2004) '"Just sustainability": The emerging discourse of environmental justice in Britain?', *Geographical Journal* 170(2), pp. 155–64.

Agyeman, J., Schlosberg, D., Craven, L., and Matthews, C. (2016) 'Trends and Directions in environmental justice: from Inequity to Everyday Life, Community, and Just Sustainabilities', *Annual Review of Environment and Resources* 41(1), 321–40.

Ahmed, S. (2012) *On Being Included*. Chapel Hill, NC: Duke University Press.

Alexander, M. (2010) *The New Jim Crow: Mass Incarceration in the Age of Colorblindness*. New York: New York Press.

Alston, D. (1991) 'The summit: Transforming a movement', *Race, Poverty and the Environment* 2(3/4), pp. 1–29.

Andreas, M. (2013) 'Must Utopia be an island? Positioning an ecovillage within its region', *Social Sciences Directory* 2(4), pp. 9–18.

Blakely, E.J. and Snyder, M.G. (1997) *Fortress America: Gated Communities in the United States*. Washington, DC: Brookings Institution Press.

Caldeira, T.P. (2000) *City of Walls: Crime, Segregation, and Citizenship in São Paulo*. Berkeley, CA: University of California Press.

Campbell, C., Greenberg, R., Mankikar, D. and Ross, R.D. (2016) 'A case study of environmental injustice: The failure in Flint', *International Journal of Environmental Research and Public Health* 13(10), p. 951.

Chitewere, T. (2010) 'Equity in sustainable communities: Exploring tools for environmental justice and political ecology', *Natural Resources Journal* 50, p. 315.

Chitewere, T. and Taylor, D.E. (2010). 'Sustainable living and community building in Ecovillage at Ithaca: The challenges of incorporating social justice concerns into the practices of an ecological cohousing community', in Taylor, D.E. (ed.) *Environment and Social Justice: An International Perspective* (Vol. 18). Leeds: Emerald Group Publishing Limited, pp. 141–76.

Chitewere, T. (2017) *Sustainable Communities and Green Lifestyles: Consumption and Environmentalism*. Abingdon-on-Thames: Routledge.

Chitewere, T., Shim, J.K., Barker, J.C. and Yen, I.H. (2017) 'How neighborhoods influence health: Lessons to be learned from the application of political ecology', *Health & place* 45(May), pp. 117–23.

Communities Magazine (2018) 'Class, Race, and Privilege', *Communities* 178 (Spring), pp. 1–65.

De Genova, N. (2018) 'The "migrant crisis" as racial crisis: Do Black Lives Matter in Europe?', *Ethnic and racial studies* 41(10), pp. 1765–82.

de Souza Briggs, X. (2007) '"Some of my best friends are … ": Interracial friendships, class, and segregation in America', *City and Community* 6(4), pp. 263–90.

DiAngelo, R. (2018) *White Fragility: Why It's so Hard for White People to Talk about Racism*. Beacon Press.

Douglas, S. and Massey, D. (1993) *American Apartheid: Segregation and the Making of the Underclass*. Cambridge, MA: Harvard University Press.

Elms, C. (1972) *Communities Magazine* (1). Fellowship for Intentional Communities.

Feagin, J. (2013) *Systemic Racism: A Theory of Oppression*. Abingdon-on-Thames: Routledge.

Feagin, J.R. (1999) 'Excluding blacks and others from housing: The foundation of white racism', *Cityscape* 3(4), pp. 79–91.

Flores, D., Falco, G., Roberts, N.S. and Valenzuela III, F.P. (2018) Recreation equity: Is the Forest Service serving its diverse publics?', *Journal of Forestry* 116(3), 266–72.

Florida, R. and Mellander, C. (2015) *Segregated City: The Geography of Economic Segregation in America's Metros*. Martin Prosperity Institute.

Frantz, G.R. (2021) 'The progressive city in the neighborhood context', in Bryson, J.R., Kalafsky, R. and Vanchan, V. (eds.) *Ordinary Cities, Extraordinary Geographies*. Cheltenham: Edward Elgar Publishing, pp. 23–43.

Germaine, C., Chopin, I. and Farkas, L. (2014) *Ethnic Origin and Disability Data Collection in Europe: Measuring Inequality-Combating Discrimination*. Boston, MA: Policy Commons.

Glotzer, P. (2020) *How the Suburbs Were Segregated: Developers and the Business of Exclusionary Housing, 1890–1960*. New York: Columbia University Press.

Gooblar, A. (2002) 'Outside the walls: Urban gated communities and their regulation within the British planning system', *European Planning Studies* 10(3), pp. 321–34.

Gregory, S. (1999) *Black Corona: Race and the Politics of Place in an Urban Community*. Princeton, NJ: Princeton University Press.

Grover, D. (2006) 'Would local currencies make a good local economic development policy tool? The case of Ithaca Hours', *Environment and Planning C: Government and Policy* 24(5), pp. 719–37.

Jacob, J., Brinkerhoff, M., Jovic, E. and Wheatley, G. (2004) 'HOUR town: Paul Glover and the genesis and evolution of Ithaca HOURS', *International Journal of Community Currency Research*, 8, pp. 29–41.

Kerney, K. (1998) How to Build Community Text: Members SCW Community Artist: Karen Kerney, watercolor. SCW©. https://www.syracuseculturalworkers.com/products/notecard-how-to-build-community.

Kovács, Z. and Hegedűs, G. (2014) 'Gated communities as new forms of segregation in post-socialist Budapest', *Cities* 36(February), pp. 200–9.

Lewis, J.A., Mendenhall, R., Ojiemwen, A., Thomas, M., Riopelle, C., Harwood, S.A. and Browne Huntt, M. (2021) 'Racial microaggressions and sense of belonging at a historically white university', *American Behavioral Scientist* 65(8), pp. 1049–71.

Litfin, K.T. (2014) *Ecovillages: Lessons for Sustainable Community*. John Wiley and Sons.

Lodge, R. E. (2016). *Why I Am No Longer Talking to White People about Race*. London: Bloomsbury Circus.

Massey, D. S., and Denton, N. A. (2019) 'American Apartheid: Segregation and the Making of the Underclass', in Grusky, D. (ed.) *Social Stratification, Class, Race, and Gender in Sociological Perspective*, Second Edition. New York: Routledge, pp. 660–70.

Md Sakip, S.R., Johari, N. and Mohd Salleh, M.N. (2018) 'Sense of community in gated and non-gated residential', *Asian Journal of Environment-Behaviour Studies* 3(9), June, pp. 151–9.

Moos, M., Whitfield, J., Johnson, L.C. and Andrey, J. (2006) 'Does design matter? The ecological footprint as a planning tool at the local level', *Journal of Urban Design* 11(2), pp. 195–224.

Mychajluk, L. (2017) 'Learning to live and work together in an ecovillage community of practice', *European Journal for Research on the Education and Learning of Adults* 8(2), pp. 179–94.

Orfield, G. (2004) 'Why segregation is inherently unequal: The abandonment of Brown and the continuing failure of Plessy', *New York Law School Law Review* 49(4), p. 1041.

Osidipe, O. (2011) *Race and Disorder: Addressing Social Disadvantages through State Regeneration in a Multi-Ethnic Community in Leeds*. University of Northumbria at Newcastle (United Kingdom).

Paisley, F. (2003) 'Introduction: White settler colonialisms and the colonial turn: An Australian perspective', *Journal of Colonialism and Colonial History* 4(3), https://muse.jhu.edu/pub/1/article/50782.

Pickerill, J. (2015) 'Building the commons in eco-communities', in Kirwan, S., Dawney, L. and Brigstocke, J. (eds.) *Space, Power and the Commons*. Abingdon-on-Thames: Routledge, pp. 43–66.

Pickerill, J. (2017) 'Critically interrogating eco-homes', *International Journal of Urban and Regional Research* 41(2), pp. 353–65.

Pulido, L. (2017) 'Rethinking environmental racism: White privilege and urban development in Southern California', in Anderson, K. and Braun, B. (eds.) *Environment*. London: Routledge, pp. 379–407.

Ratcliffe, P. (2002) 'Theorising ethnic and "racial" exclusion in housing', in Somerville, P. and Steele, A. (eds.) *'Race,' Housing and Social Exclusion*. London: Jessica Kingsley Publishers, pp. 22–39.

Reeves, B., Keeling, B., Pilaar, D. and Kuchar, S. (2020) 'The best privately owned public open spaces in SF', Curbed (website). Available at: https://sf.curbed.com/maps/sf-parks-private-popos-public-owned-spaces-downtown. Accessed 19 February 2020.

Reeve, K. and Robinson, D. (2007) 'Beyond the multi-ethnic metropolis: Minority ethnic housing experiences in small town England', *Housing studies* 22(4), pp. 547–71.

Rothstein, R. (2017) *The Color of Law: A Forgotten History of How Our Government Segregated America*. New York: Liveright Publishing.

Ross, K.M. (2020) 'Call it what it is: Anti-blackness', *The New York Times*, 4 June. Available at: https://www.nytimes.com/2020/06/04/opinion/george-floyd-anti-blackness.html.

Samkange, S.J.T. (1967) *On trial for my country* (No. 33). Portsmouth, NH: Heinemann.

Schindler, S. (2017) 'The Publicization of Private Space', *Iowa Law Review* 103, pp. 1079–153.

Silver, H. and Danielowski, L. (2019) 'Fighting housing discrimination in Europe', *Housing Policy Debate* 29(5), pp. 714–35.

Stasko, T.H., Buck, A.B. and Gao, H.O. (2013) 'Carsharing in a university setting: Impacts on vehicle ownership, parking demand, and mobility in Ithaca, NY', *Transport Policy* 30(C), pp. 262–8.

Taylor, D.E. (2000) 'The rise of the environmental justice paradigm: Injustice framing and the social construction of environmental discourses', *American Behavioral Scientist* 43(4), pp. 508–80.

Taylor, D. (2014) *Toxic Communities: Environmental Racism, Industrial Pollution, and Residential Mobility*. New York: New York University Press. DOI: 10.18574/nyu/9781479805150.001.0001

Taylor, P., Morin, R., Cohn, D. and Wang, W. (2008) *Americans say they like diverse communities: Election, Census trends suggest otherwise*. Washington, DC: Pew Research Center. Available at: https://www.pewresearch.org/social-trends/2008/12/02/americans-say-they-like-diverse-communities-election-census-trends-suggest-otherwise/.

Taylor, D.B. (2020) 'George Floyd protests: A timeline', *The New York Times*, 5 November. Available at: https://www.nytimes.com/article/george-floyd-protests-timeline.html.

Trounstine, J. (2018) *Segregation by Design: Local Politics and Inequality in American Cities*. Cambridge: Cambridge University Press.

Walker, L. (2005) *Ecovillage at Ithaca: Pioneering a Sustainable Culture*. Gabriola Island: New Society Publishers.

Webster, C., Glasze, G. and Frantz, K. (2002) 'The global spread of gated communities', *Environment and Planning B: Planning and Design* 29(3), pp. 315–20.

Wilkerson, I. (2020). *Caste: The Origins of our Discontents*. New York: Random House.

Wilson, S., Bullard, R., Patterson, J. and Thomas, S.B. (2020) 'Roundtable on the Pandemics of Racism, Environmental Injustice, and COVID-19 in America', *Environmental Justice*. 13(3), pp. 56–64.

8

Settling in colonial ways? Eco-communities' uncomfortable settler colonial practices

Adam Barker and Jenny Pickerill

What does it mean to be ethical in relation to the land as part of an eco-community? Eco-communities are often premised on the need to materially confront the environmental degradation caused by late-stage industrial capitalism, and in this, eco-communities have a claim to a particular ethical foundation. However, there are forms of oppression and hierarchy that, while entangled with the systems to which eco-communities are often opposed, also need distinct recognition and negotiation. If those building eco-communities are not aware and careful they can reinforce processes of settler colonial dispossession. In this chapter we outline briefly what settler colonialism is, why it is relevant to eco-communities, and how eco-communities can include settler colonial analyses and critiques in their planning and practices.

What is settler colonialism?

Settler colonialism, as described by a growing body of literature that grew out of Indigenous Studies, is a colonial formation with global implications. As historiographer Lorenzo Veracini outlines (2014), settler colonialism is a 'distinct' formation from 'colonialism' as it is commonly defined (and which has also been called, for example 'metropole colonialism' or 'extractive colonialism'; see Barker 2021), meaning the overseas control of territory and resource extraction by imperial powers. Settler colonialism is the permanent settlement and replacement of what existed there before.

Settler colonies almost always start as the project of larger empires, but become self-perpetuating and self-determining over time as colonial settlement becomes entrenched and reproduced. Common examples of contemporary states that were founded on colonization and continue to operate according to settler colonial logics include Canada, the United States and Australia. The Scandinavian states of Sweden, Norway and Finland, along with Russia, all claim parts of Sapmi, the Sami homeland, due to settler colonization that began before the creation of those modern states and continues to shape state-Sami policy. Increasingly, Latin American states are also being understood as being at least partially constituted by settler colonization, albeit obscured by complex dynamics around race and class (Castellanos 2017; Taylor & Lublin 2021).

All of these states were exempted from – in many ways benefitted – the post-Second World War decolonization of European empires. The 'salt water thesis' (also called the blue water thesis) held that colonies were only considered as colonized if they were separated from the homeland by a sea or ocean. As such, decolonization was not applied to many nations, including – for example – the Haida of the Pacific northwest (now Canada). The Haida homeland, Haida Gwaii was annexed by the British in 1853, merged into the Colony of British Columbia in the 1860s, and in 1871 merged into the Dominion of Canada as British Columbia became the sixth province in the state. The Haida never consented to these transfers of territory or to the violence and discrimination that followed, nor were these territorial transfers within the British Empire ever conducted with the expectation that the Haida would survive in the contemporary world. Haida Gwaii was treated as terra nullius – empty land, open to claim and settlement – despite the real and continued opposition of the Haida.

Yet when the British Empire, along with the other European powers following the Second World War, began 'decolonizing' or handing over local control to colonies in Africa (an entirely separate and fraught process), Canada and the Haida were no longer considered colonies because, like Australia, they had been so effectively settled (both physically and metaphorically). It is not surprising, then, that many of the most powerful contemporary states include those that were built on and continue to benefit from settler colonialism. Haida Gwaii is an important example here because it is the exact sort of 'out of the way', 'wilderness' and rural location that are so often chosen for eco-communities. Yet violet processes of land dispossession and settler colonialism are not always immediately visible to the untrained eye.

In the words of Veracini, we now live in a 'settler colonial present' in which settler colonization plays a key and often unrecognized role in shaping cultures and political economies globally (2015). Settler colonization results in particular and distinct effects, even when deployed simultaneously alongside other colonial strategies by the same imperial power. Most importantly, settler colonization results in the creation of new settler societies, with distinct relationships to the land and ambitions for social development and personal gain. While there is no single form that a settler society takes, they are commonly defined as a form of place-based colonialism in which extraction from the lands benefits settlers (rather than Indigenous occupants) on the land, rather than being simply removed for the profits of a distant metropole.[1]

Settler colonization is the driving force behind the development of new settler societies and polities which displace Indigenous peoples from their lands. Several key aspects of settler colonialism are common across its many specific instances and warrant specific mention here. First, settler colonization 'destroys to replace' (Wolfe 2006) – as a form of conquest settler colonialism does not seek primarily to invade and subjugate, but rather to physically, conceptually and legally replace one population

---

[1] Much of the theory of settler colonialism has been developed since Patrick Wolfe's first book on the subject was published in 1999. The theoretical field of settler colonialism is now very large and expanding, so this section is a necessarily brief and partial sketch. The works referenced in this chapter by Wolfe, Veracini, Tuck and Yang, Moreton-Robinson and Barker are all recommended for further background reading.

with another. This brings us to the second point, which is that 'the settler comes to stay' (Veracini 2010) – differentiated from both colonial agents who intend ultimately to return to their imperial core, and from migrants who intend to continue moving and/or returning to another home, settlers are motivated by an 'animus manendi', or 'intent to stay' and make a life in the place they colonize. Third and crucially, when settlers to these lands locate a place to settle and call home, they do not join Indigenous political regimes or remain dependent on the original homeland, but rather 'carry their sovereignty with them', either founding new settler communities or investing in existing and expanding settler communities with which they have a connection (Barker 2021; Veracini 2011). Finally, settler colonialism often operates to strengthen and entrench white supremacy, building on the deeply racialized approaches of colonialism *per se* (Moreton-Robinson 2015).

Wolfe famously argued that settler colonization is 'a structure, not an event', meaning that it endures across time and outlives the initial 'event' of colonization (1999). As settler colonization creates permanent spaces designed to displace Indigenous people and their claims to land and replace them with newcomer societies, Wolfe further argues that the structure of settler colonization is premised on the 'elimination of the Native' (Wolfe 2006). Here Wolfe does not just mean elimination in the form of physical violence, ethnic cleansing and genocide, although that does commonly happen in settler colonial contexts. Rather, he refers to the elimination of Indigenous peoples' abilities to function and perpetuate themselves *as peoples* – especially as polities capable of holding and exercising counter-claims to land and territory.

From these analyses, Barker (2021) has articulated settler colonialism as a decentred project in which even politically opposed ideologies – e.g. capitalism and communism – can and do participate. Settler colonialism is a means of gaining claim to, and power over, territory. It is not a tactic of the Right or the Left, and is as often as not pursued by 'ordinary' people who are not aware that is what they are doing (they are simply working within the social structures that they are given). Would-be 'allies' and progressives are sometimes the most intractable when critiqued for behaving in a settler colonial way, as Boggs (2024) has aptly demonstrated in the context of outdoors recreational enthusiasts in the American southwest. Boggs notes how trail runners and climbers in traditional Dine and Hopi territory, currently subsumed into park spaces in Arizona, simultaneously admire and work to preserve nature and also displace Indigenous spiritual traditions and histories, and actively work to prevent Indigenous reclamation of territorial autonomy when it might infringe on their recreation. In these, and many other, ways well-intentioned 'ordinary' (meaning settler) people continue to contribute to the colonization and erasure of Indigenous peoples.

Why does settler colonialism matter for eco-communities?

Eco-communities are incredibly diverse, and exist in a wide variety of political and social contexts. Not all will have the same connection to and overlap with settler colonialism, but it is a potential pitfall for all eco-communities and some more than others. First and most crucially, eco-communities have, by definition, a direct, material and explicit relationship to land. Eco-communities are often articulated as being *for* (the benefit of) the land rather than *for* the residents – that is, it is acknowledged that living in an eco-community can be hard and inconvenient (see Pickerill, Chapter 5), but the motivation of caring for the environment and connecting with the land offsets those issues. Yet, the articulation and practice of eco-communities as material places and practices can overlap with patterns of settler colonization.

Eco-communities are a form of migration, an attempt to escape undesirable elements of contemporary society by moving to places considered to exist on the edges of society, often rural, 'undeveloped' or 'unused' places filled with opportunity and potential. However, it is not so much what is motivating this movement that can be problematic, as the act of relocating and what it implies in a settler colonial context. Freifelder (2022), a co-founder of Dancing Rabbit Ecovillage (see Lockyer and Jones, this volume), argues 'advocates of sustainable living generally tend of value connection to place. Yet usually the process of founding an intentional community, especially a rural one, involves plans to relocate' (12), a mobility that also stems from privilege.

As Young (2013) has written in his critique of the works of Gilles Deleuze, leftist, progressive and radical articulations of social change often imply or openly advocate for a 'flight' to a new frontier – Deluze's 'lines of flight' needs to be going *somewhere* – which is very much the motivation behind most settler colonization. Rifkin has described the idea of a 'frontier', still often associated with freedom and liberty beyond the reach of systems of power like that of late-stage capital, as a 'movable space of exception' (2014). This means that settler colonization often begins with would-be settlers identifying a promising frontier, erasing or excusing any Indigenous claims to that place, and then moving a settler collective to that frontier to begin developing it in a way that will advantage themselves (Barker 2021). The placing and perception of these frontiers is itself shaped by the forces eco-community activists are likely to oppose – the identification of 'empty space' by eco-communities that is unused by industrial, capitalist settler societies is again a form of settler colonial seeing (Barker and Pickerill 2012). It is the perception of terra nullius, land that has not been 'developed', and can therefore be claimed, 'improved' and benefitted from in some way. Yet in places like the United States, 'our "tenancy" is more like squatting – that is our "landlords" did not consent to our being here ... I live and was born on stolen land' (Freifelder 2022, 14 and 17).

Even if eco-communities are able to source a site that is ethically acceptable, the transformative efforts of community members do not simply affect themselves and their lifestyles. Bratman et al. (2018) propose that eco-communities must be aware of how their political economies are inserted into landscapes in which people already live, which are contested, and politicized through histories of treaty making and breaking, and therefore having ripple effects with unintended consequences. Specifically tying together the concepts of colonialism and gentrification, they argue:

> Building utopia, Greek for "no place," cannot be done without impacting topia, the places where everyone else lives. That ill dynamic will follow us into Brooklyn, where we call it gentrification, and it will follow us into the countryside just as well.

When we with the privilege of money and mobility build our communities among the habitat of those less privileged, government and markets rush to attract more consumers with privilege like ours. When we go for undeveloped property instead, the gravity of our privilege draws resources away from existing neighborhoods, bringing disproportional benefit to those of us with the means to travel, to move away from family, to choose where and with whom we live. In either scenario, the less privileged are excluded from the plans and usually also from their fruition. In either scenario, we gather up privilege until we have enough to drop it somewhere, like our own little money bomb.

(Bratman et al., 2018, 36)

One practical example provided by Bratman et al. is the effect of solidifying land as property. As historian Greer (2018) has argued, mass settlement in the Americas initiated a situation that he calls 'land tenure pluralism', meaning multiple and at times competing ways of being and belonging on the land were being asserted at once. Some of these were distinctly European, others were obviously Indigenous to their territories, and crucially some developed out of European thought but altered to respond to changed conditions of place in the settlement colonies. An example is that of private property, often associated with European Enlightenment rationalism, but which historian Bhandar has demonstrated was actually developed in the colonies of the Americas – as a way of quickly and easily dividing up and profiting from the sales of abundant 'empty land' – before being exported back to Europe (Bhandar 2018; 2016). Owning property holds a revered place in settler societies, so much so that Tuck and Yang's seminal article 'Decolonization Is Not a Metaphor' focuses on both the ways that settler colonialism produces property as a primary function, and the ways that the settler colonizer's imagination, even when motivated by radical social and material justice, cannot accept what it would mean to return the lands stolen through settlement (Tuck and Yang 2012, 23–8).

The creation and occupation of private property by settler collectives have an impact not just on the space being claimed. States use the existence of material developments as evidence in support of their claims for territory even when they do not directly control or occupy that territory – colonization through the perception of occupation, even in the absence of physical occupation (Barker 2021). For example, the state of Chile uses the existence of a Marine Protected Area (MPA) around the island of Rapa Nui to extend their claim to territory thousands of miles into the Pacific Ocean while denying Indigenous claims to the island (Young 2021). This is similar to the ways that the creation of national parks in settler colonies, whether in Queensland, Australia, or Banff, Canada, reinforces settler sovereignty and property. Banivanua Mar (2010) describes how the creation of 'protected' spaces for 'nature' was both driven by and helped to normalize the idea that all land in the state would eventually be dominated by settlers. Settler societies choose to preserve in part because they know that they can change or destroy the landscape if they so wish. Conversely, while protected spaces are at least nominally protected for the 'public good', private property is just that: private. Private property is so important that, during the British Columbia Treaty

Process,[2] any private property, no matter how it was claimed up to and including being claimed illegally according to the state's own laws, was not subject to negotiation – the private property was 'settled', so to speak.

An eco-community that is built on private property, whether cooperatively owned or otherwise managed, continues to serve this function of blocking discourses around the return of land. As Bratman et al. provocatively ask: 'Does the community of my dreams begin with finding land for sale so we can take control of it?' (2018, 36), and reply to themselves by saying:

> This is where colonialism, all too often, manifests on the road paved with our good intentions. After all, the intentional communities movement is drawn from the history and lore of 19th-century utopians, who were themselves inspired by the first European colonists, seeking a "New World" to shape according to their values and interests. We tend to forget how these pioneering experimental colonies were part of the so-called Manifest Destiny project that destroyed countless indigenous worlds and people. By neglecting that history, might we doom ourselves to repeat it?
>
> (Bratman 2018, 36)

To summarize, beyond the act of voluntary migration, eco-communities can further entrench settler colonial dynamics in pernicious ways such as the legal and economic 'possession' or ownership of land. It is frequent among eco-communities to be purposefully built in rural spaces through land purchased privately, without consideration of Indigenous land claims or ownership. Eco-communities that are not conscious of wider histories of colonization may in fact be contributing to the 'transfer' of land from Indigenous control.

This situation may be exacerbated because eco-communities are often established by incomers to a place who are ignorant of local histories and previous clearances or uses of land, especially those that have been actively suppressed under settler colonialism. The impact of the new eco-community on the local or regional economy may be significant; it may compete with local Indigenous communities for scarce resources and interfere with local economies by (for example) attempting to support the eco-community economy by selling produce that directly competes with local Indigenous producers. This is what Bratman et al. mean by dropping 'our own little money bomb' – the creation of an eco-community has impacts on surrounding economies, and Indigenous economies (due to centuries of settler colonial dispossession) are often vulnerable. This underscores the degree to which eco-communities, even as they often require significant work and sacrifice, can and do wield a great deal of power and privilege in comparison to Indigenous communities.

---

[2] The British Columbia Treaty Process was developed following the Supreme Court hearing of the case Delgamuukw v. British Columbia (1997). Delgamuukw is the traditional name of one of the Gitxsan chiefs who lead the plaintiffs in the suit, which itself asserted that Canada had claimed the now province of British Columbia without treaties conferring title, and thus had never properly and legally taken possession of Gitxsan territory. The plaintiffs argued that their territories should therefore be sovereign from the rest of Canada. The Supreme Court was unable to reach a clear decision and the federal government was advised to begin negotiating 'modern' treaties to secure title to these territories. For more on this, see Wood and Rossiter (2022).

Eco-communities and practices of assimilation and exclusion

We would be remiss if we did not also discuss the ways that eco-communities engage in acts of assimilation and exclusion as ongoing features of their practices. Here we highlight three sets of problematic practices: appropriation of knowledge and culture, co-opting relationships with nature and entrenching white supremacy.

Appropriation of knowledge and culture

Usually rooted in respect for the aspects of these cultures that are apparent to outsiders,[3] eco-communities have been known to undertake what is in reality a partial and piecemeal appropriation of Indigenous spirituality, knowledges and practices. In eco-communities, this appropriation is often most obvious through the uses of particular material symbols, shapes and practices. Material symbols include dream catchers, prayer flags, medicine wheels, ornate clay pipes, shell rattles, hand drums and similar 'tribal' affectations.

Although almost always justified as showing 'respect' to Indigenous peoples and traditions, these practices contribute directly to settler colonization. As Barker (2021) has described, settler colonization requires three simultaneous and mutually reinforcing practices: elimination, occupation and bricolage. The third, bricolage, speaks to the settler creation of both conceptual and material worlds made in part from material and concepts appropriated from Indigenous people. This has several effects. First, it reinforces eliminatory narratives by positioning Indigenous culture as something that can be owned or consumed by non-Indigenous people. Second, the bricolage of Indigenous cultures becomes confused for actual Indigenous cultures, erasing detail and specificity – for example, how many people who are conceptually supportive of Indigenous rights and, relatedly, have a dreamcatcher on display, can actually name which specific nation originated dreamcatchers, their full purpose, or the ways they should actually be used?

Indicative of this cultural appropriation of material symbols are the use of a dreamcatcher-inspired willow-weaving hanging in the doorway to a bedroom at Panya Project (Thailand) and other examples elsewhere in the community. Panya Project, established in 2004, is a 10-acre eco-community with self-built eco-buildings that hosts permaculture training in the Chiang Mai region of northern Thailand. It is near the rural village of Moo Bahn Mae Jo, two hours drive north of Chiang Mai city. While the climate (tropical wet and dry) and local vernacular building designs have

---

[3] As has been extensively discussed by Indigenous scholars and knowledge keepers, many aspects of Indigenous knowledge and culture are not freely accessible to everyone. Important knowledge of, for example, medicine plants may be restricted – not to restrict access to medicine, but rather to ensure the proper rituals and practices around harvesting of the medicine are performed (ensuring it does not die off from overuse), and similarly that the proper rituals and practices around treating a patient are performed (ensuring the medicine is being used in the correct way). It may take a lifetime to gain this specialist knowledge, and sharing it in fragments may cause great harm. Other aspects of Indigenous culture are held sacred, and not shared with any outsiders, such as particular spiritual rituals (Smith 2021). However, anthropologists (professional and amateur) have documented parts of these practices over many years, and some non-Indigenous people – especially settlers – take these as free to use.

influenced the construction of open-sided teak wood and bamboo structures at Panya, their introduction of permaculture is new to the region (Pickerill 2016). Panya, and its neighbouring eco-community Pun Pun, has attracted tourists and volunteers to this otherwise quiet village (Pickerill 2010). Dreamcatchers are not part of the local heritage or cultural practices.

See also a carving into the front door of a house at the Lama Foundation (USA), Figure 1, which resembles the iconography of nearby Northern Tiwa Indigenous communities. Lama Foundation, established in 1967, started as a spiritual centre but has also become an eco-community, with natural building methods and materials, use of permaculture, solar power and rainwater harvesting. Lama Foundation was created

Figure 1 Carving into a house door at The Lama Foundation, New Mexico, USA. (Source: Jenny Pickerill.)

by settler migrants from New York. Co-founder Jonathan Altman privately purchased the land. It is a rocky, exposed, sparsely populated place with minimal infrastructure, but significant Indigenous importance (Cox 2014). It is in the Sangre de Cristo Mountains, 17 miles north of Taos (the location of the famous Indigenous Taos Pueblo, a World Heritage Site) and a destination for artists and writers since the 1920s.

The Lama Foundation also uses, produces and sells numerous prayer flags (alongside medicinal herbs and smudging products). These are prominently displayed on a pole as you enter the community. Embracing many spiritual traditions (including Buddhism, Islam, Hinduism, Judaism and Christianity), they include an 'Elk Heart Prayer Flag' which they claim is from a pottery design by 'the Mimbres Indians from 1200AD', and 'The Earth is Alive' flag they claim is a 'Native American design celebrating the nourishment of the earth' (Lama Foundation 2023). These flags were also hung from tipis on the site (Cobb 2008).

Lama is deliberately open to all religious and spiritual traditions (and the only expectation being to participate in daily meditation), 'so each individual can discover his or her own unique form of relationship to the divine' (Cobb 2008, 96). Yet there is also a danger in the way that 'Lama embraces … Native American ways' (Cobb 2008, 97) and celebrates its links with Indigenous elders such as Telesfor Reyna Goodmorning in ways that are piecemeal and mixed together with partial elements of an array of religions and spiritualities.

Co-opting relationships with nature

Many eco-communities employ a particular language which expresses kinships with nature and non-human beings. Much of this is extracted from Indigenous thought, but rarely acknowledged as such, despite the prevalence of phrases such as 'all my relations', an invocation of relationship with the more-than-human world, which is directly lifted from the traditions of Indigenous people such as the Lakota and Blackfoot (in now the United States/Turtle Island) and exemplified by the incorporation of an elephant and tree design into an eco-community home in Thailand.

This co-option of Indigenous ontologies by non-Indigenous people is far from unique to eco-communities and is also prevalent in much of contemporary human geography in its relations and post-humanism turns (Barker and Pickerill 2020). Yet, eco-community practitioners often articulate their development of mutual interdependencies and co-fabrications of reciprocal society-nature relationships, and their experiments in multi-species justice as novel and innovative (Molfese 2023). For example, permaculture – a holistic design of self-sustaining ecological systems – is a cornerstone of many eco-communities in how they manage and restore ecosystems, cultivate produce and minimize waste (Taylor Aiken 2017). Only recently have practitioners acknowledged that 'permaculture owes the roots of its theory and practice to traditional and Indigenous knowledges' (Hall 2022). Indeed, Bill Mollison (1988), who along with David Holmgren 'created' the concept and practices while in Tasmania (Australia) in the 1970s, acknowledged its Indigenous influences and cited Indigenous sources, but claimed to 'repurpose' and synthesize incorporating ecosystem modelling and European scientific practices, for contemporary non-Indigenous use. The extent of any Australian Indigenous active involvement, consent and recognition in the sharing of this knowledge is unclear and certainly Mollison and Holmgren, both white settlers, receive all the credit.

Watts (Mohawk and Anishinaabe) makes a critique of a parallel and increasingly common practice: the making of land acknowledgements or use of Indigenous prayer and smudging to open events, followed by the events in no way representing Indigenous peoples' views or interests. As Watts explains in her scathing 2016 article titled 'Smudge This: Assimilation, State-Favoured Communities and the Denial of Indigenous Spiritual Lives', the use of Indigenous concepts and frameworks for relating to the land without the attendant practices to uphold those frameworks runs the very real risk of trivializing Indigenous tradition and practice. Watts (2013) further has argued that Indigenous place-thought is so specific and complex that non-Indigenous people often think they understand it, but lacking the lived experience of place-relationship that informs place-thought, they are very likely to understand it crudely or partially.

What is crucially missing, in addition to the lack of acknowledgement, is the deep, reciprocal relationship between Indigenous peoples and their lands that shapes and guides practices over time. On the failures of 'New Age' spirituality in the 1980s to 2000s, Aldred (2000) wrote a prescient critique of these practices, calling out especially the use of sweat lodges as tourist attractions or money-making schemes, which is important given sweat lodges and similar practices are not uncommon in eco-communities (for example at Brithdir Mawr eco-community, Pembrokeshire, Wales and at Findhorn eco-village, Scotland). While Aldred's critique of the commodification of these practices for individual profit would likely resonate with eco-community members, her further point about the dangers of misusing fragmented knowledge should be heeded. In 2009, James Arthur Ray, a white settler North American, was leading a spiritual retreat that included a sweat lodge. As a result of Ray's misuse of the sweat lodge, three participants died and in 2011 Ray was convicted of negligent homicide.

Entrenching white supremacy

Regardless of the degree to which an eco-community consciously or unconsciously co-opts symbols or practices from Indigenous groups, they may work to entrench white supremacy as a dominant social construct, even in communities seeking to radically rupture from other dominant social constructs (like capitalism). This happens when eco-communities repeat white supremacist tendencies, consciously or unconsciously, that exclude Black, Indigenous and other People of Colour members and shape understandings of belonging around white-coded practices.

These exclusionary processes can manifest in how food, work, home and community are defined and collectively understood, and therefore who is allowed authority, who is allowed access and who is excluded. Settler colonialism is generally understood to socially revolve around subjective 'sorting' into three categories: 'settlers' (the in-group with power that claims the land); indigenous Others (not actual Indigenous people, but the settler colonial perception of them); and, exogenous Others (sometimes called 'arrivants', this includes migrants and enslaved peoples). Aileen Moreton-Robinson (2015) argues that settler colonialism relies on narratives of ownership and possession, premised on white-coded European traditions of building and transforming empty land, commanding the labour of exploited peoples, and claiming the results as their own. As she demonstrates through critical analysis of the history of how Australia became a 'white' settler society, these practices of possessiveness are enacted in legal and political realms, but also in social and cultural practices. The stories white people tell about themselves, their homes, how they have earned them and struggled to seize their opportunities, all inform social understandings of who is 'like us' enough to be considered a settler (see Pickerill's chapter in this volume for further examples).

Conclusions

None of this means that eco-communities are synonymous with settler colonialism – eco-communities built by Indigenous peoples on their own lands, for example, are decolonial in nature, and there are many possibilities of eco-communities developing a very different set of place-relationships to those entrenched in settler societies. Freifelder (2022) suggests eco-communities should pay rent (voluntary land tax) to Indigenous people, share resources, enable Indigenous access to the land and support justice activism. Crucially she also questions the need to move to new places to create eco-communities, advocating working more in existing neighbourhoods and communities, as she says of her struggling blueberry bushes, 'I'll try to improve other aspects of their living conditions without moving them' (17). Eco-communities are not 'bad' because they occasionally mirror settler colonization, but we must be aware that this happens and the potentially negative effects.

This also applies most clearly to places where there are specific Indigenous communities on whose lands the eco-communities are situated. While we have discussed some of the ways that eco-communities can and do reinforce settler colonialism even at a distance, issues around private property and the settler colonial transfer of land are place-specific. However, the dynamics of settler colonialism going unobserved in eco-communities suggests other intersectional patterns of domination. There are still patterns of – often Anglo-European heritage eco-community members – establishing new eco-communities in countries including India, Mexico and Thailand that extends existing colonialities of land acquisition in previously colonialized countries, ongoing colonialism in Israel, and normalizes colonizer cultures (e.g. by failing to speak local languages). Indeed, the Panya Project discussed here was founded by North American 'expats' – voluntary migrants – to Thailand and only one resident was of Thai descent and spoke the local language.

Eco-communities cannot be understood as disconnected from the world around them, whether intended as utopian or not (Bratman et al., 2018). In a world structured by settler colonialism, racial capitalism, and other profound forms of exclusion, oppression and dispossession, eco-communities cannot assume that a withdrawal to a (often rural) place can truly result in escaping these structures. This goes doubly so for settler colonialism which is premised on the promise of a better – perhaps utopian – life on the other side of the frontier. Eco-communities would do well to learn from the settler people who have gone before, so many of whom thought they were escaping an unequal or dying society to make a new, better, special existence elsewhere, and instead observe, identify and challenge these ongoing settler colonial practices.

References

Aldred, L. (2000) 'Plastic shamans and astroturf sun dances: New age commercialization of Native American spirituality', *American Indian Quarterly* 24(3), pp. 329–52.

Banivanua Mar, T. (2010) 'Carving wilderness: Queensland's national parks and the unsettling of emptied lands, 1890–1910', in Banivanua Mar, T. and Edmonds, P. (eds.) *Making Settler Colonial Space: Perspectives on Race, Place and Identity*). London: Palgrave Macmillan, pp. 73–94.

Barker, A. (2021) *Making and Breaking Settler Space*. Vancouver: UBC Press.

Barker, A. and Pickerill, J. (2020) 'Doings with the land and sea: Decolonising geographies, indigeneity, and enacting place-agency', *Progress in Human Geography* 44(4), pp. 640–62.

Barker, A.J. and Pickerill, J. (2012) 'Radicalising relationships to and through shared geographies: Why anarchists need to understand indigenous connections to land and place', *Antipode* 44(5), pp. 1705–25.

Bhandar, B. (2016) 'Possession, occupation and registration: Recombinant ownership in the settler colony', *Settler Colonial Studies* 6(2), pp. 119–32.

Bhandar, B. (2018) *Colonial Lives of Property: Law, Land, and Racial Regimes of Ownership*. Durham, NC: Duke University Press.

Boggs, K. (Forthcoming 2025) *Recreational Colonialism and the Rhetorical Landscapes of the Outdoors*. Columbus: Ohio State University Press.

Bratman, E., Brooks, B., Mercedes, T., Jancourtz, J. and Rothschild, J. (2018) 'Can We Have Communities without Gentrification? Perspectives from the Ecovillagers Alliance', *Communities* 178(Spring), pp. 36–9.

Castellanos, M.B. (2017) 'Introduction: Settler colonialism in Latin America', *American Quarterly* 69(4), pp. 777–81.

Cobb, A (2008) *Early Lama Foundation*. San Cristobal: Lama Foundation.

Cox, M. (2014) 'Modern disturbances to a long-lasting community-based resource management system: The Taos Valley acequias', *Global Environmental Change* 24(January), pp. 213–22.

Freifelder, R. (2022) 'Sense of place and land back in a transient Culture', *Communities Magazine* 195 (Summer), pp. 12–17.

Greer, A. (2018) *Property and Dispossession: Natives, Empires and Land in Early Modern North America*. Cambridge: Cambridge University Press.

Hall, B.M. (2022) 'Is permaculture appropriated from Indigenous knowledge? Shales of Green', 23 November, https://shadesofgreenpermaculture.com/blog/permaculture-101/is-permaculture-appropriated-from-indigenous-knowledge. Accessed 15 September 2023.

Lama Foundation (2023) Prayer Flags. https://store.lamafoundation.org/collections/prayer-flags-all-flags. Accessed 15 September 2023.

Molfese, C. (2023) 'Going back-to-the-land in the Anthropocene: a more-than-human journey into anarchist geographies'. Unpublished PhD thesis, University of Plymouth.

Mollison, B. (1988) *Permaculture: A Designers' Manual*. Stanley: Tagari Publications.

Moreton-Robinson, A. (2015) *The White Possessive: Property, Power, and Indigenous Sovereignty*. Minneapolis: University of Minnesota Press.

Pickerill, J. (2010) Pany Project, Mae Taeng, Thailand. Eco-homes blog, https://ecohomes.blog/2010/07/03/panya-project-mae-taeng-thailand/.

Pickerill, J. (2016) *Eco-Homes: People, Place and Politics*. London: Zed Books.

Rifkin, M. (2014) 'The frontier as (movable) space of exception', *Settler Colonial Studies* 4(2), pp. 176–80.

Smith, L.T. (2021) *Decolonizing methodologies: Research and indigenous peoples*. London: Bloomsbury Publishing.

Taylor Aiken, G. (2017) 'Permaculture and the social design of nature', *Geografiska Annaler: Series B, Human Geography* 99(2), pp. 172–91.

Taylor, L. and Lublin, G. (2021) 'Settler colonial studies and Latin America', *Settler Colonial Studies* 11(3), pp. 259–70.

Tuck, E. and Yang, K.W. (2012) 'Decolonization in not a metaphor', *Decolonization* 1(1), pp. 1–40.

Veracini, L. (2010) *Settler Colonialism: A Theoretical Overview*. London: Palgrave Macmillan.

Veracini, L. (2011) 'Isopolitics, deep colonizing, settler colonialism', *Interventions* 13(2), pp. 171–89.

Veracini, L. (2014) 'Understanding colonialism and settler colonialism as distinct formations', *Interventions* 16(5), pp. 615–33.

Veracini, L. (2015) *The Settler Colonial Present*. New York: Springer.

Watts, V. (2013) *Indigenous Place-Thought and Agency amongst Humans and Non Humans (First Woman and Sky Woman Go on a European World Tour!)*. Decolonization: Indigeneity, Education & Society, 2(1).

Watts, V. (2016) 'Smudge this: Assimilation, state-favoured communities and the denial of indigenous spiritual lives', *International Journal of Child, Youth and Family Studies* 7(1), pp. 148–70.

Wolfe, P. (1999) *Settler Colonialism and the Transformation of Anthropology: The Politics and Poetics of an Ethnographic Event*. London: Cassell.

Wolfe, P. (2006) 'Settler Colonialism and the Elimination of the Native', *Journal of genocide research* 8(4), pp. 387–409.

Wood, P. and Rossiter, D. (2022) *Unstable Properties: Aboriginal Title and the Claim of British Columbia*. Vancouver, BC: UBC Press.

Young, A.T. (2013) 'Settler Sovereignty and the Rhizomatic West, or, the Significance of the Frontier in Postwestern Studies', *Western American Literature* 48(1), pp. 115–40.

Young, F.W. (2021) 'Unsettling the boundaries of Latin America: Rapa Nui and the refusal of Chilean settler colonialism', *Settler Colonial Studies* 11(3), pp. 292–318.

9

Eco-communities and feminism(s): Who cares? An ethnographic study of social practices in three French eco-communities

Nadine Gerner

Introduction

Eco-communities provide fruitful insights into how we can live together differently, away from a growth-oriented consumerist and productivist capitalist society (Lockyer 2017; Wallmeier 2015). The knowledge they offer is based on many years of experiences with alternative ways of relating to nature, experimenting with dissident practices, questioning the hegemonic culture and creating community life. Eco-communities are also often considered to be practitioners of the degrowth movement. However, 'there is theory and there are small experiments broadly inspired by degrowth, but there is no spatialised "degrowth world" in its full plentitude' (Kallis and March 2015, 361). I therefore view eco-communities as small-scale, spatialized living experiments displaying how degrowth might look in practice (D'Alisa et al., 2014).

> In a degrowth society everything will be different: different activities, […] different relations, different gender roles, different allocations of time between paid and non-paid work, different relations with the non-human world.
>
> (Kallis et al., 2014, 4)

Looking at social practices (of degrowth) in eco-communities creates new imaginaries of socio-ecological transformation. Yet, in degrowth literature and intentional community research, there remain significant gaps with regard to gender, care (work), hierarchies and power. Supposedly, the progressive and emancipatory label often associated with eco-communities makes them more likely to challenge power structures or even transcend gender biases (Pickerill 2015). However, assuming that fixing the ecological problem 'would automatically fix the other' is, according to ecofeminists, a causal fallacy (Plumwood 2002, 197).

This chapter offers qualitative ethnographic and ecofeminist insights into the everyday life practices of three French eco-communities. First, I draw upon existing research on intentional communities and degrowth identifying the lacunae in eco-community research from a feminist perspective. Secondly, I introduce my conceptual framework based on ecofeminism combined with a social practice theory approach. Thirdly, I present the methods and the ethnographic research design of this multi-case study. Finally, this chapter critically engages with questions of social reproduction, unpaid care work and the gender-biased structures and practices in eco-communities. It challenges possible assumptions that eco-communities are more inclusive per se.

My aims are both to highlight how eco-communities may contribute to more 'care-full' and gender-sensitive practices, pointing out areas with high potential, and to identify the challenges which have to be tackled.

Consumption, production and reproduction? On the role of gender in eco-communities

Whereas eco-communities are extensively studied in terms of their eco-performance, democratic decision-making or their consumption patterns (Daly 2017; Litfin 2012, 2014), very little scholarship has studied gender concerns in eco-communities.

What is most compelling about alternative lifestyles are the transformative consumption and production patterns: Self-provision, organic food production and ethical consumption are central to most eco-community projects. However, especially when it comes to consumption several scholars underline that 'consumption decisions are not made by gender-neutral private households, but rather overwhelmingly by women' (Bauhardt 2014, 65). Actually, green(er) consumption practices or a shift in diet (e.g. healthier, more ecological) both involves a change in preparation and cooking methods which are likely to be more time-intensive and requires a certain knowledge often left to caregivers[1] (Martens and Casey 2016).

Several authors also view reduction, alongside renunciation of technological items through low-tech practices, as problematic since it runs the risk of constituting an additional burden of care work:

> I don't think many degrowthers realize how heavy a burden care work will be without domestic equipment – cookers, washing machines, hot water, vacuum cleaners, etc. It is not an argument to keep them, but domestic work is going to take a lot of the day. In most communities, this falls to women. I am troubled by how much attention in the literature is given to welcoming increased leisure time by male authors.
>
> (Mellor 2015)

Low-tech practices and a low-impact lifestyle sometimes go hand in hand with more localist and rural realities. Rural eco-communities risk idealizing and romanticizing a

---

[1] Such as women or other structurally marginalized groups. I henceforth prefer the term 'caregivers' as a more gender-inclusive term including manifold gender identities which are structurally discriminated and more likely to carry the burden of (additional) carework.

rural back-to-nature imaginary (inspired by the back to the landers movement in the 1960s and '70s). The exaltation of the peasant localist lifestyle obliterates associated gender roles (Adler and Schachtschneider 2010; Mellor 2015). Further, feminist scholars stress that localization risks 'a revival of "natural" gender divisions of labour as a result of the contingencies of local production and familial reproduction' (Kish and Quilley 2017, 314). Hence, there are contradictions between ecologically sound lifestyles and feminist concerns.

One of the works that have published on this matter is Tummers and MacGregor (2019), who studied if Dutch and UK co-housing projects succeed in transforming gender roles, redistributing carework and moving towards a post-patriarchal change. Moreover, Pickerill (2015) addresses the gender-bias in the field of eco-building. She identifies a significant gendered division of certain activities, especially linked to eco-building but distinguishes also a gender bias in terms of visibility and value of certain contributions or bodies. Furthermore, Leitner and Littig (2017) study an Austrian co-housing project and argue that even when gender is a factor in the organization of certain communities gender stereotypes, roles and performances remain. Research suggests that eco-communities have the potential to transform patriarchal culture and practices such as gender roles and feminized carework (Tummers and MacGregor 2019), yet much further work is required.

Ecological and also feminist! Ecofeminism(s) as an integral perspective

Focusing on production and consumption as one of the anchor points of 'living differently' neglects the sphere of social reproduction which is central to the continuity of societies. Social reproduction includes the socially devalued and invisible tasks and labour which is needed to sustain societal life on a daily basis but also to enable its regeneration over time and generations (Tummers and MacGregor 2019). This chapter particularly focuses on unpaid carework such as cleaning tasks, diet planning, child-raising, and food preparation and supply in eco-communities.

Both gender relations and the divide between the spheres of production and reproduction are a pillar of ecofeminist theories. This division is constitutive to modern capitalist societies and is highly gendered (Hofmeister and Biesecker 2010): whereas the productive sphere is connotated with male attributes, the reproductive sphere is linked to women, racialized people, the marginalized, and nature – and literally nourishes and sustains the latter (nature) with (un-)paid invisible care work and ecosystem services. The concept of dualism understands society as structured by hierarchically ordered exclusive, oppositional categories (male/female, nature/culture, production/reproduction, reason/emotion). Dualisms can explain why women, racialized persons and the animal(istic) are opposed to the so-called Master Model (Plumwood 2002) – the dominant, valued and visible. However, although ecofeminism views the exploitations and oppressions of nature and the marginalized as interlinked, this does not mean that women are somehow closer to nature. In ecofeminism several explanations for this women–nature connection exist (Merchant 1980; Salleh 2017;

Shiva and Mies 1993). I advocate for an ecofeminism which distances from the biologization of bodies, essentialization of gender and uniformization of experiences. The ecofeminist perspective I adopt here is coherent, care-full, non-essentialist and sensitive to the various forms of oppressions, or to put it in Plumwood's words:

> The quest for coherence is not the demand that each form of oppression submerges its hard-won identity in a single, amorphous, oceanic movement. Rather it asks that each form of oppression develop sensitivity to other forms, both at the level of practice and that of theory.
>
> (Plumwood 2002, 14)

A gender-just and ecofeminist practice would therefore imply the transcending of a dualist vision by visibilizing and revaluing the reproductive sphere, reorganizing care between the genders and the generations and thus deconstructing gender norms, roles and performances (Bauhardt 2014).

From theory to praxis: An ethnographic study on social practices in eco-communities

Drawing upon social practice theory, I consider that neither do structures fully determine our actions nor are we (as rational-choice approaches suggest) independent individuals acting freely in a power-free space: 'Practices do not float free of technological, institutional and infrastructural contexts' (Randles and Warde 2006). Social practice theory views the structure–agent relation as entrenched and recursively linked. It suggests that the materialities and structures in which individuals are embedded have an impact on the agency of individuals and the practical careers they follow. Elizabeth Shove's approach views social practices as made up of three elements: materials, meanings and competencies (Shove et al., 2012). I examine social practices in three eco-communities, putting social practice into dialogue with the feminist interrogations and concepts described above.

Ethnography as a 'way of seeing' (Wolcott 1999) makes it possible to go beyond data collection and to get physically and emotionally involved as a researcher. In order to study social practices and to gather lived experiences I needed to be right in the middle of the 'doings' and 'sayings' of the researched.

I conducted field work in three small-scale eco-communites[2] in France where I spent twenty-seven days getting immersed in workshops, gardening, plenary sessions, birthdays and open house days. Data was collected during the aforementioned events,

---

[2] The eco-communities were selected after a prior study of community listings (such as Global Ecovillage Network, Foundation for Intentional Community, Mouvement Colibris) and limited to the closer surrounding of the researcher (max. 600km). Subsequently, several eco-communities with various profiles could be identified and were contacted via mail. After getting in touch with several projects, the final selection represents one vegan eco-village (seven residents), a rather spiritual ecovillage (twenty residents) and an ecological co-housing community (fourteen residents). The study was conducted with scarce resources and under Covid-19 circumstances, so the ultimate selection was made pragmatically with regard to time, availability and resources.

but also in informal conversations and by 'hanging around' (Thomas 2019, 83) with the research subjects. Prior to my stay all the members agreed to be part of the research project. During my stay all the interviewees signed an informed consent form. The members were asked who they would recommend to interview in relation to my topic. The qualitative research is based upon participant observation collected via field notes and ten semi-structured interviews with fifteen people. I refer to the eco-communities respectively as EC1, EC2 and EC3 due to anonymization of the communities and the participants. Despite that anonymity one can highlight a few specificities with regard to the geographic context that communities are embedded in: particularly, in the French regions of Ariège and Ardèche there is a dense concentration of intentional communities due to trajectories of the back-to-the-land movement, low prices of land, constant rural exodus and a recent neo-rural excitement. Hence, taking private property from the market and into collective hands, forging links with the local population, (re-)vitalizing communal spaces and offering educational work are amongst the (respectively more or less radical) motives which make people settle down in a certain territory. Likewise, more ecological factors such as the quality of the soil, access to water or even distance to nuclear infrastructures also come into play in the French context.

Potentials of eco-communities: Towards ecological and 'care-full' practices

To begin with, let me address the role of care in the eco-communities: each of the three eco-communities accorded somehow a central place (both material and symbolic) to the needs of each and every one. Community life is characterized by caring relationships between humans and with the more-than-human (e.g. animals or plants) via anti-speciesism, veganism or permacultural techniques. Furthermore, care is fundamental in the community activities. Plenary sessions do not have a purely organizational character but are accompanied by an emotional round, with active listening to what each member shares. 'Caring about' and 'taking care of' in the sense of Fisher and Tronto (1990) play an important role in everyday life. Likewise, all the eco-communities name emotional care and self-care as central pillars and share a definition of care that comprehends self-care (Winker 2015). Thus, daily meditation, personal development workshops and mantra chanting are part of the everyday life, especially in EC1. They have developed several brochures on community and couple relationships and regularly propose workshops to visitors to share their knowledge.

Through collectivization EC3 and EC2 also make reproductive tasks visible. Regular 'clean-up Mondays' or 'community Saturdays' create a positive event of taking care of the common spaces such as the community kitchen, the garden and so forth. Collectivizing such tasks might be conducive to distribute tasks in a more gender-just way since everyone is involved. EC1 offers a basic community income, so if one does cleaning or building, each task has the same value for the community economy. Other volunteers and I could observe how manifold activities and tasks are valued and considered as work. One volunteer said that spending a week in EC1 changed her relationship with work. She thought it was better to do gardening, but then she did several days of handicraft to decorate the place. As people were encouraging her so much, she said to herself, that creation is worth something too. Hence, in all three communities cleaning tasks, taking care of others, and self-care as carework were given a more positive connotation and became re-valued.

Less is more: Embracing the common materialities

From an ecofeminist perspective, materials can be crucial to make reproductive work visible. For Shove, materials are an element of a social practice representing tools, artefacts, objects, infrastructures and even the body as an instrument (Shove and Walker 2010; Shove et al., 2012). The above-mentioned 'carefulness' materializes literally: construction plans and buildings centring common spaces diminish the individual's charge of care, for instance via a community kitchen, a common children's room, a shared laundry and so forth. Eco-communities take several care tasks out of the single dwelling (if existent) into common spaces which has the potential for a more gender-just distribution.

EC3 had the highest amount of shared spaces which was directly reflected in a diminished and visible charge of carework. The material arrangement of EC3 is partially able to create new visibilities. First, their outside kitchen is directly visible for visitors when arriving and sometimes became a central place for gatherings and informal discussions around the cooking place. Second, EC3 visibilizes the person in charge of the meal by noting the name on a board in the common living room. Further, the person in charge of co-parenting is also written on that board. Organizing domestic tasks via boards and rota is a very common way to organize tasks in all three communities. In EC2 and EC3 residents share shopping errands preparing lists for the ones who go to the market or the local food store. As a result, less carework for the individuals could be observed in terms of shopping, cleaning, or cooking once spaces and errands were shared. EC3 suggests an interesting shift in the meaning of meals motivated by health, practical and ecological issues. The community decides upon a common, wholesome, vegan meal at around 4 pm that is prepared by the person on the board. One common meal per day is meant to liberate time for other tasks and activities and to make the day less food-centred. Previously the community shared two meals a day and often finished late at night, creating the impression of spending the whole day eating. Here, reduction of reproductive tasks is one solution in organizing care and lightening the care burden. However, it cannot be seen as a universally applicable solution to organize care in general, especially for person-related care tasks (Dengler and Lang 2018). Material arrangements are likely to favour an environment of sharing and caring; however, the latter are not sufficient to deconstruct the prevailing assumptions and gendered distribution of tasks.

Different but the same? Gendered competencies

Space is not the same for everyone. A lot of places in the three eco-communities are common places but they are not used by residents equally.

As he is Mr. DIY, there is not necessarily the space to experiment, even if he really doesn't want to. He wants everyone to feel free to explore this impulse. It's just that he has this passion. So it's more practical reasons, for him it's easier to see 'ah we should have a shelf there' and in two hours, you have a shelf there, while when I'm getting into it, it may take me more time. It will be there one day, but it will take longer. And so, it's true that sometimes, I notice that we have a bit like a DIY monopoly.

(Resident EC3)

As the quote shows, a gendered use of certain spaces was observed: traditionally male members could be observed in the garage or carrying heavy stuff, whereas female residents would gather in the garden and the kitchen to interact with light(er) objects.

Likewise, low-tech practices were performed mainly by male members. For example, the maintenance and reparation of a solar shower or the low-tech laundry in EC1 would need certain competencies. Whenever there was a problem or questions concerning those gadgets, residents directly referred to the oldest, technically skilled male members. Here, skills, knowledge and materials remained monopolized by these male members. I observed where ecologically sound features created by men create barriers, preventing other (often female) members from being able to make use of them independently. This dependency was enhanced by the fact that EC1 opts for fixed roles to organize community tasks, and by the fact that male members had longer experience living in the community or even were the owners of the land. Such organization of property and roles (instead of rota) results in knowledge hierarchies, dependencies and asymmetries that are highly gendered. The latter was not perceived as something negative since every resident could contribute where the person has the most competencies. It is, however, problematic that gender roles persist in reproducing traditional role models without challenging them. Residents explained that if someone wants to learn how to build, one has just to ask one of the male members and they would instruct with pleasure. This leaves the individual responsible for challenging structural imbalances.

As social practice theory suggests our practical consciousness is restrained, therefore 'doing gender' as a set of routines and unintentional 'doings' are often barely conscious and the result of social construction (Garfinkel 1967; West and Zimmermann 1987). 'Doing gender' is deeply inscribed in our bodies and thus, perceived as natural (Jonas and Littig 2016). The incorporated bodily aspects were often referred to when I asked about gender and the distribution of tasks. Bodily features as a barrier to the equal distribution of tasks were named by older and several female residents in EC 2 and C3. For instance, emptying the (heavy) bucket of the compost toilet demanded a certain physical strength. Instead of adapting the material part of the practice (e.g. lighter smaller buckets), gender asymmetries remained and were accepted as somehow naturally given. When I asked a resident why they had only men applying to live in the community, she explained:

Maybe it's because we were looking for people who know how to do something, that there were more guys who came. At that time we were looking for people who knew how to do things.

(Female resident EC1)

Such claims are linked to a naturalization of difference between the genders attributing certain physical skills and competencies respectively to men and women.

Challenging the 'natural' and the free distribution of tasks

It depends so much on the personalities of the people present it's hard to go out and say 'wait, but ok, he takes a lot of space, she fades away', it depends on what it is, because it is a man, because it's just his personality. It's complicated.
(Male resident, EC1)

The place invites us to fulfill our life mission. So, often, it goes beyond the traditional.
(Female resident, EC1)

Tracing gendered outcomes back to one's personality or interests is a common explanation (Leitner et al., 2015), as well as assuming that accomplishing one's interests would automatically benefit everyone. Such explanations contain a strong neoliberal ethos (Argüelles et al., 2017) and neglect that personality or interest is a product of socialization which can lead to gender ignorance or cultural appropriation sometimes reinforced by spiritual argumentation:

At the same time there is an undeniable correlation on the part of culture-nature, […] yin means to welcome so that life can develop, it's only a woman who can do that. Surely there is a set of hormonal, physical factors etc. Which means that socially, it means having a greater tendency to be more manifesting in a form of feminine energy for a woman, yin energy. I say indistinctly yin and feminine. For me, it's not me, it's not an invention. […] For example, I am very yang professionally and very yin intimately. It's complicated for me: Serving people, taking care of a place, taking care of the cleaning, the aspects, the food. I really know it's not my quality at all or I need to have those energies there. I don't care if it's men or women, I don't care who is the one who takes care of this feminine energy so that there is a place that is welcoming, safe for people who propose a more confrontational work as I do.
(Male resident, EC1)

Such ways of justifying affinities and task distribution can be viewed as naturalizing the social and existing domination and power structures (Biesecker et al., 2000; Ruether 1975). Essentializing gender and clinging to binaries perceptualizes a dualistic vision. It views women as closer to nature and imposes them a 'natural' responsibility and affinity based on their (presumed) biological disposition to raise children, for example.

Even if she and I share a large part of the responsibility for [Child1], she remains the mother. [Other woman] is a single mother … [Child 2] and [Child1] are just more attached to their mothers. So there's a kind of mental charge that can be overwhelming. For me, it might be easier to break free from that. Concerning the fairness [of caring responsibility] I think that's also why [not equally distributed].
(Father EC3)

Whereas EC3 opts for co-parenting and raising children in a gender-neutral way, EC2 does not consider child care as something to share. If parents do feel a certain relief thanks to being in the community then it is a side effect, the result of both a common playground and the presence of other children ensuring that 'they do not see their children anymore' (EC2). One interviewee stresses that organizing and scheduling child care on a communal board do not correspond to the reality. Parents cannot plan when they are tired and need some relief. By organizing shifts in this way, a person in need is unlikely to ask for additional support and hence care responsibility falls back on caregivers (EC1). This reveals the limits of a 'free', 'need-based' and often referred to as 'natural' way of organizing. In such circumstances a backlash is more than probable and (child)care risks remaining a feminized domain. Queer ecologists call into question the women–nature–mother nexus which maintains this invisibility and devaluation of women's work (Bauhardt 2017). Therefore, a defeminization of care, overcoming hegemonic constructions of masculinity and thriving towards 'caring masculinities' (Heilman and Scholz 2019) are necessary.

On gender blindness, denial of difference and privilege

The very practice of retreating, practising voluntary simplicity and being able to 'be the change you want to see in the world', a Gandhian slogan many eco-communities adhere to, is in itself shaped by environmental and social privilege (see Pickerill in this Book). EC1 and EC3 are strongly committed to spirituality, personal development strategies, sociocracy[3] (EC 2, EC3) and non-violent communication (EC 2, EC3). These tools are used against sexism and racism, as I was told that one has to 'heal one's own problems and incoherences with racism or men' (EC1). Yet, these are individualist tools for tackling structural problems, which remain unseen.

> Racism or things like that, there is not one person here who has even a shred of racism. For me, we have already reached this ... I don't even want to come back to it.
>
> (Female resident EC1)

> I mean, I want trans people and black people to come here, so much the better, if that happens, but on the other hand, ten people out of 60 million, chances are low, ... we are not a so representative sample of society.
>
> (Male resident EC1)

Understanding for the structural origins of the problem and reflecting on one's standpoint and privileges were lacking in many observations. Despite celebrating diversity in their discourses and in their spiritual rituals (EC1) there were significant inconsistencies between the 'doings' and 'sayings' in eco-communities. Residents

---

[3] Sociocracy is a way to self organize as a collective. It offers many methods to structure group meetings and decisions, for instance by holding up meetings in a circle, active listening, a certain speaking order or through consensual decision-making.

denied difference (Eräranta et al., 2009). However, when referring to each other I observed practices of 'doing gender' with a strong group identification to 'the boys' and 'the girls': 'Women are talking and men are doing the technical, haha.' On top of that, the uniformization of all individuals as humans poses problems from a queer-feminist point of view, moulding binary gender constructions and eliminating queer identities from discourse, practice, imaginaries and space. Although not explicitly adopting the lens of class or race for my research, field work confronted me very quickly with the societal structures that eco-communities are embedded in. Eventually, patriarchal capitalism and white supremacy also trickled down into their (alternative) mentalities, their day-to-day interactions, the collective infrastructures and the division of work conceived by the members of the communities.

Towards queering eco-communities? The long path to becoming a safer space

One resident explained to me that she felt the community was not ready to break with the cultural norms and to truly share responsibility for children away from the nuclear (heterosexual) family. Family is an important element in eco-communities. Nonetheless, this image of families is not without bias. Heteronormativity and a certain procreation pressure could be observed in all three communities. In their discourses, each eco-community wishes to welcome more families with children. In an in-depth discussion with one queer member he noted that it was difficult to be the only member representing the queer community in a context where the heterosexual nuclear family is the only visible configuration. Queer invisibility pervades in language, corporalities and materials. For example, even if compost toilets have the potential to be gender-inclusive, EC1 opted for gendered toilets: a wooden plate with a drawing showing a blond girl in a dress was attached to the entrance. In contrast to that, EC3 has a drag room to challenge gender norms through fashion. The studied eco-communities did try to queer the community projects, for instance by hosting LGBTQIA+ community events. However, these efforts were seen as delicate as even a queer member was not sure if the place could be considered safe:

> So there were trans people as well, […] but it was a bit exotic anyway, a bit fun and actually a light-hearted get-together. But at the same time, I don't think there was a deep understanding of what it was. […] There was something that was a bit beyond the scope, which was not so easy to live with, to talk so much about sexuality. We talked about polyamory, transgenderism. It was all, a bit too much, I don't know why. It has a little bit to do with the fact that it's not what the place wants to spread.
>
> (Resident EC1)

The studied eco-communities work at different levels being more or less familiar with queer-feminist vocabulary. Whereas EC1 and EC2 have few points of contact with terms such as 'cis-gender' or separate spaces without cis-men, EC3 had several meetings on queerness. Along these lines, I recommend eco-communities exploit their full spatial and transformative potential by creating spaces to explore gender-sensitive practices. This can be temporary (separated workshops without cis-men) or permanent in order to share skills or exchange experiences of discrimination, and thus to eventually create safer spaces. Yet, there is still some way to go to make eco-communities safer spaces, the following quote reflects the challenge on point: 'It's been really well received, but it hasn't changed the DNA of [EC3]. The word "queer" just didn't resonate for some people' (Male Resident EC3).

On the quest for (eco-)feminist eco-communities

For eco-communities to truly become 'pioneers of change' (Wagner et al., 2012), renegotiating gender and privilege is required. I have shown that the three eco-communities in France that were studied present new materialities, transformative care practices and partially break with common gender norms. Nevertheless, just as Tummers and MacGregor (2019) argue, physical infrastructures are not sufficient. I view the self-reflecting and critical individuals opting for a life in eco-communities and sometimes adhering to personal development both as a barrier and as a chance to reflect upon their privileges and deconstruct them critically. As 'trickle over' from ecological consciousness to gender consciousnesses failed to appear, a truly gender-just redistribution of tasks inevitably raises the question of privilege, since the most privileged would need to acknowledge and then abandon them. For eco-communities to become a (serious) interlocutor with feminism(s), binary visions of gender and a defeminization of care work are required (Gregoratti and Raphael 2019). Yet, the latter cannot be achieved if transformation happens only at the individual level of the community members. Reorganizing the structures of a community constitutes an essential step towards a more care-full living together. The studied community projects lack sensitivity and concern for gender bias, racism and (re)distribution of care as central elements of a (eco)feminist practice. These findings resonate a lot with ongoing debates amongst degrowth scholars, centring understanding feminism as not an 'add on' but as an integral part of degrowth theory and practice (Dengler and Strunk 2018). Deeper investigation, more diverse empirical insights, and eventually transformative and participative research are required to centre feminism(s) in eco-community projects. Finally, additional effort is needed to put feminism(s) on the table 'from the start' (Perkins 2010) in order to truly live up to a practice of 'living together differently'.

References

Adler, F. and Schachtschneider, U. (2010) *Green New Deal, Suffizienz oder Ökosozialismus. Konzepte für gesellschaftliche Wege aus der Ökokrise*. München: Oekom.
Argüelles, L., Anguelovski, I. and Dinnie, E. (2017) 'Power and privilege in alternative civic practices: Examining imaginaries of change and embedded rationalities in community economies', *Geoforum* 86(November), pp. 30–41.
Bauhardt, C. (2014) 'Solutions to the crisis? The green new deal, Degrowth, and the Solidarity Economy: Alternatives to the capitalist growth economy from an ecofeminist economics perspective', *Ecological Economics* 102(C), pp. 60–8.

Bauhardt, C. (2017) 'Living in a Material World: Entwurf einer queer-feministischen Ökonomie', *GENDER-Zeitschrift für Geschlecht, Kultur und Gesellschaft* 9(1), pp. 99–114.

Biesecker, A. and Hofmeister, S. (2010) 'Focus: (Re) productivity: Sustainable relations both between society and nature and between the genders', *Ecological Economics* 69(8), pp. 1703–11.

Biesecker, A., Mathes, M., Schön, S. and Scurrell, B. (2000) *Vorsorgendes Wirtschaften. Auf dem Weg zu einer Ökonomie des Guten Lebens*. Bielefeld: Kleine Verlag.

D'Alisa, G., Demaria, F. and Kallis, G. (Eds.) (2014) *Degrowth: A Vocabulary for a New Era*. Abingdon-on-Thames: Routledge.

Daly, M. (2017) 'Quantifying the environmental impact of ecovillages and co-housing communities: A systematic literature review', *Local Environment* 22(11), pp. 1358–77.

Dengler, C. and Lang, M. (2018) 'Feminism Meets Degrowth: Sorgearbeit in einer Postwachstumsgesellschaft', in Knobloch, U. (ed.) *Ökonomie des Versorgens*. Weinheim: Beltz Juventa Weinheim, pp. 123–6.

Dengler, C. and Strunk, B. (2018) 'The monetized economy versus care and the environment: Degrowth perspectives on reconciling an antagonism', *Feminist Economics* 24(3), pp. 160–83.

Eräranta, K., Moisander, J. and Pesonen, S. (2009) 'Narratives of self and relatedness in eco-communes: Resistance against normalized individualization and the nuclear family', *European Societies* 11(3), pp. 347–67.

Fisher, B. and Tronto, J. (1990) 'Toward a feminist theory of caring', in Abel, E. and Nelson, M. (eds.) *Circles of Care: Work and Identity in Women's Lives*. Albany, NY: State University of New York Press, pp. 35–62.

Garfinkel, H. (1967) 'Passing and the managed achievement of sex status in an intersexed person', in *Studies in Ethnomethodology*. Englewood Cliffs, NJ: Prentice Hall, pp. 116–85.

Gregoratti, C. and Raphael, R. (2019) 'Maria Mies's and Marilyn Waring's Critiques of Growth', in Chertkovskaya, E., Paulsson, A. and Barca S. (eds.) *Towards a Political Economy of Degrowth*. Washington, DC: Rowman and Littlefield, pp. 83–98.

Harcourt, W. and Bauhardt, C. (2018) 'Introduction: Conversations on care in feminist political economy and ecology', in Bauhardt, C. and Harcourt, W. (eds.) *Feminist Political Ecology and the Economics of Care*. London: Routledge, pp. 1–15.

Jonas, M. and Littig, B. (Eds.) (2016) *Praxeological Political Analysis*. Milton Park: Taylor & Francis.

Kallis, G. (2017) *In Defense of Degrowth: Opinions and Manifestos*. London: Uneven Earth Press.

Kallis, G., Demaria, F. and D'Alisa, G. (2014) 'Introduction: Degrowth', in D'Alisa, G., Demaria, F. and Kallis, G. (eds.) *Degrowth*. Abingdon-on-Thames: Routledge, pp. 1–18.

Kallis, G. and March, H. (2015) 'Imaginaries of hope: The utopianism of degrowth', *Annals of the Association of American Geographers* 105(2), pp. 360–8.

Kish, K. and Quilley, S. (2017) 'Wicked dilemmas of scale and complexity in the politics of degrowth', *Ecological Economics* 142(December), pp. 306–17.

Leitner, M. and Littig, B. (2017) 'Towards sustainable practices: A practice-theoretical case study of a cohousing project', in Backhaus, J., Genus, A., Lorek, S., Vadovics, E. and Wittmayer, J.M. (eds.) *Social Innovation and Sustainable Consumption*. Abingdon-on-Thames: Routledge, pp. 115–27.

Leitner, M., Markut, T., Mandl, S. and Littig, B. (2015) Nachhaltiges Wohnen und Arbeiten in einem Wohnprojekt. [Research Report] p. 156.

Litfin, K. (2012) 'Reinventing the future: The global ecovillage movement as a holistic knowledge community', in Kutting, G. and Lipschutz, R. (eds.) *Environmental Governance: Power and Knowledge in a Local/Global World*. London: Routledge, pp. 138–56.
Litfin, K. (2014) *Ecovillages: Lessons for Sustainable Community*. Oxford: John Wiley & Sons.
Littig, B. and Spitzer, M. (2011) Arbeit neu-erweiterte Arbeitskonzepte im Vergleich: Literaturstudie zum Stand der Debatte um erweiterte Arbeitskonzepte (No. 229). Working Paper.
Lockyer, J. (2017) 'Community, commons, and degrowth at Dancing Rabbit Ecovillage', *Journal of Political Ecology* 24(1), pp. 519–42.
Martens, L. and Casey, E. (2016). *Gender and Consumption: Domestic Cultures and the Commercialisation of Everyday Life*. Abingdon-on-Thames: Routledge.
Mellor, M. (2015) Contribution to GTI Roundtable 'On Degrowth,' *Great Transition Initiative*.
Merchant, C. (1980) *The Death of Nature*. London: Wildwood House.
Mies, M. and Shiva, V. (1993). *Ecofeminism*. London: Zed Books.
Perkins, P.E.E. (2010). 'Equitable, ecological degrowth: Feminist contributions', in Conference Proceedings of the 2nd Conference on Economic Degrowth for Ecological Sustainability and Social Equity, Barcelona.
Pickerill, J. (2015) 'Bodies, building and bricks: Women architects and builders in eight eco-communities in Argentina, Britain, Spain, Thailand and USA', *Gender, Place & Culture* 22(7), pp. 901–19.
Plumwood, V. (2002) *Feminism and the Mastery of Nature*. Abingdon-on-Thames: Routledge.
Randles, S. and Warde, A. (2006) 'Consumption: The view from theories of practice', in Green, K. and Randles, S. (eds.) *Industrial Ecology and Spaces of Innovation*. Northampton, MA: Edward Elgar Publishing, p. 220.
Ruether, R.R. (1975) *New Woman, New Earth: Sexist Ideologies and Human Liberation*. New York: Seabury Press.
Salleh, A. (2017) *Ecofeminism as Politics: Nature, Marx and the Postmodern*. London: Zed Books.
Scholz, S. and Heilmann, A.S. (2019) Caring Masculinities. *Männlichkeiten in der Transformation kapitalistischer Wachstumsgesellschaften*. Oekom, München.
Shove, E. and Walker, G., (2010). 'Governing transitions in the sustainability of everyday life,' *Research policy* 39(4), pp. 471–6.
Shove, E., Pantzar, M. and Watson, M. (2012) *The Dynamics of Social Practice: Everyday Life and How It Changes*. London: Sage.
Thomas, S. (2019) 'Ethnografische Datenerhebung', in *Ethnografie*. Wiesbaden: Springer VS, pp. 67–93.
Tummers, L. and MacGregor, S. (2019) 'Beyond wishful thinking: A FPE perspective on commoning, care, and the promise of co-housing', *International Journal of the Commons* 13(1), pp. 62–83. Available at: https://www.thecommonsjournal.org/articles/10.18352/ijc.918/
Wagner, F., Andreas, M. and Mende, S. (2012) 'Research in community: Collaborating for a culture of sustainability', *RCC Perspectives* 8, pp. 95–8.
Wallmeier, P. (2015) 'Dissidenz als Lebensform. Nicht-antagonistischer Widerstand in ÖkoDörfern', in Partzsch, L. and Weiland, S. (eds.) *Macht und Wandel in der Umweltpolitik*. Nomos: Verlagsgesellschaft mbH KG, pp. 181–200.

West, C. and Zimmerman, D.H. (1987) 'Doing gender', *Gender & Society* 1(2), pp. 125–51.
Winker, G. (2015) *Care Revolution: Schritte in eine solidarische Gesellschaft*. Bielefeld: Transcript Verlag.
Wolcott, H.F. (1999) *Ethnography: A Way of Seeing*. Walnut Creek, CA: Rowman Altamira.

10

Uneven equity and sustainability in intentional communities in the United States: A national-level exploratory analysis

Christina Lopez and Russell Weaver

Introduction

Calls for a more 'sustainable' built environment are regularly informed by recognition that the climate crisis is intimately connected to society's other systemic problems (Agyeman 2013), such as structural racism, social and economic injustice, and widening levels of inequality (Jafry 2018). In other words, if we are committed to building a more 'charming' and 'livable' world for present and future generations (Buck 2015; Hester 2006), then it is essential to look beyond purely environmental considerations and instead grapple more holistically with visions for how the built environment can be reorganized into patterns of settlements that are at once more welcoming, diverse, equitable, just, inclusive and sustainable relative to conventional neighbourhoods (Lopez and Weaver 2019a; Pickerill 2020a).

Towards that end, recent research suggests that *intentional communities* (ICs) such as eco-villages and eco-communities are alternative, 'actually-existing socio-spatial configurations that depart from mainstream modes of living in ways that are likely to produce different – potentially more just, equitable, and sustainable – social, economic, political, and environmental outcomes' (Lopez and Weaver 2019a, 198). Stated another way, ICs offer scholars and practitioners real-world case studies for researching settlements that are purposefully designed and formed by people to 'collectively enact bottom-up solutions' to one or more of the systemic problems that plague conventional communities (Lopez and Weaver 2019a, 205; Lopez and Weaver 2019b). To the extent that ICs successfully realize these ambitions, studying their physical, spatial, socio-institutional and cultural arrangements can uncover potentially scalable insights to inform society-wide strategies for addressing the intersecting crises of the twenty-first century.

Yet, for all of the promise that ICs and IC research offer, there is little if any empirical work to suggest that existing ICs are universally more inclusive and socially and environmentally desirable spaces than their conventional counterparts. At least part of the reason for this lack of evidence is that data on ICs can be elusive – as such, IC research is often based on individual case studies that have produced mixed results to date (Lopez and Weaver 2019b). This chapter puts forward the first national-level empirical analysis of ICs in the contiguous United States. To accomplish this goal, we draw on the web-based directory of ICs maintained by the Foundation for Intentional Community (FIC). While the FIC directory relies on self-reporting, and it therefore does not represent an exhaustive inventory of all ICs across the globe, it is arguably the most comprehensive source of information on ICs presently available. Consequently, we use it to (1) map the geography of ICs in the conterminous United States and (2) analyse the degree to which ICs (fail to) perform stronger on selected social, economic and environmental indicators relative to their neighbouring geographies. With respect to the latter, we ask, specifically: do census tracts[1] containing ICs exhibit significant differences from their surrounding census tracts on selected indicators of *sustainability*, *diversity*, and *equity*?

Purpose and aspirations of intentional communities

Intentional communities (ICs) are small groups of people that live together – intentionally – to pursue specific goals (Brown 2002; Shenker 1986). ICs exist in many countries and landscapes, from urban high-rises in Australia to small rural villages in New York state. Based on their 'specific goals' or objectives, ICs tend to be classified into four broad, non-mutually exclusive categories: ideological, ecological, practical and communal (Lopez and Weaver 2019a; Meijering, Huigen, and Van Hoven 2007; Sanguinetti 2012; Shenker 1986). Generally speaking, ideological ICs have a religious or spiritual purpose; ecological ICs, or eco-village/eco-communities, strive for low-impact living and to forge connections with nature; practical ICs are typically where members live together (co-housing) for financial or social reasons; and communal ICs are organized to promote shared living experiences, work and income. Regardless of type, though, one 'commonality among [all] ICs is that they present alternative moral claims about the arrangement of society' (Rubin, Willis, and Ludwig 2019, 183).

As of 2019, there were approximately 1,085 active or forming ICs in the United States (Foundation of Intentional Communities 2019). A preponderance of these ICs – especially ecological intentional communities – maintain goals of inclusivity, equity, diversity, and social and environmental sustainability (Bhatia 2023; Cooper 2013; Dawson 2006; Kunze 2012; Lockyer 2007; Sanguinetti 2012; Sargisson 2009). As implicated above, aspects of social and environmental sustainability need to be addressed in tandem because 'a truly sustainable society is one where wide questions of social needs and welfare, and economic opportunity, are integrally connected to environmental concerns' (Agyeman, Bullard, and Evans 2003, 78). Thus, ecological

---

[1] Tracts were chosen over block groups for this study insofar as pertinent income inequality data (namely, the Gini coefficient) are provided by the US Census Bureau for the former, but not the latter geographies.

intentional communities, according to the Global Ecovillage Network, 'use local participatory processes to holistically integrate ecological, economic, social, and cultural dimensions of sustainability in order to regenerate social and natural environments' (Global Ecovillage Network n.d.). Scholars have demonstrated that some eco-villages are capable of reducing consumption of electricity and water and trash production to an amount that is a mere 10 per cent of the average North American (Jones 2014; Lockyer 2017). Further, ICs not only attempt to reduce consumption, but, according to Rubin, they alter relationships with technology and modernism to fit their needs: 'Pooping in a bucket is as innovative and important as using the internet for fundraising and recruitment, since both are key to achieving the mission of the eco-village and their use is informed by the ecological motivator' (Rubin 2019, 15). For these reasons, ICs are often seen as 'place-based sustainability initiatives' (Pisters, Vihinen, and Figueiredo 2020, 2).

ICs offer a model of low-impact living through environmentally responsible design, including aspects of energy consumption or production, food production, renewable or savaged housing materials, and overall reduced resource consumption (Choi 2008). ICs have also been associated with improvements in quality of life (socially) for their residents, as well as higher degrees of individual happiness compared to residents in conventional communities (Grinde et al., 2017; Mulder, Costanza, and Erickson 2006). More generally, ICs attempt to: 'facilitate a national dialogue on how we live by modelling an alternative to urban sprawl', combat the breakdown of social institutions, and address environmental degradation (Chitewere 2006, v; Putnam 2000; Trainer 1997).

Discourses on inclusivity, equity and diversity are present in the majority of IC mission statements and/or community descriptions. While most such statements include vague concepts (e.g. 'radical acceptance', 'cultural diversity' and 'tolerance of diversity'), some ICs list specific criteria for their diversity objectives: ethnicity, gender, generation, household composition and income (Arkin 2012). For example, an IC in Arizona states they 'embrace and nurture diversity', striving to be a lesbian, gay, bisexual and transgender (LGBT) welcoming community (Foundation for Intentional Communities 2019). Recent research on equity (in terms of governance) and (racial) diversity demonstrates these features are integral to the success – meaning the ongoing operation and existence – of ICs and the satisfaction of community members (Rubin et al., 2019). First, there is a positive relationship between egalitarian decision-making structures and satisfaction with community governance (Rubin et al., 2019, 187). Second, communities with low levels of racial diversity reported lower levels of satisfaction. To be sure, Rubin and colleagues found that 'predominately white (over 75%) communities fare worse than the more diverse' in terms of community member satisfaction. The authors conclude that, in modern ICs, racial diversity is a key to success (Rubin et al., 2019, 190).

In more general terms, Trainer (1997) suggests that community is crucial to a sustainable society. To Trainer, such a society is an amalgam of highly self-sufficient communities characterized by thriving local (small) economies, institutions of sharing and minimal within- and between-community levels of inequality. These ideas and observations are highly consistent with streams of literature that are rooted in urban and community planning. Namely, concepts from scholarship on New Urbanism and Activist (Advocacy) Planning exhibit considerable overlap with motivations and ideals identified in ICs and IC research. This overlap is briefly introduced in the remainder of this section and then summarized in Table 1 by way of concrete examples from the mission statement excerpts taken from selected ICs that are represented in the Foundation for Intentional Community (FIC) directory.

New Urbanism refers to a school of thought in urban planning and design that advocates for compact, high-density living in economically and racially diverse communities (Congress for New Urbanism 2008; Trudeau 2013; Trudeau and Kaplan 2015). New Urbanism – like many ICs – is anti-sprawl (Choi 2008; Duany and Brain 2005; Garde 2006; Lehrer and Milgrom 1996). Similar to ICs, New Urbanist communities seek to promote internal social bonds that are not limited to family, are joined voluntarily and typically involve some degree of shared property or common spaces. Both New Urbanist communities and many ecological ICs seek to be environmentally sustainable through reducing personal automotive transportation and creating safe, walkable neighbourhoods (Gallimore, Brown, and Werner 2011). In addition, both New Urbanism and many ICs share overarching social goals such as building community, social equity and enhancing the common good (Talen 2002). Key indicators used by researchers to evaluate how well-aligned existing New Urbanist

Table 1 Overlap between selected planning concepts and ICs using real-world examples

Location	Related concept	Excerpts from community descriptions/mission statements:
Name	Type	
	New urbanism	
Santa Cruz, California, USA *Walnut commons*	*Practical / ecological*	'An all-age community, contained in a 3-story LEED compatible building with underground parking. There are 19 units, 700–1400 square feet, plus a large common area and terrace. We commit to being a vibrant community, sharing meals 3 times a week, living in a location where we are far less dependent on cars since we can bike and walk to shops, restaurants, the beach and incredible hiking trails.' '[An] urban community that fosters mutual support and cooperation while respecting privacy. We encourage ecologically responsible living, nonviolence, a healthy living environment, and we value active participation in the local and larger world.'
	Activist planning	
St. Louis, Missouri, USA *Eco Village StL*	*Ecological*	'We aim to provide a safe place for community members' to sleep or live, whether it be travelers, those in crisis, activists needing housing to continue working in the movement, or a street musician needing a couch to crash on for a few weeks. We have an open door and open arms. We love everyone. Welcome Home.'

Table 2 IC and related concepts of communal/social arrangements, with relevant indicators

Concepts related to ICs	Major overlap with ICs relating to sustainability, equity and diversity	Indicators used in research
New urbanism	• Bonds are not only by family • Voluntarily join • Sharing of some portion of property or common space • Dense development • Less dependent on individual automotive transportation • Lower dependence on fossil fuels and lower impact living	• Income (in)equality • Education • Ethnicity • Density • Biking/walking • Fewer private cars • Telecommuting or working from home
Activist Planning	• Centred on loyalty to a group or community • Commitment to a strategic cause • Aim to improve the relationship between social groups or interests	• Diversity • Community self-sufficiency (self-employment)

communities are with these goals include income, ethnic diversity, economic (in) equality, resident education levels and density (as a proxy of compactness) (Day 2003; Mason 2010; Trudeau and Kaplan 2015).

Activist (or Advocacy) Planning involves a commitment to strategic causes that are generally geared towards improving or bringing awareness to inequitable social relations (Bratt and Reardon 2013; Leal 2010; Sager 2016). Advocacy planners value a democratic society with strongholds in personal freedoms, openness, tolerance and inclusion (Sager 2017). Such values are evident in many ICs. Dogwood Hollow Homestead, an IC in Missouri, for example, is prefiguring a society in which no non-renewable resources will be available, and where maximal freedoms facilitate community-scale self-sufficient living (Foundation for Intentional Communities 2019).

Taken together, the foregoing engagements with relevant literature suggest that ICs – similar to the type of planned communities being advocated by Activist and New Urbanist urban and community planners – are often formed to pursue progressive social and environmental goals related to ecological sustainability, social and economic equity, and diversity and inclusion. Table 2 summarizes some of the specific social and institutional arrangements that are implicated by these goals, along with tangible indicators that researchers have used to evaluate how well communities are accomplishing those goals in practice. The remainder of this chapter employs those indicators in an empirical analysis of ICs in the United States.

Data and methods of analysis

Data for this project were acquired through three secondary sources. First, the Foundation for Intentional Community (FIC) provides an online directory with communities' approximate location. In 2018, the geographic coordinates of established ICs were extracted from that directory and used to create a geographic data layer. In total, 860 records were included in that data layer for the United States. However, further inspection revealed that numerous ICs were entered into the directory more than once, resulting in extensive duplication of some records. After de-duplicating the dataset and spatially selecting only those ICs in the study area (the conterminous United States), we were left with 673 IC point locations distributed across 594 census tracts. Figure 1 maps the distribution of those ICs.

Next, the data for selected demographic and socioeconomic variables were obtained from two sources: the US Census American Community Survey (ACS) Five-Year Estimates for 2014–18 and Esri Business Analyst 2019. Variables selected from these sources for our exploratory study were drawn directly from the indicator list developed in Table 2 in consultation with instructive literature. The precise set of variables, as well as the data source from which each was acquired, is presented in Table 3. Table 3 further summarizes the broader IC concepts (e.g. sustainability, diversity, equity) to which each individual indicator is connected.

Prior to moving on, note that the variables listed in Table 3 were obtained at the census tract level of analysis. In the US Census Bureau's geographic framework, census tracts are data collection units that 'generally have a population size between 1,200 and 8,000 people, with an optimum size of 4,000 people' (US Census Bureau). Importantly, while census tracts are regularly used to represent 'neighbourhoods' or 'communities' in quantitative social science research, administratively delineated tract boundaries

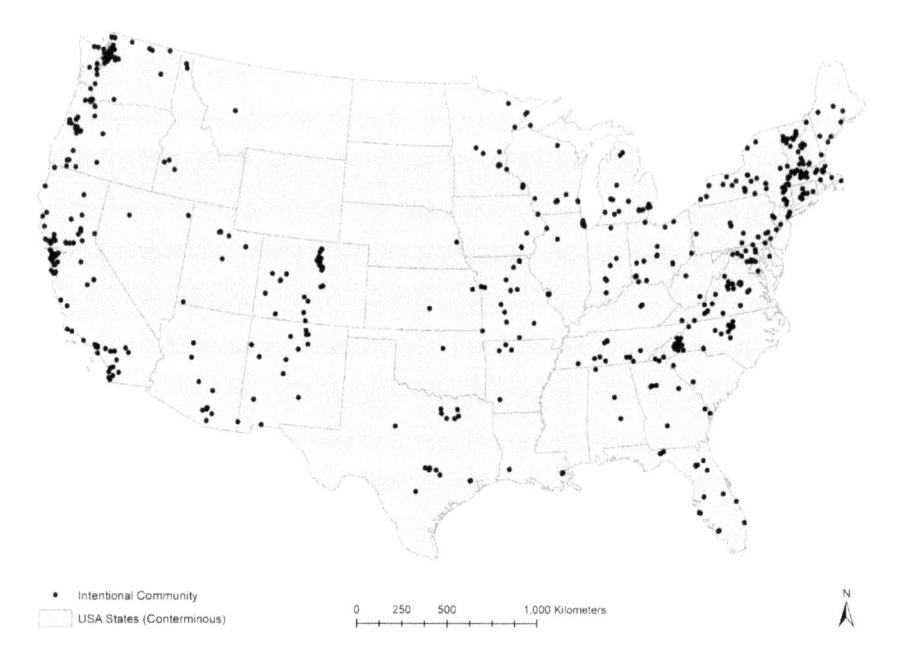

Figure 1 Distribution of intentional communities in the contiguous United States. (Source: Christina Lopez and Russell Weaver.)

Table 3 Indicators and data sources

Variable	Potential indicator of:	Related to broader IC concept of:	Data source
Population density (persons per square mile)	Compactness	Sustainability	Esri Business Analyst 2019
% Private car commuters	Greenhouse gas emissions	(un)Sustainability	US Census ACS 2014–18
% Carpool commuters	Lower reliance on automobiles	Sustainability	US Census ACS 2014–18
% Biking or walking commuters	Lower reliance on automobiles	Sustainability	US Census ACS 2014–18
% Work from home	Lower reliance on automobiles	Sustainability	US Census ACS 2014–18
% Self-employment income	Local self-reliance	Sustainability	US Census ACS 2014–18
Housing Affordability Index (100=average; higher values indicate greater affordability)	Cost of living	Equity	Esri Business Analyst 2019
% with Bachelor's degree or higher	Socioeconomic status	Equity and Diversity	US Census ACS 2014–18
Wealth Index (100=average; higher values indicate wealthier population)	Socioeconomic status	Equity and Diversity	Esri Business Analyst 2019
Gini Index of Income Inequality (higher values indicate greater inequality)	Socioeconomic status	Equity	US Census ACS 2014–18
Racial diversity (0=homogeneous; 100=maximum diversity)	Demographics	Diversity	Esri Business Analyst 2019
% Persons of colour	Demographics	Diversity	US Census ACS 2014–18

rarely if ever coincide with social perceptions or definitions of neighbourhood or community spatial footprints (Weaver 2014). It is almost certain that members of the ICs represented in Figure 1 would not draw their home census tracts when asked about the spatial boundaries of their communities. Consequently, the results presented herein must be taken with the appropriate amount of caution. That being said, we note that, without operationalizing ICs using political or administrative units for which secondary data have been collected, a national-extent empirical study would not be possible. To facilitate such an exploration, we therefore caution that: (1) because the

FIC directory only provides spatial coordinates for IC locations, not areal boundaries, (2) ICs are proxied in our analyses using the census tracts in which their FIC-reported coordinates fall.

Recall from the introduction that this chapter has two key objectives – to:

1. map and describe the geographic distribution of ICs in the conterminous United States and
2. analyse the degree to which ICs (fail to) perform stronger on selected social, economic and environmental indicators relative to their neighbouring geographies.

Whereas Figure 1 attended to part of the first objective, insofar as it mapped ICs using data from the Foundation for Intentional Community (FIC) web-based directory, there is certainly more to be said about the resultant pattern. On that note, given the exploratory aim of this investigation, it is beyond our scope to dive into explaining the variation in the distribution of ICs shown in Figure 1. Instead, we simply ask two follow-up questions here, answers to which can inform and motivate future research. Namely, (i) is the spatial pattern of ICs from Figure 1 (non)random? And, (ii) where in the United States do there appear to be the highest concentrations or densities of ICs? To answer these follow-up questions, we perform a simple point pattern analysis using Ripley's K function to describe the distribution of ICs; and we use kernel density (with 1km^2 grid cells) to convert the distribution from Figure 1 into a heat map with which eyeball estimates can point out areas that might be of interest for closer examination of the IC phenomenon in the United States.

Next, to address our second objective, we used a spatial selection procedure to identify every census tract in the conterminous United States that contains at least one of the IC point locations we extracted from the FIC directory. There were 594 such tracts in our study area, which we coded as 'IC tracts'. To explore how these IC tracts compare on our selected indicators to similarly-situated tracts, we used spatial selection once more to identify tracts that are adjacent to the 594 IC tracts. We used a common definition of adjacency to mean any tract that shares at least one point with a given IC tract. There were 3,399 of these adjacent, 'comparison tracts' that featured nonzero population data (i.e. we used only tracts that contain people). Finally, to compare the IC tracts to their neighbouring tracts, we relied on a combination of parametric t-tests to examine differences in variable means between the two groups, and nonparametric Mann-Whitney tests, which loosely look for differences in the medians of the two groups (and are used in cases of highly skewed variable distributions) (Weaver et al., 2016). In both cases, the null hypotheses are that IC tracts and comparison tracts do not exhibit differences in the indicator variables – rejecting those hypotheses suggests that IC tracts are meaningfully different from their surroundings on the selected indicators.

Interrogating sustainability, equity and diversity

Exploratory point pattern analysis using Ripley's K function over a range of spatial distances revealed unambiguous evidence of clustering in the distribution of intentional communities (ICs) in the conterminous United States. Whereas some of this clustering can plausibly be explained by variation in population distribution (e.g. there are relatively more ICs near population centres on both coasts of the United States), the heat map in Figure 2 flags a few other possibilities for future research. Namely, some of the highest densities of ICs in the United States are relatively proximate to prominent natural and/or cultural features, including (from east to west) the Appalachian Trail, the Mississippi River, the Continental Divide National Trail and the Pacific Crest Trail.

The results from carrying out the t-tests and Mann-Whitney tests outlined above are shown in Table 4. The tests are grouped into the three major categories of goals or values that have featured throughout this chapter: [environmental] sustainability, equity and diversity (Table 4). Recall that the tests evaluate the broad null hypotheses that IC tracts and their adjacent neighbourhoods do not differ in the selected indicators. Rejection of that null hypothesis is indicated with asterisks in the table, and means that IC tracts, on the whole, are different from their neighbouring tracts in ways that cannot be explained by chance alone.

The results from further exploring the spatial pattern of intentional communities (ICs) in the continental United States show evidence of clustering (see Figure 2), with relatively high densities near coastal population centres and in relatively close proximity to noteworthy natural and cultural features, i.e. the Mississippi River (largest watershed) and three longest hiking trails (Alltrails.org)

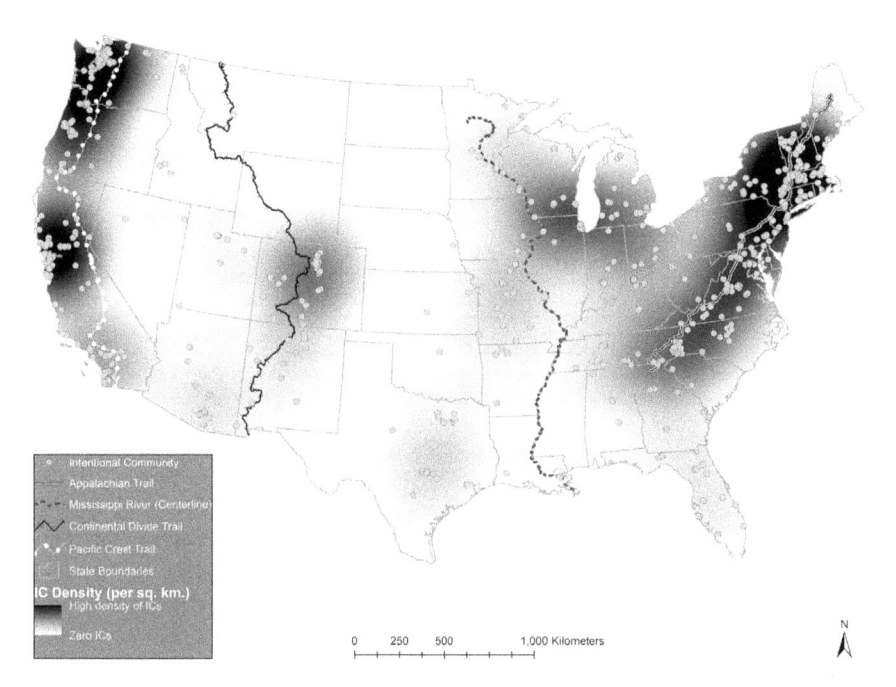

Figure 2 Heat map of intentional communities in the conterminous United States relative to selected natural and cultural features of potential interest for future research. (Source: Christina Lopez and Russell Weaver.)

Table 4 Sustainability indicators in IC tracts and neighbouring tracts

Goal	Outcome/indicator	IC tracts Median	IC tracts Mean	Neighbouring tracts Median	Neighbouring tracts Mean	p
Sustainability	Population density (persons per square mile)	564.6[a]	4,527[a]	812.9[a]	4,748[a]	0.255
	% Private car commuters	74.0	69.6	76.1	71.0	0.065*
	% Carpool commuters	8.0	8.6	8.5	8.8	0.235
	% Biking or walking commuters	3.3[a]	7.3[a]	2.8[a]	6.5[a]	0.002***
	% Work from home	6.3	7.1	5.6	6.6	0.037**
	% Self-employment income (indicator of local self-sufficiency)	13.2	13.8	12.4	13.1	0.009***
Equity	Housing Affordability Index (100=average; higher values indicate greater affordability)	102	108.5	110	114.4	0.009***
	% with bachelor's degree or higher	34.3	38.4	30.7	36.0	0.013**
	Wealth Index (100=average; higher values indicate wealthier population)	80	103.0	78	100.2	0.384
	Gini Index of Income Inequality (higher values indicate greater inequality)	44.5	45.2	43.3	43.7	<0.001***
Diversity	Racial diversity (0=homogeneous; 100=maximum diversity)	38.9	41.6	39.7	42.2	0.576
	% Persons of colour	20.0	27.7	21.3	30.0	0.031**
n		594		3,399		

[a]The test summarized in this row is a non-parametric Mann-Whitney test due to highly skewed distributions of this variable. All other tests are parametric t-tests.

***p<0.01; **p<0.05; *p<0.10.

in the United States. Nearness to these features might be a reflection of 'back-to-the-land' and counterurbanism movements that have been linked to some ICs whose members desire to get away from society, establish alternative, small-scale, self-sufficient economies and reconnect to nature (Halfacree 2001; Mitchell 2004). If these sorts of tendencies are indeed factoring into IC formation and spatial decision-making in the United States, then ICs might not be quite as accessible, dense and diverse as some of the more urban-centred literature would suggest (see above).

To add greater perspective to the notion that actually existing ICs might be somewhat more exclusive than most of them set out to be, observe that eight of the twelve statistical tests summarized in Table 4 reveal significant differences between IC and neighbouring tracts. In four of those eight cases, IC tracts are found to be more *exclusive* than what would be expected by chance alone. Specifically, relative to their neighbours, IC tracts: (1) have less affordable housing and (2) greater income inequality, with residents who are (3) more educated and (4) less likely to be persons of colour. These findings are highly consistent with existing literature. Qualitative research on ICs in the state of Texas, for instance, found that communities lacked diversity (Lopez and Weaver 2019b). Empirical research on New Urbanist communities recurrently finds that residents tend to be somewhat homogeneously white and affluent (Day 2003; Mason 2010; Markley 2018).

On the other hand, the remaining four tests for which we rejected the null hypothesis suggest that ICs in the continental United States might indeed have fewer negative environmental impacts relative to their conventional neighbouring communities. More precisely, compared to surrounding tracts, IC tracts contain (1) fewer single-occupancy vehicle commuters, (2) more commuters who bike or walk to work, (3) more workers who telecommute or otherwise work at home (and therefore do not rely on gas-powered automobiles for their day-to-day occupations) and (4) more households with self-employed earnings. The former three of these results imply that IC residents may emit fewer greenhouse gases into the atmosphere than residents of traditional communities, while the latter finding is consistent with the notion that some ICs seek to establish locally self-reliant communities that are less dependent on conventional capitalist employment relations (Trainer 1997). In these respects, all four findings offer emerging evidence that the physical, spatial, social, cultural and/or institutional arrangements in ICs might help them to function more environmentally sustainably than conventional American settlements.

Conclusions, limitations and moving forward

Academic researchers have a long history of studying intentional communities (ICs) such as eco-villages and eco-communities; however, only recently have these settlements been reframed as 'radical spaces of innovation' (Pickerill and Maxey 2009) that might hold the keys to scalable solutions to the manifold, intersecting crises of the Anthropocene (Lopez and Weaver 2019a). Although these communities often do facilitate lower impact and more environmentally sensitive ways of life (Chitewere 2006) (also see Table 4), consistent with findings from research on New Urbanist neighbourhoods, buying into these ways of life can be costly and inaccessible to most people, and therefore, not 'inclusive'. Our findings that the highest densities of ICs tend to be found near 'in demand' natural and cultural features like celebrated scenic trails makes it somewhat unsurprising that we found housing costs in IC tracts to be higher than their surroundings. The logical consequence of higher housing costs is that residents of IC tracts tend to be more affluent, educated and less diverse (i.e. whiter) than residents of surrounding neighbourhoods. The upshot is that, if ICs or any other planned communities are going to serve as models for reconfiguring the built environment in response to the climate crisis, then it is critical to engage more directly with the forces that make such communities exclusive places that cater primarily to the privileged few (Pickerill 2020b). That is, urban and community design can only go so far in isolation. ICs and other low-impact communities can certainly offer important on-the-ground examples that help us to envision the shapes that a more sustainable world might take, but without simultaneously fighting for systems change to open up that world to everyone, those shapes are bound to continue bending towards inequality and exclusivity (Weaver 2019).

As a final matter, we acknowledge that our broad, national-scale approach potentially masks important state- or region-level differences in outcomes. Also, because our initial explorations were aimed mostly at understanding race and class structures of IC spaces relative to their surroundings, we did not engage with other forms of identity that are essential for building a fuller picture of IC social composition, such as gender, sexual orientation or family type. Whereas our initial results suggest that actually existing ICs might not be as inclusive as rhetoric surrounding ICs would lead observers to believe, further evidence for or against this claim must be guided by future research that engages directly with intersections of race and gender. For, if ICs are to be(come) models of lower impact living for navigating future climate crises, then it must be acknowledged that women, especially women of colour, are 'particularly vulnerable' to the hazards of climate change (Bhatia 2023; Tanner, Mitchell, and Lussier 2007). Importantly, gender equity has been a focus of at least a handful of ICs (Bhatia 2023), flagging the topic as a vital one for future research.

Despite these limitations, though, this chapter arguably established a starting point for empirical research that compares ICs to conventional neighbourhoods. From such a national starting point or baseline, deeper investigations into subnational patterns can be launched for the purposes of developing richer theory and revealing more nuanced practical implications, to move IC scholarship and on-the-ground experiments forward in pursuit of more sustainable, equitable and just futures. On that note, we invite readers to join the growing efforts to understand how ICs such as eco-villages and eco-communities might prefigure a more 'charming' and 'livable' Anthropocene (Buck 2015). Onward.

References

Agyeman, J. (2013) *Introducing Just Sustainabilities: Policy, Planning, and Practice*. London: Zed Books.

Agyeman, J., Bullard, R.D. and Evans, B. (eds.) (2003). *Just Sustainabilities: Development in an Unequal World*. Cambridge, MA: MIT Press.

Arkin, L. (2012) 'Diversity issues in Los Angeles eco-village', *Communities* 155(1), pp. 14–18.

Bhatia, M. (2022). 'Gender and sustainability in ecological intentional communities', *Environmental Sociology* 8(2), pp. 199–210.

Bhatia, M. (2023) 'Work and Sustainability at Twin Oaks Intentional Community', in Delbridge, R., Helfen, M., Pekarek, A. and Purser, G. (eds.) *Ethnographies of Work*. Leeds: Emerald Publishing Limited, pp. 73–93.

Bratt, R.G. and Reardon, K.M. (2013) 'Beyond the ladder: New ideas about resident roles in contemporary community development', in Carmon, N. and Fainstein, S. (eds.) *Policy, Planning, and People: Promoting Justice in Urban Development*. Philadelphia, PA: University of Pennsylvania Press, pp. 356–81.

Brown, S. (2002) *Intentional Community: An Anthropological Perspective*. Albany, NY: State University of New York Press.

Buck, H.J. (2015) 'On the possibilities of a charming Anthropocene', *Annals of the Association of American Geographers*, 105(2), pp. 369–77.

Chitewere, T. (2006) *Constructing a Green Lifestyle: Consumption and Environmentalism in an Ecovillage*. PhD Dissertation. State University of New York at Binghamton.

Choi, J.S. (2008) 'Characteristics of community life in foreign intentional communities focus on the differences between ecovillage and cohousing', *International Journal of Human Ecology* 9(2), pp. 93–105.

Congress for the New Urbanism (2008) Canons of sustainable architecture and urbanism: A companion to the charter of the new urbanism. http://www.cnu.org/canons.

Cooper, L. (2013) *Sustainability through Community: Social Capital in Australia's Inner Urban Eco-communities*. PhD Dissertation. The University of Melbourne.

Dawson, J. (2006) *Ecovillages: New Frontiers for Sustainability*. Foxhole: Green Books.

Day, K. (2003) 'New urbanism and the challenges of designing for diversity', *Journal of Planning Education and Research* 23(1), pp. 83–95.

Duany, A. and Brain, D. (2005) 'Regulating as if humans matter: The transect and post-suburban planning', in Ben-Joseph, E. and Szold, T. (eds.) *Regulating Place: Standards and the Shaping of Urban America*. London: Routledge, pp. 301–40.

Foundation for Intentional Communities (2019) URL: https://www.ic.org/directory/listings/.

Gallimore, J.M., Brown, B.B. and Werner, C.M. (2011) 'Walking routes to school in new urban and suburban neighborhoods: An environmental walkability analysis of blocks and routes', *Journal of Environmental Psychology* 31(2), pp. 184–91.

Garde, A. (2006) 'Designing and developing New Urbanist projects in the United States: Insights and implications', *Journal of Urban Design* 11(1), pp. 33–54.

Global Ecovillage Network. (n.d.). *About GEN*. Retrieved January 7, 2025, from https://ecovillage.org/about/about-gen/.

Globe Ecovillage Network (2017) URL: https://ecovillage.org/.

Grinde, B., Bang Nes, R., MacDonald, I.F. and Wilson, D. (2017) 'Quality of life in intentional communities', *Social Indicators Research* 137(2), pp. 625–640. DOI: 10.1007/s11205-017-1615-3.

Halfacree, K. (2001) 'Going "back-to-the-land" again: Extending the scope of counterurbanisation', *Repopulation and Rural Mobilities* 19(1), pp. 167–70.

Hester, R.T. (2006) *Design for Ecological Democracy*. Cambridge, MA: MIT Press.

Jafry, T. (2018) *Routledge Handbook of Climate Justice*. London: Routledge.

Jones, K.B. (2014) *Toward Sustainable Community: Assessing Progress at Dancing Rabbit Ecovillage*. MA Thesis. University of North Texas.

Kunze, I. (2012) 'Social innovations for communal and ecological living: Lessons from sustainable research and observations in intentional communities', *Journal of Communal Societies* 32(1), pp. 50–67.

Leal, P.A. (2010) 'Participation: The ascendancy of a buzzword in the neo-liberal era', *Development in Practice* 17(4), pp. 539–48.
Lehrer, U.A. and Milgrom, R. (1996) 'New (sub)urbanism: countersprawl or repacking the product', *Capitalism Nature Socialism* 7(2), pp. 49–64.
Lockyer, J. (2017) 'Community, commons, and degrowth at dancing rabbit ecovillage', *Journal of Political Ecology* 24(1), pp. 519–566. DOI: 10.2458/v24i1.20890.
Lockyer, J.P. (2007) *Sustainability and Utopianism: An Ethnography of Cultural Critique in Contemporary Intentional Communities*. PhD Dissertation. The University of Georgia.
Lopez, C. and Weaver, R. (2019a). 'Placing intentional communities in geography', *Journal of Geography* 118(5), pp. 197–209.
Lopez, C. and Weaver, R. (2019b) 'A conceptual model for assessing environmentally responsible practices in ecological intentional communities: Examples from Texas, USA', *Journal of Communal Societies* 39(2), pp. 93–105.
Markley, S. (2018) 'Suburban gentrification? Examining the geographies of New Urbanism in Atlanta's inner suburbs', *Urban Geography* 39(4), pp. 606–30.
Mason, S.G. (2010) 'Can community design build trust? A comparative study of design factors in Boise, Idaho neighborhoods', *Cities* 27(6), pp. 456–65.
Meijering, L., Huigen, P., and Van Hoven, B. (2007) 'Intentional communities in rural spaces', *Tijdschrift voor economische en sociale geografie* 98(1), pp. 42–52.
Mitchell, J.A.C. (2004) 'Making sense of counterurbanization', *Journal of Rural Studies* 20(1), pp. 15–34.
Mulder, K., Costanza, R. and Erickson, J. (2006) 'The contribution of built, human, social and natural capitals to quality of life in intentional and unintentional communities', *Ecological Economics* 59(1), pp. 13–23.
Pickerill, J. (2020a) 'Eco-communities as insurgent climate urbanism: Radical urban socio-material transformations', *Urban Geography* 42(6), pp. 738–43.
Pickerill, J. (2020b) 'Making climate urbanism from the grassroots: Eco-communities, experiments and divergent temporalities', in Broto, V.C., Robin, E. and While, A. (eds.) *Climate Urbanism*. Springer Nature, Cham, Switzerland: Palgrave Macmillan, pp. 227–42.
Pickerill, J. and Maxey, L. (2009) 'Geographies of sustainability: Low impact developments and radical spaces of innovation', *Geography Compass* 3(4), pp. 1515–39.
Pisters, S.R., Vihinen, H. and Figueiredo, E. (2020) 'Inner change and sustainability initiatives: Explore the narratives from eco-villages through a place-based transformative learning approach', *Sustainability Science* 15, pp. 395–409. DOI: https://doi.org/10.1007/s11625-019-00775-9.
Putnam, R. (2000) *Bowling Alone: The Collapse and Revival of American Community*. New York: Simon and Schuster.
Rubin, Z. (2019) 'Ecovillagers Assessment of Sustainability: Differing Perceptions of Technology as a Differing Account of Modernism', *Sustainability* 11(21), p. 6167.
Rubin, Z., Willis, D. and Ludwig, M. (2019) 'Measuring success in intentional communities: A critical evaluation of commitment and longevity theories', *Sociological Spectrum* 39(3), pp. 181–93. DOI: https://doi.org/10.1080/02732173.2019.1645063.
Sager, T. (2016) 'Activist planning: A response to the woes of neo-liberalism?', *European Planning Studies* 24(7), pp. 1262–80.
Sager, T. (2017) 'Planning by intentional communities: An understudied form of activist planning', *Planning Theory* 17(4), pp. 449–71.
Sanguinetti, A. (2012) 'The design of intentional communities: A recycled perspective on sustainable neighborhoods', *Behavior and Social Issues* 21(1), pp. 5–25.

Sargisson, L. (2009) 'Sustainability and the intentional community: Green intentional communities', in Leonard, L. and Barry, J. (eds.) *The Transition to Sustainable Living and Practice, Volume 4*. Bingley: Emerald Publishing, pp. 171–92.

Shenker, B. (1986) *Intentional Communities: Ideology and Alienation in Communal Societies*. London: Routledge and Kegan Paul.

Talen, E. (2002) 'The social goals of new urbanism', *Housing Policy Debate* 13(1), pp. 165–88.

Tanner, T., Mitchell, T. and Lussier, K. (2007) *We Know What We Need: South Asian Women Speak Out on Climate Change Adaptation*. London: ActionAid.

Trainer, F.E. (1997) 'The global sustainability crisis: The implications for community', *International Journal of Social Economics* 24(11), pp. 1219–40.

Trudeau, D. (2013) 'New urbanism as sustainable development?', *Geography Compass* 7(6), pp. 435–48.

Trudeau, D. and Kaplan, J. (2015) 'Is there diversity in the New Urbanism? Analyzing the demographic characteristics of New Urbanism neighborhoods in the United States', *Urban Geography* 33(3), pp. 458–82.

US Census Bureau (n.d.) 'Glossary: Census Tract'. URL: https://www.census.gov/programs-surveys/geography/about/glossary.html#par_textimage_13

Weaver, R. (2014) 'Contextual influences on political behavior in cities: Toward urban electoral geography', *Geography Compass* 8(12), pp. 874–91.

Weaver, R. (2019) *Erasing Red Lines: Part 2-Systems Thinking for Social and Community Change. Cornell University ILR Buffalo Co-Lab*. URL: https://digitalcommons.ilr.cornell.edu/buffalocommons/417/

Weaver, R., Bagchi-Sen, S., Knight, J. and Frazier, A.E. (2016) *Shrinking Cities: Understanding Urban Decline in the United States*. New York: Routledge.

11

Confronting racial privilege: Questioning whiteness in eco-communities

Jenny Pickerill

The problematic positionality of eco-communities – at once activist movements on the margins of society that create vibrant alternative futures, and simultaneously movements able to secure themselves against climate change by building retreat spaces for their future – remains largely unexplored (Taylor Aiken and Mabon 2024). Eco-communities deliberately employ low-tech, grassroots, low-cost alternatives, yet the outcomes of their attempts at transformation are often worryingly similar to neoliberal practices – eco-enclaves, exclusionary spaces, rising house prices and so on.

Participants in eco-communities often assertively reject or deny that they may hold class or racial privilege. They argue instead that their lack of financial assets balances or erases other aspects of their relative security and that they are precariously positioned. There remain intractable silences around environmental racism from eco-communities – silences about ongoing inequity, insecurity and injustice (see Chitewere Chapter 7 for more on this). This chapter explores the damage that this positioning of privileged-as-precarious does to the ability of eco-communities to effectively contribute to socio-ecological transformations.

This chapter draws on examples predominantly from the UK, United States and Australia. There is an obvious focus here on Anglophone countries. In addition, as a white English woman, I share much of the privilege I am seeking to challenge. It should be the privileged who do the work of social change in eco-communities, to actively listen to critiques about exclusionary practices, and not to expect marginalized others to do additional work to make these spaces inclusive. Therefore, this chapter is purposefully focused on challenging the centres of privilege.

Although eco-communities have potential to create futures otherwise, many also have a narrow inward-looking focus that does not necessarily centre questions or priorities of social justice. Eco-community residents tend to place foremost effort on transforming their daily lives rather than necessarily engaging in broader projects of socio-ecological transformation. Eco-communities do offer potential to tackle social or climate injustice, but they can also be spaces of exclusion and privilege. This privilege is rarely acknowledged. In this sense eco-communities share a critique that is also levelled at white environmentalism:

> White environmentalism is environmentalism that is Euro- or Western-centric in its vision for climate action. Environmentalism that has tunnel-vision on emissions, and leaves out ideals of justice. Environmentalism that proposes 'solutions' that can actually have unjust consequences.
>
> (Loach 2023, 72)

White environmentalism, and many eco-communities, advocate for, and celebrate solutions such as renewable energy transitions without fully acknowledging the uneven spatial implications of these technologies (Swyngedouw 2019). Unfortunately, renewable energy remains reliant on the extraction of labour and resource extraction of the already marginalized, for example, the mining lithium needed for electric car batteries, generating new forms of carbon colonialism (Lennon 2017). This reinforces ongoing forms of 'domination, displacement, degradation and impoverishment' (Sultana 2023, 61) from people of colour in the Global South and North. As Loach (2023), Sultana (2022, 2023), Begay (2023), Penniman (2020), Pellow (2016), Whyte (2018) and numerous other Black, Indigenous and PoC authors have extensively detailed unless environmentalism (and by implication eco-communities) start from a critique of colonialism, white supremacy, racial capitalism and existing inequalities, then they will continue to replicate existing systems of injustice and real harm to the 'occupied, post-colonial, and settler-colonial subjects' (Sultana 2022, 4).

While environmentalisms, then, might appear to be seeking an improved environment for all, it has unfortunately tended to mainly benefit white people. This is much more than a critique of who is 'included' in environmentalism activism, but rather a critique of who ultimately *benefits* and is *disenfranchised* by the goals, intents and outcomes of white environmentalism per se (Pickerill 2024). Loach (2023) argues that until there is recognition that 'white supremacy has both created this problem and held us back from solving it' (Loach 2023, 66), white environmentalism won't realize the need to centre questions of justice, challenge the 'oppressive principles of whiteness' (ibid, 84) and radically reconfigure the alternative futures they are seeking. Therefore, eco-communities need to be explicitly anti-racist if they are to adequately generate socio-ecological transformations. Otherwise, there is a real risk that their form of environmental protection is little more than the elite looking after themselves.

There are a variety of practices of exclusion at play in eco-communities through which they become rather homogeneous, lacking racial or class diversity in particular, which in turn facilitates the adoption or development of practices that fail to tackle white supremacy and carbon colonialism. These processes interweave and overlap but will be explored here primarily through analysis of the (lack of) racial diversity and wealth, tied together by an acknowledgement of the ways in which eco-communities can replicate neoliberal and colonial rationalities.

Spaces of racial exclusion

Eco-communities often celebrate their diversity. Despite noble intent and often positive beginnings, many develop a disjuncture between their imagined projects and their realization. While some (Los Angeles Eco-Village, USA; LILAC, England) are well positioned and structured to attract diverse residents, many (EcoVillage at Ithaca, USA; Findhorn, Scotland; Hockerton, England; Lancaster Co-housing, England, to name just a few) struggle to reach beyond the white upper-middle-class cohort. In the Global North eco-communities are too often dominated by a narrow demographic – often highly educated, white, able-bodied and with a predominance of women (Bhakta and Pickerill 2016; Chitewere 2018). Even when emerging in the Global South there are similar processes of exclusion that delimit them to the wealthier middle classes, certain ethnicities and often expatriate communities. Consequently, the outcomes of eco-communities' attempts at transformation can look worryingly similar to other forms of gentrification – eco-enclaves, rising property prices and exclusionary bounded places – which entrench rather than ameliorate existing inequalities (Rice et al., 2020). Chitewere (2018) classifies the EcoVillage at Ithaca as a green gated community, an exclusive commodified space of experiences and a form of green flight. With any radical project it is therefore vital to ask, 'Who or what is really being transformed, and to what ends?' (Last 2012, 710).

In their discussion of exclusions based on diverse bodies, race and wealth, eco-communities can replicate neoliberal rationalities. This mirrors other seemingly radical experimental spaces – what might initially appear as alternative can be built on neoliberal rationalities, reproducing neoliberal conditions that undermine their radical potential (Argüelles et al., 2017). Indeed, many eco-communities replicate, repeat and mirror conventional society in multiple ways (gender relations, the way money is used, etc.), and rely on state support. At the same time, projects that start with racial difference as a key defining factor have developed more radical alternatives (Bledsoe et al., 2019).

There is a strong class element to this, but also a presumption of individual empowerment (rather than structured privilege) in being able to reject state infrastructures and welfare. Argüelles, Anguelovski and Dinnie (2017) summarize such rationalities as a focus on individual responsibility rather than calling for state intervention, which in turn 'might help to legitimize neoliberal attempts of disposing the state from its economic and societal functions' (38). This ability to retreat from the state is reliant on the 'privileged progressive whiteness that permeate' (40) these experiments, an environmental and social privilege that enables such individuals to self-provide, self-organize and improve their quality of life.

In the Global North eco-communities are predominantly white, and the absence of Black participants is rarely critically interrogated. Indeed, it is in some places consciously created, as one interviewee at EcoVillage at Ithaca noted, 'You have a lot more … control about who your neighbours are' (Chitewere 2018, 95), suggesting that some eco-communities are deliberately created as places of escape from differentiated others. For context, in New York State (where EcoVillage at Ithaca is located) only 55.2 per cent of residents in 2020 were white and 14.8 per cent Black or American African out of a total of 44.5 per cent identified as non-white (United States Census Bureau 2021). Although there has been little explicit research on racism in eco-communities, they mirror the important analysis of alternative food networks (AFNs), another space of radical socio-ecological transformation, as being spaces of white privilege

(Lockie 2013). This is not to suggest a lack of Black farmers, Black food networks or Black social justice food campaigning, but to acknowledge that such spaces are rarely visible in discussions of radical transformatory projects in the same ways that white-dominated AFNs are (Alkon 2012). Even when the inequitable implications of demand for, for example, organic food are proved to rely on precarious work regimes that have racialized inequality built into them, AFN still uses 'a moral economy framing [which] can obscure systemic inequities in precarious farm employment and dampen the impetus for structural change through collective food movement organizing' (Weiler et al., 2016, 1140). In other words, it is dismissed as an unfortunate case of a few 'bad apple' farmers, rather than a structural problem.

The inclusion of race in eco-communities is too often tokenistic or through forms of racial-cultural appropriation (such as use of Indigenous spiritual symbols or practices, see Barker and Pickerill, Chapter 8). The lack of racial diversity is explained as an individual failure either for Black people to 'want to join' eco-communities or a lack of affordable housing (thereby assuming all Black people have less wealth). The lack of racial diversity is rarely articulated as a complex socio-cultural question where structures of belonging, identity, racism and social justice hinder broader participation, and that eco-communities rarely attempt to tackle racial capitalism (Chitewere 2018). Yet as Joe, a long-term member of Hart's Mill Ecovillage North Carolina, argues, often the guise of being radically alternative obscures the realization for participants that they are reproducing white supremacy culture:

> I see many intentional communities reproducing a lot of elements of white supremacy culture, especially the sense of urgency, paternalism, fear of conflict, worship of the written word, and quantity over quality. Consensus and sociocracy are often used in a way that unconsciously reproduces white supremacy culture (and patriarchal culture). What's worse, when participants perceive themselves as doing something different but don't recognize how they are continuing patterns of racial exclusion and dominance ... so there can be a tension or paradox in groups that are creating something new while reproducing elements of mainstream, patriarchal, white supremacy culture.
>
> (Quoted in Cole, Horton, and Pini 2019, 55)

Inequities in wealth are recognized in eco-communities to some extent but tend to only be approached as a problem of affordability of housing at the joining stage of community formation. Several eco-communities have explicitly sought to radically reduce the cost of housing. Yet few have done this in a way that fundamentally challenges the market-based approach to housing in the long term. The majority have started as low cost but failed to prevent a reversion to market valuations of property prices, which has obviously curtailed who can then buy into the community. Others are privately owned properties (Kailash Ecovillage) then rented, or community-owned but still rented (Los Angeles Eco-Village [LAEV], Christie Walk, Australia), albeit at below market rates. It is only Low Impact Living Affordable Community (LILAC) where all residents pay 35 per cent of their income for housing (purchasing shares they can eventually sell) that has sought to prevent long-term cost inflation while also giving residents security and capital growth in their investment (Chatterton 2013).

Eco-communities can reduce the costs of everyday living in other important ways, benefitting from economies of scale in energy-generating infrastructures, having smaller home units but access to large shared spaces and facilities such as laundry rooms, bike storage, cars, gardens, visitors' rooms and entertaining space as well as tools and equipment (Jarvis 2019). Residents can also benefit from shared social responsibilities where LILAC, LAEV, Kailash, Springhill Cohousing (UK), Cascade Co-housing (Australia) and Christie Walk share childcare and elder care, shopping errands and cooking.

Class and identity of its residents also act to exclude differentiated others. Seemingly subtle assumptions about participation, common values, lifestyle and food choices shape who gets to be part of eco-community experiments. Indeed, the very intent to generate collectivity, a necessity in creating and maintaining eco-communities, can drive a racial division in that the very claim of being equal is only possible in a white space, yet this remains unacknowledged. In this sense, the seeking of collectivity can override the question of race.

Understanding white privilege

Privilege is a structural advantage that benefits those of particular race, class, gender or identity categories (Bhopal 2018). Privilege is systematically produced through ongoing processes of dominance and uneven geographies that materially and socially benefit certain populations. Privilege requires attending not just to historical conditions but also to the ongoing processes and logics (such as settler colonialism) that continue to support and ensure privilege and the consequent erasure of others. For example, whiteness remains an invisible normative category (Bonnett 2000; Joshi, McCutcheon, and Sweet 2015; Pulido 2015), one that intersects with the logics of class but ultimately 'takes precedence over all other forms of identity'; in other words, 'the identity of whiteness is … the first determinant of how groups are positioned' (Bhopal 2018, 27).

The limitation of privilege as a concept is that it can be a way to claim an innocence (Leonardo 2004; Wekker 2016), to shift responsibility from the individual to the category and simultaneously suggest that its acknowledgement resolves its advantage (Ahmed 2004), without materially changing any existing structures of oppression (Gilmore 2002). The term is therefore used here cautiously to articulate a problem, rather than tightly define its remit. As Joe (quoted above) articulates, it is necessary at times to employ more explicit language – such as white supremacy – when reflecting on certain forms of racial privilege and 'the presumed superiority of white racial identities' (Bonds and Inwood 2016, 719) that actively produces white privilege and the power relations and material conditions of advantage (Berg 2011). Likewise, authors such as Roediger (2019) have suggested a shift to using the term 'white advantage' in an attempt to acknowledge the complexity of how poverty and misery is not always racially discriminating. Rothman and Fields (2020) likewise raise the dilemma that to use white privilege as a broad-brush term potentially alienates those who might otherwise seek productive alliances and commonality with fellow Black citizens. Therefore, the term 'privilege' is purposefully used here as a tool to frame important conversations in eco-communities about structural advantage, while simultaneously acknowledging the limitations of its definition.

Eco-communities are spaces of exclusion in large part because of the ways in which they have failed to acknowledge and respond to their privileges. These privileges are inherited from, and structured by, some of the broader mainstream environmental activisms that many have emerged from (Pickerill 2024; Taylor 2016). Environmentalism, for example, is built on a troubling colonial history and a 'fortress' conservation approach where nature is protected by the exclusion of humans (Paperson 2014). This can be seen in how some environmental campaigns purposefully focus on saving iconic species (whales, old growth trees, etc.), without paying enough attention to the social justice implications (people's livelihoods, traditional practices) of how this will likely disadvantage particular (often racialized) groups of people. The privilege of whiteness has facilitated the production of the 'white savior' environmentalist who determines how others should live, sometimes drawing on Indigenous or Black environmental approaches, but ultimately creating stereotypes or co-opting them rather than including them as equals. Consequently, environmentalisms often exemplify a variety of types of 'othering' in their discourses and exclusion in their political narratives (Erickson 2020; Paperson 2014), generating a long-held and ongoing suspicion among, for example, Indigenous activists, that the protection of the environment will ultimately be prioritized over Black people (Pickerill 2009; 2024). This is reflected in eco-communities when their ecological rationale erodes the social justice politics that many of them began with.

The structural advantages that many residents in eco-communities (particularly in the Global North, but globally too) benefit from, through whiteness and class, position participants as relatively wealthy. Even if they have not secured financial savings (with which to purchase land or homes), they are able to access loans or secure professions (which often also support part-time or working from home) and have access to higher education systems and qualifications. By seeking like-minded participants in order to more easily build common intentionality and collectivity, there is also an ongoing tension between celebrating diversity and yet purposefully seeking homogeneity in order to more easily build community (Christian 2003). At Ecovillage at Ithaca, for example, a resident argued that low-income families would complicate communal decision-making because they might hold different values (Chitewere 2018).

Although many of these privileges are acknowledged, they are rarely considered a result of structural advantage but one of individual good fortune and/or are articulated as interchangeable and equivalent with other types of disadvantage that residents experience. The individualization of privilege enables residents to deny that they have benefitted from a system such as racial capitalism, that has by definition caused the oppression of differentiated others. It enables participants to reject any obligations or responsibilities for their privilege, a denial of its social injustice implications and a denial of their role in structures of systemic racism. As such, as Chitewere (2018) argues, living at EVI appears to enable residents to avoid facing their own contradictions, with many asserting by virtue of membership that they were doing their bit for the greater environmental good. This positioning negates residents having to engage in any acts of real sacrifice or systemic change – the consumption of the eco-village is used to signal that they have contributed 'enough' towards socio-ecological transformations.

Taken further, this individualization is also applied by members in explaining a lack of racial diversity in eco-communities. The lack of Black eco-community residents is justified by predominantly white participants as a lack of environmental concern. This is a deeply flawed but often repeated belief that the lack of Black participants in environmental projects and eco-communities is because of a lack of prosperity – that it is only once people have their basic needs met that they can afford to be concerned about environmental matters (Gomez 2020; Hickcox 2018).

There is, of course, plenty of Black and people of colour concern for environmental issues, such as Black-led environmental movements and environmental justice organizations (Carter 2016; Guha and Martinez-Alier 1997). Black, Indigenous, Latinx and other People of Colour environmentalisms have always existed but have done so, with different priorities and intent than white environmentalism and therefore have too often been ignored or considered as separate from 'environmentalism' per se (Dungy 2009; Mendez 2020; Penniman 2023; Pulido 2006; Wald et al., 2019).

Indeed, given the critiques of white environmentalism this is not itself surprising, but the ways that environmental justice movements – which centre calls for social and climate justice – have been considered as a distinct and separate movement belie the lack of attention paid in white environmentalism to questions of justice. This is in part because centring social justice in environmentalism would require making visible and then dismantling the colonial-capitalist systems that extract from, harm and then dispose of people and places deemed sacrificial for the benefit of the elite (majority white) few in the Global North (Sultana 2023).

Black, Indigenous, Latinx and other People of Colour environmentalisms have tended to frame environmental problems not as questions of how to protect 'wilderness', certain biodiverse places, a narrow focus on reducing CO_2 emissions or particular species, but as questions of mutual survival for all beings, recognizing the interconnectedness of human survival with that of the earth and other beings. This framing then centres tackling human health (such as air pollution, cancer clusters, etc.) as an environmental problem, ensuring land rights (and resisting land grabs), working towards poverty alleviation and sustainable livelihoods, soil care and seeking multispecies justice (Pellow 2016; Whyte 2018). These environmentalisms are also rightly critical of how many in the Global North ignored climate change precisely because the Global South nations were hit first and hardest, demonstrating an entrenched environmental racism through which 'the humanity and value of Black lives is disregarded' (Loach 2023, 69). Likewise, Finney (2014, 2020) has carefully examined how the concept of outdoor nature and the environment have been racialized and are now being reclaimed by African Americans, despite the persistence anti-Blackness.

The reticence of Black involvement in eco-communities is more likely reflective of the unacknowledged white privilege on the part of many residents, a colonial history of violent conservation and the failure of white environmentalism to acknowledge structural problems, inequality and the need for social justice (Pellow 2016). As Chitewere (2018) argues, unless capitalism and colonialism are structurally challenged, in eco-communities, then issues of diversity, especially of race and class, will not be resolved. White environmentalism will not alter the culture of capitalism nor result in broad-scale environmental justice.

Yet silences remain around environmental racism, inequity and injustice in eco-communities. Instead, onus is placed on the individual resident to (voluntarily) engage in training, notably not seen as necessary until Black people arrive: 'We're encouraging all members to do substantive training in white supremacy and racial equity, but for now it's optional. It remains to be seen what adjustments we may need to make in our governance practices should we start attracting Black members. But we definitely need to raise our awareness of the elements of white privilege and power now' (Hope quoted in Cole, Horton, and Pini 2019, 56).

Furthermore, when privilege was explicitly discussed during my fieldwork, eco-community residents have been quick to articulate their insecurity, most often financially. They position themselves as precarious as a way to reject any privilege. Yet such limited financial capital or income is often purposeful – a form of voluntary simplicity or voluntary poverty (Vannini and Taggart 2013). Even if it is not, such vulnerability is not interchangeable and equivalent with that of white supremacy (as argued, because race dominates as a privilege), and it cannot be allowed to erase residents' multiple other forms of privilege.

Challenging the privileged

Eco-community residents are quick to individualize and seek to reduce notions of privilege, thereby erasing their structural and systemic advantages. This perpetuates racial exclusion and class exclusivity:

> There are limits on how cooperative a group can be if it's bringing old habits and practices from the dominant culture of competition. There are always many dimensions of power, rank and privilege present in any human group, and it's important to cultivate individual and group consciousness about these power differences, and have conversations about how to address them …. Both [decision-making systems – consensus and sociocracy] may therefore entice participants into a false sense of 'instant equality' without addressing the unequal power relations within the group.
>
> (Joe in Cole, Horton, and Pini 2019, 53)

An absence of a critical analysis of racial privilege and power in eco-communities means the broader political possibilities of transformative change are limited. There is a need to be vigilant to the politics of eco-communities and to their justice. If the structural dynamics of privilege (especially the structures of capitalism and colonialism) are not acknowledged and challenged, eco-communities can become time and energy sinks that distract from participating in broader social justice and environmental struggles and instead become focused on protecting the privileged few. This, of course, limits eco-communities' capacity for resistance to neoliberalism and social and political norms, or rather forecloses which elements of contemporary society are challenged and which are left as is. This produces new spaces that might be more ecological but are also more privileged, exclusionary and far from transformative.

White-centred eco-communities should use their privilege more productively to collectively challenge conventional ways of being and organizing, and more assertively reject the 'old habits and practices' that Joe laments (Cole, Horton, and Pini 2019). This is not about 'letting more Black people in', or making homes 'more affordable', or even ensuring that decision-making forums or work distribution processes are more inclusive. It requires eco-communities to become assertively anti-racist (Kendi 2019), to use their racial privilege, resources and power to share and reach out and join Black-led initiatives. This is a multi-staged process that requires the privileged to acknowledge the problem and move past their own discomfort. As Rios (2020) argues, in putting into practice Nieto's (2014) strategy, there are many missteps on this route. It is only when 'we become effectively anti-racist through participating in individual, institutional, and structural change that is envisioned and led by BIPOC' (55) that effective change can begin.

This radical anti-racist praxis should draw on the work of Black radical feminism, which enables the structures of privilege to be questioned (Lorde 2017; Oluo 2019). This involves centring Black, Indigenous and other People of Colour and following their lead, creating Black spaces, running trainings for eco-community residents about cultural appropriation, racism, white supremacy and so on, and exploring what reparations and land back might look like (Begay 2023; Johnson and Wilkinson 2020). This work has started, albeit tentatively. For example, a workshop was held at Brazier's Park eco-community (Oxfordshire, England), in 2024. Organized by Black activists it was explicitly aimed as an 'entry point to the topic suitable for those of you who are racialised as white' and where

> talking about race may lead to challenging feelings which we experience in our bodies. We use somatics as an aid to lengthy immersion and deep diving. We hope its trauma-informed lens will help support you through the more difficult parts by integrating mind and body where they meet. You won't be alone – we're expecting this will be an introduction for some of you.
>
> (Braziers Park 2024)

Such an approach requires building new forms of radical and racial relationality.

In practical terms there are numerous starting points for how to do anti-racist work in eco-communities. This requires resisting the material and social processes that facilitate the unevenness of the impacts of environmental change and instead generating equitable and accessible alternatives. Building anti-racism requires internal reflection and external action – actively asking Black activists what the priority issues are for them and co-creating equitable solutions to problems, but without relying on Black activists to educate or lead initiatives. This step of asking and then listening to, not assuming, what matters, and then acting on these issues, has been vital in the praxis of anti-racism. Just as white environmentalism has to reconsider how it defines an 'environmental problem' to incorporate a more diverse set of issues (for example, beyond biodiversity to questions about livelihoods), so eco-communities have to understand what their neighbours' priority concerns are.

As Pellow (2016) argues, this is not an optional addition to environmental or transformative politics; rather, People of Colour are indispensable to the future of all, 'indispensability demands dramatic change but does so from the perspective that all members of society and socioecological systems have something to contribute to that process and to our collective futures (231).' Or rather white people cannot survive without Black liberation because we are all interconnected.

There are many lessons that can be learned from work in environmentalism that has challenged racism, such as in explicitly Black environmental groups including Black2Nature, Black Environmental Network, Black Girls Hike, Outdoor Afro, Green Worker Cooperatives and the specifically climate-focused group Climate Reframe. For Indigenous peoples, acknowledging and maintaining the interconnections and interdependencies between all living things (including the land) enable self-determination, (energy) sovereignty, liberation and climate justice. For Begay (2023) the solution is to 'build a regenerative Indigenous economy' that enables 'having a mutually beneficial relationship with our land' (69). This is only possible if they have access to their land and are free to use in how they wish.

Directly reaching out to these groups and offering to share resources (material and land, but also time and energy) in supporting their initiatives is just a first step. While 'inviting in' to white spaces is not enough, if eco-communities include green spaces, gardens and natural play areas, then sharing access to these is an important step in acknowledging the inequity of opportunities to engage with nature. Likewise, making it clear that communal spaces, meeting rooms and eco-community resources can be used for initiatives and projects of Black activists' choosing is a small but inclusive step.

A bigger and vital step is to consider what eco-communities generate that could be shared. This could include renewable energies, locally grown organic food, childcare, editing and publishing abilities, or skills and expertise. Or it could mean sharing the residents' privilege to give Black activists media platforms, stepping aside and letting other people speak, co-creating possibilities of funded positions in eco-communities, and validating the lived experiences of Black activists in determining how to enact social and environmental change. It is also about sharing the land that eco-communities are built on. This approach requires that eco-communities ask themselves what contributions they can make in environmental sustainability, new environmental job creation, or the transition to democratic, collectively owned energy systems.

This, then, is the radical potential of eco-communities for social and climate justice – spaces that not only offer social and environmental alternatives in practice, that generate spaces for experimentation and hope in a climate-changed world, but also confront their white privilege through anti-racist praxis and in so doing seek to ensure that everyone and every being flourishes.

References

Ahmed, S. (2004) 'Declarations of whiteness: The non-performativity of anti-racism', *Borderlands e-Journal* 3(2), p. 1–6.

Alkon, A.H. (2012) *Black, White, and Green: Farmers Markets, Race, and the Green Economy*. Athens, GA: University of Georgia Press.

Argüelles, L., Anguelovski, I. and Dinnie, E. (2017) 'Power and privilege in alternative civic practices: Examining imaginaries of change and embedded rationalities in community economies', *Geoforum* 86 (November), pp. 30–41.
Begay, J. (2023) 'An Indigenous Systems Approach to the Climate Crisis', in Solnit, R and Young Lutunatabua, T. (eds.) *Not Too Late: Changing the Climate Story from Despair to Possibility*. Chicago, IL: Haymarket Books, pp. 66–72.
Berg, L. (2011) 'Geographies of identity I: Geography – (neo)liberalism – white supremacy', *Progress in Human Geography*, 36(4), pp. 508–17.
Bhakta, A. and Pickerill, J. (2016). Making space for disability in eco-housing and eco-communities. *The Geographical Journal*, 182(4), pp. 406–17.
Bhopal, K. (2018). *White Privilege: The Myth of a Post-Racial Society*. Bristol: Policy Press.
Bledsoe, A., McCreary, T. and Wright, W. (2019) 'Theorizing diverse economies in the context of racial capitalism', *Geoforum* 132(July), pp. 281–90.
Braziers Park (2024) 'Hidden reality of racism embodied', https://www.braziers.org.uk/programme. Accessed 25 October 2024.
Bonds, A. and Inwood, J. (2016) 'Beyond white privilege: Geographies of white supremacy and settler colonialism', *Progress in Human Geography* 40(6), pp. 715–33.
Bonnett, A. (2000). *White Identities: Historical and International Perspective*. London: Prentice Hall.
Carter, E.D. (2016) 'Environmental justice 2.0: New Latino environmentalism in Los Angeles', *Local Environment* 21(1), pp. 3–23.
Chatterton, P. (2013) 'Towards an agenda for postcarbon cities: Lessons from Lilac, the UK's first ecological, affordable cohousing community', *International Journal of Urban and Regional Research* 37(5), pp. 654–1674.
Chitewere, T. (2018) *Sustainable Community and Green Lifestyles*. London: Routledge Press.
Christian, D.L. (2003) *Creating a Life Together: Practical Tools to Grow Ecovillages and Intentional Communities*. Gabriola Island: New Society Publishers.
Cole, J., Horton, H. and Pini, M. (2019) 'Culture change or same old society? Consensus, sociocracy, and white supremacy culture', *Communities Magazine* 184 (Fall), pp. 53–6.
Dungy, C.T. (Ed.) (2009) *Black Nature: Four Centuries of African American Nature Poetry*. Athens, GA: University of Georgia Press.
Erickson, B. (2020) 'Anthropocene futures: Linking colonialism and environmentalism in an age of crisis', *Society and Space D* 38(1), pp. 111–28.
Finney, C. (2014) *Black Faces, White Spaces: Reimagining the Relationship of African Americans to the Great Outdoors*. Chapel Hill, NC: University North Carolina Press Books.
Finney, C. (2020) 'The perils of being black in public: We are all Christian Cooper and George Floyd', *The Guardian*, June 3. Available From: https://www.theguardian.com/commentisfree/2020/jun/03/being-black-public-spaces-outdoors-perils-christian-cooper, 2020.
Gilmore, R.W. (2002) 'Fatal couplings of power and difference: Notes on racism and geography', *Professional Geographer* 54(1), pp. 15–24.
Gomez, K.L. (2020) 'Confronting White Environmentalism', *Toyon Literary Magazine* 66(1), p. 22.
Guha, R. and Martínez-Alier, J. (1997) *Varieties of Environmentalism: Essays North and South*. London: Earthscan.
Guha, R. and Alier, J.M. (2013) *Varieties of Environmentalism: Essays North and South*. London: Routledge.

Hickcox, A. (2018) 'White environmental subjectivity and the politics of belonging', *Social and& Cultural Geography* 19(4), pp. 496–519.

Jarvis, H. (2019) 'Sharing, togetherness and intentional degrowth', *Progress in Human Geography* 43(2), pp. 256–75.

Johnson, A.E. and Wilkinson, K.K. (Eds.) (2020) *All We Can Save: Truth, Courage, and Solutions for the Climate Crisis*. New York: One World.

Joshi, S., McCutcheon, P. and Sweet, E.L. (2015) 'Visceral geographies of whiteness and invisible microaggressions', *ACME: An International e-Journal for Critical Geographies* 14(1). https://acme-journal.org/index.php/acme/article/view/1152.

Kendi, I.X. (2019) *How to Be an Antiracist*. London: One World, 2019.

Last, A. (2012) 'Experimental geographies', *Geography Compass* 6(12), pp. 706–24.

Lennon, M. (2017) 'Decolonizing energy: Black Lives Matter and technoscientific expertise amid solar transitions', *Energy Research & Social Science* 30(August), pp. 18–27.

Leonardro, Z. (2004) 'The color of supremacy: Beyond the discourse of "white privilege"', *Educational Philosophy and Theory* 36(2), pp. 137–52.

Loach, M. (2023) *It's Not That Radical: Climate Action to Transform Our World*. London: Publisher DK.

Lockie, S. (2013) 'Bastions of white privilege? Reflections on the racialization of alternative food networks', *International Journal of Sociology of Agriculture and Food* 23, pp. 409–18.

Lorde, A. (2017) *Your Silence Will Not Protect You*. London: Silver Press.

Méndez, M. (2020) *Climate Change from the Streets: How Conflict and Collaboration Strengthen the Environmental Justice Movement*. New Haven, CT: Yale University Press.

Nieto, L. (2014) *Beyond Inclusion, beyond Empowerment: A Developmental Strategy to Liberate Everyone*. Olympia: Cuetzpalin.

Oluo, I. (2019) *So You Want to Talk about Race*. New York: Seal Press Hachette.

Paperson, L. (2014) 'A ghetto land pedagogy: An antidote for settler environmentalism', *Environmental Education Research* 20(1), pp. 115–30.

Pellow, D.N. (2016) 'Toward a critical environmental justice studies: Black Lives Matter as an environmental justice challenge', *Du Bois Review: Social Science Research on Race* 13(2), pp. 221–36.

Penniman, L. (2020) 'Black Gold', in Johnson, A.E. and Wilkinson, K.K. (eds.) 2021. *All We Can Save: Truth, Courage, and Solutions for the Climate Crisis*. London: One World, pp. 301–10.

Penniman, L. (Ed.) (2023) *Black Earth Wisdom: Soulful Conversations with Black Environmentalists*. New York: HarperAudio.

Pickerill, J. (2009) 'Finding common ground? Spaces of dialogue and the negotiation of Indigenous interests in environmental campaigns in Australia', *Geoforum* 40(1), pp. 66–79.

Pickerill, J. (2024) 'Lived environmentalisms: Everyday encounters and difference in Australia's north', *GEO: Geography and Environment* 11(1), e00141, pp. 1–19.

Porter, J. (2014) *Native American Environmentalism: Land, Spirit, and the Idea of Wilderness*. Lincoln, NE: University of Nebraska Press.

Pulido, L. (2015) 'Geographies of white supremacy and ethnicity 1: White supremacy vs. white privilege in environmental racism research', *Progress in Human Geography* 39(6), pp. 809–17.

Pulido, L. (2006) *Black, Brown, Yellow and Left: Radical Activism in Los Angeles*. Oakland: University of California Press.

Rice, J.L., Cohen, D.A., Long, J. and Jurjevich, J.R. (2020) 'Contradictions of the climate-friendly city: Nnew perspectives on eco-gentrification and housing justice', *International Journal of Urban and Regional Research* 44(1), pp. 145–65.

Rios, M. (2020) 'Centering Blackness in our soils and our souls to promote climate justice', *Communities: Life in Cooperative Culture Magazine* (187), pp. 53–7.

Roediger, D. (2019) 'White privilege, white advantage, white and human misery', Verso Books blog, Available From: March 8. https://www.versobooks.com/blogs/4262-white-privilege-white-advantage-white-and-human-misery.

Rothman, A. and Fields, B. J. (2020) 'The death of Hannah Fizer', *Dissent* magazine, Available From: July 24. https://www.dissentmagazine.org/online_articles/the-death-of-hannah-fizer.

Sultana, F. (2022) 'The unbearable heaviness of climate coloniality', *Political Geography* 99(November), 102638, pp. 1–16.

Sultana, F. (2023) 'Decolonizing Climate Coloniality', in Solnit, R. and Young Lutunatabua, T. (eds.) *Not Too Late: Changing the Climate Story from Despair to Possibility.* Haymarket Books, pp. 58–65.

Swyngedouw, E. (2019) 'The Anthropo (Obs) cene', in Antipode Editorial Collective (ed.) *Keywords in Radical Geography: Antipode at 50.* Oxford: John Wiley & Sons, pp. 253–8.

Taylor Aiken, G. and Mabon, L. (2024) 'Where next for managed retreat: Bringing in history, community and under-researched places', *Area* 56(1), e12890, pp. 1–9.

Taylor, D. (2016) *The Rise of the American Conservation Movement: Power, Privilege, and Environmental Protection.* Durham, NC: Duke University Press.

United States Census Bureau (2021) 'Race and Ethnicity in the United States: 2010 Census and 2020 Census', https://www.census.gov/library/visualizations/interactive/race-and-ethnicity-in-the-united-state-2010-and-2020-census.html.

Vannini, P. and Taggart and Jonathan, T. (2013) 'Voluntary simplicity, involuntary complexities, and the pull of remove: The radical ruralities of off-grid lifestyles', *Environment and Planning A* 45(2), pp. 295–311.

Wald, S.D., Vázquez, D.J., Ybarra, P.S. and Ray, S.J. (2019) 'Introduction: Why Latinx Environmentalism?', in Wald, S.D., Vázquez, D.J., Ybarra, P.S., Ray, S.J., Pulido, L. and Alaimo, S. (eds.) *Latinx Environmentalisms: Place, Justice, and the Decolonial.* Philadelphia: Temple University Press.

Weiler, A.M., Otero, G. and Wittman, H. (2016) 'Rock stars and bad apples: Moral economies of alternative food networks and precarious farm work regimes', *Antipode* 48(4), pp. 1140–62.

Wekker, G. (2016) *White Innocence: Paradoxes of Colonialism and Race.* Durham, NC: Duke University Press.

Whyte, K. (2018) 'Settler colonialism, ecology, and environmental injustice', *Environment and Society* 9(1), pp. 125–44.

12

In defence of eco-collaborative housing communities: Porous boundaries and scaling out

Anitra Nelson

Eco-collaborative housing communities, i.e. self-governing, resident-designed multiple-household communities sharing certain spaces and facilities, attract increasing worldwide interest from residents and housing policymakers. This interest is generally based on the potential for such housing to be more affordable, environmentally friendly and community-oriented, with co-benefits such as neighbourhood care and cohesion. The growing array of models includes intentionally ecologically sustainable cohousing, community land trusts, certain housing cooperatives, political squats (occupiers) and urban and rural ecovillages.

In northern European countries, such as Germany, Denmark and Sweden, eco-collaborative housing models are familiar to planners, construction firms, city councillors, housing policymakers and financiers under different regionally dependent names and models. However, development of such eco-communities has been slow and mainly marginalized to rural locations in English-speaking countries such as the UK, the United States, Canada and Australia. Here professional and institutional acceptance has been weak and, in the past, projects have succeeded more by way of an exception or innovation to regulations. Many communities-in-formation have failed to get projects envisaged off the ground more because of institutional frustrations and barriers than challenges involving internal group cohesion or unity of purpose.

Cultural reasons for the slow development of eco-collaborative models include suspicions that they are cultish, inward looking and elitist, as detailed in the 'Sinister cultish and shirkers' section below. Even the entry processes to a community can lead to criticism without any sensible comparison with most households, whose members vet visitors let alone co-residents. Eco-collaborative housing is often evaluated via a spectrum of inappropriate units of analysis for both contrast and comparison. Elitist and middle-class charges are reasonable for only some eco-collaborative housing projects. Another common criticism is that, however successful they might be environmentally and socially, eco-collaborative housing models are not conducive to 'scaling up'. Once claims of marginality and an uncertain future gain ground, planners, policymakers and financiers have little interest in investing time to understand such models. This range of cultural apprehensions about eco-collaborative housing has created barriers to their establishment and expansion, indeed vicious circles of self-fulfilling (even if poorly founded) prophecies.

This chapter addresses such suspicions, using critical and discursive logic and by reference to cases of 'best-practice' eco-collaborative housing communities that are, in fact, open, affordable and can be 'scaled out'. As such, in negotiating questions of inclusion, I take a somewhat defensive position with respect to eco-collaborative housing communities, and offer a constructive way forward by proposing the development of a distinct unit of analysis for broad application to improve inclusionary standards across the cluster of such communities. Here 'best practice' refers to eco-collaborative housing communities with high levels of self-governance, and environmental sustainability and social justice values. Such eco-communities have porous boundaries and expansive influence, sharing spaces with neighbours and/or 'the public', engaging in outreach, welcoming guests and hosting and engaging in various progressive activities. They are not cultish, closed or gated but rather have porous boundaries and are engaged in and with their social and ecological environments. Questions of access and privilege are, arguably, as much (or more) the result of their market and cultural contexts as intent and internal practice.

Questions around difficulties in 'scaling up' such eco-communities indicate one-dimensional industrial perspectives, most significantly implying that they have no future and will always exist in the shadows as 'alternatives'. More importantly, many best practice eco-collaborative housing settlements can be seen as transformative, pre-figurative or hybrid institutions where residents identify as active agents of their future. They increasingly exist as implicit or explicit nodes in sets of alternative productive and exchange networks and, as such, represent forms of multi-dimensionally 'scaling out'. Questions around a 'human scale' and scaling out make more sense than scaling up. Renowned Danish architect Jan Gehl describes 'human scale' in terms of human senses, quality of life and comfort as distinct from overwhelming, alienating and monumental urban landscapes (Alonso 2017).

I conclude that judgements of eco-collaborative housing communities often occur without much knowledge or experience of them, via specious and inappropriate associations with traditional village and religious communities, boarding houses, holiday camps and large, extended family households. For instance, an intern at Dancing Rabbit Ecovillage (Shelby 2020) reports that before his visit friends jibed him that they would need to 'come up to Missouri just to get you, because you'll refuse to leave'. Their fears were vivid: 'We'll find you covered in mud and leaves, and you'll fight us trying to capture you.' Indeed, in legal, planning and financial terms in most English-speaking societies eco-collaborative housing communities do not fill a set social or built environment category but instead are marginalized with squats, communes and tiny houses as 'other', forever 'alternative', housing.

To avoid such misrepresentation and identify ways forward for practitioners, professionals and scholars of collaborative housing studies, Cohousing Australia has been promoting eco-collaborative housing as constituting a specific unit of settlement with set social and environmental characteristics in their built form and everyday operation, i.e. characteristics especially relevant for eco-urban futures. Such settlements, for instance, strive to minimize needs for car parking spaces so it is inappropriate and counterproductive for councils to demand they include them unnecessarily. Similarly, they are self-governing and prefer multi-user, environmentally friendly utility and water services, whereas authorities, following ordinary residential multi-dwelling codes, often insist on privatized household unit delivery and payment systems. Developing appropriate criteria for such a unit of settlement with respect to zoning, building and financing would enable planning for and regulating them. Such advances are especially important given growing demands for intergenerational and senior cohousing models, as well as social and affordable eco-collaborative housing.

'Eco-collaborative housing' communities

Eco-collaborative housing communities go by many names, generally associated with specific legal forms and tenures: US 'cohousing' is dominated by owner-occupier settlements whereas European 'co-housing' refers to diverse models, many incorporating tenants or tenant-shareholders in self-governing housing cooperatives. Unfortunately, few are consistent in definition: all terms need to be defined as they are used due to variations by language, country and even city, given that different histories, characteristic cases and regulations pertain.

Indeed, the broader term 'collaborative housing' is only just consolidating as appropriate nomenclature for this emergent and diverse field of studies (Czischke et al., 2020; Lang et al., 2020). Within this field I draw on specific cases to qualify as 'eco-collaborative housing', i.e. intentionally ecologically sustainable and community-oriented housing models where co-governing residents both occupy personal and private areas as well as share spaces and facilities and work together in participatory ways (Nelson 2018).

The scarcity of such models in English-speaking countries is partly due to entrenched market-based supply of housing via commercial developers, housing mortgage providers and real-estate agents who generally oppose eco-collaborative housing residents having a greater say in design, project management and construction than is the case in mainstream housing produced as a commodity and asset.

Customized eco-collaborative housing projects with on-demand production of dwellings often economize on costs through multiple economies of scale and avoid or minimize profit margins demanded by commercial developments. Note here that I exclude from 'eco-collaborative housing' projects that are neither wholly commercial or wholly housing community-driven but, rather, initiated and managed by professional developers stepping in to pre-build community-oriented and sustainability-focused housing projects to which residents buy in. In Australia such 'deliberative developments' are referred to, say by Echelon Planning (2018), as if akin to cohousing – heightening confusion among potential residents and government agencies.

The 'eco' in eco-collaborative housing

Demonstrable and effective environmental practices in the design, construction and operation of buildings, and in residents' everyday lives are requisite criteria for an intentional community to fit the category of *eco*-collaborative housing. Thörn et al. (2020a, 11) conclude that forms of ownership and tenure determine the extent to which a community can be environmentally sustainable – a function of design and building features, sharing practices and the greater capacity for a community to catalyse action from outside and within the community to create low-impact lifestyles. Sargisson (2012) finds a light green 'ecological pragmatism' even amongst mainstream North American cohousing, while Tummers and MacGregor (2019, 11–12) argue that the sharing and design aspects of European co-housing enhance other features to make their housing more ecological. Yet other models target one-planet livelihoods (Nelson 2018). Moreover, on deep social sustainability, in their article on feminist political ecology, commons and care, Tummers and MacGregor (2019, 8) assert: 'Co-housing, more than either owner-occupation or private rental housing, has potential for addressing the democratization and visibility of carework.'

Sinister, cultish and shirkers

First, I offer an erudite illustration of the kind of suspicion of 'community' that typifies certain discussions in the street and with professionals or scholars with respect to eco-collaborative housing models, which often identify as 'intentional communities'. Johannes Euler (2019, 167) wrote in a footnote to a work on commoning that critical urbanist 'Erik Swyngedouw rightly argued at the 2016 Conference on Political Ecology in Stockholm that there is something sinister about communities'. Investigating further, Swyngedouw (personal email, 28 January 2020) explained:

> Too often in planning and geography and cognate disciplines, 'community' is celebrated as a normative ideal – I disagree – it depends very much on a whole series of other factors. Sometimes the anomy of city life is to be preferred over the closeness of many communities.

He made a personal point:

> Coming myself from a rural community in Flanders in the 1950, I and many others of my kind found it stifling, oppressive, dogmatic, fixed. Going to the city is often experienced as a liberation of oppression from 'community' life.

Similar arguments are made in a theoretical and detailed context by Lars Heitman, and rebutted by Nelson in Project Society after Money (2019).

Second, the 'intentionality' in 'intentional communities' presents another barrier, so much so that when I lived in a well-established Australian housing cooperative during the late 1990s many members denied living in an 'intentional' community to ward off stigma, a negative association that they had internalized. By definition they did live in an intentional community in that 'intentionality' is simply a reference to committing to a shared purpose, certain values and cooperative practices. But they found it uncomfortable that the adjective 'intentional' attracted unwanted associations with 'cults' – all the more offensive given that this community, like many others, has been diligently open in its relations, structures and processes and accepting of a range of beliefs within a non-denominational collective.

Some twentieth-century scholars of intentional communities reinforce associations with secret societies. Sargisson (2012, 31) refers to Timothy Miller's cultish criteria for categorizing intentional communities as:

(1) a sense of common purpose and of separation from the dominant society; (2) some form and level of self-denial, of voluntary suppression of individual choice for the good of the group; (3) geographic proximity; (4) personal interaction; (5) economic sharing; (6) real existence; and (7) critical mass.

In response, Sargisson introduces a far more relaxed and appropriate definition of intentional communities in the twenty-first century, as people with a shared purpose who live together with a 'raison d'être … beyond tradition, personal relationships, and family ties'. This latter definition is specifically useful in that it correctly indicates that such communities are likely to be even more open, respectful and ecumenical than regular families and neighbourhoods.

Third, a popular slur is both alluded to and rebutted in this introduction to a post by Avi (2019):

When I tell people I live in an ecovillage, I often hear, "Like a commune?" as a response. "Commune" is often times the only concept people have to place it on their mental map, and that term frequently connotes free love, drug usage, artsyness, and a general shirking of responsibility.

Avi here, attempting to shed some light on the ways in which discipline, structure, and responsibility are essential components in the life of a thriving community member at Dancing Rabbit Ecovillage

The point is that undoubtedly there are *some* intentional communities – just like there are *some* families, workplaces and associations – that formally follow a specific ideology or informally constitute an insular clique. However, just as this fact does not impugn the family, workplace or neighbourhood precinct as a legitimate social unit, neither should it stick like mud on eco-collaborative housing communities as a whole.

A fourth prejudicial suspicion that infects thinking on eco-collaborative housing communities is that such models are generically, even intentionally, elitist. There are specific cohousing communities that appear within current housing contexts characterized by multiple layers of unaffordability that are perceived as 'privileged'. An example is a US subset of proudly homeowner cohousing typically inspired by the McCamant and Durrett model. Durrent (2019) argues for a cohousing definition to include 'no shared community economy' to form the basis of a certification programme for cohousing. Sargisson (2012, 36) points out that McCamant and Durrett are keen to separate cohousing from intentional communities, impugning the latter as prone to 'charismatic leadership, shared ideology, and an educational and/or spiritual function'. In contrast to the greater incidence of mixed tenures and demographic, social and cultural diversity of European models, Sargisson (2012, 50) concludes that US 'second wave' cohousing exists 'as a collective version of the American Dream, stemming from a liberal, property-owning ideology'. Nevertheless, North American eco-collaborative housing includes many cohousing projects, such as Jamaica Plain Cohousing (Boston), that clearly depart from the McCamant and Durrett model. Even more US ecovillage models are easily accessible in economic terms, such as Twin Oaks (Virginia) with its communal purse and shared work model. Such communities tend to be politically progressive integrating a consciousness of gender, class and race questions into their agenda.

Unfortunately, in capitalist societies operating substantially through monetary power and private property relations, many developments only happen if those with means decide to invest in them. Therefore, in relation to eco-collaborative housing communities populated by those with middle to high incomes, the question has to be asked whether the market society in which they are constructed and operate is not responsible for this outcome? Ruiu (2014) makes similar arguments. Barriers to establishing such housing conspire to make them more expensive than if planning and financing was more straightforward and less expert advice and support was necessary.

A similar intervention can be made in debates over gentrification, particularly those regarding eco-collaborative housing. Financialization of the sector reduces accessibility and drives higher prices irrespective of the intentions and values of best-practice eco-collaborative communities. In response, many communities have developed a range of mechanisms to detach from market-based dynamics. While several scholars judge collaborative housing as exclusive and akin to gated communities (Lang et al., 2020, 23), best-practice models offer opportunities to local neighbours and even the wider public to share in their activities and facilities. Prominent examples are Los Angeles Eco-Village in the United States, UfaFabrik and Spreefeld in Berlin (Germany), Cloughjordan Ecovillage in Tipperary (Ireland), Kalkbreite in Zurich (Switzerland) and Earthsong Eco Neighbourhood in West Auckland (New Zealand). Their borders are remarkably porous and accessible when compared with private homes and conventional neighbourhoods. In summary, the charge of elitism and privilege is correct only for certain cases. One needs to recognize the great diversity of collaborative housing communities, and the contexts and polities that encourage adverse outcomes.

An allied charge made of collaborative communities is that residents attract others like themselves so they are, if not ghettos, generally demographically and ethnically similar (and likely to be white and middle class). A study of social inclusion in ten cases of French collaborative housing by Bresson and Labit (2020, 128) indicated that grassroots projects tended to attract members with similar backgrounds and values – 'a rather robust socio-cultural homogeneity, which probably strengthens the social cohesion'. Tummers and MacGregor (2019, 13) write in a nuanced way that 'most co-housing projects have a homogeneous population; there is an (unintentional) lack of socio-cultural and economic diversity'. This is no so different from many mainstream neighbourhoods.

These matters of context and polity are especially stark in best-practice European cases, such as the 'young housing cooperatives' in Zurich. There, municipal law demands a composition that replicates the city's demographic characteristics. Twenty-five per cent of places are reserved for those 'disadvantaged' say by income, such as non-Swiss migrants and refugees, who, at some point in their housing cooperative residency become nationalized, falling out of the disadvantaged category, enabling more and more non-Swiss join – to keep up the quota. Thus eligibility at any particular time is conditioned by a need to fill specific profiles. Kalkbreite self-reports 'a relatively wide social diversity' of residents. Clearly, this formal requirement alone might not in and of itself encourage inclusionary relationships which, however, do benefit from the cooperatives' purposively community-based design and operation.

Usefully, Thörn et al. (2020b, 205–9) identify porous boundaries of eco-collaborative housing communities within their neighbourhoods as a function of more activist-based projects but find some anxieties and tensions around lines between personal authority and collective autonomy. They distinguish three forms of ownership: private, market-oriented ownership, which tends to be less inclusive and affordable; cooperative housing with non-speculative mechanisms or membership via non-speculative shares and generally affordable tenancy, say linked to income and, significantly, the optimum form of tenure for achieving environmental sustainability; collaborative housing projects owned by not-for-profit housing associations or government agencies with tenures similar to social housing tenants.

Thörn et al. (2020b, 207) emphasize that tenure determines affordability and scope for inclusion and, in this regard, private ownership is detrimental. Consequently, in directing governmental and other support to eco-collaborative housing communities, certain criteria are deemed necessary, such as only funding settlements that are inclusive, open and mixed or all-tenant tenures, i.e. demonstrably affordable and authentically community-oriented in internal structures and external relationships. Architectural and infrastructural designs and social acceptance are necessary to allow for a range of disabilities. For instance, the first eco-collaborative community that I lived in accommodated disabilities that prevented me from living in many other places, and was a key reason I joined in the first place. Their entry process involved negotiating costs so they were affordable given each person's own means as well.

In a subtle evaluation of a purportedly representative sample of top-down and bottom-up French collaborative housing projects, Bresson and Labit (2020, 130) conclude that independent skills development can realize and enhance social inclusion:

> [P]rofessional counselling that we observed in many of the projects plays a key role in moving beyond the concept of social diversity … of unrelated people from different backgrounds, to that of social inclusion, in other words, the constitution of a real community based on the participation and empowerment of all its members.

This is a very constructive observation, reinforcing the utility of processes that diligent becoming-communities regularly engage in, intentionally developing their personal communication skills and collective consensual self-governance practices. It seems key for stakeholders such as government agencies and not-for-profit housing associations supporting such communities to arrange independent counselling services to enhance the process of genuine social inclusion. Similarly, it is necessary to promote AIM HIGH style approaches to optimize virtuous circles of inclusion, as described by Chitewere (Chapter 12, this volume).

There is a crucial need, then, for policymakers to develop criteria and templates for eco-collaborative housing community charters that clearly define that eligibility for government funding is confined to *best-practice* eco-collaborative housing settlements. This solution leads us to a favourite question from politicians and professionals: 'How can you scale up or mainstream eco-collaborative housing settlements?'

Scaling up, scaling out and a human scale

In describing two examples of what I deem best-practice twenty-first-century eco-collaborative communities, I try to show that such models usefully 'scale-out' their spatial, ecological, social and economic benefits. Consequently, simply enabling such projects to evolve would beneficially impact on their neighbourhoods. As long as such models are permitted and lightly supported by relevant agents, they will evolve from voluntary acts of citizens.

Such self-governing complexes rely on community participation and willing and active residents. The related key quality of a 'human scale' is most relevant to eco-communities, which are humanity-rich settlements. Many models are hybrids, existing within capitalism but substantively, and in their imaginary, point towards postcapitalism. Thus, 'upscaling' in the specific sense of mainstreaming seems inappropriate or wrong-headed. 'Scaling out' is a better descriptor of their potential in urban revitalization and housing and welfare policies.

Decentralization: Urbanization

The 'smart' and 'slow' Cloughjordan Ecovillage (CE) in Tipperary (Ireland) – ninety minutes from Dublin by car or train (limited services) – has been lauded for revitalizing a rural settlement. The founders successfully advertised for appropriate land. In 2004 they purchased a 27-ha greenfield site with an entry at one end of the main street and spreading back into countryside. Planning permission took a few years, in stages, starting with a master plan before land purchase. Subsequent struggles with authorities ensued over matters such as initially rejecting an environmentally ideal drainage system. The ultimate plan included a relatively dense residential settlement, woodlands, fruit and regenerative tree planting by residents, 12 acres reserved for community-based farming and individual plots.

Food production and biodiversity were twin principles. By late 2015, the average resident achieved an ecological footprint of 2 gha (almost one-third of the Irish average) and aimed for a one-planet lifestyle of 1.7 gha. Framed as low-carbon lifestyles and low-impact living, CE member-residents had built 56 of an expected 130 dwellings (including work-cum-live units) by mid-2019. Over 20,000 fruit and native trees were planted. Ireland's largest renewable energy district heating system and fibre-optic cabling for high-speed broadband was completed in 2008, the year the member-owned horse-ploughing biodynamic Cloughjordan Community Farm traversing 5 ha of ecovillage started.

In 1999 the founders had started a company registered as an educational charity, a vehicle to establish CE, certain associated organizations, and operated as a not-for-profit cooperative. Many members came from Dublin so, once they identified the site in 2002, it was imperative that they first worked on becoming part of the existing social and geographic environment of the prospective CE. They invited considerable input from the around 500 village residents of Cloughjordan, a town established in the mid-seventeenth century in an area inhabited by humans for several millennia. A year-long consultation included local schoolchildren creatively participating in modelling the ecovillage.

The ecovillagers work on establishing food security: one resident couple run a bakery that aims to be economically sustainable, local, fair and equitable. The village Cloughjordan has been rejuvenated. When I conducted research there in 2019, I interviewed twenty-three people mainly from the ecovillage but some in the village proper, including a key CE worker–founder who could not afford to purchase a dwelling there so rented in Cloughjordan. This unaffordability was far from intentional: the global financial crisis and subsequent recession had massively impacted on CE's establishment in terms of costs and incomes. Cloughjordan has attracted many aspiring CE residents and others attracted to living in the village because of CE but with no intention of residing at CE, yet seeing it as an essential aspect of their life. These 'adjacent residents' demonstrate the porous boundaries of progressive eco-communities. CE and Cloughjordan now meld and blend with a combined population of around 700.

A July 2019 focus group created a mud map of activities and relationships within CE and the Cloughjordan locale – ranging beyond, nationally and internationally. A small sample of activities included the Village Education Research and Training association, with activities including tours; foraging; an astronomical siting basin, next to the ecovillage's arts amphitheatre; a labyrinth; CULTIVATE (originally, the Living and Learning Centre) managing the North Tipperary Green Enterprise Park and Fab Lab with national and international relationships; a WeCreate workplace for livelihoods and food hubs, aggregating value through use of kitchen and accounting services, and associated with a national co-working network; a local e-list to get/offer lifts/goods/services, facilitating people without cars; and a circus club for kids of all ages, some unicycling to school, driven by Jo who was attracted by CE but lived in a house she bought in the main street of Cloughjordan.

The exemplary exists

In Zürich, the 'young housing cooperatives' are exemplary best-practice eco-collaborative housing communities. They evolved in a very well established and conducive polity outlined in Hugentobler et al. (2016), from which the description below is substantially drawn, confirmed by research in the field and interviews conducted by the author in 2019.

In 1907, in response to needs for housing, especially affordable housing, the city of Zürich enabled non-profit housing collectives to construct residential buildings by giving them a legal, planning and policy status and by financially facilitating them. Today this sector is owned primarily by cooperatives, and secondarily by the municipality and foundations. By the mid-2010s, they managed more than 40,000 apartments or around one-quarter of the city's apartment stock. The sector confidently expanded with a 2011 referendum determining that the city support the expansion of housing cooperative apartments to one-third of all stock by 2025. As not-for-profit and non-speculative enterprises, such apartments are affordable: residents are tenant-shareholders who cooperatively self-manage their housing and housing cooperative with would-be-resident members on the waiting-list for a dwelling to inhabit.

The 'young housing cooperatives' are an innovative subset, a movement evolving in the 1990s driven by high ideals of active self-organization enacting social and environmental justice in their built and socio-political environments. An assemblage of ex-squatters, traditional construction cooperatives, inspiring utopians and practical imaginaries – floated by utopian writer P.M. (Hans Widmer) and the association INURA – realized innovative, high-quality and ecologically sustainable builds, with cooperatives operating mainly on voluntary protocol. KraftWerk 1 (2001–) and Kalkbriete (2014–) subsidize rents for low-income households and enliven their neighbourhoods. Kraftwerk 1 connects with local farmers through direct food purchases and temporary work commitments as farmer-gardeners. Kraftwerk 1 originally had 110 variously designed apartments, then developed a space in 2012 for eighty-five inhabitants, including flats for people with disabilities. The central courtyard of Kalkbreite is open to the public; diverse spaces available for all types of households are modest, progressing towards one-planet ecological footprints. Two car spaces complement a massive bike storage space. Cluster living means around ten singles can opt for a small studio attached to a large shared kitchen and living area. 'Joker rooms' can be temporarily used as bedrooms or studios.

The young housing cooperatives evolved within a broader movement of dozens of local housing cooperatives that used the sector's centenary in 2007 to launch the More than Housing (MH) construction cooperative that they and the city government financed. MH, the city and its public works agency launched, in 2008, an architectural competition attracting around 100 applicants, to design a residential estate and urban design concept for an affordable build, accommodating a diversity of household types, responding to multi-generational needs and supporting a Swiss '2,000-watt society'. The winning consortium's innovation drew on the openness and praxis of a cooperative approach. Hunziker Areal (2015–) comprises of thirteen compact and energy-efficient buildings designed by five architectural teams for around 1,200 residents and workplaces for 150 laid out in a lively neighbourhood plan, with alley ways, green spaces and vertical gardens. The MH cooperative offers 35 m² personal space per resident and access to numerous rooftop and quarter spaces.

Given this activity by citizens, the city only needs to subsidize rents for around 1.3 per cent of apartments sprinkled through such cooperatives and municipal housing. Zürich is remarkable even in Switzerland where, in the mid-2010s, housing cooperatives were responsible for some 140,000 apartments (28.5 per cent in Zürich) and Swiss national home ownership stood at 37 per cent but just 9 per cent in Zürich. As such best-practice cases of eco-collaborative housing communities in Zurich confirm that affordability, low-impact living and social inclusion are works in progress in truly collaborative milieu where government agencies, professionals and residents share decision-making and work on massive projects requiring constant attention even after they are built. Perhaps key here is the Swiss tradition of grassroots democracy?

On analytical units

Arguably, many concerns about eco-collaborative housing evolve from focusing on groups frustrated in realizing their ideals in unpropitious urban contexts and polities, whose members are drawn from a competitive and alienating society that neither equip nor skill them to govern collectively, be inclusive, or share and nurture. Eco-collaborative housing seems odd in comparison with other forms of mainstream settlement. Intentional eco-collaborative housing is not easily comparable with traditional/village communities, communities of place, communities of interest or communities of practice, even though they have some functions in common with each of those types of communities. The relationships and governance required are not comparable with conventional houses and households, even if they incorporate them. They cannot be compared with either a mainstream multi-dwelling apartment of residents or a cosmopolitan and anarchic neighbourhood precinct with mixed-uses and diverse dwelling types and households, both without formal and comprehensive organization of all users. They must be considered a unique, if multi-dimensional unit of analysis. Consequently, it would be beneficial if professionals in the field follow the recent formation of collaborative housing as a field of studies by creating clear universal legal, financial, planning and construction approaches to them.

Completely privately owned models of eco-collaborative housing are, generally, the most inaccessible and privileged (Czischke et al., 2020, 5) unless they demand or favour self-building. Yet even sweat equity is not available to all to contribute, especially those who are disadvantaged through ill health, disabilities or dependents. In their Danish study, Sørvoll and Bengtsson (2020) identify a potential and deeply troubling wedge between wholly privately owned collaborative housing communities and those in need of affordable housing. They argue that, where such interests diverge, internal solidarity is highly likely to prevent external solidarity with those less advantaged than themselves.

In terms of holistic social outcomes, collectively owned models are preferred, with affordable life-long tenancies at rental rates accessible for all. Existing models demonstrate a subset of hybrid institutions with legal standing and accountability within contemporary capitalist societies, and with the potential to readily transform into postcapitalist cells of a commons economy or a community mode of production, already endowed with skills in direct and substantive governance and sharing of all kinds (Nelson 2018, 214–37; Nelson and Chatterton 2022). As a transformative hybrid they differ in agency from the individual, the household and the urban neighbourhood precinct. Here, scaling up is a capitalist concept aligned to growth, while scaling out is a postcapitalist concept aligned to relations and qualitative impacts, such as social communality for ecological sustainability. We want a post-industrial, human scale future.

Authors such as Szemző et al. (2019, 407) and Nelson (2018, 171–5) argue for generalizing the Northern European model of which Berlin and Zürich are outstanding representatives. Here municipal governments respond to residential interest in collaborative housing by offering use of vacant land or built properties under a range of special and supportive arrangements (sometimes via competitive tendering), and facilitate planning and borrowing processes for these large and complex developments. The Berlin-based id22 Institute for Creative Sustainability has been supported by government in advisory and promotional roles for collaborative housing, a hub that encourages inclusivity, affordability and eco-sustainable living (LaFond and Tsvetkova 2017). Such projects assist local governments to fulfil their housing, social welfare, urban revitalization and development policies. Indeed, in a *Built Environment* 45(3) special issue on this topic, co-editors Palmer and Tummers (2019, 279) concluded that there was 'evidence of a maturing sector of resident-controlled or at least a highly participative and self-determining culture of residential development' and that 'the collaborative housing trend invokes a paradigm in which there is no longer room for housing as a commodity, reinstalling dwelling as a condition for citizenship and a key factor in creating liveable cities'.

Conclusion

In conclusion, it is important to point out that collaborative housing has gained such significance that, among other directions to be taken up in this under-researched area, Czischke et al. (2020, 8) call for researching the 'extent these CH [collaborative housing] initiatives compensate the retreat of the institutions that have traditionally provided social protection and inclusion in different parts of Europe – the welfare state, family or communities'. In contrast, this chapter has focused on reasons for the delayed development of eco-collaborative housing in regions such as North America, Australia and the UK. An important caveat regarding the rather defensive arguments made in this chapter: by restricting examples to a subset of 'best-practice' eco-collaborative housing I avoid generically whitewashing or green-washing eco-collaborative housing. Certain eco-collaborative housing communities do fall short of the positive descriptors used here.

However, my key points are, first, that the potential and actual functioning of the best-practice models makes a mockery of dismissive and derogatory claims and, second, that if eco-collaborative housing can be understood and identified as occupying a specific kind of category and unit of analysis, then we might more easily understand and assess them in terms of the intended specific standards of their existence. They have a distinctive form and potential role that I believe deserves serious consideration and respect within urban environments of our uncertain future.

References

All URLs. Accessed 1 September 2021.

Alonso, R. (2017) 'Jan Gehl: "In the last 50 years, architects have forgotten what a good human scale is"', *Arch Daily*, 28 October. URL: https://www.archdaily.com/877602/jan-gehl-in-the-last-50-years-architects-have-forgotten-what-a-good-human-scale-is.

Avi (2019) 'Becoming the change we wish to see: A Dancing Rabbit update', *The March Hare*, 5 June – https://www.dancingrabbit.org/becoming-the-change-we-wish-to-see-a-dancing-rabbit/.
Bresson, S. and Labit, A. (2020) 'How does collaborative housing address the issue of social inclusion? A French perspective', *Housing, Theory and Society* 37(1), pp. 118–38.
Czischke, D., Carriou, C. and Lang, R. (2020) 'Collaborative housing in Europe: Conceptualizing the field', *Housing, Theory and Society* 37(1), pp. 1–9.
Durrett, C. (2019) 'The future of cohousing in America: The case for certification', *e-Newsletter from McCamant and Durrett Architects*, The Cohousing Company (August).
Echelon Planning (2018) *Deliberative Development: Opportunities for Moreland Council*. Version 2, 31 May. Brunswick: Échelon planning – https://www.echelonplanning.com.au/deliberative-development-research.
Euler, J. (2019) 'The commons: A social form that allows for degrowth and sustainability', *Capitalism Nature Socialism* 30(2), pp. 158–75.
Hugentobler, M., Hofer, A. and Simmendinger, P. (Eds.) (2016) *More than Housing: Cooperative Planning – A Case Study in Zürich*. Basel: Birkhäuser Verlag.
LaFond, M. and Tsvetkova, L. (Eds.) (2017) *CoHousing Inclusive: Self-Organized, Community-Led Housing for All*. Berlin: Jovis.
Lang, R., Carriou, C. and Czischke, D. (2020) 'Collaborative housing research (1990–2017): A systematic review and thematic analysis of the field', *Housing, Theory and Society* 37(1), pp. 10–39.
Nelson, A. (2018) *Small Is Necessary: Shared Living on a Shared Planet*. London: Pluto Press.
Nelson, A. and Chatterton, P. (2022) 'Dwelling beyond growth: negotiating the state, mutualism and commons', in Savini, F., Ferreira, A. and Carlotta von Schönfeld, K. (eds.) *Post-Growth Planning: Cities beyond the Market Economy*. Milton Park/New York: Routledge, pp. 49–62.
Palmer, J. and Tummers, L. (2019) 'Collaborative housing: Resident and professional roles', *Built Environment* 45(3), pp. 277–9.
Project Society after Money (2019) *Society after Money: A Dialogue*. New York/London: Bloomsbury Academic.
Ruiu, M.-L. (2014) 'Differences between cohousing and gated communities. A literature review', *Sociological Inquiry* 84(2), pp. 316–35.
Sargisson, L. (2012) 'Second-wave cohousing: A modern utopia?', *Utopian Studies* 23(1), pp. 28–56.
Shelby (2020) 'Opportunity of a lifetime: A Dancing Rabbit update', *DRE* Newsletter, 27 July – https://www.dancingrabbit.org/opportunity-of-a-lifetime-a-dancing-rabbit-update/.
Sørvoll, J. and Bengtsson, B. (2020) 'Autonomy, democracy and solidarity. The defining principles of collaborative civil society housing and some mechanisms that may challenge them', *Urban Research and Practice* 13(4), pp. 390–410.
Szemző, H., Gerőházi, E., Droste, C. and Soetanto, D. (2019) 'Towards a collaborative housing initiative: The role of local authorities', *Built Environment* 45(3), pp. 398–415.
Thörn, H., Larsen, H.G., Hagbert, P. and Wasshede, C. (2020a) 'Constraints and possibilities for co-housing to address contemporary urban and ecological crises: A conclusion', in Hagbert, P., Larsen, H.G., Thörn, H. and Wasshede, C. (eds.) *Contemporary Co-Housing in Europe: Towards Sustainable Cities?* Milton Park/New York: Routledge, pp. 202–13.
Thörn, H., Larsen H.G., Hagbert, P. and Wasshede, C. (2020b) 'Co-housing, sustainable urban development and governance: An introduction', in Hagbert, P., Larsen,

H.G., Thörn, H. and Wasshede, C. (eds.) *Contemporary Co-Housing in Europe: Towards Sustainable Cities?* Milton Park/New York: Routledge, pp. 1–19.

Tummers, L. and MacGregor, S. (2019) 'Sustainable beyond wishful thinking: A FPE perspective on commoning, care, and the promise of co-housing', *International Journal of the Commons* 13(1), pp. 1–22.

Part Three

Doing it together: Collective governance

Jenny Pickerill

Eco-communities engage in multiple forms of governance – existing state systems while simultaneously creating autonomous self-governance processes. Eco-communities are also deliberately participatory – they seek to operate as a collective rather than as individuals in how they make decisions, share resources, tackle problems and complete tasks. This collectivity – doing it together – requires developing new forms of decision-making, and expanding conceptualizations of responsibility, trust and obligation. Eco-communities invest considerable time and effort into creating and sustaining these collective processes. There is an implicit articulation that formal state governance is inadequate and limited in its ability to support appropriate scales of collective participation and decision-making. In contrast, eco-communities seek to generate human-scale systems whereby individuals have a direct and accountable say in all decisions that affect them, and also a responsibility and obligation to make choices that support the collective good, not just their individual needs. In practice, eco-communities have a strategic and fluid relationship with the state – sometimes working with it, using systems it provides (such as healthcare, public transport and education systems), while at other times challenging decisions, or providing alternative infrastructures.

Collective decision-making has required eco-communities to acknowledge and challenge cultural norms, and implicit rules and assumptions, with varying degrees of success. Most eco-communities in this book consider these processes as dynamic, always needing refinement and improvement through community reflexivity. It is not unusual for eco-communities to reach moments of discord or crisis in these collective processes, and need to pause, reflect and reset (as Gavaldá and Cattaneo explore in Chapter 14). There are multiple tensions to navigate here; individual versus community needs, competing demands, uneven power relations (demarcated by longevity in a community, age, gender, perceived competencies, and/or individual self-confidence), and temporalities (residents' differing available time to dedicate to collective activities).

The contributors to this theme critically examine how eco-communities develop these processes of collective governance and how they have (or not) navigated the challenges they encountered. There remain many moments of disjuncture between the intent of governance and the reality of how in practice it requires compromise and negotiation, and can include disorder and disarray. Yet eco-communities have contributed significant and ongoing effort into recognizing the potential inequities in how their decision-making processes might inadvertently maintain uneven power and unconscious biases, and have sought to continuously improve their practices. Two examples of this navigation are explicitly explored – using deep social learning to effectively navigate group processes (as Jarvis examines in Chapter 15), and using embodied spiritual practices (such as singing, rituals, dancing, etc) to facilitate participatory consensus decision-making (as Clarence-Smith explores in Chapter 16). Eco-communities have also increasingly understood that social and material histories shape governance practices – that there is a place specificness that must be considered in devising ways of working and living collectively. Therefore, it is not always possible or desirable to replicate decision-making systems from one place to another without adjusting for these place experiences. The resulting differences are evident when reading across the examples in this section, where, for example, spiritually is highly important in Auroville but barely registers as in Can Masdeu and Kan Pasqual.

13

Contingent, contested, political: Learning from processes of environmental governance in the Global South to understand eco-communities

Natasha Cornea

In order to begin to question how eco-community participants might work together, (self) govern and relate to the state, this chapter takes as its starting point, not research on eco-communities themselves but rather the emerging and rich literature on urban environmental governance in the Global South. This body of research questions and accounts for governance as a contingent, contested and deeply political process may inform the creation of ecologically sustainable and inclusive cities in both the Global North and South, and therefore also shape the direction of eco-communities. By examining environment governance as a practice, involving actors in and beyond the state and questioning how these processes contribute to the (re)production of (in) equitable and (un)sustainable systems, we create scope to consider spaces of possibility for both incremental and potentially revolutionary changes.

In this chapter, I focus on research, often emerging from Geography and Anthropology that adopts a non-normative understanding of governance to focus on the actual processes through which environmental goals are pursued and countered, and the environmental imaginaries that underpin them are rendered and shaped in processes which are inherently power-laden. This research often draws on feminist, post-colonial and/or Foucauldian understandings of power to focus on the everyday practices and discourses through which the environment is governed, rather than (exclusively on) formal policy (Bjerkli 2013; Bjerkli 2015; Cornea et al., 2016; Desai et al., 2015; Truelove 2011; Truelove 2018). These perspectives fundamentally understand governance to be something which involves both state and non-state actors, who are in the position to adapt, hybridize and create norms, rules and regulations (Blundo and Le Meur 2009; Olivier de Sardan 2008). While the theoretical goal of governance is homogenizing, the practice and outcomes of governing are marked by temporal and spatial variation (Cornea et al., 2017; Moore 2009; Ranganathan and Balazs 2015). Legislative and legal regimes that allow for significant 'grey areas' in regard to environmental protection may further create scope for heterogeneous outcomes (Datta 2012), as does the influence of classed, casted and ethnically powerful groups (Baviskar 2003; Datta 2012). Fundamentally, this research has highlighted the complexity and politically contentious and negotiated nature of environmental governance in the Global South and has pointed towards the need for careful and nuanced analysis of these processes.

Research emerging from Southern contexts[1] offers several provocations for South-North and South-South learning. Firstly, this research demonstrates the importance of going beyond policy discourse and formal policy analysis to carefully consider processes of policy implementation and the reproduction of policy regimes by governance actors. In turn, this requires us to consider and account for the multiple rationalities and positionalities that governance actors operate from. Operating from an assumption of distortion and adaptation may create scope to allow us to consider how we may account for flexibility, innovation and change while also facilitating equitable outcomes. Secondly, and interrelated, this research recognizes and accepts that the state is a key governance actor, but demonstrates that the state is not orderly and predictable, but rather a heterogeneous and disorderly entity (Blanco et al., 2014). Even in situations where the state may appear omnipotent, it is not omniscient and the reality of governing is much messier than the theory of it. It further recognizes that a host of actors beyond the state are intimately and inseparably involved in processes of governing. Recognizing this disrupts any assumption that getting the policy right is the lynchpin for sustainable urbanization. In turn, this raises the question: what are the necessary governance conditions for supporting equitable, inclusive and ecologically sustainable communities and cities? Rather than try to artificially separate these issues, this chapter proceeds by examining what these bodies of research tell us about who governs, how actor networks and hybrid regimes interact, how governance happens in the everyday and the need to account for spatial and temporal heterogeneity. I return to these provocations at the end of this chapter to argue for the analytical and political potential of examining and accounting for processes of everyday environmental governance.

Who governs? Actor-oriented approaches to governance

Hong and Vicdan (2016, 133) have characterized governance as the 'nitty-gritty' of life in eco-communities:

> As an embodiment of social and relational dynamics in ecovillages, governance mechanisms both facilitate and convolute the transformative processes in which individual- and communal-level negotiations become the nitty-gritty of the sustainable lifestyle. The elements of sustainability as a practice often evolve from dialogues and compromises.

---

[1] It is essential here that we acknowledge the knowledge politics that shapes this research. The 'afterlife of colonial and Eurocentric power relations' (Jazeel and McFalane 2010, 109) and ongoing structural barriers to knowledge generation and dissemination – particularly in internationally accessible and valued (in the Euro-American context) outlets means that voices and experiences remained unheard. While efforts are made herein to explicitly privilege citations from author from the Global South and early career scholars where possible, this is an imperfect response to calls to consider and make visible how worldview and position produce data (Jazeel and McFarlane 2010; Siffiqi 2022).

The research on 'everyday governance' and the interconnected idea of the 'everyday state' emerging from Geographical and Anthropological studies in the Global South offer a particularly relevant and nuanced approach to understanding governance as a practice. This helps us to shift away from thinking about governance primarily as the sphere of governments and formal policy, and from what remains at times a near-fetishist obsession with 'good governance' as a panacea for all things. Instead, it encourages critical engagement with the processes of negotiation that underpin all governing practices and relationships. This shift may allow us to operate from a non-normative recognition of distortion and adaption to uncover the ways that governance as practised will always vary from governance as prescribed and that this does not necessarily imply unacceptable, inequitable or otherwise negative outcomes (though it in fact may).

To briefly situate these two conceptual fields, the *Everyday State* literature emerges primarily from research in India (Anjara 2011; Coelho 2006; Corbridge et al., 2005; Fuller and Benei 2000). These studies understand the state as a heterogeneous assembly of actors, institutions, practices and representations that are constantly reproduced through power relations and performance. Key to these investigations is a recognition that states often assert authority in and through the intimate, personal relationships between state and non-state actors. As a body of research, it challenges the boundaries between state and society and highlights the diverse range of relationships and normative registers that shape governance practices. *Everyday governance* as a concept and object of study emerges largely from anthropologists of the state in (francophone) West Africa (Bjerkli 2013; Blundo and Le Meur 2009; Eggen 2011; Hausermann, 2012; Le Meur and Lund 2001). The focus for many of these researchers is the provisioning of public goods and services and the banal workings of the local state (Bierschenk and Olivier de Sardan 2014, 3). Blundo and Le Meur (2009, 7) define everyday governance as 'a set of interactions … resulting in more or less stabilized regulations, producing order and/or disorder … and defining a social field, the boundaries and participants of which are not predefined'. Somewhat more succinctly, Le Meur & Lund (2001, 2) broadly define everyday governances as 'the actual practices of how interests are pursued and countered, authority exercised and challenged, and power institutionalised and undermined'. These bodies of research examine how the state works, and recognize and examine the multiplicity of actors who act in state-like ways. While these bodies of research have resonance between each other, and certainly with other conceptualizations of the state, such as Painter's (2006) understanding of the prosaic geographies of the state, crossover between them and with research focused on the Global North is surprisingly limited. However, there is significant analytical utility in these conceptualizations for critically engaging with governance as a practice and identifying spaces of opportunity for change.

Webs of power: Governance practice and hybrid regimes

Everyday approaches to understanding governance focus specifically on practices and questions of power, often drawing on feminist, post-colonial and/or Foucauldian understandings of power and in doing so are often deeply situated and embedded (Bjerkli 2013; Bjerkli 2015; Cornea et al., 2016; Desai et al., 2015; Truelove 2011; Truelove 2018). These approaches may give particular attention to the ways that actors racialized, gender (Desai et al., 2015; Truelove 2011) or caste/community-based (Cornea et al., 2016; Truelove 2018) identities are constituent to these power relations. Adopting these perspectives serves to centre everyday forms of control (Ekers and Loftus 2008) and recognize that such control may be wrought by a multiplicity of overlapping actors. While recognizing that each place and each situation are subject to 'continuous and contingent negotiations and shifting allegiances' (Cornea et al., 2017, 5), reading across this research attunes researchers to consider: the fragmented nature of the state and those who govern, and the relational webs between actors and the role of hybridized norms and rules in governing practices.

To a degree, the role of state (including bureaucrats and politicians) and state-like actors (Lund 2006; Palat Narayanan 2019) continues to dominate analysis of environmental governance, in large part perhaps due to their central role and influence. However, increasingly the 'porous' (Truelove 2020) or 'leaky' (Anand 2015) nature of state in the Global South is being recognized by researchers. Anand (2015) for example, in his work on water in Mumbai, has characterized the state and particularly state authority as porous and unstable, and produced both the material leakage of water from the system and the state's ignorance about such leakage. Even in cases where the state may seem omnipotent, it is not omniscient. Rather, the more common arrangement is of a fragmented state, who governs in tandem, alongside and in differing, overlapping spaces with other political, but 'non-state' actors.

Increasingly, researchers have begun to characterize and capture the 'webs of power' (Cornea et al., 2016), or relations between state and non-state actors who govern (urban) environments in heterogeneous, overlapping and contingent formation. Such research recognizes the multiple ways that such non-state actors can influence governance outcomes and exist in 'parallel to, and in complex relations to, state space' (Truelove 2020, 3). Actors may adapt, adopt and are perceived to have 'stateness' and in doing so through everyday processes 'blur rather than clearly differentiate, the boundary between state and society' (Truelove 2020, 5). Neves Alves (2019), in the context of a largely absent state in Guinea-Bissau, demonstrates the ways that the state itself is constituted through the erratic recognition of the state by international non-state organizations on the one hand, and on the other hand how state actors continue to have influence not through policy but rather through their informal decisions and interactions with non-state organizations. Others have variously explored the complex relationships and power relations between the state and wide range of actors including social clubs (Cornea 2020; Kundu and Chatterjee 2021), gangs (Pilo 2019) and local leaders (Palat Narayanan 2019). By recognizing the political assemblages that characterize the ways and means through which the environment is governed in the everyday, we create space to challenge the dualisms inherent in much analysis of governance – those of formal-informal, public-private, legal-illegal and in doing so recognize the multiple forms of legitimacy produced through these processes on the one hand and the ways that they may (re)produce 'social power relations and embodied forms of gendered, classed, and racialized difference in the city' (Truelove 2019, 5). This is important for eco-communities and the scope for more equitable urban futures because of the recognition of hybrid regimes and the need to consider not just the ways that the state may govern but also the role and power-laden relationships with and between other actors deemed legitimate. It is necessary, therefore, to critically examine both internal and external structures and relations of governing.

Here it is useful to recognize and remind ourselves that hybrid regimes[2] not only characterize governance of the Global South. Bulkeley et al. (2018, 2) have recognized that urban living laboratories as a modality of urban governance recognize that 'the capacity to govern is … fragmented' and subject to contestation and uncertainty. In doing so, the city is recognized as an 'emergent and heterogenous assemblage' (Evans 2016, 429 in: Bulkeley et al., 2018, 2). Recognizing these hybrid regimes of environmental governance in the everyday brings to fore questions of identity and subjectivity, and norms, modes and rules (de facto and de jure) through which governance occurs – in short, questions of how, when and where governance happens.

Processes of governing: Norms, subject positions and territory

Much of the research examining everyday governance practices in the Global South recognizes that both state and non-state governance actors adapt, hybridize and create norms, rules and regulations (Blundo and Le Meur 2009; Olivier de Sardan 2008). These adaptations and hybridizations are not understood to be negative or undesirable deviations, but rather to capture the messy reality of governing. These messy realities in practice conform to particular logic(s) and rule(s) which may not be fixed or singular, but are in fact present. Olivier de Sardan (2008; 2014), employs the concept of 'practical norms' to capture the *rules on the ground*; these are the informal rules that underpin practices of public actors which may not conform to professional/bureaucratic norms and often happen at the unconscious level. Often these *rules on the ground* are shaped in part by the multiple identities and loyalties of governance actors which shape their interactions and decisions (Osella and Osella 2000) At times what seems like competing norms and logics may in fact create the space in which different actors can mobilize to support their own agendas and needs (Pihljak et al., 2019). This recognition encourages us to not ask or not only ask, 'Do people follows the rules?' but also and more fundamentally 'What are the actual rules?' and 'How did these rules come to be?'.

One can also question how it is that people become governable, and what those processes are. In order to govern, through a range of practices, discourses and ideologies, actors construct a governable public. Some of these processes are relatively well explored in the literature, for example, practices of governmentality along with structures such as the law and as citizenship may ensure people are subject to the state[3],

---

[2] The use of hybrid regimes here differs from the use in some politics writing to describe more or less authoritarian 'democratic' states.
[3] See, for example, Foucault (1980; 1991).

and the ways that patronage politics may ensure acquiescence to broad and structural systems of government;[4] what has received less attention is the ways that non-state actors create governable publics. In examining the role of neighbourhood social clubs as governance actors in urban West Bengal, I have argued that it is only through a set of active and continued practices that these groups can establish governable territory and reproduce a 'club subject'. It is a population who understand themselves to be either voluntarily or by coercion subject to the authority of the club as governance actors. In turn this allows these clubs to act as both an alternative to and intermediary with the state (Cornea 2020). Elsewhere, Schramm and Ibrahim (2020, 12) have explored the ways that Water Action Groups (WAG) constituted in Nairobi function largely as 'a space for the cultivation of good, compliant, submissive citizens'. Privatization alone is not enough to turn citizens (who claim rights) into customers who earn commodities and are governed under that system. The WAGs produce a governable public who have a hybrid identity, one of the customers who must earn water and citizens who must also monitor the water suppliers on behalf of the state (see also Pilo 2020). In the same ways that systems are hybrid, people have multiple political subjectivities and allegiances. As we consider more sustainable urban futures and the roles of eco-communities in these, these insights open up questions about and recognition that governance is dependent on people acquiescing to the systems of governance and understanding themselves to be part of and subject to that system. Moreover, that such systems are continually reproduced and in flux. We cannot assume that there is a static identification with the goals and norms of an eco-community, nor that relationships between state and non-state actors and those they govern remain stable.

There has been an increased recognition of the ways that actors may strategically pivot their subject positions within governance strategies. This may include groups who act strategically as intermediaries with the state at particular moments, whilst serving as alternatives to the state at other points (Cornea 2020). In doing so, these governance actors strategically use their position as both political and non-political in strategic ways. However, it is not only non-state actors who pivot. Elected officials, for example, may variously mobilize their position as political actors and/or as citizens to secure services for the publics they govern (Truelove 2020). This ability to pivot subject positions contributes to the complex and flexible nature of everyday governance strategies. In making things work, in ensuring that services are secured and order maintained, governance actors use the relationships, identities and types of social capital or resources available to them in complex and strategic ways. To capture this and to fully comprehend and respond to the potential and limitations of current governance practices researchers must recognize and account for the multiple identities of members governance actors and the political potential[5] of those identities. Equally

---

[4] Chatterjee's (2004) distinction between populations who interact with the state as citizens (the minority) and those who interact with it as populations in systems of patronage (the majority) has been influential in understanding governance and the creation of governable publics in the Global South. There is insufficient scope here to discuss these ideas, or the criticisms of them (see Kalaiyarasan (2017); Routray 2014).

[5] The political potential of governance actors' identities may not align easily with more conventionally understood forms of capital or social power. At times, governance actors can mobilize otherwise marginalized identities in particular circumstances (Cornea et al., 2016).

important, though less explored in the current research, is the need to understand how the decisions to pivot, to employ different identities or draw on different relationships are made.

Governing temporal and spatial heterogeneity

All the hitherto explored processes in the Global South occur in the context of significant spatial and temporal heterogeneity. While the theoretical goal of governance may be homogenizing, the practice and outcomes of governing are marked by temporal and spatial variation (Cornea et al., 2017; Moore 2009; Ranganathan and Balazs 2015). Recognizing and accounting for this variation is crucial for considered analysis of the ways that inequality is produced and developing appropriately nuanced and flexible policies and interventions contributing to more sustainable and equitable urban futures. To a certain extent the material and social afterlives of post-colonial infrastructure and planning underpin a degree of spatial variation in practices and outcomes of environmental governance in the Global South (Allan et al., 2017; Mukherjee 2015; Schramm and Ibrahim 2020). For example, several scholars have demonstrated that the 'infrastructural ideal', that of a modern, universal network was in fact neither the norm nor the goal in most cities of the Global South, neither during the colonial or postcolonial period (Pilo 2019; Truelove 2020). Further reminding us that despite how it may be perceived, material infrastructure (around which much environmental governance in cities is organized) is not static (Pilo 2019). The heterogeneities that characterize cities of the Global South (though not just those) and the complex and differentiated politics of these cities have led Zimmer (2010) to argue for the need to understand the urban political ecologies that characterize post-colonial cities. Reminding us that different groups experience and inhabit very different landscapes. Similar ideas have been captured by other researchers, for example through the idea of archipelagos of water services, rather than homogenous networks (Bakker 2003). Interconnected to these ideas is a recent provocation by Lawhon et al. (2018) to look at infrastructural artefacts not as individual objects but rather as socio-technical configurations involving multiple technologies, relationships and capacities (amongst other factors). Systems thinking as suggested by the heterogeneous infrastructure configurations (HIC) concept may also help us think across the socio-technical configurations (which may include how they are governed) that characterize different eco-communities and initiatives aimed at sustainable urban futures to avoid one-size-fits-all 'solutions'. Instead we should recognize the characteristics that have proven successful (however we define it) and how those characteristics/processes may be transferred or learned from. Analytically it also points to the need to recognize and trace different social and material histories, alongside contemporary realities to comprehend both what exists and the future potential or challenges.

Far less accounted for in the literature is the issue of temporal variation. People don't inhabit the same cities, the same political ecologies both materially but also temporally. For example, Truelove (2016) through careful analysis of water practices in Delhi slum de-centres the normalized accounts of the gendered nature of urban water experiences as she finds the greatest embodied hardship is for single working men who are only rarely able to access the intermittent and unreliable water that serves their community. Elsewhere, researchers have documented the ways that the influence of actors may wax and wane temporally or situationally; this may follow a relatively regular pattern with particular actor configurations at certain times of day or seasonally (Schindler 2014) or reflect the rise and fall of actors influence over time and reflection of broader changes (Kundu and Chatterjee 2021; Palat Narayanan 2019). Actor assemblages in environmental governance are fluid and shifting; recognizing temporal variations in governing practices is thus key to understanding the city as lived environment.

Conclusions

Research on environmental governance in cities in the Global South has clearly demonstrated the analytical utility of paying close and careful attention to everyday practices and relationships of governance. Understanding governance as a relational process situated in particular material, social and political realities creates scope to consider how equitable urban futures may be constructed and facilitated in ways that go beyond getting policy right and towards accounting for relationships of power. To summarize the key arguments of this chapter, I return to the two provocations offered at the beginning of the chapter as key themes for South-North and South-South learning that I see arising from the research on environmental governance in cities of the Global South. Fundamentally, these provocations relate to questions of who governs, and how and with what rules do they govern.

Firstly, this research orients us as researchers towards questions of who governs. The state is and remains a key actor in the heterogeneous and disorderly processes that characterize environmental governance in cities in the Global South. This research has clearly demonstrated that governance occurs in processes between webs of actors in and beyond the state. This includes state and state-like actors (i.e. bureaucrats, politicians, traditional authorities with state-like authority and organizations that substitute for the state in its absence) but also formalized non-state actors (i.e. NGOs), and informal actors (i.e. strong men, locally influential groups and gangs). The divisions between such groups are often unclear and an individual actor or public may be loyal to more than one group. Such governance actors operate in heterogeneous, overlapping and contingent formations and these webs of power are constantly in flux, shaped by a range of structural factors (including those of community, caste and gender) and situated dynamics. This body of research further demonstrates that state, in its role and ability to govern, rather than being monolithic is in fact fragmented and porous. The boundaries between state and society are unclear and the reality is one of hybrid regimes.

Secondly, governance research from the Global South demonstrates the importance of questioning not just who governs, but how they govern. What are the rules on the ground and how are they reproduced? What power relations do they reproduce? The practices of governance actors align to a range of hybridized norms and rules. While governance may not conform to formalized rules in practice (i.e. those found in legislation established by the state), it does conform to systems of practical norms that whilst unwritten shape the rules of the game and the ways that people access the state, and navigate the webs of power between actors and the processes that shape everyday life. In order to produce and reproduce systems of rules and norms, governance actors draw on multiple forms of legitimacy. This legitimacy is built on and reproduced through complex configurations of identity and allegiance. This body of research has demonstrated that the practices of governance actors are shaped by their multiple identities and in the process of governing actors may pivot and employ identities with the most political potential in pursuit of particular outcomes. Equally, governed publics may pursue relationships with a multitude of actors in pursuit of their goals, drawing strategically on different relationships to pursue their needs. This research also increasingly recognizes that the ability of governance actors to govern depends on interlinked processes that (re)produce governable publics and governable territory. Careful attention to these processes begins to illuminate the specificities of political subjectivities that shape people's lives and in turn the city as a lived environment.

Moving away from assumptions of stability helps to reveal not only the analytical relevance of these insights but also their political potential. Engaging with governance as a practice allows us to identify spaces for opportunities for equitable and sustainable change. Accounting for and recognizing the multiple political and socio-material landscapes that shapes existing cities and eco-communities allows for careful and considered political and material interventions with the aim of equity. If, following the cues from this research in the Global South, we consider the political assemblages and overlapping landscapes of governance what emerges as key is getting relationships right. Recognizing and accounting for the multiple forms of legitimacy and multiple, overlapping subject positions that shape how those inside and outside of the state govern, creates the opportunity to facilitate relationships of equity (which can, and arguably should, be defined across multiple axis and dynamics. However, given that the contingent, shifting nature of governance relationships and networks produce and reproduce power relations, there is also scope for these relations to entrench or produce inequity. Actors and networks can pivot, governable publics can oppose being governed and governable territory may erode. All of this can subvert attempts at equity.

The deeply situated, everyday analysis that has characterized the research discussed here helps to highlight the need to consider systems and what characteristics support the goals of governing and in turn to act on those. Whilst wholesale replication, getting the policy right, or model projects may represent an easy-to-understand way forward, this research has clearly demonstrated the need to address underlying complex socio-material relationships that (re)produce conditions of (in)equality. This points then to the relevance of not only how we understand eco-communities, but also (perhaps) how eco-communities can understand themselves. If we accept that all governance relationships, and indeed all relationships, are contingent, not inherently stable, multiple and power-infused, then we can begin to consider ways and means to support these relations to be equitable. This enables us to negotiate the way we work together – both inside communities and with external governance actors (such as the state) with an ethos where possible of equity and transparency of networks.

References

Allen, A., Hofmann, P., Mukherjee, J. and Walnycki, A. (2017) 'Water trajectories through non-networked infrastructure: insights from peri-urban Dar es Salaam, Cochabamba and Kolkata', *Urban Research & Practice* 10(1), pp. 22–42.

Anand, N. (2015) 'Leaky States: Water audits, ignorance, and the politics of infrastructure', *Public Culture* 2(76), pp. 305–30.

Anjaria, J.S. (2011) 'Ordinary states: Everyday corruption and the politics of space in Mumbai', *American Ethnologist* 38(1), pp. 58–72.

Bakker, K. (2003) 'Archipelagos and networks: Urbanization and water privatization in the South', *The Geographical Journal* 169(4), pp. 328–41.

Baviskar, A. (2003) 'Between violence and desire: Space, power, and identity in the making of metropolitan Delhi', *International Social Science Journal* 55(175), pp. 89–98.

Bierschenk, T. and Olivier de Sardan, J.-P. (2014) 'Studying the dynamics of African bureaucracies: An introduction to states at work', in Bierschenk, T. and Olivier de Sardan, J-P. (eds.) *States at Work: Dynamics of African Bureaucracies*. Lieden & Boston, MA: Brill, pp. 3–33.

Bjerkli, C.L. (2013) 'Governance on the ground: A study of solid waste management in Addis Ababa, Ethiopia', *International Journal of Urban and Regional Research* 37(4), pp. 1273–87.

Bjerkli, C.L. (2015) 'Power in waste: Conflicting agendas in planning for integrated solid waste management in Addis Ababa, Ethiopia', *Norsk Geografisk Tidsskrift – Norwegian Journal of Geography* 69(1), pp. 18–27.

Blanco, I., Griggs, S. and Sullivan, H. (2014) 'Situating the local in the neoliberalisation and transformation of urban governance', *Urban Studies* 51(15), pp. 3129–46.

Blundo, G. and Le Meur, P.-Y. (2009) 'Introduction: An anthropology of everyday governance: Collective service delivery and subject making', in Blundo, G. and Le Meur, P.-Y. (eds.) *The Governance of Daily Life in Africa: Ethnographic Explorations of Public and Collective Services*. Leiden: Koniklijke Brill NV, pp. 1–38.

Bulkeley, H., Marvin, S., Palgan, Y.V., McCormick, K., Breitfuss-Loidl, M., Mai, L., von Wirth, T. and Frantzeskaki, N. (2018) 'Urban living laboratories: Conducting the experimental city?', *European Urban and Regional Studies* 26(4), pp. 317–35.

Chaterjee, P. (2004) *The Politics of the Governed: Reflections on Popular Politics in Most of the World*. New York: Columbia University Press.

Coelho, K. (2006) 'Tapping in: Leaky sovereignties and engineered (dis)order in an urban water system', *Sarai Reader* 6, pp. 497–509.

Corbridge, S., Williams, G., Srivastava, M. and Véron, R. (2005) *Seeing the State: Governance and Governmentality in India*. Cambridge: Cambridge University Press.

Cornea, N. (2020) 'Territorialising control in urban West Bengal: Social clubs and everyday governance in the spaces between state and party', *Environment and Planning C: Politics and Space* 38(2), pp. 312–28.

Cornea, N., Véron, R. and Zimmer, A. (2017) 'Clean city politics: An urban political ecology of solid waste in a small city in West Bengal, India', *Environment and Planning A* 49(4), pp. 728–44.

Cornea, N., Zimmer, A. and Véron, R. (2016) 'Ponds, power and institutions: The everyday governance of accessing urban water bodies in a small Bengali town', *International Journal of Urban and Regional Research* 40(2), pp. 395–409.

Datta, A. (2012) 'India's ecocity? Environment, urbanisation, and mobility in the making of Lavasa', *Environment and Planning C: Government and Policy* 30(6), pp. 982–96.

Desai, R., McFarlane, C. and Graham, S. (2015) 'The Politics of open defecation: Informality, body, and infrastructure in Mumbai', *Antipode* 47(1), pp. 98–120.

Eggen, O. (2011) 'Chiefs and everyday governance: Parallel state organisations in Malawi', *Journal of Southern African Studies* 37(2), pp. 313–31.

Ekers, M. and Loftus, A. (2008) 'The power of water: Developing dialogues between Foucault and Gramsci', *Environment and Planning D: Society and Space* 26(4), pp. 698–718.

Evans, J. (2016) 'Trials and tribulations: Problematizing the city through/as urban experimentation', *Geography Compass* 10(10), pp. 429–43.

Foucault, M. (1980) *Power/Knowledge: Selected Interviews and Other Writings 1972–1977*, Gordon, C. (ed.) New York: Vintage Books.

Foucault, M. (1991) *Discipline and Punish: The Birth of Prison*. London: Penguin.

Fuller, C.J. and Benei, V. (2000) *The Everyday State and Society in Modern India*. New Delhi: Social Science Press.

Hausermann, H. (2012) 'From polygons to politics: Everyday practice and environmental governance in Veracruz, Mexico', *Geoforum* 43(5), pp. 1002–13.

Hong, S. and Vicdan, H. (2016) 'Re-imaging the utopian: Transformation of a sustainable lifestyle in ecovillages', *Journal of Business Research* 69(1), pp. 120–36.

Jazeel, T. and McFarlane, C. (2010) 'The limits of responsibility: A postcolonial politics of academic knowledge production', *Transactions of the Institute of British Geographers* 35(1), pp. 109–24.

Kalaiyarasan, A. (2017) 'Populism and party: Society developmental Regimes in Tamil Nadu and West Bengal', in Nagaraj, R. and Motiram, S. (eds.) *Political Economy of Contemporary India*. Cambridge: Cambridge University Press, pp. 98–124.

Kundu, R. and Chatterjee, S. (2021) 'Pipe dreams? Practices of everyday governance of heterogeneous configurations of water supply in Baruipur Municipality, a small town in India', *Environment and Planning C* 39(2), pp. 318–35.

Lawhon, M., Nilsson, D., Silver, J., Ernstson, H., Lwasa, S. (2018) 'Thinking through heterogeneous infrastructure configurations', *Urban Studies* 55(4), pp. 720–32.

Le Meur, P-Y. and Lund, C. (2001) 'Everyday governance of land in Africa', *Bulletin de l'APAD [en ligne]* 22, n. p.

Lund, C. (2006) 'Twilight institutions: Public authority and local politics in Africa', *Development and Change* 37(4), pp. 685–705.

Moore, S.A. (2009) 'The excess of modernity: Garbage politics in Oaxaca, Mexico', *The Professional Geographer* 61(4), pp. 426–37.

Mukherjee, J. (2015) 'Beyond the urban: Rethinking urban ecology using Kolkata as a case study', *International Journal of Urban Sustainable Development* 7(2), pp. 131–46.

Neves Alves, S. (2019) 'Everyday states and water infrastructure: Insights from a small secondary city in Africa, Bafatá in Guinea-Bissau', *Environment and Planning C: Politics and Space* (online first).

Olivier de Sardan, J-P. (2008) *Researching the Practical Norms of Real Governance in Africa*. London: Africa Power and Politics Programme.

Olivier de Sardan, J.-P. (2014). 'The delivery State in Africa: Interface bureaucrats, professional cultures and the bureaucratic mode of governance', in Bierschenk, T. and Olivier de Sardan, J.-P. (eds.) *States at Work: Dynamics of African Bureaucracies*. Leiden & Boston, MA: Brill, pp. 399–429.

Osella, F. and Osella, C. (2000) 'The return of King Mahabali: The politics of morality in Kerala', in Fuller, C.J. and Benei, V. (eds.) *The Everyday State and Society in Modern India*. New Delhi: Social Science Press, pp. 137–62.

Painter, J. (2006) 'Prosaic geographies of stateness', *Political Geography* 25(7), pp. 752–74.
Palat Narayanan, N. (2019) 'The production of informality and everyday politics', *City* 23(1), pp. 83–96.
Pihljak, L., Rusca, M., Alda-Vidal, C. and Schwartz, K. (2019) 'Everyday practices in the production of uneven water pricing regimes in Lilongwe, Malawi', *Environment & Planning C: Politics and Space* (online first).
Pickerill, J. (2015) 'Bodies, building and bricks: Women architects and builders in eight eco-communities in Argentina, Britain, Spain, Thailand and USA', *Gender, Place & Culture* 22(7), pp. 901–19.
Pilo, F. (2019) 'Negotiating networked infrastructural inequalities: Governance, electricity access, and space in Rio de Janeiro', *Environment & Planning C: Politics and Space* (online first).
Pilo, F. (2020) 'Material politics: Utility documents, claims-making and construction of the "Deserving Citizen" in Rio de Janerio', *City & Society* 31(1), pp. 71–92.
Ranganathan, M. and Balazs, C. (2015) 'Water marginalization at the urban fringe: environmental justice and urban political ecology across the North–South divide', *Urban Geography* 36(3), pp. 403–23.
Routray, S. (2014). 'The Postcolonial City and its Displaced Poor: Rethinking "Political Society" in Delhi', *International Journal of Urban and Regional Research* 38(6), pp. 2292–308.
Siddiqi, A. (2022). 'The missing subject: Enabling a postcolonial future for climate conflict research'. *Geography Compass* 16(5), e12622, pp. 1–13.
Schindler, S. (2014) 'A New Delhi every day: Multiplicities of governance regimes in a transforming metropolis', *Urban Geography* 35(3), pp. 402–19.
Schramm, S. and Ibrahim, B. (2020) 'Hacking the Pipes: Hydro-political currents in a Nairobi housing estate', *Environment & Planning C: Politics and Space* (online first).
Truelove, Y. (2011) '(Re-)Conceptualizing water inequality in Delhi, India through a feminist political ecology framework', *Geoforum* 42(2), pp. 143–52.
Truelove, Y. (2016) 'Incongruent waterworlds: Situating the everyday practices and power of water in Delhi', *South Asia Multidisciplinary Journal* 14, pp. 1–26. https://journals.openedition.org/samaj/4164.
Truelove, Y. (2018) 'Negotating states of water: Producing ilegibility, bureaucratic arbitrariness, and distributive injustices in Delhi', *Environment and Planning D: Society and Space* (online first).
Truelove, Y. (2019) 'Gray Zones: The everyday practices and governance of water beyond the network', *Annals of the American Association of Geographers* (online first).
Truelove, Y. (2020) 'Who is the state? Infrastructural power and everyday water politics in Delhi', *Environment & Planning C: Politics and Space*. DOI: 10.1177/2399654419897922.
Zimmer, A. (2010) 'Urban Political Ecology. Theoretical concepts, challenges, and suggested future directions', *Erdkunde* 64(4), pp. 343–54.

14

Organizing together: Coexisting, time economies, money and scale in Barcelona eco-communities

Marc Gavaldà and Claudio Cattaneo

Introduction

What are the insights we can gain from different organizational approaches within eco-communities? We both live in one of them and, although very similar, they have important differences, with one based on spontaneous organization and the other more structured. Our case compares two similar 'rurban' communities in Barcelona but with very different models: Kan Pasqual and Can Masdeu (Cattaneo and Gavaldá 2010), with a focus on organizational patterns, the role of the assembly, how time is used, how is work carried out for the collective, its reward and its control. Both Can Masdeu and Kan Pasqual are representative cases from Iberia and are well established (2001 and 1996 respectively). They are also both squatted projects and active social centres (Hodkinson and Chatterton 2006; Martínez 2013; Mudu 2004). They can be seen as squats, as social centres or as eco-communities. Their internal organization – which is the focus of this chapter – has a lot to do with being squats and that the community members are also the managers of their respective social centres. The phenomenon of neo-rural communities formation can be compared with 'utopian migrations' (Sayadi 2010, 10); that is, examples of urban exodus and voluntary marginalization rejecting modernization processes and instead establishing more intimate human relationships.

Can Masdeu and Kan Pasqual subscribe to this ambivalence in their origins. They have both been inspired by anarchist movements and community autonomy, such as the Zapatista movement for the construction and defence of Indigenous autonomy, as practised by the EZLN (Mexico), the Cauca Indigenous Regional Council (Colombia) or, before them the Popular Communities of Resistance (CPR) of Guatemala. Other foundational sources of inspiration were Zibechi (2006), who approaches community empowerment from the bottom up and the postulates of agroecology (Altieri 1995) and permaculture (Mollison 1988). On the other hand, a foundational principle shared by both these communities is the development of collective tools that will free from, or at least reduce the dependency upon, the state and capitalist markets. They are therefore both living as community and a social centre where they project antagonistic political and cultural activities. The borders between spheres, identities and practices are blurred and redrawn with the passage of time.

It is essential to understand the geographical position of both projects that lay in the outskirts of Barcelona City – Catalonia's capital – with its antagonist history, rooted in its anarchist experience as well as in its long-term confrontation with the Spanish State, so strong that has even reached the highest level of Catalan institutions. This is essential to understand the social *milieu* where these communities are set.

They are located in the Natural Park of Collserola, the mountain range that runs parallel to the sea. Higher on the hills, Kan Pasqual is less reachable by public transport or bike, while Can Masdeu is only a 15-minute walk from the metro station, where the city ends and the park begins. Both estates have agricultural infrastructure and are early examples of the squatters movement meeting the ecologist movement. But they are also close to the city, therefore they are defined as *rurban* projects – and they constitute examples where a battle against the growth of the neoliberal city has been won. They have resisted the wave of privatization and the real estate speculation bubble which severely hit Barcelona between the late 1980s and 2008, a period of intense capitalist urban renovation. As a post-industrial city limited on one side by the sea and on the other by the hills, renovation through privatization has been collectively condemned by its social movements (UTE 2004). In Can Masdeu, privatization and enclosures have been prevented since the failed eviction attempt in 2002 and the following victories in court against its owner, the Sant Pau Hospital, a public entity. Similarly, when in 2006 large parts of Collserola were declared a Natural Park as a result of a long-term battle in which members of both collectives have been active along other civic moments, the green and anti-capitalist squatters could celebrate a moral victory.

The socialization spaces of social movements (demonstrations, concerts, parties, talks) have been environments where the desire to squat among young people has spread. This is driven by a desire to emancipate themselves from family dependencies, and the demands of rent, to implement a way of life more coherent with fighting against the capitalist system. The period 1995–2005 was a glorious decade for the squatting movement in Barcelona, with more than forty social centres and fifty homes established (Debelle at al., 2018).

Both collectives are also committed to social activism that goes beyond the defence of the spaces they squat; such as participating in the Barcelona squatters movement and its assembly, in anti-capitalist and alter-globalization struggles, in local and global ecologist movements, in housing struggles, in immigrant and refugee support, participation in neighbourhood activities, and in structuring social activities offered in their spaces. Kan Pasqual has been offering workshops, talks or the use of its oven for baking bread, or its living room for neighbourhood-cinema sessions. It has often hosted gatherings such as the rural squatting meeting or educational visits to people and groups, and organizing a mutual support network among the different rural squatting projects of the Iberian Peninsula. At the same time, its accomplishments in energy autonomy (solar and wind) have been a referent for other emerging projects.

Can Masdeu has structured its social centre activities around three projects: (1) a community garden collective (started in 2002) where thirty-five allotments are allocated to neighbours who are collectively organized in the community gardens assembly; (2) an environmental education project (established in 2003) in which members offer visits and activities and has a garden plot for hands-on learning; and

(3) a social space, located in one part of the building and its patio (established in 2003) which has since then worked mainly on Sunday openings – around twenty-five per year – where free workshops, talks and activities are offered and a bar-restaurant serves food and beverages at popular prices contributing to the kitty of the collective who runs the space. The social space is also used for gatherings of activist groups or camps who might use the space overnight – about six times per year. Running a social centre and supporting the activism of its members constitutes a further element of complexity with respect to the internal organization of these eco-communities.

Co-existence and collectivity

Members who in the first place decided to squat the properties, and also those who have later joined the projects, have done so not only out of the necessity of precarious living conditions, but also for political ideals. Politically, this includes, from a feminist perspective, the challenge of living together, inserting personal lives into a collective dimension. These are highly motivated strong-minded people who have decided to cut ties with their previous apolitical or consumerist life-styles and follow their ideals. Bauman (2001, 4) points to the trade-off between freedom and security – while more freedom means less sense of community, more security means gaining a community at the cost of freedom. This trade-off also represents the dilemma between community and individuality. Therefore, community is not only born out of a utopic vision, it also consolidates into a structure, with obligations and rights, that protect those who belong to it (Robes 2010).

The result is a delicate situation in which individuals want to create their ideal place while at the same time have to deal with other strong-minded highly motivated comrades who might pursue their own ideal. In order to make the Can Masdeu project work in its day-to-day activities, being pragmatic and solution-driven is more important than making decisions based on ideals that would cost long hours lost in philosophical debates. Once each individual has followed her own ideals and decided to join one of these projects, it is important to be pragmatic and compromise in the day-to-day in order to allow for a better co-existence.

Coexistence in a collective is a process of self-learning. Many of us have been born and raised in single-family homes where life has been lived within the boundaries of a delimited private space and, often, with patriarchal behaviours within the family. Coexistence in a collective, then, is an inhospitable terrain to in which walk, where many difficulties arise. In both groups, there have been personal conflicts that have led to the resignation or abandonment of some components. Little by little, the groups have been equipping themselves with tools to navigate dynamics and personal differences that can affect the emotional health of the group. This is worked through primarily at the assembly.

The assembly is the collective communication and horizontal decision space, where the collective's news is shared and day-to-day tasks are organized, as well as long-term projects. In Kan Pasqual, a weekly assembly is held where the points to be discussed are proposed at the beginning and are ordered randomly. The recurring themes are: organization of the tasks of bread making, the garden, maintenance and improvement of the solar system, and visits and organization of events of the social centre. Social relational issues have little space and it is one of the weaknesses identified in the group. From time to time, attempts are made to address these issues in special meetings, but again, the lack of experience in streamlining these processes means that differences are not resolved in these spaces either. On the other hand, the convivial sharing of time and spaces, such as the meals in a small kitchen, offers the opportunities to exchange information and viewpoints. Sharing a meal is often something much more than simple feeding.

In Can Masdeu, assemblies are organized on a monthly basis; they are not as frequent because the project is organized in working groups and responsibilities that, initially instituted by the assembly with the design of a protocol of actuation, have allowed for decentralized decision-making. Also, the use of an email list and more recently of different WhatsApp groups have allowed for the day-to-day communication of news beyond the assembly.

In both cases despite the assembly being a formal instrument of horizontal decision-making by consensus, there are repeated manifestations of power, such as the abuse of the veto or false consensus.[1] Some people monopolize turns, or project a stronger tone of voice, or the security of the issuer may in practice exercise power that has not been granted. To this extent, another tool that is used in Can Masdeu is the emotional assembly, in which people come to listen to how community members feel rather than to debate decisions.

Since 2020, there has been a rebellion led by a group of women against the failure to define a common vision for Can Masdeu and against the further establishment of protocols that are derived from 'false consensus' taken in the assembly. To solve this *impasse*, Can Masdeu hired experts from a cooperative consultancy specializing in process work and deep democracy (Mindell 1995), that is helping the collective to find its common vision starting from the sharing of emotions and improving group tolerance.

Kan Pasqual has not used process work to solve its conflicts; with the passing of time, people have learned to become more tolerant, that is, lowering the demands on each other to avoid conflicts for the common good of the whole group. In this way, mechanisms of mutual tolerance are built in which one learns to accept the annoying behaviour of one other and vice versa. This mechanism is valid as long as the tolerance and discomfort are kept in balance with the well-being and the conviviality of the experience of living together.

Time economies and monetary flows

From an economic standpoint, these eco-communities consider income as just a means to an end: the good life. This approach connects with the Indigenous concept

---

[1] For instance, when some participants agree to a decision not because they are truly convinced, but because they are tired of overly long discussions.

of *buen vivir (Sumaq Kawsay)* that overrides the capitalist search for growth and profit. Well-being is a holistic act of care that embraces health, community, mutual respect, ecology, water and territory. There is also a specific anti-capitalist perspective That motivates the community members to avoid extra consumption and spending money, while the counter-cultural dimension that is common to most of the squatters movement is that of the D.I.Y. (Do It Yourself) and Do-It-Together. Rather than selling time to the labour market, there is a tendency to invest time in the satisfaction of the individual and community necessities. Time assumes an important dimension in that of an embedded non-monetary economy (Polanyi 1944). What stands out as a marked difference between Kan Pasqual and Can Masdeu is the extent to which the time economy (that is an accounting of workload that is equitable for everyone) is formalized.

The workloads at Kan Pasqual are informal and voluntary. Therefore, there is a very different use of time among the members of the collective. Each week, an average of two to three hours are devoted to gardening, firewood collection and the orchard; about two hours to cleaning and cooking; about three hours to reading and using the internet; and about three hours a day of socializing and eating. There are also differences in the time spent working outside the community to earn money for the individual economy. Thus, 30 per cent of the community members work a few hours a week in teaching, 30 per cent work sporadically on temporary jobs and the rest do not work externally.

In Can Masdeu, the workload is similar – about 12–14 hours per week – but is a formalized process. Each community member has to cook twice per month, work six hours per week in gardening, maintenance or cleaning, work about two to three hours per week in his/her responsibility area, dedicate three weekends (45 hours) per year in cooking and attending the restaurant bar on those Sundays the social centre is opened by the house collective and 25 hours for the festival held in May and finally, attend the assemblies (both the ordinary monthly ones and the emotional ones when these are called). At the end of the year, statistics are calculated and shared and each one should comply with the minimum requirement, otherwise, there is a compensatory mechanism which can be in money (pay for the work not done) or in kind (do extra hours to reach the minimum). There are also options to request a lower workload – in particular those with a full-time employment – in exchange for extra money.

In Kan Pasqual and Can Masdeu, there is time dedicated to earn money *for* the collective: Kan Pasqual bakes and distributes bread each week, and three to four people dedicate their entire day to these tasks. With five to seven hours of work every week, 50–70 kilos of bread are baked, of which 40 are sold for a net income of €100. Approximately €6 an hour is paid to the workers. In Can Masdeu, work *for* the community is 45+25 hours per year – which can also be exchanged for money (not working one weekend is equivalent to €120 which is the mean income from the work of one person on a Sunday opening).

Most people in Can Masdeu now work externally – in the past it was more like in Kan Pasqual – so that now 50 per cent have a full-time job (employed or self-employed), 35 per cent a part-time job, and only two or three are self-employed from home: brewing beer, organizing courses in Can Masdeu or, in the past, selling bread or doing carpentry. Time is saved by shared gardening, cleaning and cooking work. Collective living reduces financial burdens as well as domestic burdens compared to single-family living.

Society imposes moral values about the virtues of work that are manifested in wealth, status-symbols and social positioning. Those who do not have a 'meaningful' job are considered worthless. However, in Kan Pasqual, and still to a large extent in Can Masdeu, external employment is perceived as a necessary process to fund individual expenses such as leisure activities, drink, travel, fashion or means of transport (car), as well as the family expenses of members who have children (schooling, after-school, transportation, dentist).

On the other hand, working for the community (be it in the garden, in the social centre, in the facilitation of a collective process or any other task that you would not normally consider normal in mainstream lifestyles) are all unpaid tasks (in financial terms), but with a high 'sense of utility', because their contributions increase social capacity (Almendro 2019). Although these tasks are not translated into monetary gains, they are part of the economy, for they (1) order supplies to the community (food, drink); (2) increase the capacity of collection and storage of physical resources for the maintenance of the community infrastructure (water tanks, batteries, cellar, warehouse spaces); (3) improve the quality of life of the households (insulation, heating, furniture); (4) increase the recycling and recirculation of materials (composting, purification of grey water) and (5) fulfil household chores (maintenance, cleaning, health).

These tasks generate benefits in terms of quality of life and therefore challenge the logic of neo-classical economics. We call them 'anti-monetary benefits': those products of work that reduce dependence on the market and therefore on money and we propose here an analytical framework. In economic terms, these benefits can be seen as 'negative Euros', in that they don't contribute to the monetary market and instead constitute an example of how to measure the degrowth effect of these communities. Several examples are offered in Table 1, which is an example from Kan Pasqual:

For the four tasks exemplified, in the columns to the left we have represented the benefits and in the last two columns to the right the costs. In turn, they are expressed with respect to their eventual contribution to GDP and to the community. These cases are each explained below.

For the building of a tiny wooden house, €3000 have been saved by not paying an external worker – instead unpaid work was put into it (we have here €3000 negative Euros). The materials for its construction have been bought in the market (this cost is reflected as a community monetary expenditure and no negative € are generated here). On the other hand, potatoes and firewood are obtained without any monetary expenditure at all (€210 and €150 negative Euros are generated). Finally, bread is baked and sold to the market. Individual labour, here too, is not paid for, resulting in €262 negative Euros; this unpaid labour time and the use of 40 kilograms of flour allow for 210 Euros of collective income. In turn, the selling price of this bread (€3.5/kg) is about half of the equivalent type of bread normally sold in the market. Rent of land is not included, because these eco-communities are squatted places. Neither are tools and machines because, in line with the idea of 'tools for conviviality' (Illich 1973),

Table 1 Example of negative Euros: Anti-monetary benefits and costs

		Work		Goods and materials	
Collective Task	GDP-equivalent in the labour market (Spanish mean income)	Actual money flow for the eco-community		Equivalent money flows in the market	Actual money flows for or from the eco-community
Construction of a wooden tiny house	200 hours *15€/h = 3000 €	0		Materials: 1500 €	Materials: 1500 € from the community
Cultivating a potato garden	20 hours * 9€/h = 180 €	0		300 kg *0,7€/kg= 210 €	0
Collecting 1 ton of firewood	20 hours * 12 €/h = 240€	0		150 €	0
Baking 60 kg of bread	21 hours * 12€/h = 262 €	0		Cost: 40 kg flour * 1€/kg = 40 € Revenue: 60 kg * 7€/kg = 420€	Cost: 40 kg flour * 1€/kg = 40 € Revenue: 60 kg * 3.5€/kg = 210€ for the community

activities are mainly done with the employment of manual tools that are durable, cheap to buy and maintain. The use of simpler tools is, in turn, evident in the monetary comparison and an apparent paradox: why would these eco-communities save 210€ in not buying potatoes and another 150€ in not buying firewood, if the hours employed in these tasks could be sold in the respective labour market (agricultural work and forest work) and a larger income generated?

The answer is multidimensional. First, working from home is preferred to working for a boss: it allows for autonomy in the choice of the pace, the time and the shifts. It saves time in going to and from work. Second, it produces an important environmental benefit because the bio-cultural heritage is conserved (Tello and Gonzalez de Molina 2023), the land is not abandoned, and the forest is managed diminishing the risk of fires (Cervera et al., 2016). Third, there is a communal understanding that these activities are useful and meaningful work for the eco-community. If rent was to be acknowledged and the hours dedicated to the maintenance of the tiny house, we could estimate that 300€/month is saved (negative Euros) thanks to the squatting of land. There is, however, a time expenditure associated to the DIY tasks of maintaining the tiny house which must be counted against the 300€ saved each month. However, within a certain range estimating the amount of hours is not relevant: they can be zero or 50 per month but as long as they constitute meaningful work that improves the social capacity within the eco-community members, there is no need to compare them with the cost of rent.

The work of building collective infrastructure generates many more benefits than the simple Euros that are saved (monetary degrowth), primarily, social capacity and meaningful work. In turn, in order to enhance unpaid collective work, a deeply rooted cultural shift is needed: the communal in this case is like a rewarding space that opens between the solitude of individual work and the alienation of labour market. Since most market relationships are dominated by capitalist firms,[2] we understand the creation of these demonetized living spaces as one of the bases for the construction of anti-capitalism, as spaces for demonstration and collective affirmation that there is life beyond capitalism.

Both places are examples of mixed economies. In Kan Pasqual, there is a collective kitty (only filled from collective work, mainly from the bakery) with some contributions from individuals when the kitty is empty; but the income generated in external work remains the property of the person who earns it. In Can Masdeu, the kitty is filled from collective work (Sunday openings of the social centre and festival in May, and some sporadic subventions[3]) and individual contributions (€100–125/month in 2020, but it used to be €60 until 2016 and €80 from 2018). Like in Kan Pasqual, personal income is not collectivized and it can also be generated by self-employment (see also Gavaldá and Cattaneo 2020). Among Can Masdeu members, as the time dedicated to external work has increased and therefore also personal income, a few mechanisms have been implemented. This includes the option to financially compensate for the hours one does not work in the collective tasks (in place since 2018). Due to the Covid-19 crisis, the 2020 festival was cancelled, which is the main source of collective income. So an increase of the monthly quota was agreed, from €80 to €100–125 / month. Overall, the collective economy in 2018 and 2019 was around €80,000 annually (that is, €250/person/month), of which €36,000 from the festival (nothing in 2020), €8,000 from the Sunday openings (€2000 in 2020), €26,000 from individual quotas (including contributions from guests) and €8000 in subventions (€2500 in 2019, nothing in 2020).

Can Masdeu is a collective economy that is growing fast, particularly the spring festival which every two to three years needs to be re-invented and down-scaled to avoid its mainstreaming. It is a resilient economy that in the Covid-19 context is re-adapting: returning to a more austere diet and increase individual quotas, avoiding extraordinary expenditures in infrastructures or gardens, and designing new ways to generate collective income, away from catering and festivals and towards training and education.

In Kan Pasqual, the monetary trend has been more constant over time, with a limited collective economy of around €5–6,000/year and a culture of recycling food and materials, simplicity and avoidance of the use of the market that Can Masdeu used to be in its beginning (Cattaneo and Gavaldá 2010).

Scaling up

Knowing that these experiments have been already in place for a long time (twenty-four and nineteen years respectively), if some scaling up was to happen, this would

---

[2] In Can Masdeu, where collective money flows more than in Kan Pasqual, there is a spending policy oriented towards the purchase of products from cooperatives rather than capitalist corporations.
[3] These one-off subventions came from the municipality for doing environmental education, from a couple of International NGOs for putting beehives and from their participation in a couple of Erasmsus+ network projects.

have already occurred. These models are not easy to replicate because long-term squatting is an exception and because joining a social political project with an eco-community can be challenging. The rurban context is also quite unique in its abrupt shift from Barcelona city to the Collserola Natural Park.

In the past five to ten years, there have been many cases of the squatting of empty properties in Collserola Park, with a new generation of activists belonging to collectives that are loosely organized as eco-communities. Primarily they resemble the DIY culture that would dumpster-dive and recycle food in the market before building a garden. Whether our rurban experiences have an impact beyond Barcelona and Collserola, we do not know. Rural squatting is frequent in the Iberian Peninsula and the networking with those projects constitutes a sort of a movement of landless neo-farmers that has been going on for more than four decades. Also, the largest squat in Europe (ZAD, in Notre-Dames des Landes, France) resembled an eco-community that emerged from what originally had been established as a land occupation to resist the development of the Nantes airport.

As long as grassroots and direct action remains an exception and individuals are colonized by the mainstream concepts of meaningful work, aesthetics and individualistic faith in the market, the scalar impact of eco-communities will be limited. Yet, we believe these experiments are seeds that could flourish if a radically different context emerged (a likely scenario with climate change, Covid and peak oil economies).

More visible are the effects of scaling-up one of the elements of the Kan Pasqual and Can Masdeu experiments. For instance, urban agriculture is a phenomenon that is scaling up from our initial experiments: in 1996, reclaiming food sovereignty was only done by Kan Pasqual; in 2001, Barcelona had no other community gardens than those of Can Masdeu. Now there are numerous examples in squatted places, in self-managed allotments that the municipality is offering to collectives, and in institutional allotment gardens for retired people. Something similar can be said with respect to the autonomous energy system in Kan Pasqual and the movements for energy sovereignty that have later emerged (e.g. xse.cat).

Another element that is quickly scaling up in Barcelona is living together: the phenomenon of housing coops is quite new to the city (which lags several decades behind Northern European countries) and, in the case of La Borda, the first housing coop in a city-context, several members are joining from the squatters movement. Cal Cases, the first housing coop on the Iberian Peninsula (established in 2008), is also an example of an eco-community with straw-bale houses, renewable energies and activists that have moved from Barcelona to inner Catalonia.

From a spatial perspective, there is potential for the proliferation of a money-free culture, which creates the opportunity for developing mutual trust, a much needed therapeutic process in the shift from individualism to community. The Nowtopia reality (Manning and Carlsson 2010) offers good examples; a useful indicator is how money is moving per square meter of urban space (€/m2), a notable indicator of demonstrations against prohibitive rents in Barcelona. Thanks to the 2008 crisis and the declaration of parts of Collserola as a natural park, urban growth fuelled by rent-seeking and real-estate speculation has diminished and now professional farmers and sheep herds are starting to proliferate.

On organization and scalability, the more structured approaches are easier to scale where social contracts and norms related to work and money are maintained, but they are established collectively and managed as a commons. The more spontaneous and informal organization requires a strong maturity and expertise by individuals in the engagement with the collective and where the sacrifice of individual needs is accepted. To this extent, the smaller the community the easier it is for mutual trust to work.

Conclusions

We have analysed and compared two eco-communities that share very specific characteristics: both are located on the hills of Barcelona in a rurban space, both are open to the public as they are social projects and both are squatted, and still remain after nineteen and twenty-four years respectively. However, there are also key differences because of the way they are organized and to a lesser extent, the number of inhabitants. We highlight the sense of being useful to the community, of contributing with time and work for the common good and how this challenges market logics and contributes to the creation of an anti-capitalist society. Also, we highlight the virtues of the 'anti-economy' understood as working and dedicating time to reducing monetary expenditures instead of increasing income, as a radical, transformative and hopeful path for the future.

However, during the time-lapse since this chapter was initially written in 2022, Can Masdeu has experienced the collapse of its household community. Although the social centre project is still quite lively, since spring 2021 people have started to move out, or stop participating (as an act of protest) in collective decision-making and chores. The result is that only five of the old members – all male – are still participating in the assembly and day-to-day work, plus two new recruits.

The reasons for this community collapse, also ironically named as *Fracasdeu* (*failure* in English), are multiple – the main ones are related to gender and power issues (all women and families have left); to an irresolvable conflict between two very opposed sub-groups; and to different visions over prioritizing the public social project or the household community project. The fact that male (as well as pioneer) participants tend to stay for a longer period, while females eventually move out, is common to other long-term squatted projects in Barcelona. It reinforces the ideas in Tummers and Mac Gregor (2019) that truly embracing the gender issue – as informed by Feminist Political Ecology – is an open challenge for eco-communities. For instance, 'Dona CanMasdeu' – the group of the female members constituted in early 2020 – announced that it would stop participating in several of the social centre activities and decision-making process because it found that serious reflection was needed for them, and other members, to find motivation again within the community. Their proposal was to temporarily stop public activities held in the social centre to focus on internal debates aimed at restructuring decision-making processes – too often made of false-consensus – and at improving interpersonal relationships which, in some cases, were toxic and even violent. Although some male members were opposed to this proposal, the Covid lockdown made it imperative to stop.

The conflict could not even be resolved when professional facilitators, recommended that all members leave the community for a new group; a proposal agreed by the large majority of the members but that has been vetoed by the three 'founding fathers'.

In late 2022, as a new group of mainly women moved in, the five old male members were invited to move out until spring 2023, leaving the project run by an experiment of ten young members – none of whom had inhabited the place for longer than one year – generating new dynamics and good interpersonal relationships. Facing the despair of the collapse, the hope in the maintenance of these new dynamics will mainly rely on the capacity to keep the balance of power between the new and the old members.

References

Almendro, R. (2019) Social capacity in the struggle for degrowth. MSc thesis, ICTA-UAB.
Altieri, M. (1995) *Agroecology: The Science of Sustainable Agriculture*. Boca Raton, FL: CRC Press.
Bauman, Z. (2001) 'Identity in the globalising world', *Social Anthropology* 9(2), pp. 121–29.
Cattaneo, C. and Gavaldá, M. (2010) 'The experience of rurban squats in Collserola, Barcelona: What kind of degrowth?', *Journal of Cleaner Production* 18(6), pp. 581–9.
Cattaneo, C. and Martínez López, M.A. (2014) *The Squatters' Movement in Europe. Commons and Autonomy as Alternatives to Capitalism*. London: Pluto Press.
Cervera, T., Pino, J., Marull, J., Padró, R. and Tello, E. (2016) 'Understanding the long-term dynamics of forest transition: From deforestation to afforestation in a Mediterranean landscape (Catalonia, 1868–2005)', *Land Use Policy* 80(October), pp. 318–31. DOI: 10.1016/j.landusepol.2016.10.006.
Debelle, G., Cattaneo, C., Gonzalez, R., Barranco, O. and Llobet, M. (2018) 'Squatting cycles in Barcelona: Identities, repression and the controversy of institutionalisation', in Martinez, M.A. (ed.) *The Urban Politics of Squatters' Movements*. New York: Palgrave Macmillan, pp. 51–73.
Gavaldá, M. and Cattaneo, C. (2020) 'Feeding together: The revolution starts in the kitchen', in Stavrides, S. and Travlou, P. (eds.) *Housing as Commons: Housing Alternatives as Response to the Current Urban Crisis*. London: Zed Books, pp. 95–110.
Hodkinsons, S. and Chatterton, P. (2006) 'Autonomy in the city? Reflections on the social centres movement in the UK', *City* 10(3), pp. 305–15. DOI: 10.1080/13604810600982222
Illich, I. (1973) *Tools for Conviviality*. New York: Harper and Row. Available at https://co-munity.net/system/files/ILLICH%201973_tools_for_convivality_1.pdf.
Martinez, M.A. (2002) *Okupaciones de viviendas y centros sociales: Autogestión, contracultura y conflictos urbanos*. Barcelona: Virus.
Martínez López, M.A. (2013) 'The squatters' movement in Europe: A durable struggle for social autonomy in Urban politics', *Antipode* 45(4), pp. 866–87.
Mindell, A. (1995) *Sitting in the Fire: Large Group Transformation Using Conflict and Diversity*. San Francisco, CA: Deep Democracy Exchange.
Mollison, B. (1988) *Permaculture – A Designer's Manual*. Tyalgum: Tagari Publications.
Mudu, P. (2004) 'Resisting and challenging neoliberalism: The development of Italian Social Centers', *Antipode* 36(5), pp. 917–41. DOI: 10.1111/j.1467-8330.2004.00461.x

Ortiz, M. (2020) *La Comunidad*. Masters thesis. Universidad de Barcelona.
Polanyi, K. (1944) *The Great Transformation: The Political and Economic Origins or Our Time*. Boston, MA: Beacons Press.
Robes, M. (2010) A Manual for having fun while changing the world. Masters Thesis. University of Applied Sciences, Tel Aviv.
Sayadi, S. (2010) 'Ciudad versus campo: El papel de los neorurales en el desarrollo rural sostenible de la comarca de la Alpujarra', *CEDDAR: Informes* 16. Available at: http://ceddar.org/content/files/articulo_319_01_Informes-2010-1.pdf. Accessed 31 July 2022.
Tello, E. and González de Molina, M. (2017) 'Methodological challenges and general criteria for assessing and designing local sustainable Agri-Food systems: A Socio-Ecological approach at landscape level', in Fraňková, E., Haas, W. and Singh, S. (eds.) *Socio-Metabolic Perspectives on the Sustainability of Local Food Systems*. Cham: Springer, pp. 27–67.
Tello, E. and González de Molina, M. (2023) 'Agrarian metabolism and socio-ecological transitions to agroecology landscapes', in *The Barcelona School of Ecological Economics and Political Ecology: A Companion in Honour of Joan Martinez-Alier*. Cham: Springer International Publishing, pp. 93–107.
Tummers, L. and MacGregor, S. (2019) 'Beyond wishful thinking,' *International Journal of the Commons* 13(1), pp. 62–83.
UTE Unió Temporal d'Escribes (2004) *Barcelona Marca Registrada: Un model per desarmar*. Barcelona: Virus.
Zibechi, R. (2006) *Dispersar el poder*. Madrid: Traficantes de sueños.

15

How eco-communities grow through social learning, social permaculture and group transformation

Helen Jarvis

Introduction

A useful way to define an eco-community is to depart from the land-use planning focus of the 'eco-village' and to focus instead on the micro-social and mesoscale phenomena that it takes to *form and sustain* (grow) socially and ecologically just *systems of interdependence*. Most scholars define eco-communities and ecovillages interchangeably, as self-governing groups or projects that seek to provide alternative dwelling, typically in a rural or semi-rural location. Similarly, the umbrella term 'intentional community' (IC) is widely used to encompass groups that often define themselves largely by their socio-spatial or legal structure, as with cohousing, cooperatives, community land trusts and the like, while recognizing that stated intentions frequently coincide with a strong ecological ethos.

Living together in greater ecological harmony is core to the *intentions* of the groups featured in this chapter, whether they identify as an eco-community or not. The common denominator is active participation in collective governance. This entails collaboration in micro-structures of social *organizing* whereby formal and tacit 'group work' shapes and adds local meaning to the design and maintenance of private and shared resources (common spaces, food growing, shared meals, renewable energy systems) and deep learning made possible by inhabiting a community of practice. Non-hierarchical structures of self-governance rely on decisions made jointly in an open and fair process. This excludes, from this study, authoritarian, ideological communities governed by one leader or one group according to cultural hierarchy.

This chapter highlights group-work as a way to translate niche research on ICs to a wider variety of community organizing and educational settings (Jarvis 2019, 62). For example, a distinct rural bias persists in the literature and popular imagination of eco-communities. Yet there is nothing intrinsically 'anti-urban' in activist groups actively seeking change. During the Covid pandemic, many of us witnessed people engaging in networks of mutuality around the world. Ecologists evoke this interdependence in a pattern language of permaculture (Taylor Aiken 2017, 175).[1] This plural movement recently began to encompass *social* permaculture education and practice, recognizing that ecological design can only be fulfilled by learning to think and act empathetically with respect for the common good (Orr 2004). Social permaculture is evident within environmental education programmes where personal empowerment and a sense of responsibility are key elements to 'scaling up' sustainable communities everywhere. According to Joubert and Alfred (2007, 177), freedom to act for the common good must be embedded in the culture of 'growing' communities so that empowerment is happening in all directions all the time. Social permaculture is relevant to the research featured here because it describes a *system of interdependence* that is necessary for successful eco-community formation and longevity.

Critically, the social dimensions of phenomenology (understanding lived experience) remain underdeveloped, especially the integration of housing and ecological issues with debates on place-making, sustainability and mutual support. Phenomenological approaches to housing, for instance, tend to privilege individual agency even where housing involves groups and communal settings (Leith 2006). Some attention has been paid to social dimensions that transcend a permanent residential setting (attending to the 'hard' green architecture) in ethnographic studies that help to reveal the 'soft' social architectures that groups negotiate together. This is evident in the ways that eco-communities evolve (people come and go) in a complex meshwork of individual and collective endeavour. This is their 'origin story'. Prolonged formation, as a community of practice, endows each group with a unique history and stock of experience and memory. This chapter examines how these origin stories are coincidentally bound up with formal and tacit relationships of influence, inspiration and networks of learning.

What follows is a conceptual framework proposing a social phenomenology of growing eco-communities, and a brief outline of the data collection and analysis underpinning this approach. The discussion sheds light on influential aspects of group formation and group work: it reveals a complex interplay of intentions and orientations linking individual pioneers, forming groups and influential eco-communities enduring since the 1970s. Discussion acknowledges that many eco-communities champion 'better' systems of interdependence. As such, insights on recruitment, retention and shared goals have wider relevance for understanding and advancing anti-racist approaches and a sense of place and belonging that can be applied in schools, colleges and civil society organizations.

Proposing a social phenomenology of group-work

Phenomenology offers a humanistic theoretical framework within which to explore the process of 'growing' ICs. It is valuable because it draws attention to structures of

---

[1] Permaculture is an umbrella term for a 'permanent agri-culture' design approach that seeks to 'work with nature rather than against'. Practitioners (who might be ecologists, gardeners, architects or activists) look for and emulate patterns and rhythms in nature. They seek to understand how nature works and consciously, and ethically, shape human patterns to mimic this (Taylor Aiken 2017, 175).

consciousness, notably orientation (formative emotional connections, with the natural environment for example, of *leaning toward*) and intention (purpose) (Ahmed 2006). In the classical approach, intentions are conceived from a first-person point of view. Hence, in qualitative research, phenomenology emphasizes relative 'self-awareness' and personal development in the narration of lived experience. This can be criticized for privileging first-person accounts that frame the individual subject as inherently introspective and without social ties. This is not to say that group work is necessarily 'social' and reliant on extrovert behaviour. Indeed, the paradox has been reported elsewhere that introverts are disproportionately attracted to IC (Glass and Frederick 2016). Intentions and orientations are contingent upon collective deliberation as much as individual consciousness: group outcomes are greater than the sum of the individuals involved. This points to an underdeveloped understanding, in classic phenomenology, of collectively negotiated social learning systems[2]: some call this the 'community glue' of interdependence (Jarvis 2011; Jarvis 2019).

This chapter proposes an explicitly *social* phenomenology (and permaculture) to shed light on the richness and fragility of public associational life. People yearn for a sense of identity and connection, and form attachments in social situations and places. Groups and alliances are characterized by strong relational cultures. Proposing a social phenomenology of collective responsibility challenges the atomized 'self' of state-sponsored 'self-organising', 'do-it-yourself' and 'self-help'. In mainstream place-making and community development, it is expected that public life will flourish if we cultivate multiple spaces (social and material) for people to organize and effect social change. While human connections are necessary they are not sufficient. Arguably, just as 'do it together' group work and 'people power' are essential to 'growing' green homes and communities in the future, the same is necessary to mobilize social and ecological justice at large (Strauss 2008).

Social phenomenology highlights the embeddedness and entanglement of this agency alongside the 'we-intentions' that shape mutual concern, group goals and joint action (Tuomela 2005). Inevitably, some facets of association are more progressive, participatory and transformative than others. While intentions and actions intersect, relational cultures are more likely to be transformative where self-awareness shifts from 'who I am' to 'what I do' and to intentions consciously negotiated in ethical discernment with others (Zammit 2017, 192). This highlights the significance of group-work obligations and deeper learning (including challenges to unequal power and voice) as impetus for transformative action.

---

[2] The IC can be viewed as a social learning system because people are working and learning together – even without any formal educational expectations. Social learning is characterized by open communication and informal, unrestricted participation, as a function of observation and imitation, learning from each other and social situations that benefit mutually agreed purpose (litter-picking, watching children at play, planning a visit to another IC, etc.). Reed et al. (2010, 1) argue that to be considered social learning, a process must (i) demonstrate that a change in understanding has taken place in the individuals involved, (ii) demonstrate that this change becomes embedded in wider communities of practice and (iii) occur through interactions cultivated by this community of practice.

Research design: origin stories and composite vignettes

Discussion now draws on ethnographic insights from a programme of visits with established and forming eco-communities from the period 2010–14. Care is taken not to romanticize eco-communities that have endured from the 1970s. Even where origin stories and life-course events place them at the 'mature' end of a continuum, the participatory heart of group work is continuously pulsing (Ochre 2013). Social learning is not a linear or one-way process. Individual and collective intentions vary in resolve such that they ebb and flow with changing experience of inter-personal cooperation and conflict. This is what makes them dynamic.

Research visits ranged from one to eight days spent living with each community, making use of the Willing Worker on Organic Farm (WWOOF) scheme (McIntosh 2006). This chapter draws on a subset of this larger itinerary, focussing on the transmission of social learning in mature eco-communities from the 1970s to 'growing' ICs and autonomous groups elsewhere.

Table 1 lists six Australian ICs. Four are selected from a remarkable concentration of IC development in and around the small town of Nimbin in the Northern Rivers region of New South Wales (NSW 1–4). Two represent ICs in the neighbouring states of Victoria (VIC1) and Queensland (QLD1) with historic connections to Nimbin. All provide opportunities for visitors to participate as guest worker or volunteer, to encounter life in community for one or more day(s), weeks or months, understanding that direct participation is the most effective way of transmitting the function and meaning of collective solidarity.

The research includes equivalent ethnographic visits with Findhorn Foundation, Scotland, claimed to be the best-known IC in the world (Metcalf 2004). By contrast with the 'closed' approach of some Australian ICs from the 1970s, with by-laws used to prevent any researcher or journalist locating their community by name, Findhorn Foundation consciously trades on its origin story and scenic location on the Moray Firth in North East Scotland. Unease among some Australian ICs reflects the negative impact of sensational journalism. The research explores this tension between group-preservation and outward ambitions to change society.

Interpersonal group phenomena are interpreted and communicated using a composite vignette method (Jarvis and Bonnett 2013, 2355). This succinctly conveys the rich complexity and intersection of individual biography and myriad group-work situations while masking individual subject identities. Vignettes incorporate real lived experience and people's voices (from interviews recorded and transcribed with informed consent, applying pseudonyms) but in composite form, triangulating observations and combining this original ethnographic research with additional secondary source material. Data on visitors and forming groups was collected from participation in educational courses, together with individual interviews and focus groups, equivalent to those generated from visits with established communities (as listed in Table 1).

Table 1 Australian Intentional Communities (IC) selected to represent eco-community activity in the Northern Rivers Region of New South Wales, listed to indicate discrete waves of development

1970s	
VIC1	1975, 33 unit, 6 cluster community settlement cooperative
NSW1	1973, 85 unit (in clusters) legalized 'multiple occupancy'
NSW2	1973, 15 unit 'multiple occupancy'
NSW3	1976, 25 unit 'multiple occupancy'
1990s	
QLD1	1989, 85 unit (clusters) ecovillage
NSW4	1996, 13 unit 'community trust' cohousing
Since 2000	
A new generation of eco-communities (notably urban cohousing and student cooperatives) face barriers with respect to land, finance and time to invest in self-organizing work. While learning from earlier eco-communities, many forming groups additionally pursue technically advanced modern methods of construction that call for a wide range of expertise. This new generation recognize that they must respond to criticism that eco-communities are predominantly white and middle class. New structures of social organizing are needed to challenge persistent cultural biases, structural inequalities, and barriers to affordability, diversity and inclusion.	

Australian eco-community origins and networks of social learning

The NSW dairy farming town of Nimbin became notable as an alternative lifestyle destination in 1973 when the Australian Union of Students held its Aquarius Festival there. It was intended to foster 'participation rather than consumer entertainment'. Co-founders published a manifesto encouraging 5000 festivalgoers to build low-cost housing from recycled materials in 'ecologically oriented' communities and to 'live in harmony with the natural environment' (Dunstan 1975). Concentrated IC development in the 1970s coincided with deep restructuring of the dairy industry and this enabled groups of young people with limited assets to collectively purchase cheap farmland. The region was permanently transformed by autonomous groups building hundreds of intentional eco-communities and networks of social learning that practised new forms of collective behaviour within a 'community of communities' (Illich 1973). This concentration of 'do it together' mutual aid is what distinguishes the Northern Rivers Region ICs and arguably contributes to their longevity.

In the early 1970s, the Northern Rivers Pan-Community network advertised regular communal gatherings and 'total learning situations'. A 'learning exchange' operated for several years with the intention that it 'could be the most powerful transmitter in Australia (as) an experiment in a new way of life' (Cock 1979, 121). This level of community organizing led to the election of at least two IC residents as members of the Australian Parliament and others serving on the local council. The festival was additionally credited with being the first event that sought the permission to use the land from Traditional Owners and Australia's first Welcome to Country ceremony.

This illustrates the paradoxical impact of eco-pioneers regarded by Indigenous Australians and local farmers simultaneously as outsiders and as agents of change.

The sample of ICs listed in Table 1 suggests three discrete waves of development. The decision to explore ICs occupying sites within and beyond proximity to Nimbin follows strong evidence that ICs develop and grow through relationships of social learning that transcend a single place of dwelling. This is illustrated in the way that ideas on group-work have travelled between eco-communities (see Vignette 1). For example, founding members of VIC1 attended the Aquarius Festival but sought greater order and security in a less remote cooperative in the rural hinterland of Melbourne. The community development skills demonstrated by VIC1 have helped many new-generation eco-communities to form. Founding members of NSW3 and VIC1 contribute to a sustainable living festival and alternative magazine that is known to all ICs in the sample. NSW1, 2 and 3 are all part of the Nimbin Pan-Community Council. NSW4 regularly employ an experienced community engagement facilitator from NSW3 to run workshops on the 'community glue' aspects of collective governance (Joubert and Alfred 2007, 51). Barry (QLD1) explains how, despite having no prior connection with the counterculture or rural living, he was drawn to Nimbin and the desire to adapt his engineering training to new ideas circulating around permaculture. He attended many IC gatherings over the years before meeting a like-minded group. This group went on to design and occupy QLD1 in 1989 as Australia's longest-running permaculture community, today with the highest concentration of social permaculture facilitators anywhere in the world (vignette 2).

Vignette 1: Sharing group ethos in the work of community

Living together as a self-governing group requires practical and ideological agreement on key aspects of common ground. Eco-communities that began in the 1970s have retained remarkably enduring 'vision statements' while at the same time routinely reinventing their enactment. Lorna explains that when she moved into NSW1 in 1983, ten years after the community began, the needs and ethos had matured with the changing age profile. This reflects the way that eco-communities must design and maintain both 'task' and 'well-being' functions (Ochre 2013). The task function refers to the work and activities that the group undertakes to fulfil their purpose (to share resources, to live lightly on the planet). This typically involves physical labour to build and repair low-cost homes from recycled materials, and agreement on how to fairly distribute mundane administrative tasks. The well-being function requires advanced social learning, emphasizing the affective dimensions of group wellbeing (Jarvis 2011, 572).

The social learning required to balance these functions is evident in outreach activities intended both to engage new pioneers in the work of community and to establish wider credibility and acceptance in the surrounding area. It is sometimes difficult to differentiate 'outreach' activities from new member recruitment. For eco-communities created by people in their twenties in the 1970s, now with a core population in their seventies, attracting younger members is a priority and a source of apprehension. It is not uncommon to hear stories of how new members encountered

ICs as a WWOOF volunteer, or by attending a retreat, before feeling drawn to a permanent home. Becoming a member typically involves regularly attending social events, meetings and workdays. The aim is to show a level of commitment and to allow a deeper understanding of life in community to develop. Yet, the introduction of a younger cohort has not always resulted in the intended diversity and harmony of 'older and younger together' (Jarvis 2019).

A statement of shared vision and common values is what establishes and maintains the intentions and meaning of the IC and holds individuals to account as a collective. While this constitutes a written document, the content is *practised* in ways that set the tone for everyday interactions including how to talk and think about everyday concerns. Each IC has its own shared ethos. NSW3 explain theirs in a handbook for guests and visitors:

> We originally came together with a deep concern for self-exploration, mainly through meditation. We aspire to live harmoniously with each other and the land, with a general philosophy of respect and non-violence. We live in a cooperative and supportive manner and use a consensus decision-making process. Our work projects are many and some are communal.

The handbook goes on to welcome the visitor, encouraging them to share in the life of the community, especially by participating in joint work projects.

Visitors are told that it 'takes a lot of work and a lot of intention' to create eco-community (Pat VIC1). The simple act of working together and sharing meals is a primary bonding experience. Guests are routinely expected to 'participate in community life, to become completely involved and immersed in it' and this forms a vital source of new member recruitment. Balancing group task and maintenance functions, while demonstrating a critical source of inward and outward transformation, can be fraught. Efforts to reach out to others (by hosting willing workers and paying guests) sometimes clash with community well-being, which takes time in relative seclusion to deepen relationships and resolve conflicts that may arise. For example, Sally (VIC1) explains that 'for years we took it in turns every Monday to build each house, so I know what I did down at this and that house, and I know what other people did on my house, and those relationships have been vital to who we are'. Newcomers building their homes today no longer follow this practice, in part because some new methods of green building are technically advanced, but also because they attract visitors who are willing to exchange casual labour for the experience of living in community.

While none of the ICs reported here rely solely on visitors for their source of livelihood, they are busy places built on collective endeavour. It is difficult to prioritize and protect the inter-personal work of solidarity. As Jude explains of NSW3; this place 'may seem like a place of peaceful isolation, but people are busy ....there's a very keen awareness of the need for social change (in Australian society), a strong commitment towards achieving that change in many different fields. This can increase levels of stress and diminish the time we spend with each other and on the land'.

This vignette explores the social phenomena of orientation and intention within and between groups. Contrary to the pejorative view of eco-communities as islands of escape, we see how the visitor and forming group observe and imitate the pulsing participatory heart of group-work in mature eco-communities, as part of a larger social learning system. At the same time, this vignette highlights the fragility of group well-being and the social ties that constitute community 'glue'. Arguably, groups must attend to their own collective well-being if they are to contribute wider social learning on task-specific goals, such as challenging structural barriers to affordability, diversity and inclusion. In this we observe a paradox. The intimate scale of belonging and trust that is necessary for intentional communities of practice can also unintentionally inhibit efforts to challenge structural inequalities, notably racism. Tensions between inward and outward credibility and cohesion reinforce unintended 'homophily' – the regressive tendency to attract like-minded newcomers.

Vignette 2: Social permaculture

The principles of permaculture can be adopted in large and small ways, such as developing a sustainable pattern of land use or planting gardens for wildlife diversity. Common goals work with, not against, the intricate balance and grain of eco-systems (soil type, sunlight, rainfall and the like). A similarly holistic ethic of care should guide social systems. Yet relationships between plants, insects, soil and water, complex as they may be, are relatively easy to deal with: people are more challenging and all activist groups including eco-communities need diversity to thrive. Because the systems of oppression (racism, sexism, homophobia, ageism, etc.) are interlocking, holistic understanding is needed to replace oppression with social justice and equity. Our understanding of soil biology or water harvesting techniques is typically more advanced than our skills at living and working with unrelated others. Our needs and goals often clash, and we don't have the tools we need to resolve conflicts cooperatively.

A recurring theme of *social permaculture* is the balance between unity of purpose (cultivating shared spaces of everyday encounter), and diversity of traditional practice (what some call the vernacular knowledge that people have of people and places) (Orr 2004). A practical example is the Channon Craft Market, NSW, which began in 1976 and continues to thrive today as a large (250 stall) not-for-profit enterprise (motto, 'make it, bake it, grow it'). Each month, on rotation, a local IC charity can fundraise from a community kitchen at the market venue (The Channon Market 2011). This is a vivid example of shared commitment to cultivate both unity of purpose and diversity of practice.

One reason why human relationships are so difficult is that we are embedded in larger regimes and systems of livelihood and citizenship that rarely encourage mutual benefit. We learn from Human Rights Education and Training literature that an explicit and holistic anti-oppressive relational education is vital, even on a small scale of IC (or school, college, or civil society organization), for culturally inclusive governance to thrive. Vignette 1 above shows that long-established ICs often lack patterns and rhythms of collective well-being because they remain bound up with wider capitalist regimes (education and employment) that neglect investment in social learning and inter-personal skills.

Findhorn Foundation eco-community: Trading on inspiration, experience and new stories

Discussion turns now from Australia to the iconic eco-community of Findhorn, Scotland. This comparative dimension serves an expansive purpose, intended to generate a fuller, richer account of culturally nuanced circuits of social learning for similar groups in different places. Since the 1970s, the non-profit Findhorn Foundation has occupied a caravan park and a former military site, several retreat sites and a large old hotel, Cluny Hill (until 2024). It is best known for the 'field of dreams' eco-homes and the Park, named after the Findhorn Bay Caravan Park on the Moray Firth, close to the small town of Forres.

How Findhorn became a world-famous eco-community is a story of mythical proportions. Andrew Rigby (1974) provides one of the most comprehensive ethnographic accounts of the early years when a previously run-down caravan became known as a 'Centre of Light'. Aside from colourful details of the co-founders (Eileen and Peter Caddy, the esoteric teaching of Peter's ex-wife Sheena, her disciple Dorothy Maclean, Eileen's divine meditations, and rumours of an organic garden with cabbages 'higher, larger, greener and more vibrant than ever seen before') (Hawken 1975, 112), Findhorn attracted thousands of guests. A charitable foundation, the Findhorn Trust, was established in 1970 to receive donations (notably caravans and building materials) (Riddell 1990). This contributed to its far-flung sphere of influence, expanding the resident community, and developing its shared spaces and social infrastructure. Today there are some 1000 residents on the park, yet fewer than 100 participate in the shared social infrastructure (e.g. shared meals). The larger population are 'on site' community organizations and individuals living in privately owned eco-homes. This loose affiliation commits to a 'statement of common ground' as members of the New Findhorn Association (Findhorn Foundation website 2019). Further afield is a 20,000-strong 'virtual village' of supporters who receive the quarterly digital newsletter and donate funds.

Findhorn Foundation held its first Experience Week in 1975 and this residential programme attracted over 30,000 participants (Vignette 3) (Findhorn Foundation website 2019). The structure and format changed little, catering for a group of (six to thirty) participants fifty weeks a year (until 2024). It is common to hear visitors say that they have heard about Findhorn from stories in circulation, while acknowledging that Experience Week encourages them to question sensational stereotypes and develop deeper learning. Evidence of the way that individuals and groups learn from direct experience is well established in research on social pedagogy and environmental education (Jackson 1999). There is nevertheless more to discover from the social phenomenology of group work.

Vignette 3: The Cook, the Guest and the Focalizer

Findhorn Foundation's intentional design has evolved through six decades of group work. Capacity to reverse established policies and procedures and embark on new projects, adopting a 'new story' in response to contemporary social justice and environmental crises, for instance, is attributed to the flexibility of the underlying spiritual eco-vision (Findhorn Foundation website 2019). The following vignette shows this by making connections between several participants on Experience Week. It illustrates tensions in the group process of social learning between the 'real' motivations, conditions, aspirations and relations of people living and working together, and the 'imagined' (felt and thought) impulse and yearning for a 'new story for humanity'.

The Cook: For those of us (on a Findhorn Foundation allowance, receiving meals and housing) what we do here has to be about 'love as service in action'. This is where I have my friends. It feels very comfortable and meaningful, and I think that relationships here are much deeper than outside and you tend to disclose more and it feels safe. Whether if I left here, I'd be able to sustain that, I'm not sure. But I think sometimes we do present this 'love' in a slightly sanitized version to guests. My commitment here, it's a two-way thing: the work I do here has to serve and fulfil me as something I feel nourished by, not blindly serving Guests to keep this place going financially.

The Guest: being able to try out living in community is transformative. Before attending Experience Week I had previously only visited for the day. I wanted to tap into the community spirit, join in a community dinner, but we were only able to wander around looking at rather dilapidated buildings. There was nothing really to judge the place on, beyond what I had read in books. But following Experience Week I felt drawn to live here in community permanently. I felt this sense of belonging, a resonance and connection with the land and people talking about stuff I found intensely interesting.

The Focalizer: The idea of Findhorn is very different from the reality, and it sometimes feels hypocritical, knowing that there is a degree of 'impression management' for guests participating in Experience Week. But the spirit of this place is bigger than any group or setting on its own and it's vital to communicate this bigger picture if we are to play any part in addressing social justice and climate emergencies. We have to set aside individual ego if we are to be part of the change that is needed.

This vignette highlights a pattern of deep and shallow encounters that distinguish 'guest facing' from 'deep community' relationships. Some people are required to perform the outward face of Findhorn – much as with the task functions of any forming IC, sharing their vision with the world. Intentions and subjectivities are neither one-dimensional nor defined by 'insiders' and 'outsiders' but instead negotiated through a meshwork of association. This explains how forming groups adapt their projects to local contexts. Significantly, the well-being function of group-work relies on interdependent patterns and rhythms of transformative social learning.

Orientation and disorientation

While intentions vary in strength and focus (and they may evolve or diminish over time), IC origin stories have at their heart some sense of stated ethos and core values. This is not true of speculative housing and community development. The concept of the origin story usefully conveys a version of truth (which is always compressed and partial) about how each eco-community came into being – and how new core groups establish a sense of community before living together. A common narrative from the research identifies one or two 'founding members' who share their enthusiasm with others, gathering a core group of 'burning souls'.

The analysis highlights intense reflexivity and constant questioning in this negotiated process of shared intentions. Evidence that this process includes moments of acute discomfort and disorientation resonates with claims elsewhere that 'lively dialogues' help introduce non-binary and non-adversarial orientations that unlock transformation (Ahmed 2006, 157). While much that is revealed in the micro-sociology of group-work appears inherently practical and parochial (how to organize childcare for meetings so that no-one is excluded from the decision process), it is important to acknowledge disorientation with respect to shifting mental outlooks. Coincidentally, idiosyncrasies of language observed in Findhorn (love in action) crop up in Australian ICs from the 1970s. Much like the Findhorn Focaliser, Bill (VIC1), regards the tacit dimensions of mutuality as *being attuned* with others:

> I get a sense from *being* here that it is important to listen and to be patient with (the origins of this group). When you hear something that resonates it's got a different sound to it and different people pick up on that different sound … so I think this whole process is mysterious and wonderful. There is a heartbeat here within the group and also in the land and the relationship between (the two) and *once you live here* you start to feel the heartbeat, the pulse that's here.

Crucially, 'growing a group' is not a matter of conducting regular meetings in a respectful manner (the socio-legal aspects of collective governance) but rather 'living together every day' through a process that allows concrete plans to develop in unexpected ways. Forming groups need time and space to engage openly with power and inter-personal competence.

Conclusions

By exploring different facets of relational 'group-work', this chapter suggests a phenomenological framework that might help explain how intentions, orientations and associations are as foundational to citizen-led social justice and environmental movements, as they are to ICs. Whereas conventional phenomenology would explain self-governing eco-communities with reference to individual motivations (such as voluntary simplicity), this chapter reveals a neglected mesoscale of formal and tacit 'group-work' in forming and sustaining (growing) eco-communities. By revealing a dynamic interplay of individual and collective endeavour in the microsociology of 'we-intentions', this chapter sets the stage for closer scrutiny of relationships and circuits of social learning at this mesoscale in public spaces of civil society. The origin stories and interactions featured in the vignettes highlight tensions between internal processes of well-being and outward ambitions to change society. This should alert us both to the limits to organizing 'better' systems of interdependence and the problems of power relations and oppression *within* communities that remain embedded in wider regimes.

Given the context of the climate emergency and social division, more people are likely to be attracted to forms of intentional eco-community in the future. At the same time, growing eco-communities must challenge the tendency to reproduce the power and privilege of predominantly white, middle-class networks of learning and outreach. In vignette 2 above, for instance, it was apparent that group or associational outcomes can be greater than the sum of the individuals involved, but only if tensions between individual and group orientations are resolved to reconcile 'task' and 'well-being' functions over the long run. This tension entails moments of disorientation and conflict without which it is unlikely that eco-communities can cultivate essential diversity (with respect to gender, age, class and Black Minority Ethnic populations). Newly forming groups need to actively participate in a divided world (learning to disagree better) if the deep learning and new structures of social organizing that they develop are to challenge oppressive structural inequalities. This cannot be achieved by imitating iconic ICs from the 1970s.

The discussion above shows that 'growing' eco-communities rely on empathetic skills of thinking and acting for the common good that mainstream regimes of individualism and materialism fail to cultivate. Arguably, there is more at stake here than the capacity to build green homes and communities through collective endeavour. We need to consider what it will take to build sustainable communities everywhere: how can people raised in an atmosphere of competition, alienation and separation become fit for community? (Joubert and Alfred 2007, 25). We are unlikely to achieve an alternative, better future if learning is limited to 'doing things better' (Perlman 2014). Instead, 'doing better things' calls for deeper learning and a rich ecology of shared spaces and social time within which to harness the power of groups.

References

Ahmed, S. (2006) *Queer Phenomenology: Orientations, Objects, Others*. Durham, NC: Duke University Press.

Channon Market (2011) *Community Groups* [website] Available at: https://thechannonmarket.org.au/community-groups/. Accessed 01 September 2011.

Cock, P. (1979) *Alternative Australia: Communities for the Future?* Melbourne: Quartet Books.

Dunstan, G. (1975) 'Nimbin: The vision and the reality', in Smith, M. and Crossley, D.(eds.) *The Way Out: Radical Alternatives in Australia*. Melbourne: Lansdowne Press, pp. 19–27.

Findhorn Foundation (2019) Website. Available at: https://www.findhorn.org/common-ground/. Accessed 01 July 2019.

Glass, A.P. and Frederick, N. (2016) 'Elder cohousing as a choice for introverted older adults: obvious or surprising?', *The Gerontologist* 56(3), p. 172.

Hawken, P. (1975) *The Magic of Findhorn*. London: Fontana/Collins.

Illich, I. (1973) *Tools for Conviviality*. London: Marion Boyars (2009 reprint).

Jackson, H. (Ed.). (1999) *Creating Harmony: Conflict Resolution in Community*. White River Junction, VT: Permanent Publications.

Jarvis, H. (2011) 'Saving space, sharing time: Integrated infrastructures of daily life in cohousing', *Environment and Planning A* 43(3), pp. 560-77.

Jarvis, H. (2019) 'Social architectures of age-friendly community resilience: lessons from "niche" intentional community development', in Trogal, K., Bauman, I., Lawrence, R. and Petrescu, D. (eds.) *Architecture and Resilience: Interdisciplinary Dialogues*. London: Routledge, pp. 61-76.

Jarvis, H. and Bonnett, A. (2013) 'Progressive nostalgia in novel living arrangements: a counterpoint to neo-traditional new urbanism?', *Urban Studies* 50(11), pp. 2349-70.

Joubert, K.A. and Alfred, R. (Eds.) (2007) *Beyond You and Me: Inspirations and Wisdom for Building Community. The Social Key of the Ecovillage Design Education*. East Meon: Permanent.

Leith, K.H. (2006) 'Home is where the heart is ….or is it? A phenomenological exploration of the meaning of home for older women in congregate housing', *Journal of Aging Studies* 20(4), pp. 317-33.

McIntosh, A. (2006) 'Willing workers on organic farms (WWOOF): The alternative farm stay experience?', *Journal of Sustainable Tourism* 14(1), pp. 82-99.

Metcalf, B. (2004) *The Findhorn Book of Community Living*. The Park, Findhorn: Findhorn Press.

Ochre, G. (2013) *Getting Our Act Together: How to Harness the Power of Groups*. Melbourne: Groupwork Institute of Australia.

Orr, D.W. (2004). *Earth in Mind: On Education, Environment, and the Human Prospect*. New York: Island Press.

Perlman, J. (2014) Sustainable humanity, sustainable nature: Our responsibility pontifical academy of sciences. Pontifical academy of Social Sciences, Acta 19 www.pas.va/content/dam/accademia/pdf/es41/es41-perlman.pdf (cites Aleem Walji, Director, Innovation Labs., WBI, author of Striking Poverty).

Reed, M.S., Evely, A.C., Cundill, G., Fazey, I., Glass, J., Laing, A., Newig, J., Parrish, B., Prell, C., Raymond, C. and An Stringer, L.C. (2010). 'What is social learning?', *Ecology and Society* 15(4), pp. 1-10. Available at: http://www.jstor.org/stable/26268235.

Riddell, C. (1990) *The Findhorn Community: Creating A Human Identity for the 21st Century*. The Park, Findhorn: Findhorn Press.

Rigby, A. (1974) *Communes in Britain*. London: Routledge.

Strauss, K. (2008) 'Re-engaging with rationality in economic geography: behavioural approaches and the importance of context in decision-making', *Journal of Economic Geography* 8(2), pp. 137-56.

Taylor Aiken, G. (2017). 'Permaculture and the social design of nature', *Geografiska Annaler: Series B, Human Geography* 99(2), pp. 172-91.

Tuomela, R. (2005) 'We-intentions revisited', *Philosophical Studies* 125(3), pp. 327-69.

Zammit, M. (2017) 'The long shadow thrown over the actions of men', in Borg, C. and Grech, M. (eds.) *Pedagogy, Politics and Philosophy of Peace: Interrogating Peace and Peace-Making*. London: Bloomsbury, p. 181.

16

Prompting spiritually prefigurative political practice: Collective decision-making in Auroville, India

Suryamayi Aswini Clarence-Smith

Intentional communities and prefigurative practice

This chapter contributes a unique case study of how collective governance is inspired by spirituality in Auroville, an intentional community in India. Intentional communities are known for embracing participatory decision-making processes (see Firth 2012; Sanford 2017), and have recently been framed as sites of 'prefigurative practice', given that they experiment with reformulating society while guided by specific ideals (2019; Farias 2017; Monticelli 2018). Indeed 'prefiguration' refers to the embodiment of modes of organization, social relations, attitudes and culture that a collective envisions for its future, through 'experimental and experiential' means (van de Sande 2015, 189). While prefigurative scholars are beginning to map a broad spectrum of prefigurative practices – from solidary economies and holistic education to ecological and social sustainabilities (see Monticelli 2022) – most research using this theoretical framework is focussed on participatory decision-making processes in politically left social movements (Graeber 2010, 2013; Maeckelbergh 2009, 2011; Yates 2015).

Interestingly, spirituality was interwoven with the participatory decision-making practice of such prefigurative social movements, notably Occupy Wall Street (see Writers for the 99% 2012) – although this phenomenon has not been emphasized in the literature on prefiguration. While spiritual philosophy and practice have been critiqued for rendering individuals apolitical (Žižek 2001), there is a burgeoning body of work which points to the potential for spirituality to inform political action and participation (see Chari 2016; Rowe 2015, 2016). In this chapter, I will be exploring the role of spirituality in articulating prefigurative collective governance in the context of Auroville, which is the largest intentional community in the world – and whose overarching ideal is to spiritualize society as a whole. An autoethnographic exploration of a participatory decision-making process will examine the lived experience of experimenting with implicit and explicit articulations between spiritual and political practices in this community, of which I am a long-term member, and in so doing reveal singular insights into how spirituality can encourage political engagement. These insights underlie the importance of including experiences in the Global South when endeavouring to map the promise of intentional communities as laboratories for social change.

Auroville: A spiritually prefigurative intentional community

Auroville is situated in India's south-eastern state of Tamil Nadu, eight kilometres north of the coastal town of Puducherry, on a plateau ecologically restored since its founding in 1968. Land for the project of a spiritual township was initially purchased by the Sri Aurobindo Society, an Indian not-for-profit organization (see Sri Aurobindo Society), from local farmers cultivating low intensity seasonal crops such as peanut, on an arid landscape deforested during the colonial rule of the British Raj. Fifty years later, private land in and around the Auroville area remains largely agricultural, with plantations such as the 'cash crop' cashew in predominance. However, a growing trend is the sale and development of ancestral, family-owned farmland as real estate property, given the proximity of the urban centre of Puducherry and the construction of highways, while younger generations seek professional employment. On Auroville land, a unique focus has been to restore the Tropical Dry Evergreen Forest, a rare forest type endemic to peninsular India (see Blanchflower 2005; Pohl 2020), while concurrently developing a township with an innovative urban design concept, inspired by the shape of a galaxy (see Majumdar 2017). This urban development has been slow-going and sporadic, in part due to financing and land ownership challenges, and in part due to disagreements within the community around how to translate the urban design concept for Auroville onto ground realities, with key concerns being the protection of ecologically sensitive areas and the integration of local Tamil settlements (see Clarence-Smith 2023).

While far from its originally envisaged population of 50,000, today Auroville is nonetheless the largest, and amongst the oldest, of active intentional communities in the world. Its current population of 3300 people – of which approximately half is Indian – contain an exceptional diversity of sixty different nationalities ('Census'). Recognized by the Indian government, UNESCO and other international governmental and non-governmental bodies (see Auroville Media Liasion 2022) for pioneering progressive practices, Auroville has a wide range of activities, concentrating on alternative education, sustainable architecture and renewable energy, communal economy and participatory democracy, rural development and environmental restoration. Based on the Integral Yoga tradition, the overarching aim of Auroville is to enact a spiritualized transformation of society, in all fields and practices the community engages with. Integral Yoga is a philosophy and practice developed by Sri Aurobindo (1872–1950), a political leader in India's independence movement who later turned to spirituality to work towards a holistic, transformative evolution of human society. Aurobindo was joined in this endeavour by Mirra Alfassa (1878–1973), a French mystic whom he referred to as 'The Mother' in recognition of her spiritual embodiment of a universal consciousness.

To create a field of exploration for such a project, The Mother first founded the Sri Aurobindo Ashram (late 1920s) 'with another object than that ordinarily common to such institutions, not for the renunciation of the world but as a centre and a field of practice for the evolution of another kind and form of life' (Sri Aurobindo 2011, 847). One of Sri Aurobindo's iconic phrases is 'All life is yoga' (1999, 8); all aspects of life were to be imbued with a higher consciousness in 'an effort to create a new life-formation which will exceed the ordinary human society' (Aurobindo 1970, 1060). In the ashram, to this day, there are no set rites or practices for the ashramites to follow, instead they engage in numerous secular activities of 'ordinary' life and seek to make them a part of their yoga, or spiritual practice. Sri Aurobindo referred to the ashram as 'a first form which our effort has taken, a field in which the preparatory work has to be done' (1970, 13). This sheds some background insight as to how and why The Mother came to found Auroville in 1968, as a second 'form' through which to realize Sri Aurobindo's vision of a life divine: an experimental township. While she acted as a managing guru of the Sri Aurobindo Ashram, Auroville was to be a community developed by its own members, with no predetermined organizational structures and rules (see 'The Mother on Auroville'). The Mother went so far as to envisage 'a place which no nation could claim as its own, where all human beings of goodwill who have a sincere aspiration could live freely as citizens of the world' (1954, n.pag.). While recent scholarship points out that early foreign members of the Sri Aurobindo Ashram and Auroville were able to join thanks to 'privileges of colonial mobility and wealth' (Namakkal 2021, 3), it unfortunately fails to grasp not only the significant Tamil demographic presence in Auroville, but also the range of backgrounds in terms nationality, class and caste. That said, there are ongoing tensions that stem from Auroville's predicament of being a multicultural, utopian experiment embedded in a postcolonial context that harbours its own, innate challenges around inclusion and social equity, ones that are observed across fault lines of foreign to Indian, North Indian to South Indian, and even Tamil to Tamil – in which race, gender, class and caste play an important role. An in-depth, scholarly analysis of this complexity is yet to be produced, and should ideally be undertaken by a researcher who is not a member of the community.

A few years after Auroville was established (1968), The Mother was asked what political organization she envisaged for the township. Her response was 'a divine anarchy' (2003, 219): the premise of the project was to be a spiritually prefigurative experiment guided by an evolution in universal consciousness. Forms of collective organization would emerge out of this process, and continue to develop alongside it, they could not be anticipated and ought not be prescribed – on the contrary, space for them to manifest, unfettered, ought to be safeguarded. Rather than comprehensively defining how Auroville should function, therefore, The Mother insisted on there being no fixed rules in Auroville (2003, 261-6), and that its organization be 'flexible and progressive' ('The Mother on Auroville', 71). While the Indian government did award the project the status of an 'autonomous Foundation' in 1988 (see 'Auroville Foundation'), with the passing of a unique Act of Parliament that gave decision-making powers over the community's internal affairs to its residents, the freedom that the community and its members have experienced to date is currently being impinged upon by central government authorities in a drive to accelerate the development of

Auroville, which community members argue is in disregard of environmental concerns as well as democratic values (Venugopal and Mistri-Kapoor 2021).

This chapter will be examining spiritually informed practices in the context of one of Auroville's key participatory decision-making processes: the Selection Process for Auroville's Participatory Working Groups. I consider the Auroville project as a whole to be 'spiritually prefigurative' (Clarence-Smith 2019): for prefiguration is the praxis of experimentally and experientially anticipating cultures of being, relating and organizing for a desired future (Boggs 1977; Maeckelbergh 2011; van de Sande 2015), and in Auroville that future is spiritually informed. This spiritually anticipatory dimension harks back to the original use of the term 'prefiguration', which has its roots in religion, and refers to a prophetic foreshadowing (Raekstad 2018, 361). Given that Auroville is a polity that aspires to collectively and progressively become an embodiment of a spiritualized society, I consider many activities outside of the realm of the 'political' to be nonetheless politically significant: ones in which this spiritually prefigurative process is intentionally engaged (Clarence-Smith 2019). The specific political forum examined here exists within and is informed by the broader, spiritually prefigurative polity that it emerges from.

Spiritual practice: Empowering or disempowering political potential?

Spiritual self-development practices are being increasingly adopted in a broad spectrum of political contexts. These range from prefigurative social movements to the US Congress (Seitz-Wald 2013), while indigenous spiritual protocols have been central to protests that seek to protect sacred indigenous land, such as the Protect Mauna Kea demonstration in Hawai'i ('Protect Mauna Kea'). That said, spirituality is critiqued for rendering individuals apolitical, for two main reasons. First, it emphasizes a detachment from worldly life. Second, in making individuals responsible for their experiences of hardship – whether economic, social or psychological – it draws emphasis away from seeking out and addressing the roots of such hardship in structural inequities and social reform, framing these instead as inadequate self-management (Davies 2015; Madsen 2015; Rimke 2000; Saari and Harni 2016; Cederström 2015; Žižek 2001).

Academic work endorsing these critiques of spirituality are primarily based on Buddhism-based contemplative practices, such as mindfulness meditation – although it does extend to a broader set of practices of secularized 'eastern' mysticism, such as yoga. Yet Buddhist and mindfulness leaders have in recent decades decisively committed their spiritual practice to social, political and environmental activism. The Vietnamese Buddhist leader Thich Nat Hahn is famous for having defined an 'engaged Buddhism' to foster and support such activism, adopted in both Asia and 'Western' countries (Hahn 1993; King 2009; Queen 2012; Queen et al., 2003; Queen and King 1996). The American founder of 'Mindfulness', Jon Kabat-Zinn, has also explicitly written about the role of mindfulness practices in activism, and these are often integrated into environmentalist and social justice movements (Berila 2016; Kaza 2008; Kabat-Zinn

2018; Yang and Willis 2017). Scholars have highlighted the instrumental influence of such contemplative spiritual practices in political engagement, arguing that these can not only trigger a more conscious participation, but also 'assist in fighting burnout, political cynicism, and hopelessness' (Wilson 2014, 185).

Auroville is a community based not on Buddhism but another Indian spiritual tradition: the Vedic yoga tradition. Traditionally, yogic spiritual practice was undertaken in ashrams, centres where 'sadhaks', or spiritual practitioners, renounced and retreated from worldly lives in order to pursue contemplative and devotional practices, such as meditation, study and chanting, under the guidance of the guru. As of the nineteenth century, however, the phenomenon of 'guru organizations' (Warrier 2003a, 2003b), in which gurus and their ashrams take on missionary activities related to both spiritual education and humanitarianism, and establish centres internationally, began to emerge. In doing so, some sought to reform society, such as Swami Vivekananda, perhaps the forefather of this practice. In 1866, Swami Vivekananda founded a monastic order, the Ramakrishna Math, and the Ramakrishna Mission, a humanitarian voluntary organization in which monks and devotees continue to engage in charitable work. Another famous example of such a 'guru organization' is that of 'Amma', Mata Amritanandamayi Devi, a living female guru from Kerala (India) who has founded numerous charitable organizations and ashrams internationally, and engages in worldwide travel (see Warrier 2003a, 2003b).

The spiritual worldview of 'Integral Yoga', developed by the Indian gurus Sri Aurobindo and The Mother, and on which the Auroville community is based, is one in which all aspects not only of the self, but also of society, are to be enfolded within the purview of spiritual practice. This chapter explores Auroville's experimentation with merging spiritual and political practice specifically. Other scholars have begun to explore the phenomenon and potential of an integration of spiritual practices in political contexts, as 'embodied practices such as singing and dancing, along with spiritual forms such as prayer and ceremony, have been central to most successful social movements' (Rowe 2016, 208). In her work, political scientist and somatic facilitator Anita Chari differentiates between 'contemplative' (i.e. seated mindfulness meditation) and 'embodied' spiritual practices (i.e. tai chi; hatha yoga). She emphasizes the importance of the latter for developing relational capacities, which she argues may give rise to 'new political potentials' (Chari 2016, 236). Similarly, Karen Litfin has highlighted how the experience of individual and shared conscious states in eco-villages can act as an embodied reference to strive for in collective contexts, including political and decisional forums (Litfin 2018), something I have personally experienced as a member of the Auroville community.

What both are pointing to is that engaging in spiritual practices can create new experiences of subjectivity, ones that may inform individuals whilst participating in political forums. When adopted within these forums, spiritual practices can generate or resuscitate these experiences of subjectivity, and thus act as strategic, micropolitical interventions towards facilitating the dispositions necessary for successfully engaging in prefigurative macropolitics (see Connolly 2002; Rowe 2016).

Auroville offers a fascinating case study of how spirituality can be woven into political practice, and what effect this has, as will be explored next. While the community embraces a distinct spiritual worldview it remains secular,[1] and has adopted the direct, horizontal and participatory democratic modes common to prefigurative social movements (Clarence-Smith 2019). Its experimentation with spiritualizing the latter may therefore be relevant to other political contexts.

Prompting spiritually prefigurative political practice: The Auroville selection process

In the early years of the Auroville community, when it was made up of only a few hundred people, decision-making was undertaken collectively at weekly community meetings, in which any Aurovilian could bring a topic, and express their resonance or concern with the issues raised to arrive at a consensus. As the community grew and became more complex, groups were formed by bottom-up processes to take responsibility for specific aspects, such as funds and assets management, or town planning. Since 2014, those 'Working Groups' which have community-wide mandates are selected via a community process, typically based on consensus. The ethnographic account rendered below is from the 2017 Selection Process for Auroville's Town Development Council (TDC), which I attended as a participant-observer.

I will focus here exclusively on the integration of spirituality-based practices within this process, drawing from the more extensive analysis of Auroville's selection process and other aspects of its collective governance undertaken in my doctoral research (see Clarence-Smith 2019; Clarence-Smith 2023). The Selection Process made instrumental use of a variety of spiritually informed activities – both to induce spiritually centred and reflective individual and collective states, and to inform strategic discussions with Auroville's founding spiritual philosophy. These were based on clauses of the Auroville Charter, other statements The Mother (Auroville's spiritual founding figure) had made about Auroville or the twelve qualities she had defined as essential to living a spiritually evolved life, highlighted in the embodied session 'Awareness Through the Body' session described above (see Figure 1).

The Selection Process: An autoethnographic account

The facilitation team used Tibetan chimes to indicate the beginning of the Selection Process. They stood in silence, for quite a while, a couple of minutes perhaps, until the room fell quiet. Then one of them started, saying 'So the future of Auroville is in silence, when all is contained in silence'. The second followed on with 'Let's all in our own ways try to touch the silence for a minute'. And the third facilitator concluded with 'Maybe silence can be there for three days – that's our idea. That we don't forget the silence'.

---

[1] Auroville is a secular organization in that it is not dedicated to practising or promoting any particular religious doctrine. The Indian Supreme Court ruled as such in 198, when establishing Auroville as a Foundation under India's Ministry of Education.

Figure 1 Awareness through the Body session, Auroville. (source: Awareness through the Body, 2012).[2] © 2012 Awareness Through the Body.

What followed was a beautiful atmosphere of silence in the room, the kind that is hard to describe in words to an audience that is not accustomed to instances of religious or spiritual silence. It is a silence that is not just the absence of sound, but one of palpable presence. Some people closed their eyes, while others kept them open. It was a precious moment to me, to be able to create and share that atmosphere collectively – while I had often experienced this in Auroville, such as in Awareness Through the Body sessions, or in collective community meditations, I never had in the context of a collective-decision-making process.

To embody this shared and spiritually concentrated state in a political forum was revelatory, to me, of the already existing spiritualized polity we were attempting to prefigure. Outside of such moments reserved to spiritual connection, however, it was difficult to feel its underlying presence and potential amongst us, as we shall see. That said, such moments were successfully used to re-centre us – the Selection Committee – when the political process we were engaged in proved challenging. Reportedly, Occupy Wall Street General Assembly facilitators also used moments of silence and short meditation, and that these 'became more common as the occupation continued, and challenges intensified' (Rowe 2015, n.p.) an observation that corroborates the strategic use and role of such practices.

For much of the process, we would work in small groups, at tables set up with folders with the *Auroville Charter*, *To Be a True Aurovilian*, and *A Dream*, the three

---

[2] 'Awareness Through the Body Intensive 2012', 2012, Photograph, Awareness Through the Body digital archive.

founding documents of Auroville. After the initial moment of silence on the first day, the facilitators asked us to concentrate on the first clause of the Auroville Charter: 'to live in Auroville, one must be a willing servitor of the divine consciousness' (The Mother 1968, n.p.) – specifically in relationship to our participation in the Selection Process. They then invited us to pick out, at random, a card of the twelve qualities – Sincerity, Peace, Equality, Generosity, Goodness, Courage, Progress, Receptivity, Aspiration, Perseverance, Gratitude, Humility. We were to reflect and share how the quality we picked informed our aspiration to participate in and contribute meaningfully to the Town Development Council team. The cards were lying face down, on one side was the name of the quality, on the reverse, a quotation by The Mother of that particular quality. As we went to choose our cards, I was touched, again, by the atmosphere of reflective and collective silence

Yet, while some people seemed genuinely keen to go through this spiritually reflective exercise, others seemed to be just going through the motions. A few protested by not participating: 'I don't play card games', said one person at our table, sarcastically. Another told me she did not attend the Selection Process because at the last one she was 'sitting at a table and had to do stuff completely unrelated to the selection: journaling about the qualities', adding 'I don't understand why we can't just vote' – belying the perceived futility of such spiritual activities in and for a collective decision-making process.

For those who did participate, the exercise seemed to inform their positionality in the process: 'I picked Surrender', said a young Indian woman who was still in her 'Newcomer' process (a trial period for joining the community). 'I just closed my eyes and asked the Divine to organize my life the way it wants, because I'm feeling like I already have a lot of commitments'. Another person said his card was 'Progress', and that he felt 'the need to make inner progress for this work, that I am willing to do'. Clearly, there was a strong tendency to contextualize participation within a spiritual perspective.

As the Selection Processes progressed, similar exercises were used strategically to inform how participants related to specific areas of work of the Town Development Council, with mixed responses. A key point of frustration was what the spirituality centred activities were focussed on, when concerns pertaining to the practical skills and information required for selecting a team were not satisfactorily addressed.

In our first case-study group exercise, we were to discuss a mock town planning issue at our tables, and then share a proposal for it with the room at large. I was surprised that there was no presentation of the TDC's mandate and scope of work, or of its new structure, which had led to this very Selection Process. The introduction had been exclusively focussed on spiritual positioning. While relevant materials were provided on the day, I had expected to receive these in advance, and found that many people in the room were largely unfamiliar with the TDC. I was not the only person who found this concerning: after the exercise, several Aurovilians who had served on the TDC, or had been involved in its restructure, remarked that the Selection Committee needed to be briefed for it to be worthwhile. 'They need to participate with information, not opinion', exhorted an architect who had been on the TDC restructure team. 'I was doubting if this would be *practical*, I was even doubting coming', said another participant, who eventually left the process. 'I would have liked a presentation from the TDC: targets, difficulties – they know better than any of us! They could have made some *practical* recommendations'.

A presentation of the Town Development Council had not been programmed, and we continued with spiritualized iterations of the same exercise the facilitators had planned. They asked each group to revisit their issue, in light of one of The Mother's quotes: 'If the growth of consciousness were considered as the principal goal of life, many difficulties would find their solution'. We were prompted to notice what changed within us, and our perception of the situation. Following a period of individual reflection, we each went on to share our insights within our subgroups. A current member of the Auroville Council sitting at my table said 'A change of consciousness can be very small, it doesn't have to be big … A group can commit to do that. It's not just good or important – it's *necessary*. If we don't, we are doing the same thing as everywhere else'. At another table, I heard someone else say, 'But there is no reason to just rely on the growth of consciousness, we can also use common sense, we can also *work*'. These two comments portray the crux of the issue: focussing on the spiritual can either distract from strategic action, or inform, and perhaps, transform it. Attempting the latter is critical to Auroville's spiritually prefigurative project.

In yet another exercise, we re-examined the issue with the first article of the Auroville Charter as a point of reference:

> Auroville belongs to nobody in particular. Auroville belongs to humanity as a whole. But to live in Auroville, one must be a willing servitor of the divine consciousness.

'How can the first article of the Charter be a framework to guide the TDC's Terms of Reference and Detailed Development Plan?' prompts one of the facilitators. Within the same breath, he defends the proposed exercise, saying: 'As long as we don't make the Charter a practical tool we will not make it' implying that we will not realize the ideal society envisioned by the Auroville Charter unless it is applied in practice. I notice two of the architects of the Terms of Reference looking at each other, eyes wide with frustrated disbelief. 'What is this question?' one of them asks, recalcitrantly, belying the perceived futility of such an exercise in light of the ongoing lack of information provided on the Terms of Reference and Detailed Development Plan.

The exercise revealed a range of responses to the attempted articulation between the ideals of the Auroville Charter and the governance of the community in practice: from 'In our issues of donations, the Charter is the ideal reference document', to 'the first point of the Charter is not applied here!' a heated exclamation from a table working on the issue of privately owned land in Auroville's city plan. Whilst the ideals were able to offer clarity and guidance in some cases, agency was disabled in scenarios in which present situations so contradicted with them that participants struggled to envisage how the Auroville Charter could possibly, practically, be realized within these conditions.

Yet, many chose to attend the Selection Process to address this gap between ideals and ground realities. One candidate – among the few with professional town planning experience – expressed that she was 'frustrated and fascinated, again and again', by the issue of planning in Auroville, which she said was about 'collective growth and development to come to a new consciousness, not about building a city as quickly as possible'. Her and others' comments pointed to the perceived lack of centrality of spiritual development in the current town planning process, and a desire to address it. That the participation and candidature of Aurovilians in the Selection Process was significantly linked to a spiritually informed attitudes and motivations (see Clarence-Smith 2019) is a counter to the critique that spirituality renders individuals apolitical (see Žižek 2001).

The last stage of the process was to actually select new members for each Working Group. Participants were split into small groups of about six people and asked to arrive at consensus on which candidates they would choose. The outcomes of each table were displayed to the whole room, and candidates picked by all small groups on this first round were officially selected. In the second round, two small groups merged into one, and consensus on the remaining names was attempted again. There was no guidance from the facilitators during these discussions, which proved challenging. At one point, they called for a pause and played a recording of The Mother, Auroville's founder and spiritual guide, which succeeded in inducing a spiritually centred and receptive state. In the Auroville context, we can understand this to be a strategic intervention towards maintaining a spiritually prefigurative practice. How this palpable effect on the process may have reverberated into the final consensus decision-making, however, is hard to determine.

Conclusion: Spiritual practice and political praxis

In examining the spiritualization of a collective decision-making process in the intentional community Auroville, this chapter builds on scholarship that highlights the significance of embodied spiritual practices in prefigurative political praxis, and the potential for spiritually informed worldviews and subjectivities to prompt, inform and sustain such praxis (Chari 2016; Litfin 2018; Rowe 2016; Wilson 2014). It also contributes ethnographic insight into an experimental attempt at prefiguring a spiritualized polity as an aim unto itself (see also Clarence-Smith 2019; Vidal 2018). Previous scholarship pointed to the potential of spiritual practices – whether embodied or contemplative (see Chari 2016) – for developing new subjectivities and relational capacities that could significantly facilitate collective decision-making processes. In this chapter, spiritually centring practices, such as moments of silence, were used within the Auroville Selection Process, as strategic micropolitical interventions towards engaging in and sustaining an overarching, spiritually prefigurative political process (see Connolly 2002; Rowe 2016).

Importantly, this case study reveals an additional way in which spirituality was strategically used towards facilitating a spiritually prefigurative political praxis. The community's spiritual ideals were applied as instrumental prompts, to frame and inform the actual content of the decision-making towards prefiguring these. While it is important to note that an emphasis on such practices resulted in a failure to address a lack of practical guidance and information pertaining to the issues and process at hand – echoing the criticism that a focus on the spiritual causes an elision of worldly concerns – this attempted articulation between spiritual ideals and actual governance did have varying levels of success. The very challenge of Auroville is to prefigure the spiritual vision of Integral Yoga, one which recognizes and seeks to address this disconnect between the spiritual and material realms of existence. I remain curious about the potential for our spiritually informed political praxis to mature into doing so, seeds of which have been observed in other contexts, as when mindfulness meditation was used to identify patterns of social injustice being reproduced in Occupy Wall Street (Rowe 2015, 2016). While such meditation practices remain individual in nature, the Auroville community is committed to collectively practicing and embodying spiritually prefigurative politics, and continues to experiment despite – or thanks to – differences in how to successfully translate it into practice.

References

Auroville Media Liaison (2022) *Auroville Media Kit*. URL: https://auroville.media/press/. Accessed 23 January 2023.
Berila, B. (2016) *Integrating Mindfulness into Anti-Oppression Pedagogy: Social Justice in Higher Education*. New York: Routledge.
Blanchflower, P. (2005) 'Restoration of the tropical dry evergreen forest of Peninsular India', *Biodiversity* 6(3), pp. 17–24.
Boggs, C. (1977) 'Marxism, prefigurative communism and the problem of workers' control', *Radical America* 6, pp. 99–122.
Cederström, C. (2015) *The wellness syndrome* (Vol. 94). Bristol: Polity Press.
'Census May 2020 – Auroville population', *Auroville*. URL: https://www.auroville.org/contents/3329. Accessed 17 June 2020.
Chari, A. (2016) 'The Political potential of mindful embodiment', *New Political Science* 38(2), pp. 226–40.
Clarence-Smith, S.A. (2023) *Prefiguring Utopia: The Auroville Experiment*. Bristol: Bristol University Press.
Clarence-Smith, S.A. (2021) 'Auroville, an experiment in spiritually prefigurative utopianism', in Sargent, L.T. and Baccolini, R. (eds.) *Essays in Honour of Lucy Sargisson*. Oxford: Peter Lang, pp. 106–18.
Clarence-Smith, S.A. (2019) *Towards a Spiritualised Society: Auroville, an Experiment in Prefigurative Utopianism*. PhD Dissertation. University of Sussex.
Connolly, W.E. (2002) *Neuropolitics: Thinking, Culture, Speed* (Vol. 23). Minneapolis, MN: University of Minnesota Press.
Davies, W. (2015) *The Happiness Industry: How the Government and Big Business Sold Us Well-Being*. London: Verso.
Farias, C. (2017) 'That's what friends are for: Hospitality and affective bonds fostering collective empowerment in an intentional community', *Organization Studies* 38(5), pp. 577–95.
Firth, R. (2012) *Utopian Politics: Citizenship and Practice*. London and New York: Routledge.
Graeber, D. (2010) *Direct Action: An Ethnography*. Edinburgh: AK Press.

Graeber, D. (2013) *The Democracy Project: A History, A Crisis, A Movement*. London: Allen Lane.
Guigan, G. (2018) *Auroville in Mother's Words*. Auroville: Auroville Press.
Hahn, T.N. (1993) *Interbeing: Fourteen Guidelines for Engaged Buddhism*. Berkeley, CA: Parallax Press.
Kabat-Zinn, J. (2013) *Full Catastrophe Living. Using the Wisdom of Your Body and Mind to Face Stress, Pain, and Illness*. New York: Bantam Books.
Kabat-Zinn, J. (2018) *Meditation is not What you Think: Mindfulness and why it is so Important*. Oxfordshire: Hachette UK, Didcot.
Kaza, S. (2008). *Mindfully Green. A Personal and Spiritual Guide to Whole Earth Thinking*. Boston, MA: Shambhala Publications.
King, S.B. (2009) *Socially Engaged Buddhism*. Honolulu, HI: University of Hawaii Press.
Litfin, Karen T. (2018) 'The contemplative pause: Insights for teaching politics in turbulent times', *Journal of Political Science Education* 16(1), pp. 57–66. URL: http://doi.org/10.1080/15512169.2018.1512869.
Madsen, O.J. (2015) *Optimizing the Self. Social Representations of Self-Help*. London: Routledge.
Maeckelbergh, M. (2011) 'Doing is believing: Prefiguration as strategic practice in the alterglobalisation movement', *Social Movement Studies* 10(1), pp. 1–20.
Maeckelbergh, M. (2009) *The Will of the Many: How the Alterglobalisation Movement is Changing the Face of Democracy*. London: Pluto Press.
Majumdar, A. (2017) *Auroville: A City for the Future*. Gurugram: Harper Collins India.
Monticelli, L. (2022). *The Future is Now: An Introduction to Prefigurative Politics*. Bristol: Bristol University Press.
Monticelli, L. (2018) 'Embodying alternatives to capitalism in the 21st Century', *TripleC: Communication, Capitalism & Critique* 16(2), pp. 501–17.
Namakkal, J. (2021) *Unsettling Utopia the Making and Unmaking of French India*. New York: Columbia University Press.
Pohl, C. (2020) *Ever Slow Green*. Auroville: Brainfever Media Productions. Documentary film.
Protect Mauna Kea. URL: https://www.protectmaunakea.net. Last Accessed 13 September 2019.
Queen, C.S. and King, S.B. (Eds.) (1996) *Engaged Buddhism: Buddhist Liberation Movements in Asia*. Albany, NY: SUNY Press.
Queen, C.S. (Ed.) (2012) *Engaged Buddhism in the west*. London: Simon and Schuster.
Queen, C.S., Prebish, C.S. and Keown, D. (Eds.) (2003) *Action Dharma: New Studies in Engaged Buddhism* (Vol. 23). Hove: Psychology Press.
Raekstad, P. (2018) 'Revolutionary practice and prefigurative politics: A clarification and defense', *Constellations* 25(3), pp. 359–72.
Rimke, H.N. (2000) 'Governing citizens through self-help literature', *Cultural Studies* 14(1), pp. 61–78.
Rowe, J.K. (2015) 'Zen and the art of movement maintenance', *OpenDemocracy*, March 27. URL: https://www.opendemocracy.net/en/transformation/zen-and-art-of-social-movement-maintenance/.
Rowe, J.K. (2016) 'Micropolitics and collective liberation: Mind/Body practice and left social movements', *New Political Science* 38(2), pp. 206–25.
Saari, A. and Harni, E. (2016) 'Zen and the art of everything: Governing spirituality in entrepreneurship education', *Ephemera: Theory & Politics in Organization* 16(4), pp. 99–119.

Sanford, W. (2017) *Living Sustainably: What Intentional Communities Can Teach Us about Democracy, Simplicity and Nonviolence*. Lexington, KY: The University Press of Kentucky.

Satprem (1981) *Mother's Agenda* (Vol. 9). Paris: Institut de Recherches Évolutives.

Seitz-Wald, A. (2013) 'Meet the "mindfulness" caucus: Politicians who meditate!', *Salon*, July 10. URL: https://www.salon.com/2013/07/10/meet_the_buddhist_caucus/.

Spicer, A. (2011) 'Guilty lives: The authenticity trap at work', *Ephemera: Theory & Politics in Organization*, 11(1), pp. 46–62.

Sri Aurobindo (1999) *Complete Works of Sri Aurobindo* (Vol. 23), *The Synthesis of Yoga – I*. Pondicherry: Sri Aurobindo Ashram.

Sri Aurobindo (2011) *Complete Works of Sri Aurobindo* (Vol. 35), *Letters on Himself and the Ashram: Selected Letters on His Outer and Inner Life, His Path of Yoga and the Practice of Yoga in His Ashram*. Pondicherry: Sri Aurobindo Ashram.

Sri Aurobindo (1970) *Sri Aurobindo Birth Centenary Library* (Vol. 19), *The Life Divine – II*. Pondicherry: Sri Aurobindo Ashram.

Sri Aurobindo Society [online] URL: https://aurosociety.org. Accessed 31 May 2023.

'The Auroville Foundation', *Auroville* [online] URL: https://www.auroville.org/contents/572. Accessed 23 May 2023.

The Mother (1954) *A Dream*. Pondicherry: Sri Aurobindo Ashram.

The Mother (2003) *Collected Works of The Mother* (Vol. 13), *Words of The Mother – I*. Pondicherry: Sri Aurobindo Ashram Press.

The Mother (1968) *The Auroville Charter*. Pondicherry: Sri Aurobindo Ashram.

The Mother (1971) *To Be a True Aurovilian*. Pondicherry: Sri Aurobindo Ashram.

'The Mother on Auroville', URL: http://archive.auroville.org/vision/maonav_selected.htm. Last Accessed 14 September 2020.

van de Sande, M. (2015) 'Fighting with Tools: Prefiguration and Radical Politics in the Twenty-First Century', *Rethinking Marxism* 27(2), pp. 177–94.

Venugopal, L. and Mistri-Kapoor, T. (2021) 'Why Auroville needs to be an example of exemplary development practice', URL: https://thewire.in/urban/debate-auroville-master-plan. Accessed 27 May 2023.

Vidal, M. (2018) *Manifesting the Invisible*, MA Thesis. École des Hautes Études en Sciences Sociales.

Warrier, M. (2003a) 'Guru Choice and Spiritual Seeking in Contemporary India', *International Journal of Hindu Studies* 7(1–3), pp. 31–54.

Warrier, M. (2003b) 'Processes of Secularization in Contemporary India: Guru Faith in the Mata Amritanandamayi Mission', *Modern Asian Studies* 37(1), pp. 213–53.

Wilson, J. (2014) *Mindful America: The Mutual Transformation of Buddhist Meditation and American Culture*. Oxford: Oxford University Press.

Writers for the 99% (2012) *Occupying Wall Street: The Inside Story of an Action that Changed America*. New York: OR Books.

Yang, L. and Willis, J. (2017) *Awakening Together: The Spiritual Practice of Inclusivity and Community*. Somerville, MA: Wisdom Publications.

Yates, L. (2015) 'Rethinking prefiguration: Alternatives, micropolitics and goals in social movements', *Social Movement Studies* 14(1), pp. 1–21.

Žižek, S. (2001) 'From Western Marxism to Western Buddhism', *Cabinet* 2(2), n. p.

Part Four

Building diverse economies

Jenny Pickerill

In operating as a collective with an explicit intent to live ecologically eco-communities also seek to reconfigure engagement with the capitalist economy, formal labour employment, the notion of what constitutes 'work' and how time is valued. Many eco-communities explicitly reject the practice of fulltime wage employment: critiquing how conventional labour relations only value some activities as productive and worthy of a wage, the unevenness and inequity how labour roles are paid, while social reproduction work remain undervalued.

What constitutes work and how it is valued is redefined in attempts to generate post-capitalist economic relations where work is performed for collective benefit (more than individual income), regular labour contributions include community activities (such as land care, food production, meal preparation etc.), and ideally everyone's time is valued equally. Eco-communities are therefore building community economies (Gibson-Graham, 2006): making visible the diverse economic activities and relations which exist beyond a narrow categorization of labour-for-income exchange, and reprioritizing work which has ecological and social benefits above capital generation.

These economic experiments (or what Malý Blažek, Chapter 19, calls economic playgrounds) are often less visible than the socio-ecological transformations of eco-communities, but are vital in reducing environmental impact *while* retaining a quality of life. Indeed, redefining economies is the more radical act – it is possible to live more ecologically if wealthy by purchasing technologies or outsourcing manual labour, but to do so with limited financial resources is harder and requires significant shifts in how labour, work, money and time are understood, shared and valued.

As the contributors to this section discuss, eco-communities' diverse economic experiments are less understood than their ecological practices. Eco-communities are assumed to be anti-capitalist but in practice many engage in an extensive range of economic activities including commercial initiatives, external paid employment, social enterprises, workers' cooperatives and informal non-monetary exchanges. These economic activities operate at numerous scales, but most effectively at the smaller spaces of daily life where capitalist conventions can be more easily subverted. Economic practices are a hybrid of capitalist, anti-capitalist and post-capitalist initiatives, which involve compromises, conflict and inequalities. Yet many residents celebrate this patchwork of economic engagements as enabling a higher quality of life and a freedom from the drudgery of working-to-live.

A common outcome for eco-communities, however, is a distinct lack of capital. Most eco-communities, and certainly those examined in these chapters, struggled with generating enough surplus to cover maintenance costs of buildings, additional food costs, vehicle repair or materials. There was also a lack of financial planning for retirement, and often explicit rejection of the suggestion that retirement from work would be desirable or possible. The long-term financial sustainability of eco-communities, how these hybrid economic arrangements work (and fail) and the consequence of this partial and patchwork approach to post-capitalism are perhaps some of the least understood aspects of eco-communities and yet building such diverse economies is vital to sustaining the daily quality of life that is central to surviving well together.

17

Escaping capitalism? Time, quality of life and hybrid economies

Kirsten Stevens-Wood

I am in the kitchen and it is 1.30 in the afternoon. The lunch crew have just finished washing up and I am about to begin preparing dinner. For forty people. My starting point is the large kitchen blackboard. It lists what is 'ready' in the kitchen garden; it even has a chalk-drawn box called 'use first' which lists fruit and garden produce which is either in abundance or needs to be used before it has passed its best. It is June, so the list is long: lettuce, tomatoes, sweetcorn, peppers, spinach, some early potatoes … I will also check the large walk-in cold store for anything that needs using, things that have been opened, part used or to be reheated as part of today's meal. Many of yesterday's leftovers will have been served at lunch: soups, salads, homemade bread, and Friary Grange Cheese. The priority is home produce, food that has been grown or produced on site by the community.

Friary Grange (a pseudonym) is a rural eco-community housing forty adults and a handful of children. Situated amongst the rural villages of the East coast of England, they mirror many of the characteristics of the surrounding communities in being predominantly white and well educated. They manage over 70 acres of land in addition to substantial buildings and outbuildings. Much of the land is pasture where their small herd of dairy and meat cows graze year round. There are also sheep, chickens and sometimes pigs. The community are pragmatic about their meat consumption and see the animals as part of the wider land management and community endeavours to produce a large proportion of their own food on site. Polytunnels are bursting with summer growth, in the fields there are onions, potatoes and whole fields of cabbages and broccoli. A well-tended orchard holds apples, pears and plum trees, and there are raspberries, gooseberries and currant bushes. Time is also invested into the preservation of summer abundance; fruit is jammed, bottled and frozen, produce is pickled, dried and sealed into containers; onions are tied into strings, and apples are racked alongside potatoes in preparation for the less plentiful winter months. It is this relationship with the production of food, that somehow shifts the relative value of that same food from something purchased to something that has become directly symbolic of their time and labour. Unlike the anonymous vegetables purchased at the supermarket checkout, this community are aware of the embodied time and resources that have been invested and therefore food is treated as a valuable resource even to the point where waste becomes abhorrent (Tucker 2018).

Eco-communities are often aligned with the concepts of self-reliance and self-sufficiency (Kirby 2003). There is a rich tapestry of urban and rural groups who are attempting to reduce their impact on the earth, consume less and in many cases grow or produce more of their own food. According to Nelson (2018, 242):

> Eco-collaborative housing models that incorporate initiatives and infrastructure towards collective sufficiency at least in food, water and energy not only represent the cutting edge of more sustainable lifestyles but also seem to prefigure post-capitalist values and relations of production and exchange.

However, this self-reliance is muddied and made more complex because of pre-existing relationships with consumption, wage labour and work. Community members extol the fulfilment of working the land and reaping the fruits of their labour. Meanwhile, they also struggle with the apparent contradictions that manifest when they consider their community labour both in terms of an indirect financial exchange, and also in the way that time (and the cost/value of that time) is experienced differently by different people. This chapter is drawn from research conducted over a period of six months. Personal accounts of community members' experiences of living in an eco-community were collected through a process of interviews, discussions and observations. This chapter explores the ways in which residents of an eco-community make sense of their choices to live in a way which embraces many of their ideas of environmentalism whilst simultaneously living in a capitalist society.

What makes an eco-community?

Eco-villages are described by Cattaneo (2015, 165) as:

> specifically planned and set up for people to come and live together with the goal of living and working according to ecological principles by promoting a degree of sharing and pursuing well-being through more sustainable life-styles, direct democracy and a degree of autonomy.

However, eco-communities can encompass a much broader spectrum, of communal settings such as co-housing (McCaimant and Durrett 2012), housing co-ops and squatter communities (Haydon 2014; Jarvis 2017). Although not all of these forms of communal living will identify themselves as eco-communities, many will hold the principles associated with self-reliance and sustainability. Many will practice some form of self-sufficiency such as growing their own food, and in some cases engaging in full-scale farming and smallholding. John Seymore, the author of the 1976 book *Self Sufficiency*, describes this form of lifestyle as:

> the striving for a higher standard of living, for food which is fresh and organically grown and for the good life in pleasant surroundings for the health of

the body and peace of mind which comes with hard and varied work in the open air and for the satisfaction that comes from doing difficult and intricate jobs well and successfully.

(Seymore 1976, 7)

These concepts are evident in the descriptions that community members provide about their motivations to live in Friary Grange. Self-sufficiency is considered here as one of the elements of living a more sustainable lifestyle and as encompassing wider principles such as the reduction of waste and a lower carbon footprint.

Friary Grange is a medium-to-large intentional community that formed in the early 1970s. Many UK communities formed at that time followed a similar format of buying a large building with land with the intention of creating some type of back-to-the-land venture. Unlike the back-to-the-land projects created from the hardships of the 1930s, the 1970s wave was a reaction to growing consumption and disillusion with capitalism (Brown 2011). As such, many of their inhabitants hoped to create a community that would not only feed their bodies but would also build a community based on shared values and environmental ideals (Halfacree 2006). Today, Friary Grange maintain many of their values established at the outset and continue to espouse environmental principles which revolve around a green lifestyle and people living in community. This is evident in how members describe their community and also in the day-to-day practices of mindful consumption and prudent use of resources:

> We choose to live in a way that is lighter on the earth, so for example, by growing our food here on site we are reducing food miles, saving carbon and energy. We also try to farm organically.
>
> (Sasha, 17 years at Friary Grange)

> We are completely self-sufficient in milk and the things that come with that like cream and cheese. We have solar panels that provide a lot of our electricity, plus we do a lot of things like lift sharing, reducing car use.
>
> (Eamon, 32 years at Friary Grange)

Residents can also often be seen undertaking small acts of thrift such as mending worn out equipment or clothing, saving seed and repurposing objects. Wheelbarrows are often patched, machinery repaired and usable wood stored for future use.

The residents of Friary Grange are aware that they exist to some degree in a bubble, set outside the experience of the vast majority of people living in the UK. Friary Grange buildings are grand but well worn, set in a large network of historical buildings that in addition to personal living units includes a library, communal bathrooms, a large kitchen dining space where all meals are prepared and eaten communally, plus extensive vegetable gardens and land. As a community they share all of the common space; they also share all of the work including many of the maintenance jobs, farming, cooking, cleaning, household and community administration. This is an enormous undertaking and managed cooperatively between the members of the community through a mixture of working groups, meetings and an allocated number of community hours to be undertaken by each adult community member per week. While this conjures up utopian images of a fully cooperative lifestyle, it is not without its complications. This bubble that the community exists within has its limits; Friary Grange is subject to the same liabilities and constraints as any other home, community or business. Bills and services need to be paid for and the everyday lives of community members include the necessity of paid work, leisure and external commitments. In an attempt to create a community which engenders cooperative values and environmental principles, community members are required to exist in or between two worlds, that of the 'real world' and that created by their community:

> It sometimes feels like I live in two worlds, the one out there and the one in here. Out there feels faster and shockingly expensive, and it's easy to lose touch with that, which makes it all the more shocking when you are confronted with the cost of things.
> (Nigel, 44 years at Friary Grange)

> It's a privileged lifestyle, but one where we *choose* to have less.
> (Sasha 17 years at Friary Grange)

> I chose to live here because it allowed me to raise my children in an environment where all of *this* [gestures at vegetable garden, polytunnels and fruit trees] is normal.
> (Leah, 33 years at Friary Grange)

The residents of Friary Grange inhabit a hybrid economy where, once the initial outlay of membership has been covered,[1] day-to-day living costs are comparatively small. For example, the daily cost of meals per head (plus shared access to other resources such as dairy and home-grown produce) is around £2.50 per person per day (usually paid monthly), which is significantly lower than average UK expenditure on food and non-alcoholic drinks (ONS 2022). Other shared costs are divided by household per adult member which is almost always less (and sometimes considerably less) than the equivalent if each household were living outside of the community. This in principle means that community members are able to reduce their external paid work commitments in order to then commit those additional hours to work within the community. The cost of living, however, is not zero, and so all members are required to have some form of additional income, either earned (paid work) or unearned (savings, inheritance or some other asset-based income). This is far from a new conundrum with Farber (2013) documenting communes of the 1960s often needing to re-engage with paid work and often state benefits (Pepper 1993; Rigby 1974) once the realities of self-sufficiency started to bite. For the residents of Friary Grange, the necessity

---

[1] New members must buy into Friary Grange (in the form of loan stock). This can vary according to the size of the space needed, however as a collectively owned property, new members are unable to take out a mortgage and therefore must somehow meet the whole cost on entry. At the time of writing, a half unit (enough for two people or a small family) was £156,000.

of external, individually paid work and the time given to this bring up a number of areas of contention: allocated time, the offsetting of income for well-being and the navigation of a hybrid economy.

Not all time is equal

All community members are required to commit fifteen hours a week to the community. This is considered the minimum commitment from each member to get the 'work' of Friary Grange done. These hours include core or 'rota' jobs (jobs which are considered to be essential for the day-to-day functioning of the community such as daily meal preparation, cleaning and animal care). Outside of this are a vast number of (non-rota) manual and non-manual jobs, domestic and land-based. For example, some members may spend more time on administration such as bookkeeping or managing the volunteering or membership process, others may undertake household tasks such as additional cooking and cleaning, and others may prefer outdoor work such as wood chopping, farming or gardening. Many members move between different tasks often picking up jobs as and when they are needed. There is no formal record of hours worked or jobs done (outside of the weekly sign-up sheets) and although this is not without its tensions:

> You can't think about who has done what, or if so-and-so has done their hours because it would drive you crazy, you have to just know that you have done your bit and that's that.
>
> (Leah, 33 years at Friary Grange)

> Some people here do more, and some do less, it has always been the way. I think in general; most people do their hours one way or another.
>
> (Eamon, 32 years at Friary Grange)

> There are some jobs that are more visible than others, for example driving a tractor, whereas a job like sorting out the insurance for this place can take hours when you take into account all the calling round and quotes, but that takes place behind closed doors, out of sight.
>
> (Duncan, Friary Grange)

Unlike the regulated world of formal employment, Friary Grange chose not to formalize their community hours, instead relying on a system of goodwill and trust. Although this is a system that they have agreed, it is also a regular topic of discussion. Individual members must balance the demands of the community against the demands of their private use of time, and in many cases paid work. Members often talk about being 'seen' to complete their hours and the difficulties that the system creates in terms of fairness and the different ability of each member to meet the required number of hours.

Paula invites me to join her one afternoon in one of the large polytunnels where we are thinning some of the leafy vegetables and picking others for the kitchen. We talk about living in a community, and in particular a community with a high focus on self-reliance and ecological sustainability where food growing and land management are heavily dependent on community members' commitment:

> I work the equivalent of three days per week, but sometimes more depending on what's happening in my job. So I have to decide whether to try to do all of my community hours on either two long days or split it up over the week. Sometimes it's hard to do all of the hours; I run out of time.
> (Paula, 8 years at Friary Grange)

Paula describes her community work hours as manageable, but often squeezed in between other commitments such as paid employment and external personal commitments. As a single parent, Paula often finds her time pulled in different directions and similar to many community members, she imagines an ideal where members are able to live and work within the community without the need for external employment. However, she acknowledges that this is not currently a possibility.

Later that week, I am taking a morning break in the communal garden with Bill, a long-standing community member who is now retired. We discuss the balance between work and leisure when living in a community which aspires to self-sufficiency: 'It's not really that much when you think about it, a couple of hours a day if that, but then, I am retired'. Bill concedes that for those needing to work in addition to their community hours, it can be difficult.

These two statements provide an insight into the way that the same number of community hours can impact individual members differently. In much the same way that feminist writers have identified gender differences in the experience of work and non-work (Abbott and Wallace 1997; Odih 2007; West 1997), the experience of living and 'working' in the community differs according to the individual. Community members are often straddling at least two forms of commitment; to their community hours (fixed, and based on an ideology of 'equal distribution of work') and to necessary paid individual employment. In addition to this, paid work outside the community generates different levels of pay, where one hour's work for one person may be equal to three or four hours for another person. This temporal and economic disparity becomes problematic for communities attempting to create an environmentally and socially sustainable lifestyle as it re-creates the inequalities of the outside world (Williams 2016). The internal system, based on equality of opportunity, does not allow for the differing life circumstances of individual community members, including consideration of possible caring responsibilities such as child or elder care, and tends to fall unequally on women.

Friary Grange is not alone in this, and there have been many attempts by different intentional communities to disrupt this economic relationship, and even to break away from it. An example of this is the 'One Planet' settlements of Wales, where planning is permitted in open countryside if the applicants can show that they are able to meet the majority of their day-to-day needs directly from the products of their land (thus placing many of their products into use value) (Welsh Assembly Government 2009). Through reducing their outgoings to a bare minimum, One Planet applicants are meeting planning requirements, and decoupling their reliance on external economic demands in exchange for a simpler, more sustainable lifestyle. However, even here, a capitalist economy appears to obstruct the ability of groups to entirely disconnect. One Planet smallholder Paul Jennings articulates the difficulty of existing in a system where products created on-site for direct consumption reduce the cost of day-to-day living. However, products created in a way that is time- and energy-intensive often have a relatively low exchange value (for example locally produced honey), due to money 'leaking' out of the domestic economy in the form of external costs such as insurance or loan repayments (Jennings 2020). On a much larger scale, the eco-village of Twin Oaks in the United States has attempted to mitigate this issue by creating a closed economy (also based on community hours), but where all income is produced through community endeavour, and the external assets and wealth of incomers is frozen or donated to the community upon joining (Twin Oaks 2001). Through the attempt to exclude external economics, this community is able to create an environment where work, as well as the *value* of that work, is not subject to external forces and valuations. This enables internal labour and the products of that labour to be valued as their 'use value' as opposed to the exchange value of either the labour itself, or the products created through that labour.

The members of Friary Grange are not unaware of the effect that capitalism and the 'value' of labour have on both their time and the products of that time:

> It isn't cost effective. If you were to consider all of the hours that go into caring for our animals, say for example the chickens, the space, the building and maintenance of the coop, bought in food for them and the fact that we are mostly using them for eggs, then we might in a good year break even in terms of producing high quality organically produced eggs. But it isn't about that is it? We have chosen to live in a way that gives us a connection to the land and the production of a large quantity of our food; it's so much more than just a pound for pound comparison.
> (Simon, 4 years at Friary Grange)

Shippen (2014, 76) provides an analysis of the complex relationship between time and capitalism where time becomes 'colonized' by capital in a way which is often embedded into our consciousness (the way that we think about time) and our social structures (the ways we organize our lives around time). Friary Grange are attempting to create a way of life that places value on home production of food and other goods, and by doing so they are endeavouring to create what Sarker (cited in Pepper 1993) calls 'a quasi-independent existence' where they are able to reduce their reliance and engagement with the market through a process of self-reliance. This, however, is disrupted by the necessity to engage in the market in other ways, that is, external costs and wage labour. Community members are cognizant of this and often frame their relationship with the land and their community in terms of less quantifiable returns such as personal well-being and wider benefits to the environment.

Offsetting income for well-being, community and quality of life

I suppose you could call it posh poverty, well not even that, our lifestyle is good, the food is excellent; it's a privilege to live this way.

(Leah, 33 years at Friary Grange)

Kat is preparing the evening meal with me, and as we do so she explains how living in what she describes as a sustainable community provides her with a feeling of 'moving in the right direction'. She describes her decision-making process of joining Friary Grange as one of giving up a well-paid career to downshift her life into a more environmentally sound way of living:

I earn a lot less now by choice, but I have swapped financial wealth for a better standard of living. Not everyone would want to choose this, but for me, growing my own food, living in a community and reducing my carbon footprint was a big motivator.

(Kat, 4 years at Friary Grange)

Kat's comments tally with the work of Easterlin (2003) where factors such as health and family life are more closely aligned with levels of happiness than that of income. Mulder et al. (2006) concluded that for those living in an ecologically motivated intentional community, lower income levels were offset (in terms of quality of life) by access to green spaces and conservation of nature. When asked, many of the members of Friary Grange stated that they found fulfilment both in the activities of the community as well as the rewards of producing their own food and living in a way that was less polluting than the average household. Although the work was unpaid, the general feeling was one of placing their community labour into a separate category from that of their distinctive paid employment, of working for themselves and contributing to the wider community. In his exploration of eco-socialism, Pepper (1993) describes this differentiation between paid work and community work as the difference between alienated and unalienated labour. Through a process of re-connecting with the products of their labour (both physical and non-physical) Friary Grangers are also (to some degree) pushing back against the appropriation of time and labour by the market.

For many members of Friary Grange, there was a conflict between the need to earn money to live and the desire to invest more time in community. During an evening meal, Frances expresses her feelings of being pulled between her paid employment and being free to fully participate in community life:

I still work close to three days a week which is not ideal. There are lots of things I would like to do more of, get more involved if I had the time. I am retiring at the end of the year and I am so looking forward to being able to take on some projects I have been too busy to do in the past.

(Frances, 21 years at Friary Grange)

Frances, like many at Friary Grange, would like to commit more time to the community. It was often the case that members expressed the wish to 'take on more' or that projects were not progressed due to a lack of available time. Fin, an active community member who also needed to take on paid work outside of the community to meet his expenses, reflected on the pull of community versus the need to engage in paid work:

> There are lots of people here who would like to give up work all together and invest that time in Friary Grange. A lot of the things that people get annoyed about like tools not cared for or stuff going past its best in the garden is down to the time, or lack of it, that people have to invest in the community.
>
> (Fin, 3 years at Friary Grange)

Farber (2013) reminds us that time itself is finite, whereas the demands placed upon it can expand or contract according to an individual's social context. For individuals and groups attempting to create alternative lifestyles, these differing demands can be problematic.

Navigating a hybrid economy

Examples of people exchanging full-time paid work for a simpler or 'greener' life are well documented (Ergas 2010; Escribano et al., 2020; Mangold and Zschau 2019), as are the well-being and environmental benefits (Sanguinetti 2014; Wang, Pan and Hadjri 2021). However, the lived experience of bridging the transition from one form of lifestyle to another is still relatively unexamined. Nelson and Temmerman (2011) explore a number of experimental forms of what they term as 'non-market socialism' including the credit system used in the ecovillage Twin Oakes. Bakers' (2013) study exploring the relationship with capitalism documented eco-village members' conflicting feelings over work sharing and the pressures on younger (non-retired) members to put in community time as well as make a living. This appears to have similarities to the experiences of the members of Friary Grange. Baker concludes that due to most 'alternative' communities existing within a capitalist society, it is not possible to create a fully autonomous economy due to unavoidable external pressures such as land prices and externally purchased materials. Indeed, Mincyte and Dobernig (2016, 1771) go as far as to suggest that 'unalienated, uncommodified work never exists in its pure, ideal form, but is best understood as a hybrid process fraught with contradictions and defined by continuous slippages between de-commodification and re-commodification'. Friary Grange produce much of their day-to-day needs, but they also buy in other products (including food) which tie them into external production and consumption. Escribano et al. (2020, 12) echo this when they draw a parallel between the unsustainability of our current, dominant economic system and attempts by what they call ecological communities to consider their own long-term sustainability. They conclude that 'communities that are not economically sustainable cannot serve as viable models for environmentally sustainable forms of human settlement', and that as such eco-communities inhabit a space which is ideologically opposed to a consumer-led, marketized economy.

In her analysis of work, Weeks (2011) reminds us that for the majority, work is a necessity embedded in a social system which compels us to participate. However, she also suggests that work *can* become a site of resistance and a mechanism for creating alternatives to exploitative models of employment (2011, 29). While the members of Friary Grange would not describe themselves as anarchists, they are to some extent contesting the dominant model of both work and economics. Through their engagement with self-reliance, they are challenging the dominant ideology of work-to-live. In part this is achieved through a withdrawal from the compulsion of full-time employment. Similarities can be found within the Tiny House movement where participants have been documented as gaining both mental well-being and financial security through breaking away from the necessity of long work hours and the associated costs of maintaining that lifestyle (Mangold and Zschau 2019). The members of Friary Grange have created an environment that allows them to at least partially disengage from the dominant model of economic wealth. Although, as mentioned previously, this is predicated on an ability to 'buy in' to the community, which in itself can act as a barrier and may inadvertently create issues around a lack of diversity.

Reisch (2001) provides an analysis of the relationship between wealth and time and surmises that beyond a certain level of wealth, time becomes the more valuable commodity. Communities and individuals who are choosing to simplify and reduce their consumption may similarly be reducing the point at which wealth is considered to have been achieved, thereby freeing up time for non-market activities. This is encapsulated by Lisa, a former teacher in a Further Education College who describes her experience of giving up full-time work:

> I actually have less now than I ever have, I mean personally, the things I own, I buy very little and I am much more likely to mend things ... I worried that when I gave up full time work I would have to go without, but you rebalance, re-set your priorities and then you realise that you are no worse off and all those hours at work just ate your life.
>
> (Lisa, 17 years at Friary Grange)

In the voluntary simplicity movement, individuals have chosen to disengage with what Grigsby (2004) calls 'status consumption' through rejecting a consumerist ideology in favour of a simpler and less environmentally damaging way of life. As with Lisa's description of downshifting, it is possible to make links between levels of consumption, paid work and sustainability. Kirby (2003), in his analysis of social and environmental relations within a North American ecovillage, ascertained that as members moved away from capitalist consumer lifestyles they made clearer connections with the ecological environment and their goals of sustainability. These discourses were easily found among the residents of Friary Grange where they regularly described their lives in terms of escaping 'the rat race'[2] and shifting their priorities away from economic consumption to a more sustainable way of life.

---

[2] The 'rat race' is a way of life that is premised on achieving wealth and power through focusing on competing with others.

Intentional communities are often considered to be a response to the concerns and discontentment of the society from which they were born (Sargison 2012). In this sense, they are both radical and utopian in their purpose. Sargisson (2012, 8) suggests that many 'green' intentional communities represent (albeit small) challenges to the dominant socio-economic system and that they are creating practical alternatives. In the case of Friary Grange, they have chosen a lifestyle that embraces using less, sharing to reduce consumption and waste, as well as sharing labour.

It is easy to see capitalism as unchallengeable and all-encompassing, however, Gibson-Graham (2006) suggest that instead of capitalism being considered as a force to be overthrown and replaced, it is possible to see capitalism itself as fragmented and pluralistic and therefore small, ground-level alternatives such as the multiple and varied acts of exchange and uncommodified labour that are found in social groups are in themselves both radical and practical. As such, eco-communities can have their own validity and effectiveness despite the unavoidable compromises and hybridity. The members of Friary Grange have chosen to engage in a way of life that at least in part enables them to sidestep some of the dominant ideology of living within a capitalist society, and at the same time live a more environmentally sustainable way of life.

References

Abbott, P. and Wallace, C. (1997) *An Introduction to Sociology: Feminist Perspectives*. London: Routledge.
Baker, T. (2013) 'Ecovillages and capitalism', in Lockyer, J. and Veteto, J.R. (eds.) *Environmental Anthropology Engaging Ecotopia*. New York: Berghahn Books, pp. 285–300.
Brown, D. (2011) *Back to the Land: The Enduring Dream of Self-Sufficiency in Modern America*. Madison, WI: University of Wisconsin Press.
Cattaneo, C. (2015) 'Eco-communities', in Kallis, G., Demaria, F. and D'Alisa, G. (eds.) *Degrowth: A Vocabulary for a New Era*. New York: Routledge, pp. 165–8.
Chitewere, T. (2018) *Sustainable Communities and Green Lifestyles: Consumption and Environmentalism*. New York: Routledge.
Easterlin, R. (2003) 'Explaining happiness', *Proceedings of the National Academy of Sciences of the United States of America* 100(19), pp. 11176–83.
Ergas, C. (2010) 'A model of sustainable living: Collective identity in an urban ecovillage', *Organization and Environment* 23(1), pp. 32–54.
Escribano, P., Lubbers, M.J. and Molina, J.L. (2020) 'A typology of ecological intentional communities: Environmental sustainability through subsistence and material reproduction', *Journal of Cleaner Production* 266(September), 121803, pp. 1–14.
Farber, D. (2013) 'Building the counterculture, creating right livelihoods: The counterculture at work', *The Sixties* 6(1), pp. 1–24.
Gibson-Graham, J.K. (2006) *The End Of Capitalism (As We Knew It): A Feminist Critique of Political Economy*. Minneapolis, MN: University of Minnesota Press.
Grigsby, M. (2004) *Buying Time and Getting By: The Voluntary Simplicity Movement*. Albany, NY: State University of New York Press.
Hagbert, P. (2020) 'Co-housing as a socio-ecologically sustainable alternative?', in Hagbert, P., Larsen, H.G., Thörn, H. and Wasshede, C. (eds.) *Contemporary Co-Housing in Europe: Towards Sustainable Cities?* New York: Routledge, pp. 183–201.

Halfacree, K. (2006) 'From dropping out to leading on? British counter-cultural back-to-the-land in a changing rurality', *Progress in Human Geography* 30(3), pp. 309–36.

Hayden, A. (2014) 'Stopping heathrow airport expansion (For Now): Lessons from a victory for the politics of sufficiency', *Journal of Environmental Policy and Planning* 16(4), pp. 539–58.

Jarvis, H. (2017) 'Sharing, togetherness and intentional degrowth', *Progress in Human Geography* 43(2), pp. 256–75.

Jennings, P. (2020) *Trying to Make a Living on an Organic Smallholding: Paul Jennings, 'One-Planet' Smallholder*. Available at: https://www.lowimpact.org/make-a-living-on-an-organic-smallholding-paul-jennings-part-2/. Accessed 12 August 2022.

Kirby, A. (2003) 'Redefining social and environmental relations at the ecovillage at Ithaca: A case study', *Journal of Environmental Psychology* 23(3), pp. 323–32.

Mangold, S. and Zschau, T. (2019) 'In search of the "good life": The appeal of the tiny house lifestyle in the USA', *Social Sciences* 8(1), p. 26.

McCament, K. and Durrett, C. (2011) *Creating Cohousing: Building Sustainable Communities*. Gabriola Island: New Society Publishers.

McCamant, K. and Durrett, C. (2012) *Creating Cohousing: Building Sustainable Communities*. British Columbia, BC: New Society Publishers.

Mincyte, D. and Dobernig, K. (2016) 'Urban farming in the North American metropolis: Rethinking work and distance in alternative food networks', *Environment and Planning A* 48(9), pp. 1767–86.

Mulder, K., Costanza, R. and Erickson, J. (2006) 'The contribution of built, human, social and natural capital to quality of life in intentional and unintentional communities', *Ecological Economics* 59(1), pp. 13–23.

Nelson, A. (2018) *Small is Necessary: Shared Living on a Shared Planet*. London: Pluto Press.

Nelson, A. and Timmerman, F. (2011) *Life without Money: Building Fair and Sustainable Economies*. London: Pluto Press.

Odih, P. (2007) *Gender and Work in Capitalist Economies*. Maidenhead: McGraw-Hill Education.

|Office for National Statistics (2022) 'Family spending in the UK: April 2020 to March 2021', Available at: https://www.ons.gov.uk/peoplepopulationandcommunity/personalandhouseholdfinances/expenditure/bulletins/familyspendingintheuk/april2020tomarch2021. Accessed 14 June 2023.

Pepper, D. (1993) *Eco-Socialism from Deep Ecology to Social Justice*. London: Routledge.

Reisch, L.A. (2001) 'Time and Wealth', *Time and Society* 10(2–3), pp. 367–85.

Rigby, A. (1974) *Alternative Realities: A study of communes and their members*. London: Routledge.

Sanguinetti, A. (2014) 'Transformational practices in cohousing: Enhancing residents' connection to community and nature', *Journal of Environmental Psychology* 40(December), pp. 86–96.

Sargisson, L. (2012) *Fool's gold?: utopianism in the 21st century*. 1st ed. 2012. Basingstoke: Palgrave Macmillan.

Seymore, J. (1976) *The Complete Book of Self Sufficiency*. London: Corgi.

Shippen, N. (2014) *Decolonizing Time Work, Leisure, and Freedom First*. New York, NY: Palgrave Macmillan.

Tucker, C.A. (2018) 'Food practices of environmentally conscientious New Zealanders', *Environmental Sociology* 5(1), pp. 82–92.

Twin Oaks (2001) *Labour Policy*. Available at: https://www.twinoaks.org/policies/labor-policy?showall=1. Accessed 14 August 2022.

Wang, J., Pan, Y. and Hadjri, K. (2021) 'Social sustainability and supportive living: exploring motivations of British cohousing groups', *Housing and Society* 48(1), pp. 60–86.

Weeks, K. (2011) *The Problem with Work: Feminism, Marxism, Antiwork Politics and Postwork Imaginaries*. Chapel Hill, NC: Duke University Press.

Welsh Assembly Government (2009) *One Wales, One Planet: The sustainable development scheme of the Welsh assembly government*. Available at https://www.bridgend.gov.uk/media/1505/wd32.pdf. Accessed 12 September 2022.

West, C., Lazar, M. and Kramarae, C. (1997) 'Gender in Discourse', in van Dijk, T. (ed.) *Discourse: A Multidisciplinary Introduction*. London: Sage, pp. 119–42.

Williams, J. (2016) 'A measure whose time has come: Formalizing time poverty', *Social Indicators Research* 128(1), pp. 265–84.

18

Workshops and liberation in Freetown Christiania: Tensions in a post-growth community economy

Thomas S. J. Smith and Nadia Johanisova

Introduction

Eco-communities envision and enact practices which make a double movement: away from the ecologically destructive tendencies demonstrated by contemporary societies, and towards shared, participatory alternatives which are socially and environmentally non-exploitative. In spite of this statement, Freetown Christiania has a complex relationship with environmental sustainability, lacking many of the common understandings of that concept which underlie pro-environmental collective action (Verco 2018; Winter 2016). It also consistently deviates from many of the usual tropes or imaginaries of an eco-community, given its location in the heart of a major capital city and the absence of community-based food production. Much of Christiania's soil is contaminated after its prior use by the state as a weapons store and military testing site and is not seen by residents as safe for producing many crops. Nonetheless, this chapter explores community economic practices in Christiania, particularly focusing on tendencies towards economic democracy and solidarity economics. It argues that Christiania presents patterns for a post-growth community economy, tending away from the most destructive tendencies of capitalism. It also outlines, however, the acute challenges posed by recent developments. By doing so, we hope it contributes to a more granular, empirical understanding of the challenges and possibilities faced when building diverse and community economies.

Christiania emerged in 1971 out of a tumultuous period of housing shortages and social unrest in Copenhagen (Thörn et al., 2011). During this early 'pioneer' period, a group squatted a 32-hectare former naval base in Christianshavn, in the very heart of Copenhagen (see Figure 1), inviting others to join them and create a non-capitalist, self-ruled society in which decisions would be made by consensus and where property ownership would not exist.

Today, Christiania is home to around 1,000 people, who live in fourteen autonomous and self-administering areas. During the intervening decades, the community has developed something of a parallel society: it has its own postal service, recycling and refuse service, gardening and woodland maintenance teams, building

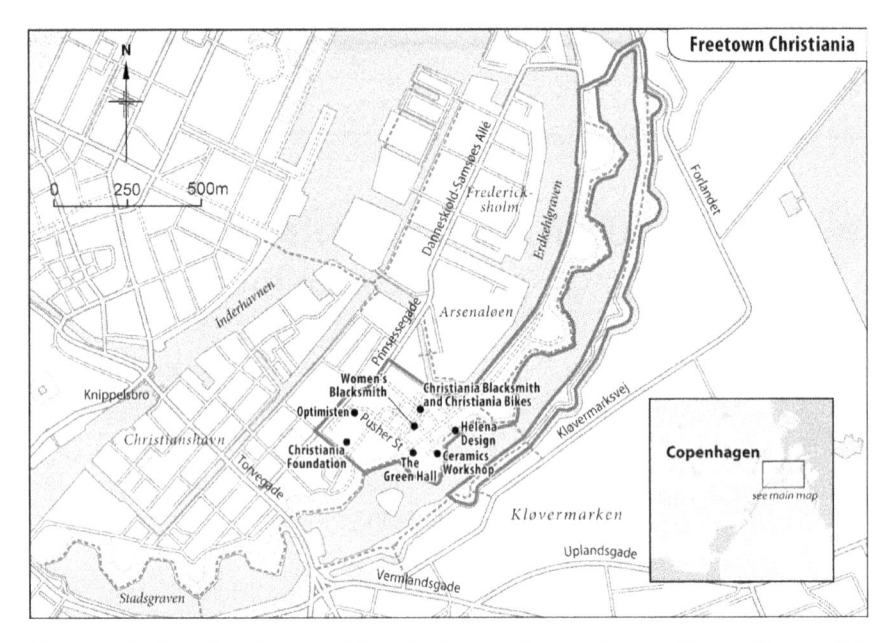

Figure 1 Outline of the Freetown's location in central Copenhagen. (Source: Thomas S. J. Smith.)

maintenance crew, bathhouse and sauna, two television stations, a community archive, and many other institutions and collective organizations. Each of the fourteen areas – distinguished through imaginative names, such as The Blue Caramel or Dandelion – meets once a month to deliberate on affairs affecting them, while a larger monthly general assembly decides on important matters pertaining to Christiania as a whole.

While the organization of daily life in Christiania takes place substantially through informal relations and volunteering (not least participating in meetings which can run long into the night), it also employs around thirty full- or part-time 'civil servants', mainly drawn from amongst its residents. All civil servants earn roughly the same, apart from the refuse collectors, who earn a little more. This, in many ways, is an inversion of the wage inequalities in capitalist societies. The community's external and internal financial obligations are paid for through individual resident contributions (making up around 70 per cent of the total Christiania budget). These contributions are now calculated according to square metres of living space, rather than a flat per capita fee. Business contributions (making up the remaining 30 per cent) are taken from the incomes of the ninety initiatives or commercial enterprises currently in operation, calculated and agreed on a case-by-case basis. In total, money received from such contributions has increased enormously, standing at about €5 million in 2019. This is more than double the amount from 2004, and four times what it was in 1996.

After more than forty years as an illegal squat, a major development occurred in 2012 when Christiania's residents came to an agreement with the state. Following protracted and tense discussions, the Christianites created a legal structure which would buy the majority of the land from the Danish government (Coppola and Vanolo 2015), a controversial decision given the fundamental hesitancy of Christianites to own land – even in a collective manner. While the fee was lower than market price, it involved raising millions of euros through the sale of symbolic shares, topped up with bank loans.

Democratic economic diversity: Christiania and *Foreningen*

Christiania is a jungle of micro-enterprises, a milder microcosm of Denmark's economy with its predominance of small and medium-sized firms, but the businesses here are run by the workers, who believe in the quality of their products, and show a genuine concern for the wellbeing of their customers.

(from the novel *Hans Christiania*)

This chapter draws from a study undertaken in Freetown Christiania in 2019, which aimed to sketch its journey from a DIY community that met many of its key needs through endogenous workshop enterprises, to the rapidly evolving economic structures to be found there today. The lead author stayed at Christiania for four weeks in March 2019, as part of the Christiania Researcher-in-Residence (CRIR) scheme, which allows artists, researchers and others to participate in the daily life of the community.

While Christiania is often imagined or framed as a radical anti-capitalist or 'alternative' space (Jonas 2016), a closer examination reveals a much more complex, intricate and pragmatic picture. Due to this complexity, a key concept underlying what follows will be that of the 'diverse economy' – a reimagining of the economy as a web of more-than-capitalist economic practices, developed by the feminist economic geographer J.K. Gibson-Graham (1996). In their work over recent decades, Gibson-Graham dislodge the tendency to fix all economic thought in relation to a system called capitalism, a tendency which would later be captured by Mark Fisher (2009) in the term 'capitalist realism'. Instead, they take a 'weak theory' approach, – remaining open to the context-specific relations which comprise an economy and which enable social reproduction, including a variety of forms of non-capitalist activity (care work, voluntary work, DIY, self-employment, barter, gifts, etc.). While Christiania has a reputation as a place run completely along the lines of anti-capitalist consensus democracy, today's enterprises are a diverse combination of worker's co-operative, informal collective, social enterprise, self-employment and hybrid forms which may defy these categorizations.

We will use a number of interrelated but distinct terms to discuss Christiania's diverse economic forms: '*Diverse economy*' is a broad category referring to the many economic forms which exist, including and beyond capitalist enterprise. This includes what we may view as good and wholesome (e.g. cooperative and social enterprise, gift relations) but also feudal, slave, black market and other modes of economy. '*Community economy*' is a more normative term, referring to those economic forms deemed to foster community and contribute to social and ecological wellbeing (Smith and Dombroski 2021). '*Economic democracy*' refers to initiatives or enterprises which take decisions out of the hands of individual capitalists or shareholders, and distribute decision-making to other stakeholders, such as workers (in a worker coop) or communities. The '*solidarity economy*' (or social solidarity economy (SSE) as it is often termed) is a broad and increasingly popular term for heterodox economic initiatives which 'foster relationships of mutual support ... shared responsibility and directly democratic decision-making' (Miller 2010, 25). SSE is often used to include credit unions, gift exchange-based groups (e.g. food sharing), fair trade networks, participatory budgeting and much besides.

Using these concepts, the chapter argues against a tendency to view Christiania as a state of exception, as a community which, due to its critical perspective on life on the 'outside', is opposed to external Danish society. The place has never been a closed enclave, but is rather more of a porous and open experiment (Coppola and Vanolo 2015). Examples attesting to this porosity abound: As has been noted elsewhere, many within Christiania have been proud of consistently meeting their external financial obligations to the state since an initial agreement to pay for water and electricity was made in 1973. A large number of people (estimated at 200 by one interviewee) come from Copenhagen to work in Christiania every day, while many Christianites travel the other way too. Christiania's older children go to school in Christianshavn, outside the community's borders, and Christianshavn's municipal recycling centre (Genbrugsstationen) is located within Christiania.

At a broader cultural level, the organizational style of Christiania draws from a strong culturally embedded tradition of 'unions' (*foreningen*) in Denmark – a term which means something akin to association, collective or society. Providing a sketch of early co-operative organizing in Scandinavia, Bernhard (1951, 633–4) noted:

> The co-operatives in Denmark have caused a peaceful social, economic, and political revolution of tremendous and far-reaching significance. They have aided in the creation of an "extra-socialistic" economy which is designed to aid the Danish people in meeting the challenges of modern society. Co-operation in Denmark is not a detached thing, as is characteristic in England or the United States, but it is very strongly ingrained in the very life of the people. The economic structure of the nation has been altered; capitalism has been weakened, but the edge of the Marxian sword has also been greatly dulled.

In the first decades of the twentieth century, as Chloupkova et al. (2003, 243) note, 'wholly voluntarily established cooperatives finally became *the* way of organizing all common practical matters among the Danish rural population'. This cooperative ethos would go on to permeate Danish society – rural and urban – with a well-known phrase noting that 'When two Danes meet, they shake hands. When three Danes meet, they form an association'.

Organizational vignettes from the field

In order to give more insight into this, we will now present findings drawn from interviews and desk research on six Christiania enterprises with a close connection to the community's autonomous DIY and workshop culture. These are purposefully selected for diversity – ranging from workers' cooperatives to self-employment – and we focus on the aspects of them which relate to the questions of workshop economies and economic democracy. Some of these organizations are well-known, with many media accounts available (Christiania Bikes and the Women's Blacksmith, for instance) while there is no evidence of any English-language writing on some of the others (e.g. Optimisten).

I The Ceramics Workshop (Keramik værksted): Artists' collective

While Christiania has been home to a ceramics workshop since the 1970s, the workshop building – located in Christiania's 'factory district' – had fallen into disrepair by 2015. The space itself was underutilized, and the building was mouldy, damp and in need of renovation. A non-Christianite was invited in to lead the rejuvenation of the space. Windows, floors, doors, heating and insulation all had to be replaced.

It reopened in 2016, with all of the work having been undertaken by the artists themselves, working in their own time, around their work schedules. Demonstrating some of the flexibility of being a commercial initiative in Christiania, for half a year, during the renovation process, the workshop didn't pay any contributions to Christiania. A loan was acquired from the Christiania community to fund acquisition of the new kiln, with further funding provided from the Christiania foundation for the replacement of windows.

Today, the ceramics workshop is fully utilized, providing a shared studio space for seven artists to work in, each with their own work bench and storage area. Consciously reflecting Christiania's non-hierarchical decision-making structures, the workshop occupants meet once a month to administer the space. Each of the seven artists – some of whom are residents, while others come in from outside Christiania to use the space – pays the same amount, plus each pays for use of the kiln separately, due to the expense of electricity.

II The Christiania Blacksmith (Christiania Smedien) and Christiania Bikes (Christianiacykler): Social enterprise

Christiania's Blacksmith – which originally made stoves, stovepipes, guttering, bikes, candlesticks and other metalwork for Christiania residents – was founded in 1978 by four friends, in a former munitions building in the heart of Christiania. The blacksmith also began to produce trailers from recycled bed frames for transporting fuel, building materials and children around the car-free site.

It was in this environment that Lars designed what would become the famed Christiania cargo bike. Originally built as a birthday present for his girlfriend, in 1984, the box bike design came to be in high demand and, as of 1990, was produced in a new factory on the outskirts of Copenhagen and sold worldwide. One estimate suggests that a third of cargo bikes in Copenhagen are Christiania bikes (Williams 2011).

Today, the space is no longer used for blacksmithing, but instead has transitioned into being the home of the social enterprise, *Christiania Bikes* (see Figure 2). This company is the result of a merger of the former blacksmith workshop and a

Figure 2 The entrance to Christiania Bikes/Smedien. (Source: Thomas S. J. Smith.)

neighbouring bike shop, in 2016. While the Christiania bike is now produced outside of Christiania, Smedien is a popular licensed seller, assembling new box bikes in their original home, while the neighbouring bike shop focuses on their maintenance. The company has also recently launched a leasing service, removing the need for personal ownership of the bikes.

Similar to Christiania' ban on housing speculation, it is not possible to profit from selling a business here, with each business operating under the discretion of the local area, according to an occupancy agreement. As Christiania property belongs to everyone and no-one, it is only possible to transition businesses from one owner to another, with the requisite recompense for any stock or materials held. After negotiations about ownership structures, in what became a five-year takeover process, Christiania Bikes is now run by two co-owners, who employ around ten others in bike assembly and maintenance. As with the Women's blacksmith (described below), the workshop is further evidence of Christiania's connections with the outside world. Christiania Bikes is involved with municipal programmes where individuals who have been unemployed long-term can train at the enterprise for a period of months, often resulting in employment at the end of the time period.

As a social enterprise, Christiania Bikes also has an associated foundation which administers 1 per cent of total revenue to benefit the wider Christiania community, as well as international charitable partners. Revenue was chosen over profit, building in guaranteed returns to Christiania. While the co-owners don't pretend that their twelve-person organization is run along consensus democratic lines, they contend that working conditions are perhaps better there than elsewhere in Christiania, given they're the only place in Christiania which is unionized according to the recognized criteria of the Union of Metalworkers in Denmark (Dansk Metal). The latter comes with minimum salary requirements and other benefits, but also ensures workers' representatives have a say in how the business is run. Worker representation is also included on the foundation board.

III Women's Blacksmith (Kvindesmedien): Collective metal workshop

Located in the Milky Way area, this woman-owned and -operated blacksmith is found in a large industrial space which had been gradually vacated during the 1990s, when the production of Christiania Bikes moved outside of Christiania. At the same time, the demand for oil-drum stoves and other household items was reducing. Charlotte – my interviewee and one of the three founding partners (along with Dorte and Gitte) – began working in the Blacksmith (Vignette II) in 1995, initially sharing with the men, before the women struck out on their own in 1997. Wasshede (2011, 196) notes that 'besides its function as a workshop and apprentice place for female smiths, [it] was a kind of feminist community'.

The idea of a women's workshop was quite novel, not least for the gender stereotypes it subverts, and the enterprise has gained substantial media attention. This has aided its growth, and it currently employs around ten people, including two men. The Women's Blacksmith has a shop which is regularly open to the public, although much of their revenue comes from commissions for sculptures, furniture, chandeliers, awards and other bespoke items. Since around 2009, they have been training (usually female) blacksmith apprentices through work placements, giving those who come to study experience in more bespoke and non-mechanized production than they may get elsewhere.

IV The Green Hall – Workers' Cooperative

The Green Hall, a large and cavernous former military riding house (see Figure 3), has long served a purpose as a clearing house for salvaged and second-hand building materials within Christiania. Today, it also houses a broad-spectrum hardware, homeware and garden shop. The Green Hall is a key supplier of the wood pellets which nowadays heat many of Christiania's buildings – in the form of district heating systems – and the gas bottles which are widely used for cooking within the community.

The enterprise is a registered workers' cooperative, run by its seven worker-owners. The majority of these are residents of Christiania, with two coming from outside. The workers meet over breakfast every Monday morning at 8.30 am to discuss the business of the week, arranging what needs to be done, by whom and when. The work shared out includes everything from staffing the checkout, to public relations, including placing submissions about the Green Hall in the Christiania weekly newspaper – the community's key internal communications source. The Green Hall runs a delivery service, to get fuel and other necessities to Christiania's residents. This is done in the form of a small electric delivery vehicle, to accord with the community's no-car ethos.

The organization operates a foundation which distributes revenue to community and solidarity initiatives. This has funded a wide range of initiatives, including building projects in Africa, the arts and local theatres, and funding the stays of doctors in countries of the Global South. This type of solidarity income distribution also happens

Figure 3 The Green Hall. (Source: Thomas S. J. Smith.)

in-kind, more locally, with the donation of materials for certain community building projects (including, for example, Christiania's popular indoor skate park).

V Helena Design: Self-employed Jeweller

Helena has lived in Christiania for thirty-three years. Her jewellery business has been running for about thirty of those, starting as more of a hobby, when she began to occasionally attend markets in Christiania and around Copenhagen. Her current house, where she has lived for the last ten years, is where her showroom/shop is located. She completely renovated the house to strict eco-standards and decided she needed a space in which to meet customers, blurring public with private. This lake-view conservatory space has evolved into a more permanent shop, signed from Christiania's main thoroughfare, reflecting the growing flow of visitors and tourists through Christiania, and the requisite growing dependence on external resource flows.

Helena initially brought her idea for a shop to her local area meeting, which approved of it on a trial basis. After a few months, they agreed on the amount that she should pay to the area every month. This contribution has risen every year, in accordance with her revenue. Displaying a lack of growth-orientation, Helena spoke about working just to 'pay her bills' so that she can use her time for things she values, primarily activism and 'community service' work in Christiania. To this end, she keeps costs down by, for example, skip diving for food. As such, she focuses on the business at the weekends, when the number of visitors and tourists is higher, using much of the rest of the week to help out around Christiania. This community work, which includes helping to organize action weekends and clean-ups around the site, is voluntary, but can include symbolic payment.

VI Optimisten (Snedkeriet Optimisten): Collective workshop/self-employment hybrid

Optimisten is a joinery/carpentry workshop (see Figure 4), founded in 1979, which holds a prominent location near the main entrance of Christiania. Kim, who is in charge of running the workshop, arrived to Christiania in 1978, age nineteen. He lives in the same house that he moved into then – a collective house with separate living spaces for multiple families, but a shared kitchen – and it was the skills obtained during the renovation of that building which started the learning process, leading to his later involvement at Optimisten in 1987.

When Kim arrived, the workshop's main focus was on taking waste beams from old houses being renovated during the city's redevelopment and housing projects, and repurposing them into tables and furniture. The latter were then sold both within and outside of Christiania, and took the form of a work integration project for young people, funded by the Danish Ministry of Education. Taking money from the state was a controversial development, however. 'It was the first example in Christiania of cooperation with the state', recounts Kim, 'So, for twenty years, [others in] Christiania thought "Optimisten, they're not good guys, they got money from the state!"' Indicating how quickly Christiania is changing on that front, he continues, 'Optimisten was ahead of its time. Now there's cooperation with everything'.

Figure 4 Optimisten's main workshop space. (Source: Thomas S. J. Smith.)

Originally the workshop was informally organized, mostly meeting domestic needs within Christiania, with interested members meeting on the first Monday of the month to decide who would make what. 'There were maybe 20 or 30 people but only very few made money off it.'

Kim complains of disorganization amongst early members and, showing some of the tensions which can arise, says he focused on building up and professionalizing the workshop. 'There were always problems about people paying. And there were always problems that they liked to drink a lot of beer and smoke lots of hash. I was the only one who said "no, no beer, no hash, you can do that after you work."'

The source of work has shifted: the workshop has professionalized and thus its products have become more expensive, and simultaneously Christiania has become less self-reliant in furniture and other everyday goods. 'Some customers are from Christiania, but they're mostly from Copenhagen or north of Copenhagen. That's where the nice old houses are', Kim notes, referring to the bespoke woodwork Optimisten supplies for house renovations.

He is the main coordinator, and the only one with a fixed salary. While some community members also pay per hour to use the workshop on an ad hoc basis, more informal arrangements are also evident. This includes a retired Christianite, for example, who helps out in-kind (cleaning around the outside of the workshop, for example), in order to have access to workshop machines for prototyping his own products.

Confronting normalization and mission drift

We are not socialists, we are not anarchists, we are not communists, and we are not capitalists. What are we? We don't define it and that is good. The undefined community is a definition in itself

(Tata, Christiania resident)

The previous vignettes, along with the quote above, demonstrate what appears to be both a great strength and a great weakness of the Freetown – its pragmatic, evolving collectivity. The community's consensus approach, for instance, has enabled inclusive decision-making, encouraged dialogue, reduced polarization and, as the community moves forward, resulted in taking multiple perspectives on board at all times. This has played an important role, for instance, in maintaining the community's integrity in the face of five decades of the state's divide-and-conquer tactics. However, while it can facilitate common understanding, such openness also appears to result in a community which can lack direction or vision, resulting in mission drift or blunting its formerly radical edge.

On the one hand, not much has fundamentally changed in Christiania's economy, even since the long battle with the state was brought to a close 2012. Private ownership of property is still forbidden, removing it from the damaging speculative dynamics which have pushed up property prices and driven gentrification throughout Copenhagen and many other large European cities. Community enterprises still take part in the enterprise meeting on the last Tuesday of each month, where they meet to discuss affairs including their mutual obligations to Christiania, how they can aid struggling businesses, and other issues which might arise. Residents conduct an annual participatory budgeting process, the results of which are published transparently in the community newspaper, distributed freely throughout the local areas. Economic democracy remains deeply grounded, furthermore, not just in the internal running of its enterprises (which, as the vignettes above show, varies significantly in scope), but in each of the fourteen autonomous areas which, ultimately, have the final say over which businesses get to operate in their back yard. This is a level of community-based democratic oversight unheard of in capitalist market economies.

However, Christiania *is* changing, and there is a vocal segment of the community which thinks that, through compromise after compromise, it is losing much of what made life there special. If true, then this appears to be the result of unconscious, creeping and systemic processes. Initially well-intended decisions bring hierarchical dynamics and unforeseen consequences, which in turn bring other hierarchies and unforeseen consequences. Agreement with the state in 2012, for instance, brought the need for lawyers, a new legal foundation to 'represent' the community, harmonization with Danish state regulations and bank loans. These developments have necessitated a more professionalized administrative structure, while bank loans have meant higher financial commitments for all residents and businesses. Such commitments and new hierarchies in turn create subtle new dynamics in everyday life. This includes the normalization of interactions with state funding, but also pressures to work more and search for employment outside of Christiania. Charlotte from the Women's Blacksmith reflected on this latter point:

> This is Christiania … we have so many relationships, and we have been building up this town together and we have been doing lots of projects together, you know? But Christiania has also changed. Many years ago when I moved to Christiania, if you were not working here then you moved [out]. It was like if you live in Christiania, you're also working here, it was an idea from the start … [Regarding increasing living costs] Most people who came to Christiania didn't come here to work. They came to be part of a community. If you work and work and work, you don't have much time for the community. It's hard to keep that balance.

In its pioneer phase, Christiania's businesses were cut off from normal markets and forms of credit, with banks unwilling to loan to businesses operating in such a risky environment. Because of this, initiatives remained small and informal: they operated in the black market, and people had to be resilient, scavenging or gleaning materials from wider society, while coming up with their own (shared) capital to invest. Due to external pressures, all of Christiania's workshops and businesses have now formalized, registered and pay tax.

The flexibility and case-by-case nature of contributions from businesses to Christiania's economy have led to 'functional diversity' (Coppola and Vanolo 2015, 1160), whereby businesses which are socially important or respected, but which can't afford to pay a huge amount, are treated leniently. Businesses will often co-operate and step in to pick up slack from others, when necessary. This form of cooperation contrasts with a purely profit-driven approach, but has come with its own down sides. One key drawback repeatedly raised by interviewees was a certain stasis or inertia, caused by the lack of incentives to pass on or close a business, thus freeing up commercial space for others to use within the community:

> [T]he system where you can't sell your business has some positive effects in terms of people not speculating too much in their businesses and it's not an unleashed sort of capitalism. But there's one side of it which is an impediment to growth in Christiania – [growth] of a social and cultural kind – which is that the people who've run their businesses, at least until now, have rarely had enough surplus to build up a pension. When you can't build a pension, you can't let go of your business ... And you have a lot of both the businesses and cultural spaces in Christiania, which sort of just wither away because people hold onto them.

Many of these 'withering' businesses take up large or prominent commercial spaces, but simply need to generate a minimal income. As such, their operation has tended towards being a hobby, rather than serving as crucial and vibrant fulcra of a community economy.

Conclusion

We have elsewhere described Christiania as a 'nowtopia' (Smith 2020), by which is meant a strategic activity involving escape from classical capitalist waged labour, to create real alternatives in the here and now (Carlsson and Manning 2010). Certainly, there have been failures, and a creep towards conformity with the outside world, which increasingly question that status. However, Christiania never claimed final utopian status, merely being one ongoing pragmatic experiment in non-hierarchical organizing.

There appear to have been certain creeping processes unleashed, which are proving difficult to contain. Once ownership of the site was formalized – albeit belonging to everyone and no-one at the same time – the need to fall into line with other regulations has seemed inevitable. The underlying ethos of freedom within collectivity may be slipping away, as financial obligations rise and bureaucracies contribute a form of democratic deficit.

That withstanding, the Freetown provides inspiring examples of what Johanisova and Wolf (2012, 563) describe as 'deep' economic democracy, transcending the understanding of the latter term as just intra-firm worker control. There is an argument to be made that Christiania is a particularly crucial case because it provides a complex picture of broad-based economic democracy in an eco-community – between residents, local area democracy, commercial initiatives, a foundation and the state – whereas much of the literature to date on 'nowtopias' or 'real utopias' remains on the level of studying isolated individual initiatives or enterprises (the Mondragon co-operative, radical squats, participatory budgeting, etc.) (see Riley 2020). Our hope, furthermore, is that the chapter shows the value for researchers of close examination of the (often complex) economic dynamics of eco-communities, rather than assuming any easy designation as post-capitalist or post-growth.

Christiania is more than the sum of its parts. This chapter drew inspiration from a diverse economy perspective, 'a project of rethinking economy, opening to and being practically affected by the wide diversity of economic activities that offer possibilities of livelihood and well-being, within and beyond the ostensibly global purview of capitalist development' (Gibson-Graham and Roelvink 2010, 323). With this in mind, the organizational vignettes help to understand how Christiania re-embeds the economy in a social-ecological web, providing many lessons regarding how this has worked (or not). What the resulting practices contribute to is a slow form of economic democracy, an economy that doesn't prioritize accumulation and growth, but connections, commoning and 'the possibilities of meaningful social connection and interaction' (Jarvis 2019, 270).

References

Bernhard, J.T. (1951) 'Empirical collectivism in Denmark', *The Journal of Politics* 13(4), pp. 623–46. DOI: 10.2307/2126319.

Carlsson, C. and Manning, F. (2010) 'Nowtopia: Strategic exodus?', *Antipode* 42(4), pp. 924–953. DOI: 10.1111/j.1467-8330.2010.00782.x.

Chloupkova, J., Svendsen, G.L.H. and Svendsen, G.T. (2003) 'Building and destroying social capital: The case of cooperative movements in Denmark and Poland', *Agriculture and Human Values* 20(3), pp. 241–52. DOI: 10.1023/A:1026141807305.

Coppola, A. and Vanolo, A. (2015) 'Normalising autonomous spaces: Ongoing transformations in Christiania, Copenhagen', *Urban Studies* 52(6), pp. 1152–68. DOI: 10.1177/0042098014532852.

Fisher, M. (2009) *Capitalist Realism: Is There No Alternative?* Winchester: Zero Books.

Gibson-Graham, J.K. (1996) *The End of Capitalism (as We Knew It): A Feminist Critique of Political Economy*. Oxford: Blackwell.

Gibson-Graham, J.K. and Roelvink, G. (2010) 'An economic ethics for the Anthropocene', *Antipode* 41(s1), pp. 320–46.

Gibson-Graham, J.K., Cameron, J. and Healy, S. (2016) 'Pursuing happiness: The politics of surviving well together', in Pike, D., Nelson, C. and Ledvinka, G. (eds.) *Essays on Happiness*. Perth: University of Western Australia Press, pp. 116–31.

Jarvis, H. (2019) 'Sharing, togetherness and intentional degrowth', *Progress in Human Geography* 43(2), pp. 256–75. DOI: 10.1177/0309132517746519.

Johanisova, N. and Wolf, S. (2012) 'Economic democracy: A path for the future?', *Futures* 44(6), pp. 562–70. DOI: 10.1016/j.futures.2012.03.017.

Jonas, A.E. (2016) '"Alternative" this, "Alternative" that … : interrogating alterity and diversity', in Fuller, D. (ed.) *Interrogating Alterity: Alternative Economic and Political Spaces*. Abingdon; New York: Routledge, pp. 43–68.

Miller, E. (2010) 'Solidarity economy: Key concepts and issues', in Kawano, E., Masterson, T.N. and Teller-Elsberg, J. (eds.) *Solidarity Economy I: Building Alternatives for People and Planet*. Amherst, MA: Center for Popular Economics, pp. 25–41.

Pickerill, J. (2016) 'Building the commons in eco-communities', in Kirwan, S., Dawney, L. and Brigstocke, J. (eds.) *Space, Power and the Commons*. London: Routledge, pp. 31–54.

Riley, D. (2020) 'Real utopia or abstract empiricism?', *New Left Review* 121(January/February). Available at: https://newleftreview.org/issues/II121/articles/dylan-riley-real-utopia-or-abstract-empiricism.

Smith, T.S.J. (2020) 'Freetown Christiania: An economic "nowtopia" at the heart of a European capital city', *openDemocracy*, 1 July. Available at: https://www.opendemocracy.net/en/oureconomy/freetown-christiania-economic-nowtopia-heart-european-capital-city/. Accessed 23 February 2020.

Smith, T.S.J. and Dombroski, K. (2021) 'Practicing wellbeing through community economies: An action research approach', in Searle, B.A., Pykett, J. and Alfaro Simmonds, M.J. (eds.) *A Modern Guide to Wellbeing Research*. Cheltenham: Edward Elgar Publishing, pp. 84–102.

Thörn, H., Wasshede, C. and Nilson, T. (2011) *Space for Urban Alternatives? Christiania 1971-2011*. Gidlunds Förlag. Available at: https://gupea.ub.gu.se/handle/2077/26558. Accessed 4 December 2018.

Vanolo, A. (2012) 'Alternative capitalism and creative economy: The case of Christiania', *International Journal of Urban and Regional Research* 37(5), pp. 1785–98. DOI: 10.1111/j.1468-2427.2012.01167.x.

Verco, N. (2018) 'Christiania: A poster child for degrowth?', in Nelson, A. and Schneider, F. (eds.) *Housing for Degrowth: Principles, Models, Challenges and Opportunities*. London: Routledge.

Wasshede, C. (2011) 'Bøssehuset: Queer perspectives in Christiania', in Thörn, H., Wasshede, C. and Nilson, T. (eds.) *Space for Urban Alternatives? Christiania 1971-2011*. Möklinta: Gidlunds Förlag, pp. 181–204.

Williams, F. (2011) 'A strange and not unpleasant experience', in Flax, P. (ed.) *The Best of Bicycling: The Very Best Stories from the First 50 Years of Bicycling Magazine*. Emmaus, PA: Rodale, pp. 71–7.

Winter, A.K. (2016) '"Environmental sustainability? We don't have that here": Freetown Christiania as an unintentional eco-village', *ACME: An International Journal for Critical Geographies* 15(1), pp. 129–49.

19

Community economies in eco-communities: Spaces of collaboration, opportunities and dilemmas

Jan Malý Blažek

Introduction

While there is evidence of concrete environmental outcomes from eco-communities and anthropological research has informed on the cultural or governance aspects of living together, relatively little research has focused on eco-communities from an economic perspective, including their economic and financial sustainability, impact on local economies and the conceptualization of different economic, organizational and co-production models and their replicable potential. In this chapter, I argue that in order to understand their potential in terms of transformation/resilience, there needs to be also a more robust elaboration of how their social and environmental goals and outcomes relate to their economies. This requires both a theoretical framework and more empirical evidence.

The research gap may be due to the diverse objectives of eco-communities, whether environmental, political, spiritual or housing (see Wagner 2012 for review). However, some stimulating studies have been conducted. Nelson (2018) or Litfin (2014) visited many global ecovillages/eco-collaborative housing projects and informed about various aspects including the economy. Cattaneo and Gavaldà (2010) investigated how two urban squats in Catalonia performed in terms of time and energy consumption, arguing that it is possible to live well in less energy-intensive economies. A study comparing intentional and unintentional communities by Mulder et al. (2006) provides an understanding of the contribution of built, human, social and natural capital to quality of life, with the results indicating that intentional communities, according to the authors, can better balance the different capitals (e.g. by substituting built capital with social capital) and therefore manage to achieve a good quality of life despite having significantly less financial means than households in unintentional communities. In their Catalan study, Escribano et al. (2020) looked at three material factors – the legal situation, the cohabitation form and the economic orientation – to demonstrate the different economic perspectives of eco-communities. And in their mixed-methods study of an Australian ecovillage, Milani Price et al. (2020) explored the relationship with the market economy, arguing that a community's alternative economic practices rely to some extent on the market economy and that market economy strategies and diverse economy practices are increasingly converging.

There are several reasons why eco-communities are important to study economically. First of all, they are residential and usually formed in a well-defined and more permanent physical location where members live, manage common infrastructure and develop their livelihoods. Second, eco-communities are linked to the dwelling not only physically but also through the financial means. They (re)create the built environment of apartment blocks, former schools, restored farmhouses with hectares of land or abandoned factories – environments that are usually the domain of neoliberal investment (whether in the hands of the state or corporations), often ending up demolished and rebuilt with profit-maximizing motives. Third, the scope of economic activities is broad and covers, depending on the size of a project practices of, sharing, care, social and solidarity activities, non-monetary transactions and relations, income-generating activities and self-sufficiency (Blažek 2016). In fact, many now-popular practices of community-based and sharing economies as defined by Acquier et al. (2017) have been pioneered in eco-communities.

In this chapter, I aim to contribute to the debate on eco-community economies, building on the frameworks of *diverse economy* and the *community economy* of Gibson-Graham et al. (2013) to conceptually unfold how the economic activities are structured and to consider the community economy as a space of decision-making and economic democracy, where the different economic practices are strategically discussed, negotiated and governed. I offer my experience researching eco-community economies and present examples of inspiring community economies in Europe to show how the theoretical economic promises can be fulfilled and how eco-communities imagine and transform their community economies. In the discussion, I offer some of the lessons learned from the contradictions and dilemmas that arise in the implementation of multidimensional sustainability goals on the 'wide edge of capitalism'.

I have spent the last decade studying the community economies as part of my doctoral thesis of which this chapter originally prepared for this book is part of (Malý Blažek 2024). Primarily, I use evidence from the field research, which took place between 2015 and 2018. I visited more than forty projects in six European countries, including Portugal, Spain (Catalonia), Austria, Germany, Denmark and the UK. I interviewed community members and participated in daily activities. I spent hours, days, weeks and in a few of these locations some months (with total of 184 visit days). The research was designed to study eco-communities in their diversity – from all-sharing communes to cohousing projects, from small farm collectives to ecovillages, from low-impact developments to housing syndicates. It explored projects experimenting how we can, at the community level, create economic alternatives with our own set of rules, which try and tackle our un/sustainability. I am thankful to each of the visited eco-communities.

Economies of eco-communities: Spaces of collaboration

Community diverse economies

Gibson-Graham define the economy as 'a diverse social space in which we have multiple roles' (Gibson-Graham et al., 2013, xx); a *diverse economy* which encompasses economic activities in households, local economies, regional and global economies. It encompasses market and non-market activities and a plethora of alternative ways in between (see Table 1).

Eco-communities are great examples of this economic diversity. But they are also examples of what Gibson-Graham et al. (2013, xix) call the *community economy* – 'a space of decision making where we recognize and negotiate our interdependence with other humans, other species, and our environment'. Healy, Heras and North (Healy et al., 2023, 13) explain the community in community economies – in the words of philosopher Jean-Luc Nancy – as the ability of being in common. The community economy then should allow us to *be in common in economic terms*.

The community economy is the part of the economy that is governed, negotiated and managed at the community level, including people, nature, infrastructures, networks, material and financial flows. Its importance and robustness are intentionally designed and vary considerably from case to case. So, for example in income-sharing communes, the community economy includes virtually all economic activities. In most projects, however, it exists alongside the individual economies of members, which are negotiated at the household level.

In keeping with the positive, experimental narrative typical of many eco-communities, I call community economies *economic playgrounds*. Similar to real playgrounds, they can be understood as infrastructures that enable the creation and play of concrete 'games', i.e. the creation of concrete economic practices and strategies. The *games* (economic activities), played in the playground, vary in size, purpose, rules, impact and in relating to each other. The playground serves each member, work group or community-based enterprise to play these games. It helps to (1) *negotiate* their everyday preferences and activities as well as the long-term vision and mission of the eco-community with other members; (2) *navigate* between eco-community goals – the playground holds, redirects and shifts the social, ecological and economic variables between activities, as some activities serve financial means; others have social or environmental benefits; (3) transform economic flows between the diverse economies

Table 1 The diverse economy

The diverse economy				
Labor	Enterprise	Transactions	Property	Finance
Paid	Capitalist	Market	Private	Mainstream Market
Alternative Paid	Alternative Capitalist	Alternative Market	Alternative Private	Alternative Market
Unpaid	Non-capitalist	Non-market	Open Access	Non-market

Source: Gibson-Graham et al., 2013, 13.

(market – alternative market – non-market) as means of relating in the commons but especially to the other actors.

In the next section, I shortly describe three areas of the playground: collaborative financing, collaborative provision and collaborative production. Then I present concrete examples of economic activities which are performed or even invented in eco-communities.

Financing of housing and the built environment

For the many socio-environmental, political or cultural objectives of eco-communities, this area of community economy has been maybe sometimes forgotten. And as with most individuals and families, the rising costs of land, materials and energy affect and determine the long-term socio-economic situation of residential eco-communities. In fact, the right financial and ownership plan at the outset has a fundamental impact on the economic situation, including the 'capacity' of the community economy to 'hold' and meet the social and environmental objectives.

Nevertheless, eco-communities are looking for solutions. They are together with other collaborative housing projects the early adopters of innovative financial/economic and property/legal frameworks and tools such as direct loans, assets pools, mutual home ownership, solidarity funds or tenant syndicates (CLH London 2020; Holm and Laimer 2021; Hurlin 2019). These schemes and tools allow to actively distribute capital, administer debt and allocate assets from members to the community and vice versa (see Table 2.). Other housing strategies include reduction of bank loans, advocacy with municipalities (e.g. for land rental or-co-production); active

Table 2 Diverse economies in eco-communities

Community economies					
Non-market economies					
Housing decommodification	Self-management and building	Money pooling	Solidarity funds	Income redistribution	Income sharing
Mobility sharing	Food coops	Self-sufficient farming	Homeschooling	Care sharing	Free flow
Alternative market economies					
Asset pools	Direct loans	Community supported agriculture	Alternative currencies	Micro-enterprises	Community enterprises
Public and market economies					
Subsidies	Partnerships	Shopping	Selling	Bills	Bank loans
Individual economies					
Individual household incomes, expenditures and enterprises					

and voluntary participation of members in project management and construction; and the architecture design that focuses on extensive use of common spaces or low-tech ecological solutions.

Collaborative provision of goods and services

While the financing and ownership of common property is usually a serious game with strict rules and legal regulations, it is the collaborative consumption or, rather, collaborative provision that the economic games get fun. Again, it involves the consumption of goods and services produced in all kinds of economies: in the market, in alternative markets and in the community itself. Members create, manage and join activities in many areas, including food, mobility, education or care for people and, in general for the commons. These are organized in systems based on pooling (that redistribute capital from individuals to the community and eventually vice versa), alternative value and exchange systems and local currencies (that value and record individual contributions and exchange between members), and free flow and solidarity schemes (where contributions are more open or less important to track) (see Table 2). The community playground is then the space that holds and directs all these practices, requiring one or more levels of democratic governance on the one hand and offering resource savings through *non-market economies of scale* (Pickerill 2016), e.g. by shopping in bulk.

Production for the public economy

The third area of community economies covers the production of goods and services that serve the public (non-member) economy, and generate (not necessarily financial) resources. These include food production, manufacturing, social services, education or culture, but also the rental of land or office space. They mostly operate for financial gains, but aim to be in line with the values and principles of the eco-community. Again, the democratic space of the eco-community economy offers the advantages of keeping the different practices together (economies of scale) and of switching between the diverse market and non-market economies (e.g. with volunteering and other *non-market capitals,* see Bruyn 1992); and of navigating and negotiating the objectives of production. These include individual enterprises that can be economically, legally and administratively independent to the eco-community; micro-enterprises, which can be economically and legally independent, but are dependent on the eco-community in terms of governance; and community enterprises, which are legally and economically dependent to the eco-community, in addition to their governance (cf. Johanisova et al., 2013 and their definition of primary and secondary social enterprise).

Community playgrounds in practice: Spaces of opportunities and solidarity

In the previous section I used the concept of the community playground to structure the economic practices identified in European eco-communities. I presented that eco-communities differ in the combinations of economic practices outlined in Table 2. However, community playgrounds depend on many factors related to identities, capital, infrastructure, decision-making or broader socio-technical, cultural, economic and political contexts. It is beyond the scope of this chapter to explore all these particular factors. Instead, in this section I offer to 'zoom' into the field to look at how community economies can be imagined and constructed. I present examples of European eco-communities that were interviewed and visited as part of the research. I have chosen a community centre, an income-sharing commune, a large eco-settlement, an ecological cohousing, a low-impact development and an urban building group.

It is worth noting that the current situation in the projects may differ (the field research was undertaken between 2015 and 2018). Communities never stop forming, constituting, reforming, eroding and fragmenting. However, the aim is to present some of the specialities, rather than to give full picture of the richness of each of the community economies.

Diverse European eco-communities

Makvärket is a cultural and environmental collective formed around a project to restore an old ceramics factory into a cultural community centre. It is located in the Danish countryside, well-connected by train, car and cycle-path to Copenhagen, the capital city with a vibrant history of self-organized projects such as The Floating City, Ungdomshuset or Christiania (Chapter 17), all of which combine autonomous culture, education and politics with (post-capitalist) structural and material experiments. Makvärket has translated this vibe into a large 10,000 square metre factory in the countryside, with lots of embedded material and space for material storage. The economy has been created around non-market and non-monetary practices in work (with tens of thousands of hours of volunteer work) – freegan culture and dumpster diving, slow development, co-education and the use of second-hand materials, but also around donations, cultural activities and public funds for building repairs. The collective consists of permanent – though not necessarily resident – members, and a fluctuating residential community of visitors from around the world. To support themselves, some members of the collective have worked and studied in Copenhagen or other cities or have partly been employed by a construction company that owns the building (the factory was sold to the construction company by the local municipality for a symbolic price). I have been able to visit this project several times and observe the long-term process of stabilizing and localizing of the collective in small housing communities in the villages around the factory. Today, the factory serves as a cultural and community centre, but also as a workshop for individual and community micro-businesses and to some extent as a safe space and starting point for many global newcomers to the Copenhagen area. It serves as an example of a multi-layered governance, a sensitive renewal of the local factory and the work it generates, but also of new rural (and rural-urban) relationships.

Lokomuna is an urban commune in Kassel, a historic city with a student atmosphere in the centre of Germany, which is a very special place for eco-communities, with a high density of political communes in the region, including the well-known Kommune

Niederkaufungen, founded in 1986. In Locomuna, the economy is based on a radical redistribution of income, wealth and time from the individual to the community level. Members share not only all costs, but also their time ('Neither money, nor time can be privatized', as they say). Spending money is decided and regulated by the collective, as is free time ('Everyone should have the same amount of free time'). This may be difficult to accept, but the community supports individuals in all life situations and crossroads, so that, for example, they have enough time to find the right job or study at any age. They are well connected to other communes in the Kassel area in a regional network, within which they are experimenting with a free-flow economy based on need, not cost. They are also unique in their system of wealth redistribution. When people join, they must give all their capital (if they have any) to the commune. Over time, as the loans are repaid, the house becomes an asset and anyone who wishes to leave receives a fair share of the wealth created. This system ensures that people with lower incomes are not 'trapped' in the collective economy. If they want to leave, they get enough capital to maintain a good quality of life in the future.

Cambium Leben in Gemeinschaft is a relatively new community in Fehring, a small town in rural Styria, Austria. In Austria, non-urban eco-communities are often located in areas with cheaper land, typically on the periphery near the borders with Czechia or, in this case, Hungary and Slovenia. But the group's history links Austria's two largest cities. A founding group in Vienna (Cambium) merged with a group with similar aims in Graz (Leben in Gemeinschaft) to form a single large rural project, and soon bought an old military barracks and land from the State of Styria. They successfully implemented the asset pool model, 'an alternative, interest-free, value-sustaining, legal asset cycle independent of the banking system' (Distelberger, n.d.) to acquire property worth €2 million. The system is based on diversification and permanent replacement of shareholders 'in the pool'. If some of the shareholders need money back, they are swapped with a new person. In theory, this system makes it possible to buy back the investment after it has been made, or at least at a much slower rate. Therefore, the asset pool shareholder model may guarantee the same feeling of secured housing as homeownership, but the housing security is much more connected to good relationships, community capital, trust and control, rather than to the need to own. The community is also experimenting with the solidarity economy; at the time of my visit, for example, they had a sliding scale payment system for rent and food with different levels of individual contributions. This solidarity and the high level of sharing (spaces, tasks) make living in the community relatively economically inclusive. However, as many similar projects struggle to do, also for Cambium Leben in Gemeinschaft it remains a challenge to create spaces that are inclusive in terms of other socio-demographic and cultural characteristics such as education or ethnicity.

LILAC – Low Impact Living Affordable Community in Leeds, UK is a cohousing project often cited as a successful example of ecological and affordable housing in a new urban development. The project consists of twenty households living in straw bale multi-unit houses and sharing a common house for means and other activities. The LILAC community has pioneered a Mutual Home Ownership Society, an affordable housing finance model in which community members pay 35 per cent of their income as rent (or 10 per cent once they have paid off their personal shares, with an option to pay off between 90 and 110 per cent of target shares (CLH London 2020)). As a result, individuals pay off 'their' shares at different rates and timeframe. LILAC also has an equity fund in which those who leave get back what they have invested. This solidarity takes equity out of the property market. The model is affordable across generations, but as newly built ecological housing, it is not inclusive of people on really low incomes, as there is still a minimum rent required to ensure that the loans can be repaid.

Tinker's Bubble is a small, low-impact woodland community of self-built cottages in Somerset, UK. The project focuses on a local economy, zero use of fossil fuels and an economic connection to the land, working with the resources it provides. The economy is based on voluntary simplicity and low, land-sustaining levels of material and monetary flows. In their case there are two commercial commodities – wood in the forest and apples in the orchards. So Tinker's Bubble produces hand-pressed apple juice and wooden frames using only hand tools, horses and a sawmill powered by a wood-fired steam engine. The hours devoted to this production are derived from the very low financial needs of the members (at the time of my visit, around £30–40 per person per week plus a few pounds per week to repay the property). The rest of the time is devoted to self-sufficient activities. The model proves to be socio-economically inclusive, but the radically low consumption and low-impact living conditions in the forest houses have been challenging and unacceptable for many people.

LiSA – Leben in der Seestadt Aspern is one of the many new building groups (*Baugruppe; Wohnprojekt*) in Seestadt Aspern, a model district in Vienna, Austria. A building group is a group of households (association, cooperative) that finances and maintains a collective property, individuals use their apartments and benefit from sharing (cars, tools, skills, care, rooms, etc.) and pay stable monthly payments (rent to pay loans). In LiSA, with a population of about seventy adults and twenty children, the house was purchased in a standard way (bought from a developer at a regular price, with a bank loan with a 35-year repayment horizon). But unlike other similar projects built in the city at the time, LiSA deliberately focused on the social and income diversity of the households. As a result of this solidarity, a third of the members contributed more than the target share and the community was affordable for people with little or no capital. In addition, half of the flats are small to increase the diversity of rents. Moreover, LiSA deliberately sought applicants of different nationalities, made two flats available to an adult day care centre, and set up a solidarity fund for situations, such as when a member is temporarily unable to pay the rent.

Community expectations: Spaces of dilemmas, compromises, luxuries and sufferings

In the previous text, I have argued that eco-communities implement multiple alternative economic practices, which are negotiated, navigated and transformed in what I call economic playground – a space for democratic governance of economic practices in eco-communities. Table 2 summarizes the identified practices and applies the concept of diverse economies on eco-communities.

Evidence from my research suggests that eco-communities often do not fully exploit the potential of diverse community economies. Across contexts, I have found that some of the theoretical promises are being fulfilled (especially in terms of care, sharing and (re)producing of housing). However, they differ in their capacity to prefigure practices in a social-ecological direction and often fail to find alternatives to the market economy (for interpretation of findings, see Malý Blažek 2024).

There are dozens of dilemmas that projects have to face and resolve. Sometimes they have to lower their expectations. And sometimes their solutions are contradictory. For example, if we were to compare different eco-communities in terms of their ecological outcome, it would not be surprising that projects that avoid the use of fossil fuels and/or aim at energy or food self-sufficiency (e.g. most low-impact developments and some ecovillages) would probably have more ecologically sustainable outcomes than more mainstream projects (such as some urban community developments and cohousing groups), which often adopt 'light green' approaches materialized in prefabricated ecological building materials, organic shopping or car sharing. But what if we found that some ecologically radical projects are economically dependent on an influx of visitors from far away (accumulating air miles), or their food production is dependent on volunteer programmes where volunteers are actually asked to pay for their stay, while the social innovation impact of some more mainstream projects at city or country level generates pro-environmental changes in neighbourhoods and in the housing sector and related policies? Or what if we found that some projects with strong environmental sustainability values cannot afford sustainable building solutions but are socio-economically affordable, while other projects with generally weaker sustainability values are at the top end of building ecology but are not socially inclusive? Or that some of the deep ecology back-to-the-land eco-communities have far-right and/or libertarian values and their attitude to the outside world is extremely selfish, if not threatening? These are important lessons for evaluators of community economies in eco-communities, because they show us how they are connected to their social ecologies; that non-market, alternative or local practices are not necessarily always more sustainable and ethical; and that they can create more tensions and problems than they solve.

The findings from the field confirm that eco-communities are, with words of Jenny Pickerill (2016, 32), 'incomplete, partial and sometimes problematic'. They are not resistant to dilemmas. On the contrary, these could be important moments that can shape the nexus between social/ecological and economic/financial spheres. What needs to be explored is whether the dilemmas arise from purposeful actions, from contradictions in objectives or from conditions that projects have to face.

More hopeful ontology and epistemology of diverse community economies

Eco-communities include not only examples of the inspiring projects presented earlier in the chapter, which nourish the social, solidarity, non-market or low-impact economies as their fundamental objectives. There are also projects which are economically less-innovative; in which members pay personal mortgages, have nine-to-five jobs, and in which the threshold for participation derives primarily from personal wealth. On the very top end, we find ecological community neighbourhoods full of collective luxuries and smart infrastructure, where the price of living is exclusive. How can we compare their economies and sustainabilities with projects that operate with a fraction of money, for example, political projects, such as squats and radical ecology projects, or with communities that operate as full income-sharing economies? What could we learn from such a comparative analysis and is it, in fact, desirable?

Heterodox economists, geographers and anthropologists are developing new concepts out of the need to seek answers to such and similar questions, and also to study the differences between practices that ask such questions and those that tend to ask less. As Johanisová and Fraňková (2013) discuss in their example of eco-social enterprises, there is a tendency to view economic alternatives on a mainstream–radical axis. From the mainstream perspective, alternatives are complementary to the mainstream, they act economically within the system to achieve their multifaceted goals and mitigate some of the mainstream problems; in the case of eco-communities, for example, the housing crisis, social cohesion or rural depopulation. From a radical perspective, alternatives oppose the dominant system and, to achieve their goals, develop new economic practices and legal structures that reject mainstream approaches.

Radical (as well as mainstream) strategies are implemented by most projects, although we can expect that radical ecology or strongly politically driven projects to be less willing to compromise their values. For sustainability assessments, Johanisová and Fraňková (2013) suggest that researchers should also position themselves along the mainstream–radical axis. In this text, for example, I propose that the market-based sharing economy practices are more mainstream than solidarity economy practices, even though both may have similar ecological outcomes in different contexts. For example, in *Gleis 21*, another Baugruppe project in Vienna, Austria, one of the members said that she perceives her project as very mainstream because the members are socio-economically relatively homogeneous in the (upper) middle class. However, the project is non-hierarchical, provides housing for refugees, runs a food co-operative or solidarity fund, and has built high-quality ecological housing. The project can be perceived as either radical or mainstream, depending on the context and (self-)positioning.

By no means all eco-communities (quite the opposite) claim to be 'alternatives to capitalism'. However, they create places on the wide edge of capitalism, which includes both more radical autonomous and anti-capitalist collectives or radically ecological communities that seek to maximize their self-sufficiency, and essentially more mainstream communities that actively contribute to and operate within (green) capitalism. However, I do not aim to decide which eco-communities are radical enough or too commercial. Following the radical epistemologies and ontology of community economies I argue for the study of diverse economic practices beyond capitalocentric perspectives.

As Monticelli (2022, 5) writes, whether by design or as a necessary consequence, diverse economies (including in eco-communities) exist 'within and despite capitalism inextricably intertwined with it'. Milani Price et al. (2020) even argue that the diverse economy and what they call the 'modern market economy' are becoming increasingly confluent. According to the authors, they are converging in terms of creating alternatives to capitalist modes of production, alternative measures and attitudes to economic growth, ecological responsiveness/environmental intentions and social relationality in economic transactions. While it is debatable to what extent the spheres of confluence are actually converging, the position of eco-communities 'always struggling with being with, beyond and against capitalism' (Pickerill et al., 2024) is certainly non-static, since non-static are both capitalism and economic alternatives.

As Benedikt Schmid (2018, 285) argues, this radical epistemology avoids looking at diverse economic practices and strategies from a 'capitalocentric perspective'; from the logic of the paradigm built on aspects of economic growth, technocratic efficiency or profit maximization. North (2018, 79–80) refers to the Gibson-Grahams' perspective as a 'more hopeful ontology'. The main role of the Gibson-Graham's framework is according to him to help pose emancipatory and epistemological questions to different actors, including ourselves. Gibson-Graham describe and categorize economic reality, but not for the purpose of deciding what is necessarily right and what is necessarily wrong. An example of such research that community economy epistemology enables is North's research on alternative currencies. He does not ask whether alternative currencies work, who is to blame if they do not work or what their transformative limits are. Instead, he simply asks 'for whom do the currencies work, and who struggles to use them?' (North 2014). In my research on eco-community economies, I follow this epistemology and do not aim to provide definitive answers as to whether community economies make the eco-social promises possible.

Conclusions

My intention in this chapter was neither to celebrate eco-communities, nor to criticize them for failing to achieve a certain level of commoning or sustainability outcomes. There are eco-communities that are environmentally focused but economically mainstream, just as there are projects that have not yet achieved their environmental goals but are more economically and socially inclusive, seeking new imaginaries and radical solutions based on economic democracy, solidarity, sharing and non-monetary practices. There are many that do not focus as much on economic transformation as on other issues, but there are a few that make serious efforts.

I used Gibson-Graham's community economies framework to conceptually explore how eco-communities create spaces of economic democracy. To explore how the democratic space is constructed, I have called it a community economic playground. Through democratic decision-making, community economies have an agency that enables them to play 'concrete games' (diverse economic practices) in economic playgrounds, i.e. to negotiate the preferences, navigate between goals and transform the particular economic activities between market, alternative market and non-market.

On concrete examples of European eco-communities, I have shown how the 'promise of enabling' of diverse economic practices can be performed in community economies. My research suggests that the economic playgrounds are as joyful and innovative as they can be stressful and demanding, as luxurious as they can be impoverished. Many projects are not making the most of their diverse community economies and there are also potential barriers to the economic diversity, such as the degree of initial 'lock-in' to the market economy through the required investment in built and natural capital. Lock-in to the market determines how 'big and fun' the playground will be, and how diverse a project's dilemma-solving strategies can be over time.

In the discussion, I described that eco-communities are situated on the wide edge of capitalism, and argued in favour of hopeful ontologies and epistemologies that would enable to raise critical, empowering questions to be asked that explore the possibilities rather than the limits of the inextricably intertwined relationship between capitalism and its alternatives.

Economies of eco-communities are not only spaces of collaboration and opportunities but also spaces of dilemmas, compromises and contradictions. The concept of community economy playground provides a guide to navigate through multi-layered goals and multiple voices in community initiatives, often resulting in dilemmas which require balancing or trading-off between the strategic objectives. Developing a community economy alone does not automatically lead to environmental, social or economic sustainability, but if organized well it can provide the needed space/playground for supporting sensible social and environmental decisions, and space for solving dilemmas in reaching the objectives. What eco-communities teach us, fundamentally, is that the economies we develop and represent can be reconfigured in a more sustainable manner, if we take an active role in them.

References

Acquier, A., Daudigeos, T. and Pinkse, J. (2017) 'Promises and paradoxes of the sharing economy: An organizing framework', *Technological Forecasting and Social Change* 125(December), pp. 1–10. Available at: https://doi.org/10.1016/j.techfore.2017.07.006.

Blažek, J. (2016) 'Economic micro-systems? Non-market and not-only-for-profit economic activities in eco-communities', *Human Affairs* 26(4), pp. 377–89. Available at: https://doi.org/10.1515/humaff-2016-0032.

Bruyn, S. (1992) 'A new direction for community development in the United States', in Ekins, P., Max-Neef, M. (eds.) *Real-Life Economics: Understanding Wealth Creation*. London: Routledge, pp. 372–81.

Cattaneo, C., Gavaldà, M. (2010) 'The experience of rurban squats in Collserola, Barcelona: what kind of degrowth?', *Journal of Cleaner Production* 18(6), pp. 581–9. Available at: https://doi.org/10.1016/j.jclepro.2010.01.010.

CLH London (2020) Introduction to mutual home-ownership societies (MHOS). Community led housing London. Available at: https://www.communityledhousing.london/wp-content/uploads/2020/07/CLHLondon-MHOS.pdf.

Distelberger, M. (n.d.) Wealthpool [webpage]. Available at: http://www.vermoegenspool.at/eng/.Accessed 14 July 2022.

Escribano, P., Lubbers, M.J. and Molina, J.L. (2020) 'A typology of ecological intentional communities: Environmental sustainability through subsistence and material reproduction', *Journal of Cleaner Production* 266(September), 121803, pp. 1–14. https://doi.org/10.1016/j.jclepro.2020.121803.

Gibson-Graham, J.K., Cameron, J. and Healy, S. (2013) *Take back the Economy: An ethical guide for transforming our communities*. Minneapolis, MN: University of Minnesota Press.

Healy, S., Heras, A.I. and North, P. (2023). 'Community economies', in Yi, I. (Ed.) *Encyclopedia of the Social and Solidarity Economy*. Cheltenham: Edward Elgar Publishing, pp. 12–18. https://doi.org/10.4337/9781803920924.00014.

Holm, A., Laimer, C. (2021) 'Alternative Finanzierungsinstrumente für Haus- und Wohnprojekte', in Holm, A. and Laimer, C. (eds.) *Gemeinschaftliches Wohnen Und Selbstorganisiertes Bauen*. Wien: TU Wien Academic Press, pp. 137–48.

Hurlin, L. (2019) 'Mietshäuser Syndikat: collective ownership, the "housing question" and degrowth', in Nelson, A. and Schneider, F. (eds.) *Housing for Degrowth: Principles, Models, Challenges and Opportunities*. New York: Routledge Environmental Humanities, pp. 233–43.

Johanisova, N., Crabtree, T. and Fraňková, E. (2013) 'Social enterprises and non-market capitals: a path to degrowth?', *Journal of Cleaner Production* 38(January), pp. 7–16. Available at: https://doi.org/10.1016/j.jclepro.2012.01.004.

Johanisová, N. and Fraňková, E. (2013) 'Eco-social enterprises in practice and theory – A radical versus mainstream view', in Anastasiadis, M. (ed.) *ECO-WISE – Social Enterprises as Sustainable Actors Concepts, Performances, Impacts*. Bremen: Europäischer Hochschulverlag, pp. 110–30.

Litfin, K.T. (2014) *Ecovillages: Lessons for Sustainable Community*. Cambridge: Polity Press.

Malý Blažek (2024) *Community economies: Diverse economic practices and strategies in European eco-communities*. Dissertation thesis. Masaryk University.

Milani Price, O., Ville, S., Heffernan, E., Gibbons, B. and Johnsson, M. (2020) 'Finding convergence: Economic perspectives and the economic practices of an Australian ecovillage', *Environmental Innovation and Societal Transitions* 34(March), 209–20. https://doi.org/10.1016/j.eist.2019.12.007

Monticelli, L. (2022) *The Future Is Now: An Introduction to Prefigurative Politics*. Bristol: Bristol University Press.

Mulder, K., Costanza, R. and Erickson, J. (2006) 'The contribution of built, human, social and natural capital to quality of life in intentional and unintentional communities', *Ecological Economics* 59, pp. 13–23. Available at: https://doi.org/10.1016/j.ecolecon.2005.09.021.

Nelson, A. (2018) *Small is Necessary: Shared Living on a Shared Planet*. London: Pluto Press.

North, P. (2014) 'Ten square miles surrounded by reality? Materialising alternative economies using local currencies: Ten square miles surrounded by reality?' *Antipode* 46(1), pp. 246–65. https://doi.org/10.1111/anti.12039.

North, P. (2018) 'Transitioning towards low carbon economies?', in North, P. and Scott Cato, M. (Eds.), *Towards just and sustainable economies: The social and solidarity economy North and South*. Bristol: Policy Press, pp. 73–95.

Pickerill, J. (2016) 'Building the commons in eco-communities', in Kirwan, S., Dawney, L. and Brigstocke, J. (eds.) *Space, Power and the Commons: The Struggle for Alternative Futures*. London: Routledge, pp. 43–66.

Pickerill, J., Chitewere, T., Cornea, N., Lockyer, J., Macrorie, R., Malý Blažek, J. and Nelson, A. (2024) 'Urban ecological futures: Five eco-community strategies for more sustainable and equitable cities', *International Journal of Urban and Regional Research* 48(1), pp. 161–76 https://doi.org/10.1111/1468-2427.13209.

Schmid, B. (2018) 'Structured diversity: A practice theory approach to post-growth organisations', *Management Revue* 29(3), pp. 281–310. https://doi.org/10.5771/0935-9915-2018-3-281.

Wagner, F. (2012) 'Ecovillage research review', in Andreas, M. and Wagner, F. (eds.) *Realizing Utopia: Ecovillage Endeavors and Academic Approaches*. Munich: RCC Perspectivs, pp. 81–94.

20

Being collectively transformational?

Jenny Pickerill

Eco-communities collectively act to transform the world. They can change how we dwell, provide, work, care, eat, rest, reproduce, educate, age, and do so by building different relations, practices, knowledges and materialities, with each other and more-than-humans. As the details in this book attest, however, eco-communities often struggle to realize their ambitions and are hindered by questions of inclusion, scale and replicability. While eco-communities' experiments challenge conventional ways of being, they only do so partially, often with a hybrid and messy empirics that complicate any simple notions of success. Yet despite this mixed picture of what actually-existing eco-communities are like, there is much we can learn from their attempts to engage in world-making and their compromises, negotiations and failures. Eco-communities offer inspiration, lived experience, and caution for how we might survive well together. This postcapitalist ethics and political intent in this book are to make visible the plethora of hopeful ways that people are already-challenging, already-changing and already-building different worlds, while always acknowledging (and detailing) how these possibilities might fall short.

This book is not meant as a compendium of all eco-communities, nor of all the questions they raise, but rather as a provocation, a starting point from which so many other different places can be explored, and questions must yet be asked. As Haraway so eloquently argues, 'our job is to make the anthropocene as short/thin as possible and to cultivate with each other in every way imaginable epochs to come that can replenish refuge' (Haraway 2015, 160).

In understanding these possibilities of collective transformation there are ten themes that emerge from this book, some more tentatively than others. These themes include key lessons we can learn from eco-communities (everyday rhythms and practices, sharing and caring, the value of visibility), some ongoing tensions which require further attention (seeking social justice, livelihoods and money, bodies and embodiment) and some perhaps more elements of eco-communities less understood (spirituality and the intrapersonal, living with Covid, building relations beyond, and erosion, failure and abandonment). This chapter concludes with reflections on the methods and possibilities of socio-ecological transformations offered by eco-communities.

Everyday rhythms and practices

Part of my fascination with eco-communities is their emphasis on action, 'doing', and prefiguration. They are spaces where non-conventional values are put into practice (Hansen 2019). The invention of new ways of doing is relatively easy, but as eco-communities demonstrate implementing and sustaining new practices are slow and complicated work. As Lockyer and Jones (Chapter 2) and Daly (Chapter 3) explore, eco-communities use different infrastructures to facilitate a change in practices (materialities that make it easier to cycle, reuse, share, etc), but new rhythms and patterns of repetition are also crucial in embedding new social practices, providing collective support for those practices, and making routine chores less onerous. These rhythms might be daily or seasonal, and marked by different rituals and celebrations (Manzella 2010).

Understanding these rhythms and practices also requires closer attention to the role of non-humans in reconfiguring relations. There is a need to decentre humans and inter-human relations, and in order to think through the more-than-human provocations offered by Schramm (Chapter 4) for a more relational approach that recognizes not just interdependencies but how we are affected by human others and non-human otherness. The role of animals beyond their value as weed suppressors or food source is strangely absent in existing work. There are also challenging temporalities in these processes – the incremental and often imperceptible work of everyday change (Pickerill 2022).

Sharing and caring

Eco-communities develop practices of sharing and togetherness which are 'extending human relations instead of market relations' (Jarvis 2019, 256). Indeed, there is a strong relationship between sharing and increased happiness (Lockyer 2017), and Litfin (2014) rightly argues that happiness is a necessary criterion of eco-community success. Collective care and social reproductive work is a central feature of eco-communities (Pajumets and Hearn 2021). Care is reorganized through the sharing of communal material infrastructures, interpersonal relations, forms of decision-making and responsibility, common meals and the deconstruction of gender norms, rules and performances.

Interdependencies are encouraged and generated in eco-communities through social and material infrastructures. Socially, many eco-communities focus on reconfiguring interpersonal relations through the use of the circle-shape in meetings, to encourage horizontal decision-making, but also a closeness in facing inwards and embodying the intimacy, and ethics, of face-to-face relations (Jarvis, Chapter 15). For some people this creates challenges around a lack of privacy, but for others it facilitates sharing which in turn enables mutual care relations.

As already acknowledged, eco-communities are always in-the-making and practices of sharing and care continue to evolve. There are examples of assertively feminist eco-communities, such as Twin Oaks, USA, that have sought to deconstruct gender norms and value all work (including care work) equally, though this remains a work in progress as patriarchal tensions persist (Kinkade 1994). As Gerner (Chapter 9) explores, care remains gendered, reproductive work is devalued, and there is often an additional care burden created by the quest to adopt environmentally sustainable practices, especially those that require manual, low-tech practices. But Gerner argues eco-communities can extend the meaning of care by centring it within everyday life, amplifying the need for self- and collective care, and prioritizing emotional care and wellbeing. Stevens-Wood (2022) cautions that we must adopt a non-transactional approach to sharing and care otherwise market relations are simply re-created.

Multiple and material lines of connections are built through the circular positioning of houses around communal shared gardens, with paths weaving past windows, and a lack of fences – all designed to create spaces of encounter and overlap. Care, then, can be conceived of in material terms. As Hayden (1982) and others have demonstrated, housing provision and design foreclose or generate feminist possibilities which directly impact care. Haydens' kitchenless designs were a way to enable collective cooking and resist the normative gendering of domestic labour, and are mirrored in many eco-communities' communal houses and shared infrastructures (see also Morrow and Parker 2020). McArthur and Stratford (2021), building on Power and Mee (2020), argue housing can therefore be considered as a caring act. By adopting voluntary simplicity, eco-community residents purposefully live in smaller, cheaper, eco-homes, where they enable self-care, ecological-care and create space and capacity to care for others.

Sharing and reconfiguring relations of care are a central tenant of all eco-communities and offer inspiration for building collective worlds otherwise. But there remain tensions (such as a heteronormativity in the communities Gerner worked with), and possibilities (in how some work with broader notions of kinship rather than nuclear family configurations) which we would do well to give further attention.

The value of visibility

Most eco-communities explored in this book put considerable effort and time into providing educational opportunities and acting as sites of demonstration. Yet their value is more than educational; it is how they make visible the infrastructures that support our daily lives, the politics that shape or constrain what is considered possible, and in presenting or performing actually-existing alternatives (Pickerill et al., 2024). Despite a growing body of research on the material and social infrastructures that enable our daily lives, much of this 'infrastructure largely remains obdurate' (Chester et al., 2019). Eco-communities make visible all the water, building, energy, waste and social infrastructures that support us, and demonstrate more sustainable ways of providing them (Gausset 2019). As Molfese (2023) argues there is a particular 'generosity' of infrastructures generated in eco-communities that rests on their ontological openness, flexibility, capacity to trigger generous encounters (often with more-than-human others) and that transform spaces and subjects towards post-capitalist autonomy. Likewise, as I discuss (Chapter 5), eco-communities are pivotal in making the interdependencies of socio-ecological relations visible, which in turn enables the development of more nuanced and diverse understandings of the agency of non-humans, and for humans to live more harmoniously with others.

Seeking social justice

If eco-communities are examples of grassroot efforts at socio-ecological transformation, then social justice must be central to such projects in order to ensure the flourishing and survival of all (Gerner, Chapter 9). As I explore in Chapter 11, failure to centre social justice risks eco-communities becoming the preserve of the white, wealthy and highly educated, and being a 'comfort bubble' of homogeneity or privileged enclaves (Cooper and Baer 2019).

Although most eco-communities start with intentions to centre social justice alongside reconfiguring socio-ecological relations, such ambitions are not always met and are uneven (Lopez and Weaver, Chapter 10). Cole et al. (2019) argued that the idealism of many members blinded them to their complicity in racial exclusion and inequity, and that many of his interviewees considered 'racial equity work as outside the scope of creating sustainable community'. This is rooted in an understanding of eco-communities as requiring shared intentionality to provide the commonality for them to function collectively, which can then be interpreted as requiring a degree of homogeneity in residents. As Chitewere (Chapter 7) articulates, questions of racial belonging or even racial absences remain difficult issues. Overtime commitments to social justice tend to be deprioritized. Consequently, many eco-communities have made little impact internally on social justice, nor have they supported initiatives in their neighbourhoods beyond notional contributions.

While Cole has demonstrated examples of racial equity efforts in some US communities (such as hosting workshops and trainings, addressing white supremacy, gifting income, resources and land to marginalized groups, and working with local anti-racist organizations), he noted numerous ongoing challenges. There was often a lack of sustained momentum in these efforts, they centred whiteness, were tokenistic, and failed to fully understand the 'negative impact of white words and behavior' (Cole 2022). Indeed, a focus on the slow intrapersonal work of changing our ways of being is often advocated as necessary *before* any material actions were taken, despite a recognition that anti-racist social justice work was urgent. While more hopefully there are examples of anti-racist training material and workshops being developed by the Foundation for Intentional Community (FIC) and The Global Ecovillage Network, and in 2023 a new BIPOC Intentional Community Council was established as part of the FIC, transformation is not possible through education alone. Seeking social justice, then, is an urgent yet too often deprioritized intent of eco-communities that requires further attention.

Livelihoods and money

Eco-communities try to reconfigure what money and work are, how much is necessary, and for what ends (Stevens-Wood, Chapter 17). There is a consensus in how livelihoods are approached and valued, with an emphasis on collective benefit, and seeking to minimize what money is needed (Smith and Johanisova, Chapter 18). This often includes developing micro-industries that provide for the communities' direct needs. Likewise, of growing importance in eco-communities in Catalonia and France, for example, is degrowth as a framework through which to develop different, often non-monetary, economies. Yet community-wide income sharing has declined as a practice, and several eco-communities have encountered financial problems, especially as a result of the Covid pandemic (Gavaldà and Cattaneo, Chapter 14).

Despite trying to decentre the importance of money in everyday lives, most eco-communities still rely upon it, work for it, generate it and spend it (Maly Blažek, Chapter 19). It is not money as an entity which is considered problematic, but rather profit accumulation and resource overextraction. Therefore, some eco-communities have carefully sought to prevent housing speculation and instigated approaches to retain affordable housing. Yet despite innovative examples where housing costs are minimized either by using a rental model (Los Angeles Eco-village, USA), a shared equity approach (LILAC, England), or by locating rurally where land costs are often lower (Tir y Gafel, Wales), affordability of eco-communities remains problematic. Indeed, the recent shift to working more closely with corporate for-profit developers has compounded rather than resolved this tension (Nielsen-Englyst and Gausset 2024; Temesgen 2020). These affordability problems are worsened by the way eco-community residents purposefully survive on minimal incomes, and therefore have limited savings, pensions or retirement plans, suggesting a general lack of preparedness for old age. The complex interplay between generating livelihoods, navigating money needs, self-provision and age would benefit from further attention.

Bodies and embodiment

Age is, of course, a universal – even if differential – experience and as many now live longer than before the final stages of life can be marked by physical fragility, mental decline and dependence on others (Stevens-Wood 2022). Eco-communities have struggled to plan and support ageing, not just financially as discussed above, but in the demands it places on others (Wechuli 2017). Many eco-communities are reliant upon the contributions of physically fit and able bodies (Laughton 2008). While communal living reduces loneliness and increases quality of life for older adults, there are few successful working examples beyond older age-specific co-housing (Glass 2020; Puplamp et al., 2020). Multi-generational eco-communities are struggling to navigate how to support older and ageing members in a culture of expected equal contributions and ongoing tensions in how these contributions are already shared and uneven (Bhakta and Pickerill 2016).

As Schramm (2022) argues, 'there has been close to no attention to how changing bodies (age, pregnancy, children, disability, illness, injury), or bodies changed through the repetition of practice (weariness and attrition) and changing priorities over time … affect the durability of everyday life in eco-communities' (35). While there is substantial research on disability in intentional communities this focuses on Camphill communities which are deliberately designed to support those with learning disabilities, mental health problems and other special needs (McKanan 2020). There is little work on how change is embodied, how our bodies change over time and through the endurance of repeated manual work of living in an eco-community, or the bodily discomfort of eco-community living and practices.

Spirituality and the intrapersonal

There is an interesting tension between the emphasis on 'inner work' (the intrapersonal), the collective space (the interpersonal), and broader social change activities in eco-communities (Pisters et al., 2020). This is a question about methods of transformation, to which we return below, but is rooted in embodied spiritual practices in eco-communities that seek to shift people's inner consciousness as a precondition of engaging in interpersonal and societal scale transformation (Clarence-Smith, Chapter 16). It rests on a belief that we must change ourselves before we can help others, but also a recognition of the need to shift our subjectivities in order to generate worldmaking otherwise (Hubbard 2024). As Healy et al. (2020) note, 'resubjectiviation is the process of detaching from capitalist subjection (or identification) and transforming self-representations, habits and practices'. This starts with eco-community members noticing what they need to refuse (such as capitalist relations), in order to invest in other possibilities and generate new subjectivities (even if this resubjectivation often remain incomplete).

Such an approach is often underpinned by a secular spirituality that helps residents navigate this 'feeling' or 'healing' work, and by rhythmic and repetitious daily collective practices that help support unlearning conventional practices, and embed new ways of being, thinking and doing. McKanan (2018) argues that anthroposophy (drawing on the Steiner tradition) underpins and guides many eco-communities approaches to spirituality, and for many eco-communities this spirituality is the 'community glue' that binds them together (Temesgen 2020).

The focus is often on unlearning capitalist and individualistic ways of being, rather than learning new knowledges, and that this unlearning is best achieved through praxis – practice and bodily engagement. Eco-communities provide the space and infrastructures through which these intrapersonal shifts can happen. This inner transformation takes place through rituals, daily rhythmic practice, creative play, art and music, meditation spaces, new communication and decision-making forms, and collective lived experiences. It is also often through practices such as attunement and manifesting, guided by the use of 'angel cards' (Findhorn eco-village, Meltzer 2015) or the '12 qualities' (Auroville). These spaces and processes enable intrapersonal transformation which produces relational interpersonal shifts.

These processes of unlearning (see Jarvis, Chapter 15), the slow work that they require, might be crucial in enabling deeper transformations, but they also risk delaying broader social change. Pepper's (1991) critique of the emphasis placed on spiritual and internal psychic development allow us to see how both presuppose or perpetuate an individualized and dangerously apolitical sensibility. Residents link such spirituality and the focus on the intrapersonal to increasing wellbeing and happiness, but there is less research evidencing the assumed trajectory of intrapersonal to interpersonal to societal transformation.

Living with Covid

Despite this book being written during the years of the Covid pandemic, most of us conducted the empirical work prior to the global health emergency. Some nascent work is emerging which has begun to explore the impact of Covid on eco-communities, particularly a Foundation for Intentional Community Covid19 survey (Tina 2021) and a survey of Covid response in Brazilian ecovillages (Martins Arruda and Santos Bevilacqua 2022).

Unsurprisingly, many communities turned inwards as a form of self-protection, enforcing their boundaries and separation and closing their doors to visitors (Tina 2021). Rural and more spacious eco-communities found this easier to do, whereas highly communal and urban communities struggled. This helped (re)generate a closeness of inter-community relations and for some represented a return to initial values and intents (even as meetings became virtual) and activities such as agriculture. Yet in many, decisions became more centralized and less democratic (Martins Arruda and Santos Bevilacqua 2022).

Several communities experienced significant internal discord around mask wearing, social distancing and vaccinations, which became a polarizing conflict, yet the majority followed national health guidelines (Tina 2021; Weeks et al., 2022). In Martins Arruda and Santos Bevilacqua's (2022) study, the greatest challenges faced by residents were in the interpersonal relations of dealing with uncertainty, isolation, rapid change and the reduction of in-person contact. Yet others created mutual aid task forces to ensure everyone was supported and drew upon those with professional health experience, especially in co-housing communities focusing on older adults (Weeks et al., 2022). Indeed, the co-housing design was 'Covid-19 friendly', especially the common house which enabled socially distanced meetings, shared outdoor spaces and visual connection even when in individual residences. Living with Covid, then, has helped many eco-communities re-prioritize their values and reassert their resilience, but also question their internal processes of decision-making and inclusivity.

Building relations beyond

Few eco-communities are shut off from the world in its entirety or are fully autonomous. The borders of an eco-community are sometimes porous (Nelson, Chapter 12) and at other times asserted and celebrated (see Smith and Johanisova, Chapter 18, in how Christiania has a clear 'exit' sign as you leave the site). Many eco-communities actively seek connection with non-residents and integration with neighbours (Anderson, Chapter 6). For some there are fences, gates and clear demarcations, and for others there are open pathways, welcoming signs, and multiple lines of connection and interaction with incomers. Whether materially or symbolically demarcated, however, as Cornea (Chapter 13) reflects on environmental governance, there tends to be a porosity or leakiness in asserted boundaries.

Eco-communities, therefore, have multiple mutual relations with those beyond their edges. These include relations to medical services, schools, employment, building inspectors and shops for goods they cannot self-provide. There has been limited examination of eco-community relations with the state (despite Wright [2010] clearly arguing why this is vital to understand), but greater acknowledgement of the risks of co-option by capitalism, corporate culture, individualism and the impossibility of successfully challenging the multiple vested interests of capitalists (Pepper 1991).

This tension between grassroots socio-ecological transformation and corporate efforts is further demonstrated by the rapid growth of developer-led co-housing projects, particularly in Denmark and Norway. Developer-driven projects tend to be 'non-committed' forms of communal living, with a lack of shared intentions and only voluntary participation in any collective activities. Even when developer-led projects initially intend to be communal, they have subsequently 'dropped introductory courses that aimed to equip new members with the necessary skills for shared practices and establish a common ground' (Temesgen 2020, 1). While the entry of corporate finance into eco-communities might enable a shift towards larger-scale or more numerous projects, they tend to miss the necessity of developing social connections and skills, such as conflict resolution. This weakening of collective values also undermines the development of the skills and competencies that are necessary to support eco-communities' abilities to develop communities of practice for sustainability (Temesgen 2020). One response has been the emergence of companies like Baerebo (Denmark) run by those with eco-community experience who seek to channel corporate finance into co-housing but with greater emphasis on the necessary social elements and skills. These multiple ways that eco-communities reach beyond their boundaries, and how the state and corporate interests seek to reach into eco-communities to co-opt elements, are vital to understanding the possibilities of broader transformation (Nielsen-Englyst and Gausset 2024).

Erosion, failure and abandonment

As eco-communities are ongoing, dynamic and unfinished, it is important to recognize that most also have a trajectory from pioneering to professionalism that tends ultimately to include a gradual weakening of values and intentions (Bang 2007). As eco-communities age there is a desire for more comfort, easier (potentially fewer manual) practices, a retreat from some communal commitments and sharing, and more individualism (Sullivan 2016a). As eco-communities seek to be larger scale or replicate, they risk re-introducing hierarchies through expert knowledges which might then threaten to undermine their egalitarian principles (Sullivan 2016b).

Each community takes a slightly different path, whether that be focusing more on financial stability through money generation, or more individual autonomy. The erosion of initial values and intentions often arises from the exhaustion of long-standing residents, the arrival of newcomers with different priorities,or increasing attachments beyond the eco-community site (Pepper 1991). It is often the social and communal elements of eco-communities that weaken most readily, and as residents gradually disengage and attend fewer collective activities the opportunities for re-engagement diminish (Ecker and Meyer 2022).

While failure is a crucial part of experimentation and eco-communities often fail (Christian [2003] suggests as many as 90 per cent fall apart), relatively little attention has been paid to these processes of failure. Schramm's (Chapter 4) work on endurance in eco-communities outlines how repetition and inconvenience threaten the persistence of practices in eco-communities and culminate into a slow process of abandonment. Failure and abandonment might be due to financial pressures, compliance with regulations and legal necessities or interpersonal conflict, but it is also an outcome of boredom and discomfort. There are, therefore, diverse processes of erosion, failure and abandonment that warrant further attention beyond a dichotomy of success-failure. Modification of practices may also signify satisfaction with 'making do', preferring repair or pragmatic decisions about the use of time (Schramm 2022). Understanding the cause of failure or abandonment is clearly vital to ensure new attempts are easier to sustain. What is clear is a need for balance between enjoyment and necessity; like many things in life, practices are easier to sustain if they are fun or there is space for joy.

Methods and possibilities of transformation

This book began with a claim that eco-communities inspire and challenge us to live and navigate more environmentally harmonious and collective lives. Although they are experimental, unfinished and messy, there are multiple ways in which collective change has been enacted – through new social practices, diverse economies, new socio-ecological relations and in negotiating questions of inclusion (Schelly et al., 2024). The question remains, however, how these eco-communities might enable socio-ecological transformation beyond their borders.

A common response to this question is to focus on the ways eco-communities use educational opportunities to encourage transformation elsewhere. Many eco-communities have invested heavily in being sites of demonstration, knowledge creation (producing guides) and educational activity (often as a source of income) (Anderson, Chapter 6). Unfortunately, education is not in itself a very effective strategy for change as the extensive research on the knowledge-action gap demonstrates. Eco-communities, however, offer other more hopeful, albeit also more complicated, possibilities in the way they effect change.

First, it is vital to understand the processes of socio-ecological transformation internal to eco-communities in order to know how to enact them elsewhere. This is far more complicated than simply replicating a few material or social infrastructures. As Schramm (2022) illustrates, eco-community residents go through processes of 'affective intensification' through repeated encounters between humans and non-humans and different knowledges. It is in this combination of initial political convictions (to start the process of transformation), space and time to experiment in new practices, and collective support in trying out and repeating new approaches that residents change how they live – the process of resubjectivation (Hubbard 2024).

Second, there is something vital about having the protected bounded physical and social space to experiment within. For many eco-communities are the 'tactical withdrawal' from conventional society that has been necessary for 'generating a coherent and consolidated ecosophical community' (Anderson 2017, 193). While 'this withdrawal compounds the estrangement between this community and mainstream society' (ibid) and might contradict the work of broader transformation, it points to a need for change to emerge from multiple pockets of non-capitalist experimentation. This is akin to Erik Olin Wright's (2010) notion of interstitial transformation, where alternatives are embedded in spaces on the fringes of capitalism. Here experiments can be developed, tested, demonstrated and improved, democratic egalitarian solutions evolved, and support slowly secured. Wright argues that this form of transformation might be slower than ruptural methods (direct revolutionary confrontation), but these more confrontational methods might still be employed when limits to change within eco-communities are reached. Equally, tipping points might be met which create rapid social change as novel practices and infrastructures get quicker broader take up.

Third, eco-communities are increasingly using their knowledges, skills and capacities to advocate for regional change. For example, Lebensgarten (Germany) took a leading role in energy transitions in its region and the Instituto Biorregional Do Cerrado (Brazil) was able to advocate for socio-biodiversity conservation using its voice in local politics (Roysen and Schwab 2021). This strategic role of eco-communities in local or regional politics should not be underestimated (Blue 2024).

Finally, an emerging strategy is for eco-communities to work with state agencies (such as those responsible for affordable housing provision) or corporate developers to enact transformative change. As Boyer (2015) found in his work with Dancing Rabbit, EcoVillage at Ithaca and Los Angeles Eco-Village (USA), which sought change through education initiatives, transformation was reliant on partnering with an existing developer or the state. The eco-communities were able to get others to replicate some of their approaches, which in turn represented a 'scaling-up', but wider adoption of practices was reliant on collaboration with organizations who did not necessarily mirror the intent or values of the eco-communities. Boyer also noted the process of transformation was uneven and highly contextual, even with the involvement of external agencies.

It feels apt to end a book that explores the open, unfinished, dynamic and ongoing practices of eco-communities, with a sense of the possibilities while simultaneously acknowledging that their methods of transformation require further research and praxis, and that these transformations are often temporary or fail. What I hope has been demonstrated in this book are the breadth, richness and complexities of eco-communities, how they navigate multiple challenges, and how despite often failing they still manage to inspire the possibility of world-making otherwise.

References

Anderson, J. (2017) 'Retreat or re-connect: How effective can ecosophical communities be in transforming the mainstream?', *Geografiska Annaler: Series B, Human Geography*, 99(2), pp. 192–206.
Bang, J.M. (2007) *Growing Eco-Communities: Practical Ways to Create Sustainability*. Floris Books.

Bhakta, A. and Pickerill, J. (2016) 'Making space for disability in eco-homes and eco-communities', *The Geographical Journal* 182(4), pp. 406–17.
Blue, S (2024) *Where do we Go from Here: Open letter to the Intentional Communities Movement*. https://www.ic.org/sky-blue-where-do-we-go-from-here. Accessed 1 November 2024
Boyer, R.H. (2015) 'Grassroots innovation for urban sustainability: Comparing the diffusion pathways of three ecovillage projects', *Environment and Planning A* 47(2), pp. 320–37.
Chester, M.V., Markolf, S. and Allenby, B. (2019) 'Infrastructure and the environment in the Anthropocene', *Journal of Industrial Ecology* 23(5), pp. 1006–15.
Christian, D.L. (2003) *Creating a Life Together: Practical Tools to Grow Ecovillages and Intentional Communities*. Gabriola Island: New Society Publishers.
Cole, J. (2022) Evolving racial justice strategies in intentional communities. Presented at the International Communal Studies Association Conference, Denmark, 14th July.
Cole, J., Horton, H., and Pini, M. (2019) 'Culture change or same old society? Consensus, sociocracy, and white supremacy culture', *Communities Magazine* 184(Fall), pp. 53–6.
Cooper, L. and Baer, H.A. (2019) *Urban Eco-Communities in Australia: Real Utopian Responses to the Ecological Crisis or Niche Markets?* London: Springer.
Ecker, A. and Meyer, I. (2022) How the Zegg Community in Germany Evolved Since the ICSA Conference at Zegg 2001. Presented at the International Communal Studies Association Conference, Denmark, 15 July.
Gausset, Q. (2019) 'Stronger together: How Danish environmental communities influence behavioural and societal changes', in Hoff, J., Gausset, Q. and Lex, S. (eds.) *The Role of Non-state Actors in the Green Transition*. London: Routledge, pp. 52–70.
Glass, A.P. (2009) 'Aging in a community of mutual support: The emergence of an elder intentional cohousing community in the United States', *Journal of Housing for the Elderly* 23(4), pp. 283–303.
Glass, A.P. (2020) 'Sense of community, loneliness, and satisfaction in five elder cohousing neighborhoods', *Journal of Women & Aging* 32(1), pp. 3–27.
Hansen, A.H. (2019) '"It has to be reasonable": Pragmatic ways of living sustainably in Danish eco-communities', in Hoff, J., Gausset, Q. and Lex, S. (eds.) *The Role of Non-state Actors in the Green Transition*. London: Routledge, pp. 34–51.
Haraway, D. (2015) 'Anthropocene, capitalocene, plantationocene, chthulucene: Making kin', *Environmental Humanities* 6(1), pp. 159–65.
Hayden, D. (1982) *The Grand Domestic Revolution: A History of Feminist Designs for American Homes, Neighborhoods, and Cities*. Cambridge, MA: MIT Press Press.
Healy, S., Özselçuk, C. and Madra, Y.M. (2020) 'Framing essay: Subjectivity in a diverse economy', in Gibson-Graham, J. K. and Dombrosk, K. (eds.) *The Handbook of Diverse Economies*. Cheltenham: Edward Elgar Publishing, pp. 389–401.
Hong, S. and Vicdan, H. (2016) 'Re-imaging the utopian: Transformation of a sustainable lifestyle in ecovillages', *Journal of Business Research* 69(1), pp. 120–36.
Hubbard, E. (2024) Bioregioning: building more just and sustainable livelihoods? PhD thesis, University of Sheffield.
Jarvis, H. (2019) 'Sharing, togetherness and intentional degrowth', *Progress in Human Geography* 43(2), pp. 256–75.
Kinkade, K. (1994) *Is It Utopia Yet? An Insider's View of Twin Oaks Community In Its 26th Year*. Twin Oaks, VA: Twin Oaks Publishing.
Laughton, R. (2008) *Surviving and Thriving on the Land: How to Use Your Time and Energy to Run a Successful Smallholding*. Totnes: Green Books.

Litfin, K.T. (2014) *Ecovillages: Lessons for Sustainable Community*. Oxford: John Wiley & Sons.

Lockyer, J. (2017) 'Community, commons, and degrowth at Dancing Rabbit Ecovillage', *Journal of Political Ecology* 24(1), pp. 519–42.

Manzella, J C. (2010) *Common Purse, Uncommon Future: The Long, Strange Trip of Communes and Other Intentional Communities*. Santa Barbara, CA: Preager.

Martins Arruda, B. and Santos Bevilacqua, B. (2022) Covid response in Brazilian ecovillages. Presented at the International Communal Studies Association Conference, Denmark, 15 July.

McArthur, M. and Stratford, E. (2021) 'Housing aspirations, pathways, and provision: contradictions and compromises in pursuit of voluntary simplicity', *Housing Studies* 36(5), pp. 714–36.

McKanan, D. (2020) *Camphill and the Future: Spirituality and Disability in an Evolving Communal Movement*. Berkeley, CA: University of California Press.

McKanan, D. (2018) *Eco-Alchemy: Anthroposophy and the History and Future of Environmentalism*. Berkeley, CA: University of California Press.

Meltzer, G. (2015) *Findhorn Reflections: A Very Personal Take on Life Inside the Famous Spiritual Community and Ecovillage*. Graham Meltzer (self-published). CreateSpace Independent Publishing Platform; First Edition.

Molfese, C. (2023) Going back-to-the-land in the Anthropocene: A more-than-human journey into anarchist geographies. PhD thesis, University of Plymouth.

Morrow, O. and Parker, B. (2020) 'Care, commoning and collectivity: From grand domestic revolution to urban transformation', *Urban Geography* 41(4), pp. 607–24.

Nielsen-Englyst, C. and Gausset, Q. (2024) 'From countercultural ecovillages to mainstream green neighbourhoods – a view on current trends in Denmark', *Npj Climate Action* 3(1), p. 60.

Pajumets, M. and Hearn, J. (2021) 'Doing gender by not doing gender in eco-communities', in Pule, P.M. and Hultman, M. (eds.) *Men, Masculinities and Earth: Exploring Ecological Masculinities*. Houndmills: Palgrave Macmillan, pp. 309–25.

Pepper, D. (1991) *Communes and the Green Vision: Counterculture, Lifestyle and the New Age*. London: Merlin Press.

Pickerill, J., Chitewere, T., Cornea, N., Lockyer, J., Macrorie, R., Malý Blažek, J. and Nelson, A. (2024). 'Urban ecological futures: Five eco-community strategies for more sustainable and equitable cities', *International Journal for Urban and Regional Research* 48(1), pp. 161–76.

Pickerill, J. (2022) Shifting temporalities: Environmentalists' time and the possibilities of just green transitions' Invited talk as Greenhouse Green Transitions Fellow, University of Stavanger, 5 October 2022.

Pisters, S.R., Vihinen, H. and Figueiredo, E. (2020) 'Inner change and sustainability initiatives: exploring the narratives from eco-villages through a place-based transformative learning approach', *Sustainability Science* 15, pp. 395–409.

Power, E.R. and Mee, K.J. (2020) 'Housing: An infrastructure of care', *Housing Studies* 35(3), pp. 484–505.

Puplampu, V., Matthews, E., Puplampu, G., Gross, M., Pathak, S. and Peters, S. (2020) 'The impact of cohousing on older adults' quality of life', *Canadian Journal on Aging/La Revue canadienne du vieillissement* 39(3), pp. 406–20.

Roysen, R. and Schwab, A.K. (2021) 'The potential of ecovillages for transitions in rural areas: A comparison of ecovillages in Germany and Brazil', in Arkbound

Foundation (ed.) *Climate Adaptation: Accounts of Resilience, Self-Sufficiency and Systems Change*. Glasgow: Arkbound Foundation, pp. 231–49.

Schelly, C., Rubin, Z. and Lockyer, J. 2024 'The paradox of collective climate action in rural US ecovillages: Ethnographic reflections and perspectives', *npj Climate Action* 3(1), p. 17.

Schramm, E. (2022) The space-time of post-capitalist transformation: More-than-human affects in French and Catalan eco-communities. PhD thesis, Oxford University.

Stevens-Wood, K. (2022) Intentional Communities in the UK and Their Response to an Aging Population. Presented at the International Communal Studies Association Conference, Denmark, 14 July.

Sullivan, E. (2016a) 'Individualizing utopia: Individualist pursuits in a collective cohousing community', *Journal of Contemporary Ethnography* 45(5), pp. 602–27.

Sullivan, E. (2016b) '(Un) Intentional community: Power and expert knowledge in a sustainable lifestyle community', *Sociological Inquiry* 86(4), pp. 540–62.

Temesgen, A.K. (2020) 'Building an island of sustainability in a sea of unsustainability? A study of two ecovillages', *Sustainability* 12(24), 10585, pp. 1–27.

Tina, C. (2021) Intentional Communities and Covid: A study of how intentional communities have responded to the Covid-19 pandemic in 2021. Foundation for Intentional Community. URL: ic.org/covid-report.

Wechuli, Y. (2017) 'Neighborly assistance: High expectations of multi-generation cohousing projects', *Working with Older People* 21(3), pp. 133–39.

Weeks, L.E., Bigonnesse, C., Rupasinghe, V., Haché-Chiasson, A., Dupuis-Blanchard, S., Harman, K., McInnis-Perry, G., Paris, M., Puplampu, V. and Critchlow, M. (2022) 'The best place to be? Experiences of older adults living in Canadian cohousing communities during the COVID-19 pandemic', *Journal of Aging and Environment*, 37(4), pp. 421–41. DOI: https://doi.org/10.1080/26892618.2022.2106528.

Winter, A. (2016) '"Environmental sustainability? We don't have that here": Freetown Christiania as an unintentional eco-village', *ACME: An International Journal for Critical Geographies* 15(1), pp. 129–49.

Wright, E.O. (2010) *Envisioning Real Utopias*. London: Verso.

Index

Acquier, Aurélien 286
activist planning 160–1
actor networks 204
   actor assemblages 210
affordability 7, 91, 292, 303
   barriers to 231
   lack of 113
   solidaristic funding model 94–5
   through low consumption 292
ageing 79, 89, 232–3, 303
   elder care 21, 177, 262
agency
   and community economies 295
   more-than-human 95, 301
   of groups 229
   of individuals 146, 228
   political 4, 14
   relational agency 68
agroecology 70, 215
air source heat pumps 99
Aldred, Lisa 138
Alfassa, Mirra 242
Alston, Dana 115
alter-globalization 216
alternative currencies 115, 288, 295
   local currencies 289
alternative food networks 175
alternative practices 50, 73, 108, 110, 300
Altman, Jonathan 137
anarchism 3–6, 215–16, 266
   'divine anarchy' 243
   mutual aid 3, 231
Anderson, Jon 12, 89, 99
animals, role of 300. *See* more-than-human
animus manendi 131
anthropocene 33, 85, 167–8, 299
anthropocentrism 67n.1, 95
Anthropology 3, 135n.3, 203, 205, 285, 294
anthroposophy 304

anti-capitalist 9, 224, 255. *See* post-capitalism
   ethics 11
   perspective 219
   society 224
'anti-economy' 224
anti-G8 protests 100
anti-speciesism 147. *See* anthropocentrism
apartheid 120. *See* segregation
   climate apartheid 113
Aquarius Festival, Australia 231–2
architecture 3
   design 289
   green architecture 103, 109, 228
   sustainable architecture 242
Auroville, India 9, 20, 202, 241–51, 304
autoethnography 20, 241, 246
autonomy 95, 221, 271, 305
   autonomous culture 290
   autonomous economy 265
   autonomous ethics 11
   autonomous zones 100, 110
   collective autonomy 193
   community autonomy 215
   'creative autonomy' 73
   individual autonomy 306
   post-capitalist autonomy 301
   self-governance processes 201

back-to-the-land 259, 293
   arcadia 103
   back-to-nature imaginary 145
   back-to-the-land movement 147, 166
Baerebo, Denmark 306
Baker, Ted 265
Banivanua Mar, Tracey 133
Barker, Adam 18, 89, 129, 131, 135
Bauman, Zygmunt 217
Beach Hill Community, UK 87
Bengtsson, Bo 197
Bernhard, J.T. 274

Bey, Hakim 100–1
Bhandar, Brenna 133
bioconstruction 67, 69, 72
  eco-building 145
bio-cultural heritage 221
biodiversity 35, 85, 90, 181, 194
  socio-biodiversity conservation 308
biomass 99
biomimicry 85
Black2Nature 182
Black Environmental Network 182
Black Girls Hike 182
Black, Indigenous, People of Color
    (BIPOC) 18, 302. *See* race and
    racism
  Black liberation 182
  empowerment 181
  environmental justice 119
  marginalization and exclusion 116–17,
    138, 174
Blackfoot indigenous group 137
Bledsoe, Adam 17
Blue, Sky 11, 21
Boggs, Kyle 131
Bratman, Eve 132
Brazier's Park eco-community, UK 181
Bresson, Sabrina 16, 192–3
Brithdir Mawr, UK 87, 138
British Columbia Treaty Process 133–4
British Empire 130
Buddhism 137, 244–5
buen vivir (Sumaq Kawsay) 219
built environment 86, 157. *See* material
    infrastructures

Cal Cases, Spain 223
Calafou, Spain 18, 70, 75
Cambium Leben in Gemeinschaft, Austria
    291
Camphill communities 303
Can Decreix, France 9, 18, 70–9
Can Masdeu, Spain 18, 70–9, 202, 215–25
capitalism 1, 192, 271. *See* post-capitalism
  alternatives to 294
  and capitalocentrism 294
  and ecofeminism 145
  and growth 219
  and high-tech fixes 68
  and privilege 180
  and productivism 143
  and settler society 130
  and work 167, 265, 282
  capitalist economy 20, 255
  'capitalist realism' 273
  capitalist regimes 234
  control of 282
  domination 3
  fighting against 216
  hegemony 84
  late-stage industrial capitalism 129
  more-than-capitalist 273
  patriarchal 152
  racial 174, 178
  subjectivity 304
car sharing 54, 115, 293
carbon footprint 10, 31, 42, 50, 69, 259,
    264
  greenhouse gas emissions 47, 167
care 7, 9, 286, 300–1
  and gender 114
  and sharing 300
  care work 4, 143–4, 145
  defeminization of care 151, 153
  ethic of care 234
  for land 132
  more-than-human 147
  neighbourhood care 187
  self-care 147
Cascade CoHousing, UK 11, 177
Cattaneo, Claudio 20–1, 215, 258, 285
Cauca Indigenous Regional Council,
    Colombia 215
Centre for Alternative Technology, UK 9,
    12–13, 99, 101–10
Channon Craft Market, Australia 234
Chari, Anita 245
childcare 31, 41, 92, 182, 237
Chitewere, Tendai 17, 115, 175, 178–9,
    193, 302
Chloupková, Jarka 274
Christiania Bikes, Denmark 275–6
Christie Walk, Australia 11, 176–7
Clarence-Smith, Suryamayi Aswini 20,
    202, 241
class 114, 177
  diversity 6, 174
  middle-class 6, 70, 118
  privilege 177

climate change 68, 173, 223. *See* climate crisis
  and hope 182
  and the Global North 179
climate crisis 118, 157, 168
Climate Reframe 182
Cloughjordan Ecovillage, Ireland 9, 192, 194–5
co-housing 8, 34, 50–1, 54, 56, 189, 227, 258, 286
  'Covid-19 friendly' 305
Cohousing Association of the United States 34
Cohousing Australia 189
Cohousing Research Network 8
Cole, Joe 302
collaborative housing 187, 189, 198
  and socio-cultural homogeneity 16
  collaborative housing studies 188
  eco-collaborative housing 187–98
collectivization 147
colonialism 1, 117, 120, 129, 131. *See* settler colonialism
  and indigenous land 16
  and infrastructure 209
  and privilege 180
  carbon colonialism 174
  colonial practices 89
commonality 302
  being-in-common 7, 85–6, 287
commons 2, 190, 224, 288–9
  commons economy 197
commune 8, 35, 188, 191, 290–1
communism 131
Communities Magazine 118–19
community
  'community of communities' 231
  concept of 6–7
  living in 43, 101, 108, 159, 190, 197
community economy 147, 255, 282, 286–7. *See* diverse economy
  community economic practices 271
  definition of 273
community garden 216, 223
community land trust 187, 227
community of practice 227–8
community supported agriculture 288
composite vignette method 230

composting 69
  compost toilets 18, 76–8, 87, 92, 149, 152
conflict 44, 75–6, 201, 224, 233, 236, 256, 280, 301, 307
  during Covid-19 305
  frustration 44
  over decision-making 91, 218
  over work 261
  tensions over goals 99
  with local communities 83–4, 95–6
consensus decision-making 20, 76, 92, 176, 202, 218, 233, 271, 280. *See* decision-making structures
consumerism 110
  green consumerism 124
consumption 47, 89, 118, 289
  ethical consumption 144
conviviality 101, 103, 218
cooperatives 21, 50, 54, 227, 274
  cooperative lifestyle 117, 260
  cooperative mindset 115
  housing cooperatives 187, 190, 193, 195–6, 223
  rental cooperative 50, 55
  workers cooperatives 255, 273, 277
co-optation 5
co-parenting 148, 151
Cornea, Natasha 19–20, 203, 305
counterurbanism movement 166
Covid-19 44, 68, 222–3, 227, 303, 305
cultural appropriation 18, 135, 150, 176, 181
Czischke, Darinka 198

Daly, Matthew 13, 47, 50
Damanhur, Italy 9
Dancing Rabbit Ecovillage, USA 9–11, 13, 16, 21, 33–45, 132, 188, 191, 308
decision-making structures
  and childcare 237
  collective 246
  democratic 144
  egalitarian 91, 159, 181, 217–18, 275, 300
  novel 2, 201
  participatory decision-making 241, 244

decolonization 114, 130, 133. *See* colonialism
deep ecology 293
deforestation 104
degrowth 70, 143, 220, 303
    post-growth 271, 283
Deleuze, Gilles 132
demographic composition 12, 16, 113, 232–3, 291. *See* ageing
Denton, Nancy 119
de Sardan, Olivier 207
design 3
    and exclusion 121
    and sustainability 190
    community-based 193
    ecological 228
    Whole System Design 22
Diggers and Dreamers 8
Dine indigenous group 131
direct action 223
disability 79, 89, 193, 303
    ableism 95, 113
'discursive enclosure' 85
diverse economy 4, 255, 273, 283, 286–7, 307. *See* community economy
diversity 113, 115
    and equity 41, 113
    barriers to 231, 238
    celebrating 151
    encouraging 291–2
    green flight 119, 175
    homogeneity 167, 294
    'homophily' 234
    lack of 16, 117, 157, 175, 266
    need for 234
    racial diversity 159, 179
Dobernig, Karin 265
Dogwood Hollow Homestead, USA 161
do-it-together (DIT) 201, 219, 229
    DIY community 273
    DIY culture 223
    Do-it-with (DIW) 74
    ethos 9
    mutual aid 231
double dividend 48
downshifting 266. *See* voluntary simplicity
dualism
    philosophical concept 145
    society-environment 84–5

Earth Common Equity Rental Cooperative (Earth Co-op), Australia 50, 54
Earth system boundaries 47
Earthsong Eco Neighbourhood, New Zealand 192
Easterlin, Richard 264
Echelon Planning 189
Eco Village St. L, USA 160
ecocentrism 84
eco-collaborative housing communities 187, 197
eco-communards 69
eco-fascism 5, 22, 86. *See* white supremacism
ecofeminism 143, 145, 148
ecological footprint 10, 43, 62, 194
'ecological pragmatism' 190
ecological restoration 90
economic democracy 271, 273, 281–2, 286
economic playgrounds 21, 255, 287, 290, 295
economies of scale 177, 289
eco-social enterprises 294
eco-socialism 264
ecosophy 10
eco-village 8, 122, 157, 187, 227, 293
    definition 34
EcoVillage at Ithaca, USA 9, 17, 113, 115, 175, 178, 308
education
    demonstration sites 12, 99, 109, 301, 307
    environmental education 99, 109, 216, 228, 235
    home and non-conventional schooling 89
elitism 187, 191. *See* privilege
Elms, Chris 119
energy
    consumption and production 159, 285
    efficiency 108
    infrastructure 93
    renewable 31, 37–8, 87, 92, 99, 104, 182, 223, 242
    transitions 174
Enlightenment, the 133
environmental impact 53, 271
    and wellbeing 43, 255, 285

degradation 129
   global consumption footprint 47–8
   of high consumption 34
   reduction 10, 31, 38, 62, 93
environmental justice 11, 116, 118, 122–4
   movements 179
environmentalism 84, 115, 174, 258
   and colonialism 178
   white environmentalism 17, 173–4, 179
Escobar, Arturo 84
Escribano, Paula 265
estrangement, concept of 102, 107, 308
ethnography 16, 33, 143, 146, 228, 230, 235, 250
Euler, Johannes 190
Europtopia 8
exclusion 7, 113, 120, 124, 135, 175. See diversity
   exclusivity 167, 173
   racial 180, 302
experimentation (social and practical) 2, 182. See living laboratory
   experimental spaces 9–10, 86–7, 123, 175
   for new ways of living 34, 143
   porous and open 274
   practical 286
   social experiments 2, 117
   spiritual and political 245
extraction
   extractivist farming 89
   imperial 129–30
   resource 86, 174, 303

Fab Lab 195
failure 282, 306–7
   as learning 73–4, 299
   of communities 224
   rates of 8, 306–7
   systemic 12
Fair Housing Act, USA 121
fair trade networks 274
Feagin, Joe 120
feminism 4–6, 205, 217, 262, 300
   feminist community 277
   Feminist Political Ecology 224
   queer feminism 152
Fields, Barbara J. 177

finance 94, 288
   asset pooling 288–91
   at LILAC 291
   corporate 306
   financial sustainability 256, 266, 285, 288
financialization 192
Findhorn eco-village, UK 1, 9, 11, 87, 138, 175, 235–6, 304
   Experience Week 236
   Findhorn Foundation 19, 230
Fireside Co-operative, UK 87
Fisher, Berenice 147
Fisher, Mark 273
Floyd, George 116
focus groups 102, 230
food provisioning 13, 59, 159, 271, 289
food sovereignty 223
foreningen 273–4
'fortress' conservation 178. See environmentalism
Foucault, Michel 203
Foundation for Intentional Community 8, 116, 146, 158, 161, 164, 302
Fraňková, Eva 294
freegan culture 290
   dumpster diving 223, 290
Freetown Christiania, Denmark 9, 11, 21, 271–83, 290
Friary Grange (pseudonym), UK 21, 257–67
friendship 123
frontier, idea of 132, 139

Garforth, Lisa 85
gated communities 121, 175. See segregation
Gavaldà, Marc 20, 215, 285
Gehl, Jan 188
gender 16, 114, 159, 168. See ecofeminism
   and care 143–4
   and patriarchy 16
   dynamics 70, 153, 224
   essentialization 146, 150
   inequality 2–3, 75
   neutrality 151
   socialization 150
   use of space 149
genocide 117, 131

gentrification 117, 132, 175, 192, 280
  green gentrification 113
geography 3–4, 67, 203, 294
Gerner, Nadine 16–17, 143, 301–2
Gibson-Graham, J.K. 85, 94, 267, 273, 286–7, 295
gift relations 273–4
Gleis 21, Austria 294
Global Ecovillage Network 8, 22, 34, 146, 159, 302
global financial crisis 195, 223
Global North 3, 118, 174–5, 179, 203
Global South 174–5, 179, 203–4, 207, 209, 242, 277
global warming 104. *See* climate change, climate crisis
Goodmorning, Telesfor Reyna 137
governance 63, 201–3
  and spirituality 20
  collective governance 12, 227
  environmental 3, 6, 11, 19, 203–11, 305
  'everyday governance' 205
  'good governance' 205
  governing practices 206
  institutional 13
  self-governance 193, 227
  shared governance 117
'green building' 54, 118, 233. *See* housing, architecture
green elitism 106. *See* privilege
Green Hills (pseudonym), UK 87, 92–5
Green Worker Cooperatives 182
Greer, Allan 133
Grigsby, Mary 266
Grinde, Bjørn 43

Haida indigenous group 130
Haraway, Donna 299
Hart's Mill Ecovillage, USA 176
Hayden, Dolores 301
Healy, Stephen 287, 304
Heitman, Lars 190
heterodox economics 294
heterogeneous infrastructure configurations (HIC) 209
heteronormativity 1, 152, 301. *See* LGBTQ+
Hockerton Housing Project, UK 87, 175
Holmgren, David 137–8
Hong, Soonkwan 204

Hopi indigenous group 131
housing 93, 301
  and place-making 228
  and segregation 120
  climate-resilience 83
  costs and affordability 167, 173, 176, 191, 195, 291
  decommodification 288
  design 55
  eco-collaborative 187
  intergenerational housing 189
  self-built 85, 87
  size of 48
  speculative housing 236
  sustainability 285–6, 301
Hugentobler, Margrit 195
human geography 137
humans, ecological role of 86, 95
  peopled environments 85, 95
  peopled landscapes 15–16, 83
Hunziker Areal, Switzerland 196
hybrid economy 260, 265, 273

Ibrahim, Basil 208
id22 Institute for Creative Sustainability, Germany 198
inclusivity 12, 198, 292, 299, 307. *See* diversity
income sharing 92, 287. *See* finance
indicators, social, economic, and environmental 158
indigenous communities and lands 85, 178, 182
  colonialism 120, 130–2
  cultural appropriation 18
  neo-coloniality 16
Indigenous Studies 129
individualization 91
  and spirituality 244
  creep of 95, 99, 110, 178–9
  individual responsibility 175
industrial agriculture 35, 37
industrial urbanism 101, 104
inequality 157, 209, 231, 262
innovation 167
insiders, outsiders and thresholders 100, 102, 107
Instituto Biorregional Do Cerrado, Brazil 308

intention 229
intentional communities 8, 157–8, 190, 238, 259
    and diversity 116
    and estrangement 102
    and participation 241
    and quality of life 43, 285
    and utopianism 134
    formation of 54
    research on 143
    structure of 227
interdependencies and co-existence 95
    and the more-than-human 79, 300
    systems of 228–9, 238
    visibility of 95
interdisciplinarity 3
International Communal Studies Association 8
intersectionalities 114
introversion 229
IPPC 1
Ithaca Hours 115. *See* alternative currencies

Jamaica Plain Cohousing, USA 192
Jarvis, Helen 19, 202, 227
Jennings, Paul 263
Jensen, Casper Bruun 70
Jim Crow and Sundown laws 121
Johanisova, Nadia 21, 271, 282, 294
Johnson, Jay T. 16
Jonas, Andrew E.G. 15
Jones, Brooke 13, 21, 33
Jørgensen, Dolly 84, 86

Kabat-Zinn, Jon 244
Kailash Ecovillage, USA 11, 176
Kalkbreite, Switzerland 192, 196
Kallis, Giorgos 18, 31
Kan Pasqual, Spain 20, 202, 215–25
Kehl, Konstantin 14
Kerney, Karen 124
Kirby, Andy 266
knowledge-action gap 307
Kommune Niederkaufungern, Germany 290–1
KraftWerk 1, Switzerland 196
Kumar, Ankit 7

La Borda, Spain 223
Labit, Anne 16, 192–3
Lakota indigenous group 137
Lama Foundation, USA 9, 136–7
Lammas, UK 20
Lancaster Co-housing, UK 87, 175
land acknowledgements 138
land costs 11, 288, 303
'land tenure pluralism' 133
Landmatters, UK 87
Larsen, Soren 16
Latour, Bruno 69
Lawhon, Mary 209
Leben in der Seestadt Aspern, Austria 292
Lebensgarten, Germany 308
legitimacy 206, 211
LGBTQ+ 4, 159
    queer community 152
LILAC, UK 9, 93–4, 177, 303
    and diversity 175
    and government grants 20
    as urban experiment 11, 95
    financial structure of 176, 291–2, 303
limits 92
Litfin, Karen 245, 285, 300
livelihoods 12, 87, 195, 302
    one-planet livelihoods 190
    possibilities of 283
    systems of 234
    visitors as source of 233
living laboratory 34, 56
    urban living laboratory 207
Loach, Mikaela 174
localization 13, 50, 61–2, 285
    in relation to gender 145
    of food 63, 118
    peasant localist lifestyle 145
Lockyer, Joshua 13, 21, 33
logos 103
Lokomuna, Germany 290
Lopez, Christina 12, 113, 157
Los Angeles Eco-Village, USA 11, 175–7, 192, 303, 308
low impact developments 8, 34, 90, 286
    low-impact living 106, 158, 190, 194
low-tech practices 144, 149, 173, 289
Ludwig, Ma'ikwe 35

MacGregor, Sherilyn 16, 145, 153, 190, 192, 224
Makvärket, Denmark 290
Malý Blažek, Jan 21, 255, 285
Manifest Destiny 134
manufacturing 275–80, 289, 292
Martin, Trayvon 121
Massey, Douglas 119
Mata Amritanandamayi Devi 245
material expectations 92, 95, 306
material infrastructures 92, 301, 307
    alternative 201
    and gender 148
    and interdependence 300
    and social practices 49
    building of 1, 13, 67, 75, 87, 221
    common 10, 31
    dynamic 209
    for sustainability 59
    socio-materialities 87
May Day 100
McArthur, Marisa 301
McKanan, Dan 304
meat consumption 257. *See* vegetarianism
meditation 137, 147, 233, 247. *See* spirituality
mindfulness 244, 251
Mee, Kathleen J. 301
Meijering, Louise 101
Mennonite 35
mental health 13, 95
migration 89, 132, 134, 215
Milani Price, Oriana 286, 294
Miller, Ethan 7, 85, 274
Miller, Timothy 191
Mincyte, Diana 265
modernism 159
Molfese, Carlotta 301
Mollison, Bill 137
Mondragon Cooperative Corporation, Spain 282
Monticelli, Lara 294
Monticello 120
More than Housing (MH), Switzerland 196
more-than-human 67–9, 299–300
    agency of 18, 41
    and quality of life 32
    care for 147

multispecies community 83–5, 94–5
    relationalities 5, 78, 137
Moreton-Robinson, Aileen 138–9
Morgan-Grenville, Gerard 99
Morita, Atsuro 70
Morton, Timothy 68
Mouvement Colibris 146
Mulder, Kenneth 43, 264, 285
multispecies justice 179. *See* more-than-human
municipal government 11, 14, 198, 223, 276. *See* the state
Murundaka Cohousing Community, Australia 9, 47–63
Mutual Home Ownership Model 94. *See* finance

Nancy, Jean-Luc 287
nature, relationship to 69, 84
Nelson, Anitra 7, 14, 187, 190, 258, 265, 285
neo-classical economics 220
neoliberalism 17, 19, 114, 173, 216, 286
    ethos 150
    rationalities 175
    resistance to 180
new economics 50
New Ground, UK 19
New Urbanism 160, 167
Nieto, Leticia 181
non-market (non-monetary) activities 255, 273, 286, 303
    as alternative economy 11
    as economic sustainability 10
    calculation of 220–2
    non-market economies of scale 289
    'non-market socialism' 265
North, Peter 295
Northern Rivers Pan-Community network, Australia 231
Northern Tiwa Indigenous communities 136
nowtopia 223, 282

Occupy Wall Street 241, 247, 251
off-grid 31, 87, 92
Olin Wright, Erik 3, 308
One Planet Development 90

oppression 146
  forms of 3
  liberation from 190
  systems of 234
  within communities 238
organic
  food production 144, 176, 182
  gardening 37, 60–1, 235
origin stories 237
Outdoor Afro 182
outreach activities 232
ozone depletion 104

Painter, Joe 205
Palmer, Jasmine 50, 198
Panya Project, Thailand 135, 139
participant observation 53, 70, 87, 102, 147
participation 113, 201, 230–1, 241
  participatory budgeting 274, 281–2
  participatory democracy 9
patriarchy 1, 16, 114, 217, 301
peak oil 34, 104, 223
Pellow, David N. 181
Pepper, David 264, 304
permaculture 2, 10, 60–1, 67, 85, 90–1, 135–7, 147, 215, 232
  social permaculture 228, 234
personal development 153
Pew Research Foundation 120
phenomenology 228–9, 237
  social phenomenology 235
photovoltaics 13, 93, 99
Pickerill, Jenny 1, 18, 31, 83, 113, 129, 145, 173, 201, 255, 293, 299
place
  'place-based sustainability initiatives' 159
  place-making 228–9
Plessy v. Ferguson 120
policy analysis 204
political ecology 190
political science 3
politics 95, 123, 180, 285
  and protest 99
  and spirituality 241
  knowledge politics 204n.1
  patronage 208
  political assemblages 206
  social justice politics 178

polyamory 152
polycrisis 2, 5
Popular Communities of Resistance (CPR), Guatemala 215
porous communities 14, 274, 305
positionality 173
post-capitalism 3, 20, 70, 197, 255, 283
  post-capitalist alternatives 1
  post-capitalist ethics 3–5, 22, 299
postcolonial 174, 205, 209, 243. See colonialism
post-humanism 137
post-politics 6
post-structural Marxism 3
power relations 74–6, 201, 206, 218
  and gender 224–5
  Foucauldian understandings 203, 205
  in decision-making 218
  inequity in 7, 20, 68, 79
  making visible 4, 114
  political power 116
  'webs of power' 206
Power, Emma R. 301
precarity 173, 176, 180, 217
prefiguration 4, 11, 15, 168, 188, 250, 293, 300
  prefigurative practice 241
privatization 121, 208, 216
privilege 70, 133–4, 168, 180, 197, 293. See elitism
  and segregation 106
  class or racial 173
  context for 188
  environmental and social 151
  gender and 153
  reinforcement of 113, 116, 238
  through physical and mental health 95
  white privilege 177–8
property 282
  and colonialism 133–4, 139
  relations 192–3
  resistance to 280, 282
Protect Mauna Kea campaign 244
protest 100
  camps 86. See Occupy Wall Street
Pun Pun, Thailand 136

queer ecology 151

race, also racialization 114–16, 131
    and diversity 13, 175–6
    and ecofeminism 145
    engagement with 17–18
racism 1–2, 114, 116, 118, 151, 234, 302.
        See white supremacy
    anti-racism 124, 174, 181, 228
    environmental racism 173, 179
    structural racism 120–2, 157
Ray, James Arthur 138
recruitment 228
recycling 105, 222, 277, 279
reed bed systems 99
regenerative agriculture 90
Reisch, Lucia A. 266
relational culture 229
repair 67, 72, 74, 259
reparations and land back 181
resilience 19, 113, 285, 305
resistance, to eco-communities 95
retirement 256, 262, 303
Rice, Jennifer L. 113
Rifkin, Mark 132
Rigby, Andrew 235
Right of Nature movements 84
Rios, M. 181
Roediger, David 177
Rothman, Adam 177
Rothstein, Richard 121
Rubin, Zach 16
Ruiu, Maria L. 192
rural bias 227
rurban projects 70, 216, 223

'salt water thesis' 130
Sami indigenous group 129
Sandhill Farm, USA 35
Sanford, A. Whitney 34
Sargisson, Lucy 102, 106, 190–1, 267
scale
    assumptions regarding 14–15
    'human scale' 194
    implications of 18
    insights regarding 157
    possibilities of 20, 187–8, 222–3, 299
    'upscaling' and 'scaling out' 194, 228, 308
Schmid, Benedikt 15, 295
Schramm, Elisa 18, 67, 300, 303, 307

Schramm, Sophie 208
segregation 116, 119, 121
self-building 85, 87
self-denial 18, 191
    discomfort 68, 76–9, 122, 237, 304
    of conveniences 40
    physical hardship 32, 42
self-employment 21, 273, 278–9
self-governance 188
self-sufficiency 2, 10, 60–1, 87, 159, 161, 260, 286, 292–4
    self-provision 87, 95, 144, 257–8, 288
    self-reliance 7, 87–9, 258, 266, 280
settler colonialism 3, 114, 129–31, 135, 138, 174, 177
Seymore, John 258
sharing 159, 286, 292, 300–1
    care 288
    costs 94, 260
    economy 286
    emotions 218
    food 218, 233
    land 91, 182
    mobility 54, 115, 259, 288
    property 160, 182
    skill 62, 101
    space 56, 58, 94, 188, 238
    work 265, 267
Shippen, Nicole Marie 263
Shove, Elizabeth 146, 148
Sieben Linden, Germany 9
skill (and 'enskilment') 68–9, 72, 78–9
    gender 149
    skill-sharing 101
slavery 117, 120
Smith, Thomas S.J. 21, 271
social centres 215–16
social enterprise 21, 255, 273, 275
social infrastructures 1, 56, 235, 307
    and potential exclusion 177
    and resubjectivation 307
    as institutional arrangements 161
    as micro-sociology 237
    as organizational approaches 215, 227
    as rhythm and repetition 300
    challenges of 201
social justice 113, 173, 178, 188, 236, 302
    social and economic injustice 157
social learning 10, 19, 202, 229, 232, 235

social movements 1, 4, 17, 99, 216, 246
social organizing 227
social practices 143, 300, 307
    social practice theory 3, 48–9, 53, 62, 144, 146
    sociocracy 9, 151, 176
socio-ecological transformation 178, 307
    and economic experiments 255
    and exclusion 113–14, 173–4
    and the more-than-human 68, 78–9
    facilitation of 31, 45, 109, 299, 307
    grassroots 306
Sociology 3
socio-technical transitions 22, 48
    socio-technical configurations 209
solar thermal 99
solidarity economy 241, 271, 274, 286, 291
    solidarity funds 288
Sørvoll, Jardar 197
spatial distribution of intentional communities 162–5
spatial practices 99–101
spirituality 20, 137, 151, 158, 201, 241, 248–9, 285, 304
    Indigenous spirituality 135
    intrapersonal development 304
    'New Age' spirituality 138
Spreefeld, Germany 192
Springhill Cohousing, UK 87, 177
squats 86, 187–8, 215, 258, 272, 282, 285, 294
Sri Aurobindo 242
    Sri Aurobindo Ashram 243
    Sri Aurobindo Society 242
state, the 14
    and governance 203–4, 210
    'everyday state' 205
    in relation to autonomous zones 100
    relationship to 19–20, 306, 308
    settlement with 272, 274, 279
    state's gaze 101
    support 175
    tension with 1
Stevens-Wood, Kirsten 20–1, 257, 301
Steward Woodland Community 87
Stratford, Elaine 301
SUDS waste water management 93
sustainability

'place-based sustainability initiatives' 159
sustainable consumption 13, 38, 49–50, 53, 56, 62
sustainable development 109
sustainable lifestyles and living 53, 107, 109, 115
sustainable practices 50, 92, 105, 301; direct and indirect 53
Sustainable Living Foundation (SLF), Australia 54
Swami Vivekananda 245
sweat-equity 197
Swyngedouw, Erik 190
Szemző, Hanna 197

'tactical withdrawal' 307–8
Taggart, Jonathan 69
task functions 236. See wellbeing functions
Taylor Aiken, Gerald 7, 15
techne 103
technology 19–20, 92, 159
    alternative technologies 99, 103, 106
Temmerman, Frans 265
tenant syndicates 288
terra nullius 130, 132
The Floating City, Denmark 290
The Yard, UK 87
Then, Volker 14
Thich Nat Hahn 244
Thörn, Håkan 193
Threshold Centre, UK 87
time commitment 19, 21, 72, 94, 261–2
Tinker's Bubble, UK 9, 87, 292
tiny houses 188, 221
    Tiny House movement 266
Tir y Gafel, UK 9, 83, 87, 89–91, 95, 303
'tools for conviviality' 220
transgenderism 152
Transition Towns movement 7, 34
    Transition US 34
Trelay, UK 87
Tronto, Joan C. 147
Tuck, Eve 133
Tummers, Lidewij 16, 145, 153, 190, 192, 198, 224
Twin Oaks, USA 9, 192, 263, 265, 300

UfaFabrik, Germany 11, 192
UNESCO 242
Ungdomhuset, Denmark 290
unionization 276
urban
    design 242
    experiments 11
    futures 209
    planning 160, 249–50. See New Urbanism
    sprawl 159–60
urban agriculture 223
US Census American Community Survey (ACS) 162
utopia 2, 107, 132, 134, 139, 196, 260, 267, 282
    ecotopia 101, 103
    'real utopias' 282. See Erik Olin Wright
    socio-ecological utopia 100, 102–3
    utopian imaginations 3
    'utopian migrations' 215

values 2, 40, 42, 55, 77, 113, 190, 233, 259, 289
    ethos and core values 236
    post-materialist values 48
Vannini, Phillip 69
vegetarianism 115. See meat consumption
    veganism 147–8
Veracini, Lorenzo 129
vernacular knowledge 234
Vicdan, Handan 204
'vision statements' 232
voluntary poverty 180
voluntary simplicity 11, 31, 34, 151, 180, 266, 292, 301
volunteering 18, 72, 136, 230, 233, 272, 289, 293

Walnut Commons, USA 160
Water Action Groups 208
Watts, Vanessa 138
wealth redistribution 291
Weaver, Russell 12, 113, 157
Wellbeing and quality of life 285
    and environmental impact 43–4
    and sense of fulfilment 264
    and spirituality 304
    as act of care 219
    as criterion of success 300
    at Dancing Rabbit 38–41
    collective well-being 234
    fulfilment 264
    giving up 18
    increases in 9, 13, 21, 32, 47, 159, 256
    of other species 115
    the good life 218
    wellbeing functions 232
Welsh Institute for Sustainable Education 99
Western modes of thinking 69
white flight 121
white supremacy 17, 22, 114, 116–17, 119–20, 131, 138, 152, 174, 176, 302. See settler colonialism
Widmer, Hans 196
Willing Workers on Organic Farms (WWOOF) 230, 233. Also World Wide Opportunities on Organic Farms
wind turbines 99
Wolfe, Patrick 131
work 255
    and care-full practices 147–8
    as moral value 220
    as shared labor 60, 94, 219
    as social life 40
    meaningful work 221
    need for 21
    wage employment 255, 263–5, 282

Yang, K. Wayne 133
yoga
    Integral Yoga 242, 245, 251
    Vedic yoga 245
Young, Alex Trimble 132

ZAD, France 223
Zapatista movement, Mexico 215
    EZLN 215
Zibechi, Raúl 215
Zimmer, Anna 209

www.ingramcontent.com/pod-product-compliance
Ingram Content Group UK Ltd.
Pitfield, Milton Keynes, MK11 3LW, UK
UKHW021838200625
459877UK00005B/36